Copy 2

apil association of **personal injury** lawyers ®

Guide to Fatal Accidents

TREASURY SOLICITOR'S LIBRARY

**THE TREASURY SOLICITOR
LIBRARY AND INFORMATION SERVICE**
Queen Anne's Chambers
28 Broadway
London, SW1H 9JS
Tel: 020 7210 3044/3102
E-mail: library@treasury-solicitor.gsi.gov.uk
Please return this publication on or before the latest date shown below

26/7/03

D1331420

association of
personal injury
lawyers ®

Guide to
Fatal
Accidents

Gordon Exall

Barrister

Chapter 24 on Coroners' Inquests
█████████ Partner and Head of
Personal Litigation Division
████████████████

J O R D A N S

2002

Published by
Jordan Publishing Limited
21 St Thomas Street
Bristol BS1 6JS

British Library Cataloguing-in-Publication Data
A catalogue record for this book is available from the British Library.

ISBN 0 85308 757 1

Typeset by Jordan Publishing Ltd
Printed and bound in Great Britain by Bell & Bain Ltd, Glasgow

FOREWORD

Fatal accident claims present one of the biggest challenges to personal injury lawyers. Not only do the tragic circumstances of the case require the utmost in client skills, the relevant law is complex and difficult, damages are generally modest and in some cases entirely absent. Indeed, the level of damages and the painstaking work which must be done to prove them is an aggravating factor for clients, causing upset at a distressing time.

Therefore, any book on the subject which aids the understanding and improves the skills of lawyers handling fatal accident claims is to be welcomed.

In this APIL Guide, Gordon Exall takes the reader through all that is required in a fatal accident claim from first interview, funding, taking instructions, analysis of the claim and the application of the law. The complexities of limitation, dependency and the effect of benefits are carefully and lucidly explained, illustrated by the latest case-law.

He deals with the steps needed before and after issue of proceedings and discusses the major problem areas and pitfalls.

You will find discussion of the shortcomings in the law and how the Law Commission proposals and the Human Rights Act 1998 may provide some solutions. The appendices provide very useful reference material including excellent precedents, the relevant statutes and the Ogden tables.

This guide is a model of clarity and practical application for lawyers trying to find their way through the maze of law and procedure relating to fatal claims. I cannot recommend it too highly.

Patrick Allen
President
APIL

ASSOCIATION OF PERSONAL INJURY LAWYERS (APIL)

APIL is the UK's leading association of claimant personal injury lawyers, dedicated to protecting the rights of injured people.

Formed in 1990, APIL now represents over 5,000 solicitors, barristers, academics and students in the UK, Republic of Ireland and overseas.

APIL's objectives are:

- to promote full and just compensation for all types of personal injury;
- to promote and develop expertise in the practice of personal injury law;
- to promote wider redress for personal injury in the legal system;
- to campaign for improvements in personal injury law;
- to promote safety and alert the public to hazards;
- to provide a communication network for members.

APIL is a growing and influential forum pushing for law reform, and improvements, which will benefit victims of personal injury.

Through its College of Personal Injury Law (CPIL), the association provides a recognised independent kitemark of expertise, and cost-effective, practical, specialist training for the profession.

APIL is also an authoritative information source for personal injury lawyers, providing up-to-the-minute PI bulletins, regular newsletters and publications, information databases and online services.

For further information contact:

APIL
11 Castle Quay
Nottingham
NG7 1FW

DX 716208 Nottingham 42
Tel 0115 9580585
Email mail@apil.com
Website www.apil.com

PREFACE

I have had the pleasure of being involved with the design of the APIL Guides almost from the outset. Sitting on the APIL publishing sub-committee is proof that some committees can do more than keep minutes and take hours. The idea of the APIL Guides is to be as much 'friend and mentor' as standard legal text. That is to identify problem areas and deal with them in practical ways. This book aims to be a guide rather than the definitive text.

I would like to thank many members of APIL who have provided encouragement. Similarly, APIL staff members have provided much assistance and I cannot pass up an opportunity to praise the quality of APIL staff at all levels. Many of those who have attended the CPIL Fatal Accidents Course have provided considerable assistance with the issues and questions they have raised. Tony Hawitt has been a patient and encouraging publisher. Finally, I must mention my own dependants, Rosemary, Jonathan, Thomas, Elizabeth and Ben. On issues of apportionment, I should state that all of them have provided encouragement and contributed to the delay in the production of this book in roughly equal proportions.

Any errors are my own, and I would welcome correspondence and debate. Hopefully, any errors or omissions can be put right in future editions.

Gordon Exall
Zenith Chambers
10 Park Square
Leeds
November 2002

CONTENTS

TABLE OF CASES

References are to paragraph numbers.

TABLE OF STATUTES

References are to paragraph numbers. References to where statutory material is set out in the appendices are to italic page numbers.

TABLE OF STATUTORY INSTRUMENTS

References are to paragraph numbers. References to where statutory material is set out in the appendices are to italic page numbers.

TABLE OF CONVENTIONS

References are to paragraph numbers.

PART 1

INITIAL CONSIDERATIONS

In this preliminary Part we look at the following issues.

(1)   The legal background and the development of fatal accident claims.
(2)   The various ways of funding fatal accident cases.
(3)   Initial meeting with client, taking instructions and obtaining documents.

CHAPTER 1

THE LEGAL BACKGROUND

1.1 INTRODUCTION

It is rare for the issue of damages to be at the forefront of the mind of a client who visits a lawyer's office after a friend or relative is involved in a fatal accident. There are many immediate and more pressing concerns that he, and the lawyer, will have to deal with.

However, ultimately, if a legal claim is to be brought there are three essential questions that the client will need answered.

(1)   Does this client have a claim as a result of death?
(2)   If so, how much is the claim worth?
(3)   What is the procedure for obtaining damages?

It is important that the client's immediate concerns are dealt with, and dealt with in an appropriate and compassionate way. However, the lawyer is not a counsellor; ultimately a client visits the lawyer in order to determine and enforce his legal rights.

This book deals with the three essential elements. In addition, we will look at issues surrounding fatal accident claims, such as psychological shock.

One matter to remember at the outset is that this is an area of law full of contradictions, ambiguity and uncertainty. Indeed, it is sometimes frustrating in its lack of clarity. However, this is something we have to live with and, as long as we are confident with the basic principles, we can (and must) adopt a practical approach to these issues. This work is designed to be a practical guide taking you through the important legal matters and dealing with issues such as the coroner's inquest. Equally important is the potential impact of the Human Rights Act 1998 on many of the issues in this book. In this regard, Chapter 26 is essential reading.

1.2 THE ORIGIN OF THE CAUSE OF ACTION

The key point to understanding the law relating to fatal accidents is that common law principles have been grafted onto statutory rights. Historically the common law did not allow any claim for wrongful death or any claims by the dependants – the right of action was held to have died with the victim.

The right of dependants to bring an action was first brought into being by the Fatal Accidents Act 1846. However, this was, in essence, a statute that gave a right of action to certain dependants. It permitted a jury to award 'such damages as they may think proportioned to the injury resulting from such death to the parties respectively for whom and for whose benefit such action shall be brought'.[1]

There were a number of amendments in the twentieth century, primarily designed to ensure that insurance policies, widows' pensions and the like were not deducted from damages awarded to the dependants. The Fatal Accidents Act 1976 was, essentially, a consolidating statute. That Act was amended substantially by the Administration of Justice Act 1982.

That the assessment of damages is, largely, a 'jury' point is a principle that pervades the assessment of fatal accident damages to this day. The only overall statutory guidance to the court is given in s 3(1) of the Fatal Accidents Act 1976:

> 'In the action such damages, other than damages for bereavement, may be awarded as are proportioned to the injury resulting from the death of the dependants respectively.'

1.3 THE ELEMENTS OF THE CLAIM

There are two different elements to a fatal accident claim, although they can overlap:

---

[1]   However, this does not mean that an award can be wholly arbitrary, see the judgments in *L (A Child) v Barry May Haulage* at para **11.7.7** and *Bordin v St Mary's NHS Trust* at para **11.8.2**.

(1) the Law Reform (Miscellaneous Provisions) Act 1934. This allows an action to be brought on behalf of the *estate*;
(2) the Fatal Accidents Act 1976 (as amended). This allows an action to be brought on behalf of the *dependants* of the deceased (see Chapter 4).

CHAPTER 2

FUNDING FATAL ACCIDENT CASES

2.1   INTRODUCTION

The issues relating to funding of fatal accident cases are similar to those in personal injury cases generally. Below, we shall explore the available methods of funding fatal cases and consider the issues which are particular to these actions.

2.2   PUBLIC FUNDING

It is unlikely that Community Legal Service (CLS) funding will be available, however, the possibility should not be ignored. The following checklist will enable advisers to establish whether or not the client/the case will qualify for CLS funding.

(1)   Does the accident involve a non-negligent cause of injury?
(2)   Is there a matter of public interest?
(3)   Will the case cost more than £25,000 to settlement (or £75,000 to trial) (at £70 per hour)?
(4)   Is it too difficult to decide whether the case should be taken on at all, but is it a case with some merit, large quantum and will it cost more than £3,000 at £70 per hour to investigate (investigative help)?
(5)   If confident of accepting the case on a conditional fee basis, will the costs (at £70 per hour) exceed £15,000 (litigation support)?

CLS funding may be available for representation at the Coroner's Inquest, particularly where the case involves a death in custody.

2.3   OTHER METHODS OF FUNDING

The surviving claimant may not be the best person to know whether alternative methods of funding are available and it is prudent for the solicitor to make additional enquiries. In particular, consider:

(1)   whether trade union funding is available;

(2)   whether the matter can be funded privately;

(3)   whether there is legal expenses insurance available (this can extend to looking at the defendant' s policy: see *Sarwar v Alam* [2001] EWCA Civ 1401[1]);

(4)   whether the matter can proceed on a conditional fee basis;

(5)   if you are instructed in a case where the claimant is likely to die during the course of proceedings, a situation that is very common in asbestos cases:

    (a)   there could be problems where legal expenses insurance is available (once again, it may be prudent to look at the defendant's policy: see *Sarwar v Alam* [2001] EWCA Civ 1401);

    (b)   care should be taken to ensure that the insurance taken out is capable of being transferred to the benefit of the dependants;

    (c)   it is important that the victim makes a will, naming executors who are prepared to assist with the claim.

Further guidance can be found in Harvey *APIL Guide to Conditional Fee Agreements*,[2] particularly at para 11.3).

The issue of funding is never an easy one to broach. In the absence of trade union or insurance funding, it is most likely that a decision will have to be made as to whether the client wishes to fund the matter privately or whether the legal representatives are willing to proceed on the basis of a conditional fee agreement.

2.4   PRACTICAL POINTS

(1)   Issues of funding *are* important. Although these should not be at the forefront of the discussion, they are matters that should be considered and addressed at an early stage.

---

[1]   [2002] PIQR P15.

[2]   Jordans, 2002.

(2) The lawyer should take particular care that proper enquiries have been made into the issue of whether alternative funding is available, in particular the existence of trade union funding or legal expenses insurance.

(3) If a conditional fee agreement is entered into, remember the extra risk involved in not having the victim available to instruct the firm. This should be properly reflected in the firm's uplift. This could be particularly important when the facts of the accident are in dispute.

CHAPTER 3

TAKING INSTRUCTIONS AND OBTAINING DOCUMENTS

3.1   TAKING INSTRUCTIONS

There is important and essential information that must be obtained in the first interview, in particular basic details of the accident, the dependants, the deceased and the date of any hearing by the coroner (see the lawyer's checklist at para **3.4**). In due course, it will be necessary to take detailed statements as to sometimes difficult issues of dependency. There are differing styles of obtaining detailed instructions in a fatal case, particularly in relation to thorny issues such as dependency. Some practitioners spend a great deal of time with the client; others prefer a questionnaire approach (see Appendix 1). An alternative approach is to give the client a notebook with some verbal and written guidance as to what matters are relevant. The reality is that there is no 'correct' approach and you should consider what method is best for each individual client. Some clients need a great deal of time and help in the preparation of a statement, others prefer to work alone. However, the use of a 'standard' questionnaire could be inappropriate; it is recommended that the questionnaire be specifically tailored to that client. This is not a difficult task with modern computer and word-processing facilities and prevents the client feeling he is part of a 'conveyor belt'. (A suggested questionnaire is shown at Appendix 1.)

3.2   THE RELEVANT DOCUMENTS

Whatever method is used, it is essential that the lawyer obtains copies of all the relevant documentation. In particular:

(1)   any documentation that relates to the funding of the claim in question, eg trade union membership, legal insurance, etc;

(2)   life insurance policies (although these may be irrelevant to the quantum of the claim they could be relevant if there is a Motor Insurers Bureau (MIB) claim);

(3)   marriage certificates, birth certificates (of the deceased and the dependants), the death certificate;

(4)   documents relating to the deceased's and dependants' earnings:
       (a) wage slips;
       (b) income tax returns;
       (c) documents relating to fringe benefits, eg cars, insurance, medical assistance;

(5)   documents relating to the education of the deceased's children (particularly relevant if the children are still at school and there is an issue as to whether or not they will attend university);

(6)   documents relating to the education, training and career path of the deceased:
       (a) educational certificates;
       (b) details of training courses attended and professional qualifications;

(7)   documents relating to pensions;

(8)   documents relating to funeral expenses;

(9)   was the deceased involved in any litigation from which he could have benefited? What documents are available?;

(10)   has any expense been incurred in relation to employing household assistance or assistance for other matters that the deceased used to do? If so, what documents are available?

3.3   PRACTICAL POINTS

(1)   In cases where a detailed amount of information is required, consider what approach is best for your individual client.

(2)   The use of a standard questionnaire is inappropriate; if at all possible, tailor the approach to the individual client.

(3)   Take particular care to ensure that all relevant documentation is available as soon as possible.

3.4   CHECKLIST FOR TAKING INITIAL INSTRUCTIONS

This checklist is designed for the fee earner running the case. A more 'client friendly' questionnaire can be found at Appendix 1. Remember also to seek the documents set out in this chapter.

CLIENT DETAILS
1.   Confirm identity of instructing client.
2.   Instructing client's full name and address.
3.   Best methods of contacting client (eg mobile telephone, e-mail).
4.   Instructing client's relationship to the deceased.
5.   Identify other potential dependants.
    (a) Had the deceased been married before?
    (b) Details of previous marriages.
    (c) Did the deceased have any children?
    (d) Names, addresses, ages.
6.   Is there any other person who appears to have a superior right to bring a fatal accident claim?
7.   If the client and the deceased were not married, but living together as husband and wife, how long had they been living together in such a relationship? Is there any documentary evidence available to establish the period of time they had been living together in a husband/wife relationship?

DECEASED'S DETAILS
8.   Deceased's full name and address.
9.   Deceased's date of birth.
10.   Date of deceased's death.
11.   Place where deceased died and the place of the incident that caused the deceased's death.
12.   Name and address of deceased's last employer.
13.   Deceased's job at date of fatal accident.

CIRCUMSTANCES OF THE DEATH
14.   The date of the injury or incident that caused the deceased's death.
15.   The nature of the injury that caused the deceased's death.
16.   Was the death instantaneous?
17.   If the death was not instantaneous, details of any issue of pain, suffering and other losses, prior to death?
18.   If the death was not instantaneous, were any proceedings brought, or an action compromised, by the deceased prior to

his or her death? If so, precise details of these matters must be obtained:

(a) identity of the solicitors involved, including the name of the fee earner and any reference;
(b) obtain as much detail as possible of the work done and any settlement reached.

INVESTIGATING THE CIRCUMSTANCES OF THE DEATH

19. Has the matter been referred to the coroner's court?
20. If so, ascertain which coroner's court, the address and the reference.
21. Has the matter been referred to the police?
22. If so, obtain details of police officers and police station involved.
23. Have any other agencies (eg HSE) investigated the death?
24. If so, obtain details of the relevant agency and the investigations that have been made.
25. Obtain the address of the hospital to which the deceased was taken or in which he/she was treated after the incident that led to his/her death.
26. Obtain the name and address of the deceased's GP.
27. If the accident was a road traffic accident and there is any possibility at all of this being an MIB claim, seek details of the insurance from any potentially negligent driver at once.

FUNDING

28. Does the claimant or the deceased have legal insurance?
29. Is there any possibility of trade union funding?
30. Check all relevant insurance policies.
31. Consider whether the case is appropriate for a conditional fee agreement.

PART 2

DOES THE CLIENT HAVE A CLAIM?

One matter at the forefront of the lawyer's mind should be the issue of whether the client actually has a claim. A failure to consider this could lead to cruel disappointment for the client. Further, if you are acting under a conditional fee agreement, an assessment of the risks has to be made. If there are issues about the client's basic entitlement to bring a claim, this could substantially increase the risks involved.

In this Part we look at four important elements:

(1)   limitation issues;
(2)   the statutory definition of dependant;
(3)   the type of loss that gives rise to a dependency relationship;
(4)   matters than can bar a claim.

There are aspects of the claim that are not reliant on clients being dependants. The executor or administrator of the estate can claim for the losses suffered on behalf of the estate. These claims relate to:

(1)   pain and suffering of the deceased prior to death;
(2)   any financial losses incurred by the deceased prior to death;
(3)   funeral expenses.

However, these are normally extremely limited claims and most fatal accident claims will be brought by, or on behalf of, the dependants.

Further details of these aspects of the claim can be found at Chapters 14 *et seq.*

CHAPTER 4

THE TYPE OF INCIDENT THAT CAN GIVE RISE TO A CLAIM

4.1   INTRODUCTION

Having checked whether the estate has a claim, or whether or not there is a dependency claim, consideration needs to be given as to whether the accident, or incident, that caused the death is such as to give rise to a claim.

4.2   THE ACT

Section 1(1) of the Fatal Accidents Act 1976 states:

'If death is caused by any wrongful act, neglect or default which is such as would (if death had not ensued) have entitled the person injured to maintain an action and recover damages in respect thereof, the person who would have been liable if death had not ensued shall be liable to an action for damages, notwithstanding the death of the person injured.'

4.3   STANDING IN THE SHOES OF THE DECEASED

In *Gray v Barr*,[1] Lord Denning MR summarised the effect of this section:

'If [the deceased] had lived, ie, only been injured and not died, and living would have been entitled to maintain an action and recover damages – then his widow and children can do so. They stand in his shoes in regard to *liability*, but not as to damages' (*emphasis in original*).

Section 1(6) of the Act states:

---

[1]   [1971] 2 QB 554, at p 569D.

'Any reference in this Act to injury includes any disease and any impairment of a person's physical or mental condition.'

4.4   THE NECESSARY REQUIREMENTS

The relevant requirements were set out by Swift J in *Nunan v Southern Railway Company Limited*.[1] The claimants have to prove that:

(1)   the deceased was injured by the wrongful act, neglect or default of the defendant;
(2)   the deceased died as a consequence of that act, neglect or default;
(3)   at the time the deceased died he could have brought an action to recover damages;
(4)   the dependants have suffered loss as a result of the death.

All of these matters must be established for the claim to continue.

Most personal injury lawyers will be able to recognise cases in which liability will arise, these depend on the basic principles of negligence. The reference to wrongful act also covers actions arising because of breaches of *statutory* duty.

4.5   CAUSATION

While liability may not pose particular difficulty to personal injury litigators, issues of *causation* may be more difficult. The burden is on the claimant to show that the death arose because of the negligence or default of the defendant. However, the defendant's actions need not be the *sole* cause of the death.

In *Pigney v Pointers Transport Ltd*,[2] the deceased committed suicide while in a condition of neurotic depression induced by the negligence of the defendant, which was responsible for an accident which he had sustained. The suicide was not a *novus actus interveniens* but was caused by the original wrongful act of the defendant.

---

[1]   [1923] 2 KB 703.
[2]   [1957] 1 WLR 1121.

In *Reeves v Commissioner of Police for the Metropolis*,[1] the House of Lords held that an action in respect of the negligence of the police in failing to prevent the deceased's suicide was not barred by the defences of *volenti* or *novus actus interveniens*. However, damages were reduced by 50 per cent.

In *Barrett v Ministry of Defence*,[2] the plaintiff was the widow of a naval airman who became so drunk one night at the naval base that he passed out into a coma and asphyxiated on his own vomit. The Court of Appeal held that once the deceased had collapsed and was no longer capable of looking after himself, the defendant had assumed responsibility for his care. The defendant had fallen short of the standard reasonably to be expected. To this extent the defendant was in breach of a duty of care and liable to damages to the plaintiff. However, since the deceased's own fault was a continuing and direct cause of his death, a greater share of the blame should rest upon him. The deceased's own contributory negligence was held to be two-thirds.

4.6 ILLUSTRATION OF CASES WHERE LIABILITY NOT ESTABLISHED

Clinical negligence cases often provide examples where negligence exists but liability cannot be established because of issues relating to causation. In *Barnett v Chelsea and Kensington Hospital Management Committee*,[3] a hospital casualty department failed to diagnose the fact that the patient was suffering from arsenic poisoning and he was sent home and died later the same day. The fatal accident claim failed because it was established that, even had he been treated promptly, the deceased would still have died.

4.6.1 The 'material contribution' test

As the above cases illustrate, the fact that the defendant's actions were not the sole cause of the accident does not necessarily prevent a claim being made.

---

[1]   [1999] 3 WLR 363.
[2]   [1995] 3 All ER 1995.
[3]   [1969] 1 QB 428.

It is often overlooked that the classic case of foreseeability and the 'egg-shell skull' rule was a fatal accident case. In *Smith v Leech Brain Ltd*,[1] a workman suffered a burn on his lip when working with molten metal. The employers were at fault. The burn turned cancerous and the man died. It was established that he had a predisposition to cancer; however, this predisposition may never have become malignant if he had not been burnt. The defendant was held liable for the death.

4.7   PRACTICAL POINTS

(1)   Remember that the claimant stands in the deceased's shoes. The question you should ask is whether the deceased could have brought an action?

(2)   Consider whether you can establish that the deceased died as a result of the defendant's wrongful act or omission.

(3)   Remember that the defendant need not be the *sole* cause of the death.

(4)   Check the strength of any causation argument. This is particularly important in clinical negligence cases, where there may be arguments that the deceased would have died in any event, notwithstanding the negligence of the defendant.

---

[1]   [1962] 2 QB 405.

CHAPTER 5

IS YOUR CLIENT A DEPENDANT?

5.1 THE DEFINITION OF DEPENDANT

There are two main points to consider here.

(1) The claimants must be dependants as defined by statute.[1]
(2) The claimants must have had a reasonable expectation of financial benefit from the deceased.

The second point is one of considerable practical importance. When considering who is entitled to make a dependency claim it is important to remember that just because a person is defined as a 'dependant' in the Act, this does not mean he has a claim. It is prudent to consider the entire range of potential dependants; however, it is doubtful that this imposes a duty to contact all of the potential claimants. To avoid misunderstandings and potential grievance the adviser should concentrate upon the *facts* of the financial dependency and make the decision as to who are the *actual* dependants. It is then necessary to consider whether these dependants come within the statutory criteria.

5.2 THE STATUTORY DEFINITION

The Fatal Accidents Act 1976 deals with these important definitions in s 1.

'(1) If death is caused by any wrongful act, neglect or default which is such as would (if death had not ensued) have entitled the person injured to maintain an action and recover damages in respect thereof, the person

---

[1] But see the potential human rights issues in Chapter 26.

who would have been liable if death had not ensued shall be liable to an action for damages, notwithstanding the death of the person injured.

(2) Subject to section 1A(2) below, every such action shall be for the benefit of the dependants of the person ("the deceased") whose death has been so caused.

(3) In this Act "dependant" means –
  (a) the wife or husband or former wife or husband of the deceased;
  (b) any person who –
    (i) was living with the deceased in the same household immediately before the date of the death; and
    (ii) had been living with the deceased in the same household for at least two years before that date; and
    (iii) was living during the whole of that period as the husband or wife of the deceased;
  (c) any parent or other ascendant of the deceased;
  (d) any person who was treated by the deceased as his parent;
  (e) any child or other descendant of the deceased;
  (f) any person (not being a child of the deceased) who, in the case of any marriage to which the deceased was at any time a party, was treated by the deceased as a child of the family in relation to that marriage;
  (g) any person who is, or is the issue of, a brother, sister, uncle or aunt of the deceased.

(4) The reference to the former wife or husband of the deceased in subsection (3)(a) above includes a reference to a person whose marriage to the deceased has been annulled or declared void as well as a person whose marriage to the deceased has been dissolved.

(5) In deducing any relationship for the purpose of subsection (3) above –
  (a) any relationship by affinity shall be treated as a relationship of consanguinity, any relationship of the half blood as a relationship of the whole blood, and the stepchild of any person as his child, and
  (b) an illegitimate person shall be treated as the legitimate child of his mother and reputed father.'

5.3   A MORE LIMITED DEFINITION IN RELATION TO THE BEREAVEMENT PAYMENT

The reference to a more limited definition in respect of s 1A is in relation to the bereavement payment. This is only available to:

(1) the husband or wife of the deceased;
(2) where the deceased was a minor who was never married:
  (a) his parents, if he was legitimate;
  (b) his mother, if he was illegitimate.

The bereavement payment is discussed in detail at Chapter 15.

5.4   THOSE WHO CANNOT CLAIM

The Law Commission lists a large number of people who could be considered dependants but who cannot make a claim:

'cohabitants who were living together as husband and wife but who do not satisfy the "two year rule"; same-sex couples; children who were not of the deceased but who were supported by the deceased whilst he or she was engaged in a marriage-like relationship with their parent; children otherwise supported by the deceased (such as a friend's children); certain distant relatives supported by the deceased (such as a great-nephew supporting a great-aunt); and non-relatives who live together but do not enjoy a marriage-like relationship.'[1]

The Law Commission recommended that there be added to the list any individual who was being wholly or partly maintained by the deceased. However, this is not the law at present and advisers of potential claimants, or defendants, will have to be fully aware of the nature of the statutory list and the restrictions it imposes.

5.5   SPOUSES AND EX-SPOUSES

This usually causes no practical difficulties. It is important to remember that:

(1)   a claimant has a right even if the marriage was void;
(2)   an ex-spouse has a right of action as an ex-spouse even if the couple are cohabiting. For example, in *Shepherd v The Post Office*,[2] the plaintiff had divorced the deceased and remarried but then returned to live with the deceased. It was held that she had a right of action under the Act as a former spouse; she did not have to prove that she had lived in the same household as the deceased for 2 years before his death.

5.6   'COHABITEES'

There are a number of requirements here. The claimant must establish that he/she had been living with the deceased in the same household:

(1)   immediately before the date of the death; and

---

[1]   Law Commission Report No 263 *Claims for Wrongful Death*, at para 3.16.
[2]   (1995) *The Times*, June 15.

(2)   for at least 2 years; and
(3)   during the whole of that period, as the husband or wife of the
       deceased.

This section was considered in *Pounder v London Underground Ltd.*[1]
The court was concerned with the issue of whether the deceased
lived with his girlfriend at the time of his death. The couple had two
children and a somewhat stormy relationship. For part of the time
the girlfriend had moved out into a woman's hostel and the
deceased had moved to a relative's home for one week prior to his
death and had only returned home for one week. The judge held
that:

(1)   brief absences would not necessarily break the continuity of
       'living' as defined by the Act;
(2)   when the girlfriend was at the hostel she regularly returned
       home and spent the night with the deceased. The period in
       the refuge was not, therefore, sufficient to break the period of
       living together.

This suggests that the courts may take a liberal approach as to what
is meant by 'living' together.

5.7   PARENT OR OTHER 'ASCENDANT' OF THE DECEASED

This means that parents, grandparents and (if appropriate) great-
grandparents are entitled to claim if they can establish dependency.

5.8   ANY PERSON TREATED BY THE DECEASED AS HIS PARENT

This is a surprisingly wide definition. The key point is whether the
person was 'treated' as a parent. A person who has no formal
relationship with the deceased is entitled to make a claim. There is
no requirement for any blood relationship, or indeed any marital
relationship, in respect of any of the deceased's parents. The fact
that such a person is entitled to bring a claim does not, however,
mean that any claim can be sustained. The key question here is
whether they can establish a dependency claim. The issue may be a

---

[1]   [1995] PIQR P217.

circular one – the fact that the deceased was maintaining that person could be the best evidence that he was treated by the deceased as a parent.

5.9 ANY CHILD OR OTHER DESCENDANT OF THE DECEASED

A child can be of any age. Adult offspring of the deceased can bring a claim. It is important to note that an illegitimate child is treated as legitimate and that children from different partners of the deceased are all entitled to bring a claim. While it is not difficult to ascertain the mother of an illegitimate child, the Act refers only to the child being treated as the child of the 'reputed father'. The meaning of this is unclear. It appears that the important issue is whether the deceased was the 'reputed', rather than the actual, father.

Further points arise in relation to children not actually born at the date of death.

(1) It appears to be established law that a child of the deceased born when the mother was pregnant at the date of the husband's death is a child of the deceased: *The George and Richard*.[1]

(2) There are undecided issues, however, in relation to the position where the mother became pregnant *after* the date of the accident causing death but *before* the death. Equally problematic is the 'sperm bank' situation where the mother can become pregnant after the death of the deceased.

An important point here is that some authorities suggest that the subsequent adoption of a child may put an end to the dependency claim: see *Watson v Willmott*.[2]

It is, however, arguable that the adoption comes within the ambit of s 4 and falls to be disregarded. For a full discussion of s 4, see Chapter 9.

---

[1] (1871) LR 3 A&E 466.
[2] [1991] 1 QB 140.

5.10   ANY PERSON WHO WAS TREATED BY THE DECEASED AS A CHILD OF THE FAMILY IN RELATION TO THAT MARRIAGE

As was seen from the Law Commission report above, there could be categories of dependent children here who are prohibited from making a claim, for instance the children of cohabitees.

Further, in relation to children living at the home, it is not uncommon for these to be nieces or nephews or similar relatives. In these circumstances, entitlement comes under s 1(3)(g). Remember that this applies even if the children are relatives of the surviving spouse and not the deceased, since s 1(5)(a) states that any relationship of 'affinity' shall be treated as a relationship of 'consanguity'.

There are suggestions in some texts that it is a requirement of this section that the child must be a child of the person to whom the deceased was married. However, the wording of the section does not appear to support this. Section 3(1)(f) gives the requirement as:

> 'any person (not being a child of the deceased) who, in the case of any marriage to which the deceased was at any time a party, was treated by the deceased as a child of the family in relation to that marriage.'

5.11   ANY PERSON WHO IS, OR IS THE ISSUE OF, A BROTHER, SISTER, UNCLE OR AUNT OF THE DECEASED

This gives rise to potential claims from the extended family, particularly since, because of s 1(3)(g), it includes the family of the deceased's spouse.

5.12   MEANING OF CONSANGUINITY, AFFINITY AND HALF-BLOOD

For the sake of completeness it is important that these definitions are set out.

5.12.1 Affinity

This means the relationship resulting from marriage between the husband and wife. So, for instance, a 'niece' of the deceased's wife would be considered a niece of the deceased.

5.12.2 Consanguinity

This means a relationship by blood.

5.12.3 Half-blood

This means the relationship between two persons who have one nearest common ancestor and not a pair of nearest common ancestors, eg half-sisters and brothers.

5.12.4 Step-child

This means the child of a husband or wife of a former union.

5.13 WIDENING THE SCOPE OF DEPENDANTS

As we have seen, the Law Commission suggested that a wider definition of 'dependant' should be put in place. The law can be particularly harsh in this respect. It has been suggested that children of unmarried parents who do not come within s 1(3)(f) of the Fatal Accidents Act 1976 can bring a claim by virtue of the Human Rights Act 1998.[1] For a full discussion of the potential impact of the Human Rights Act 1998, see Chapter 26.

5.14 SUMMARY: PRACTICAL POINTS

Entitlement to make a claim is dependent upon the claimant coming within the statutory criteria.

(1) The fact that a person comes within the statutory definition, however, does not mean that he is, in fact, a dependant.
(2) There may be arguments under the Human Rights Act 1998 in relation to claimants who are financially dependent, but who do not come within the statutory definition.

---

[1] Davis, Gumbel and Witcomb 'A Question of Dependency', NLJ, 6 July 2001.

(3)   Particular care must be taken in relation to:
       (a)   claims by former spouses; and
       (b)   claims by cohabitees.

CHAPTER 6

THE TYPE OF FINANCIAL DEPENDENCY THAT ENTITLES A PARTY TO A CLAIM

6.1   INTRODUCTION

Although it was statute that gave rise to a cause of action for death and dependency, there has never been a statutory definition of the type of dependency that gives rise to a dependency claim. It was soon established that the courts were concerned primarily with financial loss. The common law has never attempted to provide damages for bereavement. The position was put clearly, and bluntly, by Lord Wright in *Davies v Powell Duffryn Associated Collieries Ltd*:[1]

'It is a hard matter of pounds, shillings and pence, subject to the element of reasonable future probabilities.'

6.2   THE DEPENDANT MUST SHOW A FINANCIAL LOSS

In every case a dependant must show a loss. In *Yelland v Powell Duffryn Associated Collieries Ltd (No 2)*,[2] Du Parcq LJ stated:

'Any dependants who have suffered no such loss acquire no rights at all under the Act. If they bring an action and prove no loss, actual or prospective, the defendant is entitled to the verdict.'

---

[1]   [1942] AC 601, at p 617, [1942] 1 All ER 657, at p 665.
[2]   [1941] 1 KB 519.

6.3   THE TYPE OF LOSS THAT MUST BE SHOWN: THE 'REASONABLE EXPECTATION' TEST

The courts set about defining the type of damages that could be recovered. In *Franklin v South Eastern Railway*,[1] CB Pollock stated:

> 'Now it is clear that damage must be shown ... [these] should be calculated in reference to a reasonable expectation of benefit, as of right or otherwise, from the continuance of life ... a jury ought to be satisfied that there has been a loss of sensible and appreciable pecuniary benefit, which might have been reasonably expected from the continuance of life.'

The position was summarised in Law Commission Report No 263:

> 'damages awarded under the Fatal Accidents Act 1976 generally compensate the loss of any non-business benefit that the claimant reasonably expected to receive from the deceased had the deceased continued to live (often referred to as "loss of dependency"). Thus, damages under the Act may provide compensation for the loss of money brought into the household by the deceased, for the loss of gratuitous services performed by the deceased, (including domestic work) and for the loss of fringe benefits, such as a company car'.[2]

6.4   THE BURDEN OF PROOF

The claimant is *not* called upon to prove definitively that there *is* a financial loss. Rather he or she has to establish the loss of a chance to benefit financially. The question of the burden of proof was considered in detail by the House of Lords in *Davies v Taylor*.[3] The widow had left the deceased husband 5 weeks before he was killed. Her dependency claim was initially dismissed because the trial judge held that she had not shown that a reconciliation with her husband, had he lived, was more probable than not. The matter proceeded to the House of Lords, where it was held that a claimant in these circumstances had to show a substantial chance of financial benefit. Lord Reid stated, at p 212D:

> 'The peculiarity in the present case is the appellant had left her husband some five weeks before his death and there was no immediate prospect of her returning to him. He wanted her to come back but she was unwilling to come. But she says that there was a prospect or chance or probability that she might have returned to him later and it is only in the event that she would have

---

[1]   3 H&N 211, 517 ER 448.
[2]   At para 2.9.
[3]   [1974] AC 207.

benefited from his survival. To my mind the issue and the sole issue is whether that chance or probability was substantial. If it was it must be evaluated. If it was a mere possibility it must be ignored. Many different words could be and have been used to indicate the dividing line. I can think of none better than 'substantial' on one hand, or 'speculative' on the other. It must be left to the good sense of the tribunal to decide on broad lines, without regard to legal niceties, but on a consideration of all the facts in proper perspective.'

The House of Lords expressly rejected the balance of probability test. Lord Reid considered this issue at length:

'But here we are not and could not be seeking a decision either that the wife would or that she would not have returned to her husband. You can prove that a past event happened, but you cannot prove that a future event will happen and do not think that the law is so foolish as to suppose that you can. All that you can do is to evaluate the chance. Sometimes it is virtually 100 per cent: sometimes virtually nil. But often it is somewhere in between. And if it is somewhere in between I do not see much difference between a probability of 51 per cent and a probability of 49 per cent.

"Injury" in the Fatal Accidents Act does not and could not possibly mean loss of a certainty. It must and can only mean loss of a chance. The chance may be a probability of over 99 per cent but it is still only a chance. So I can see no merit in adopting here the test used for proving whether a fact did or did not happen. There it must be all or nothing.

If the balance of probability were the proper test what is to happen in the two cases which I have supposed of a 60 per cent and a 40 per cent probability. The 40 per cent case would get nothing but what about the 60 per cent case? Is it to get a full award on the basis that it has been proved that the wife would have returned to her husband? That would be the logical result. I can see no ground at all for saying that the 40 per cent case fails altogether but the 60 per cent case gets 100 per cent. But it would be almost absurd to say that the 40 per cent case gets nothing while the 60 per cent case is scaled down to that proportion of what the award would have been if the spouses had been living together. That would be applying the two different rules to the two cases. So I reject the balance of probability test.'

This test can have important ramifications in difficult dependency cases, such as the loss of a child: see the discussion in Chapter 12.

6.5   THE TYPE OF LOSSES THAT CAN GIVE RISE TO A CLAIM

The following types of loss should be considered.

(1)   Loss of income. This includes loss of the prospect of earned income.

(2)   Loss of gratuitous services provided by the deceased.

(3)   Loss of fringe benefits, eg a company car.

(4)   Loss of gifts which were anticipated.

(5)   Losses incurred because of the death. For instance, in *Davies v Whiteways Cyder Co Ltd*,[1] the dependants were able to claim damages for the estate duty they had to pay on gifts from the deceased as a result of the deceased being killed less than 7 years after the gifts were made.

6.6   NON-BUSINESS BENEFIT

The reasonable expectation test does not extend to benefits expected as a result of a business relationship. In *Burgess v Florence Nightingale Hospital for Gentlewomen*,[2] a husband and wife were dancing partners. The husband's earning capacity decreased as a result of his wife's death since he could no longer dance as a team; the earning capacity of a couple was greater. However, the husband could not recover for his loss of income as a dancer after her death. This decision has been the subject of some criticism.[3]

However, in *Oldfield v Mahoney*,[4] the practice of a school was to appoint a married man to the post of housemaster. Following the death of his wife, a schoolmaster recovered damages for his reduced chances of promotion.

6.7   SUMMARY: PRACTICAL POINTS

(1)   For an action to succeed there must be actual financial dependency.

(2)   The dependency must be a 'reasonable expectation of financial benefit'.

(3)   A potential dependant is not called upon to prove his claim on the balance of probabilities, the test is one of a loss of reasonable chance of benefit.

(4)   The dependency need not only be earned income. The financial value of services provided by the deceased is well-recognised.

---

[1]   [1975] QB 262.

[2]   [1955] 1 QB 349.

[3]   See *Munkman on Damages for Personal Injury* 10th edn, at pp 137–138.

[4]   (Unreported) 12 July 1968. Cited in *Kemp & Kemp*, vol 3, paras M3-055 and M3-122.

(5)   A business loss is not recoverable. However, this issue must be examined with some care.

CHAPTER 7

LIMITATION AND OTHER MATTERS THAT COULD BAR A FATAL ACCIDENT CLAIM

PART 1 – LIMITATION OF ACTIONS

7.1 THE LIMITATION ISSUES

It is important to note that not all fatal accident claims are subject to a 3-year limitation period. Most common law claims, however, are subject to the somewhat tortuous provisions of the Limitation Act 1980.

7.2 THE LIMITATION ACT 1980: AN OVERVIEW

To put the matter in simple form:

(1) (apart from the exceptional cases) the safest assumption, when the death was immediate, is that a 3-year limitation period runs from the date of death;

(2) in cases where the deceased survived for a time after the incident that eventually caused the death:

  (a) the first issue to be considered is whether the primary limitation period has expired so far as a cause of action by the deceased is concerned;

  (b) if this initial 3-year limitation period has not expired then a new 3-year period begins;

  (c) if the 3-year limitation period available to the deceased has expired prior to the death, then it will be necessary for the dependants to make an application under s 33 of the Limitation Act 1980.

7.3　SECTION 11

Section 11 of the Limitation Act 1980 states:

'Actions in respect of wrongs causing personal injuries or death

11　**Special time limit for actions in respect of personal injuries**

(1)　This section applies to any action for damages for negligence, nuisance or breach of duty (whether the duty exists by virtue of a contract or of provision made by or under a statute or independently of any contract or any such provision) where the damages claimed by the plaintiff for the negligence, nuisance or breach of duty consist of or include damages in respect of personal injuries to the plaintiff or any other person.

(1A)　This section does not apply to any action brought for damages under section 3 of the Protection from Harassment Act 1997.

(2)　None of the time limits given in the preceding provisions of this Act shall apply to the action to which this section applies.

(3)　An action to which this section applies shall not be brought after the expiration of the period applicable in accordance with subsection (4) or (5) below.

(4)　Except where subsection (5) below applies, the period applicable is three years from –
　　　(a)　the date on which the cause of action accrued; or
　　　(b)　the date of knowledge (if later) of the person injured.

(5)　If the person injured dies before the expiration of the period mentioned in subsection (4) above, the period applicable in respects of the cause of action surviving for the benefit of this estate by virtue of section 1 of the Law Reform (Miscellaneous Provisions) Act 1934 shall be three years from –
　　　(a)　the date of death; or
　　　(b)　the date of the personal representative's knowledge;
　　　whichever is the later.

(6)　For the purposes of this section "personal representative" includes any person who is or has been a personal representative of the deceased, including an executor who has not proved the will (whether or not he has renounced probate) but not anyone appointed only as a special personal representative in relation to settled land; and regard shall be had to any knowledge acquired by any such person while a personal representative or previously.

(7)　If there is more than one personal representative, and their dates of knowledge are different, subsection 5(b) above shall be read as referring to the earliest of those dates.'

7.4　WHERE THE DECEASED'S LIMITATION PERIOD HAD NOT EXPIRED

If the deceased survived for a period after the accident, or acquired 'knowledge' of a cause of action within the meaning of the

Limitation Act 1980, then the normal rules as to computing the limitation period apply, as given in s 12:

'**12   Special time limit for actions under Fatal Accidents legislation**

(1)   An action under the Fatal Accidents Act 1976 shall not be brought if the death occurred when the person injured could no longer maintain an action and recover damages in respect of the injury (whether because of a time limit in this Act or in any other Act, or for any other reason). Where any such action by the injured person would have been barred by the time limit in section 11 [or 11A] of this Act, no account shall be taken of the possibility of that time limit being overridden under section 33 of this Act.

(2)   None of the time limits given in the preceding provisions of this Act shall apply to an action under the Fatal Accidents Act 1976, but no such action shall be brought after the expiration of three years from –

(a)   the date of death; or

(b)   the date of knowledge of the person for whose benefit the action is brought;'.

7.5   KNOWLEDGE OF THE DECEASED

It is important to note that there are factors which could mean that the deceased's limitation period is more than 3 years.

(1)   If the deceased was a minor when the accident happened, then the limitation period will not start to run until his or her eighteenth birthday.

(2)   If the deceased was psychologically disabled to the extent that he or she was under a disability from the date of the accident until the date of death, then the limitation period never started to run. However, it is important to note that if the claimant was not under a disability when the action accrued, subsequent incapacity does not prevent time running.

7.6   SPECIAL TIME-LIMITS

Particular care should be taken when dealing with accidents arising during the course of air travel or travel by boat or ship. In most of these cases the court has *no discretion* to extend time periods under s 33 of the Limitation Act 1980.

7.6.1   'Nautical' accidents

The Merchant Shipping Act 1979, Sch 3 provides a 2-year limitation period for accidents caused by the carrier, his employees or agents, if acting in the course of their employment.

(1)   The limitation period is 2 years. However, if the death occurred during the journey the period is calculated not from the date of death but from the date when the deceased should have disembarked.

(2)   If the death occurs after disembarkation, the 2-year period runs from the date of death. However, there is a 'long-stop' provision: the death must be within 3 years of disembarkation.

The Maritime Conventions Act 1911 states that for actions arising out of the collision of vessels the limitation period is 2 years from the date when the injury was caused. The term vessels here also includes hovercrafts.[1]

(1)   This only applies to injuries sustained on board one vessel due to the negligence of another. Consequently the 2-year period does not apply if the death is caused by the negligence of those on the vessel on which the deceased was sailing.[2]

(2)   The vessel must be in the course of a navigation. In *Curtis v Wild*,[3] a sailing dinghy on a reservoir was used in navigation and the 2-year period did not apply.

(3)   A jet-ski is not a vessel for the purpose of the Act since the rider sits outside it and not in it.[4]

7.6.2   Accidents involving aircraft

Particular care must be taken in relation to any accident on aircraft. The Carriage by Air Act 1961 incorporates the Warsaw Convention into English law. Article 29 of the Convention extinguishes the right to damages if an action under the Convention is not brought within 2 years.

(1)   The 2-year period is reckoned from the date of arrival at the destination or the date on which the aircraft ought to have arrived, or from the date that the journey ceased.

---

[1]   Hovercraft (Civil Liability) Order 1979, SI 1979/305.
[2]   *Navarro v Larrinaga Steamship Co Ltd* [1966] P 80.
[3]   [1991] 4 All ER 172.
[4]   *Steedman v Scofield* [1992] 2 Lloyd's Rep 163.

(2) It is important that a claim is asserted *under the Convention*. Both the claim form and the particulars of claim must make it clear that the action is brought under the Convention. In most cases, the Convention action is the *sole* remedy available to the claimant.

(3) The Convention applies not only to air accidents, but also to accidents that occurred on board the aircraft and in the course of embarking or disembarking.

7.6.3 Accidents abroad

Limitation periods for accidents abroad may be different.[1]

7.7 PRACTICAL POINTS

(1) Always consider the relevant limitation period.

(2) Be particularly wary when the deceased survived for a period after the accident or incident which gave rise to the death (for instance, asbestosis cases). There could be arguments as to the date of knowledge.

(3) Remember the different limitation periods for some accidents at sea, or in the course of navigation, and accidents involving aircraft.

(4) If in doubt, assume the earliest date and issue proceedings.

PART 2 – MATTERS THAT COULD BAR THE CLAIM

7.8 PREVIOUS ACTIONS

Advisers need to be wary as to whether a previous action has been determined or settled. Section 1(1) requires the deceased to have been able successfully to maintain an action at the date of death.

7.8.1 Judgment made against the defendant

An action cannot proceed if the deceased has already obtained judgment against the defendant (see *Murray v Shuter*).[2] In this case the claim of an accident victim was adjourned so that the dependants could claim under the Act when he died.

---

[1] See Foreign Limitation Periods Act 1984.
[2] [1972] 1 Lloyd's Rep 6, CA.

It is not clear whether these principles would apply if the judgment was only on the issue of liability. However, in the absence of authoritative guidance it would be prudent not to enter any type of judgment unless you are making a claim for provisional damages.

7.8.2 Amending claims to include fatal accidents/injury claims

The fact that proceedings have been issued prior to death does not prevent them being amended to include a fatal accident claim. In *Booker v Associated Ports*,[1] the Court of Appeal held it was appropriate to allow the writ to be amended to allow the claim. Such amendment was permitted under s 35 of the Limitation Act 1980.

7.8.3 Appeals on the initial personal injury claim

An action under the Fatal Accidents Act 1976 cannot be instituted if an appeal has been lodged after judgment in the initial action for personal injury. However, paradoxically, the fact of the death after a hearing but before an appeal can be used to reduce the award of damages.[2]

7.8.4 Multiple defendants

However, if there is more than one potential defendant, the fact that the deceased had, prior to death, settled the action with one defendant could prevent a fatal accident claim even against a defendant who was not a party to the initial action.[3]

7.8.5 Previous proceedings issued but not served

In *Michael Cachia v Faluyi* [2001] EWCA Civ 998,[4] a writ was issued on behalf of the estate just before the end of the limitation period but was never served. Some years later a new writ was issued and served promptly. The Court of Appeal considered an argument that s 2(3) of the Limitation Act 1976, which states that: 'not more than one action shall lie for and in respect of the same subject-matter of complaint', meant that the second action could not proceed. The Court held that the European Convention on Human Rights (the

---

[1]   [1995] PIQR P 375.

[2]   *McCann v Sheppard* [1973] 1 WLR 540.

[3]   See *Jameson v Central Electricity Generating Board* [2000] 1 AC 455, HL. The rationale of this decision appears to be that the deceased did not have the right to bring an action at the date of his death.

[4]   [2002] PIQR P5.

Convention) gave the children a right of access to a court to claim compensation for their loss of dependency following the death of their mother. The Court was under a duty not to act in a way which is incompatible with a Convention right. It was possible to interpret the word 'action' as meaning 'served process' in order to give effect to the Convention rights of the children. Until the second writ was served in July 1997, no process had been served which asserted a claim to compensation by these children for their mother's death. Brooke LJ observed at para 21 that:

> 'This is a very good example of the way in which the enactment of the Human Rights Act now enables English judges to do justice in a way which was not previously open to us.'

7.9   PROVISIONAL DAMAGES

At one time it was possible that an award of provisional damages could bar any action by the dependants. However, s 3 of the Damages Act 1996 has made clear that a provisional damages award does not bar a claim under the Fatal Accidents Act 1976, although the award will be taken into account in assessing damages payable to the dependants under the 1976 Act.

7.10   PRACTICAL POINTS

(1)   It is prudent to check whether the deceased has been involved in any other personal injury claim prior to his death. Be particularly careful where a significant length of time has elapsed between the accident, the deceased's date of knowledge and the death. The deceased may have settled an action without the knowledge of your clients.

(2)   If there is a possibility that a claimant could die in the course of an action as a result of the injuries sustained, be very careful about entering judgment.

(3)   If there is a possibility of a living claimant dying as a result of his injuries, make sure that a claim for provisional damages is made.

(4)   The pleadings can be amended to plead a fatal accident claim if the deceased dies in the course of proceedings but prior to judgment.

PART 3

VALUING THE DEPENDENCY CLAIM

In this Part we will examine the general principles governing dependency. Thereafter, we will look at specific issues and problem areas.

In this section we look at:

(1)   basic principles of quantifying the dependency claim;
(2)   s 4 of the Fatal Accidents Act 1976;
(3)   specific examples of dependency claims:
  – loss of a wage earner;
  – loss of a carer;
  – loss of a parent;
  – loss of a child.

CHAPTER 8

BASIC PRINCIPLES OF DEPENDENCY CALCULATION

8.1 INTRODUCTION

The task of quantifying the dependency claim is one which requires a methodical approach coupled with a great deal of care and compassion. The use of a questionnaire will be helpful (see Appendix 1), but will rarely be sufficient and, as some of the cases show, sometimes lateral thinking is necessary. In this chapter we will look at:

(1) claims for loss of income;
(2) other losses;
(3) the dependency claim itself; and
(4) specific examples of loss of dependency claim.

8.2 LATERAL THINKING

Understandably, a great deal of stress is put upon the need to consider the multiplier/multiplicand approach in fatal cases. However, the calculation can go beyond a consideration of mathematics. In *Daniels v Jones*,[1] Holroyd Pearce LJ observed that:

> 'If ... arithmetically the conclusion must be that there is no loss in the case, arithmetic has failed to provide the answer which common sense demands. It must be remembered that this is a question of fact expressly left to the jury ... Since the question is one of actual material loss, some arithmetical calculations are necessary. But they do not provide a substitute for commonsense. Much of the calculation must be in the realms of hypothesis, and in that region arithmetic is a good servant, but a bad master.'

---

[1] [1961] 1 WLR 1103.

For a working example of the importance of lateral thinking, see *Cape Distribution v O' Loughlin*,[1] discussed at para **10.3**.

8.3   THE BURDEN OF PROOF IN ESTABLISHING A DEPENDENCY RELATIONSHIP

It is very important to bear in mind that a claimant making a dependency claim is not called upon to prove the fact that he was, or could have been, a dependant on the balance of probabilities; the test is one of showing a substantial chance and then evaluating that chance. See *Davies v Taylor*,[2] and the detailed discussion at para **6.3**, see also the case of *Davis v Bonner*,[3] discussed at para **12.5**.

8.4   STEP 1: ASCERTAINING VALUE OF THE LOSS OF THE DECEASED'S INCOME AND SERVICES

8.4.1   The deceased's income

One of the first matters that needs to be ascertained is the loss of income. This is the starting point in most claims. However:

(1)   the investigation should not only be based on the deceased's income at the date of death. Care should be taken to ensure that the court is presented with evidence to show the earnings that the deceased would have earned up to the date of trial;

(2)   the deceased's future income and prospects must be taken into account. For instance, a trainee solicitor may have been earning a relatively modest income at the date of death; however, it is clear that such income would increase upon the trainee qualifying.

In *Young v Percival*,[4] the deceased was a salesman at the date of his death. It was probable that he would have been promoted to general sales manager in the near future and there was a good prospect of his being promoted to director status. After reaching an annual figure for dependency of £1,100, the Court of Appeal awarded a further £8,000 to take account of the future prospects of promotion.

---

[1]   [2001] PIQR Q8.
[2]   [1974] AC 207.
[3]   (Unreported) 6 April 1995. See *Kemp & Kemp*, para M5-103.
[4]   [1975] 1 WLR 17.

In *Malone v Rowan*,[1] a strong possibility that the deceased would have been promoted in the near future was established. For loss of dependency an overall multiplier of 16 was used. After 1½ years to trial, a multiplier for future loss of 14.5 was used. Because the chance of promotion was such a strong one the lower rate of earnings was taken for only 6 months, and the remaining 14 years of the multiplier were calculated using the higher rate.

8.4.2 Other items

Remember that the losses are not confined to pure income. Other losses may be relevant, such as:

(1) the loss of fringe benefits such as a company car can be recovered: *Clay v Pooler*;[2]
(2) a loss of reasonable expectation of benefit. In *Betney v Rowland and Mallard*,[3] a daughter claimed for the loss of the contribution her parents would have made to her wedding;
(3) in *Davies v Whiteways Cyder Co Ltd*,[4] the dependants claimed damages for the estate duty they had to pay on gifts from the deceased as a result of the death occurring less than 7 years after the gifts were made;
(4) the loss of gifts which were anticipated. An example of this is cited above in *Betney v Rowland and Mallard*.[5] The loss was the contribution expected from the parents to their daughter's wedding;
(5) loss of a right of action. In *Singh v Aitken*,[6] the deceased died from a heart attack, the defendants having misdiagnosed his condition. He would have survived if a correct diagnosis had been made. He had been seriously injured in a road traffic accident and had an unanswerable claim against the MIB which had a value of £120,497.

After his death the action against the MIB was settled for £20,000. The dependants, therefore, claimed 75 per cent of the difference between that value and the sum paid under the compromise as damages under the Fatal Accidents Act 1976. The defendants contended that loss of the capital sum was not

---

[1] [1984] 3 All ER 402.
[2] [1982] 3 All ER 570.
[3] [1992] CLY 1786.
[4] [1975] QB 262.
[5] [1992] CLY 1786.
[6] [1998] PIQR Q37.

reasonably foreseeable and that damages for that loss were irrecoverable.

The judge gave judgment for the claimants. The injury to Mr Singh's dependants, resulting from the death, was the loss of the capital sum which would otherwise have been received by them from Mr Singh's personal injury damages had he survived. It was entirely foreseeable that the misdiagnosis of the heart condition would lead to Mr Singh's death. The defendants were required to take Mr Singh as they found him – a man with an unanswerable claim to a large sum which was forfeited by their negligence.

The dependants were also entitled to interest from the date which they would have received the capital sum of which they had been deprived.

(6)　*Loss of unpaid services.* This includes the 'DIY' claim which often prevails in personal injury cases. In *Crabtree v Wilson*,[1] it was said that the deceased's work around the home had an annual value of £1,500.

In *W v H*,[2] a 44-year-old man was awarded £446,084 for loss of dependency suffered as a result of his wife's death. The claimant suffered from multiple sclerosis. His wife had provided care for him at their home prior to the accident. The claimant was forced to move into a nursing home. At trial, the cost of the claimant's nursing care was found to be recoverable from the defendant.

8.5　STEP 2: THE DEPENDENCY CALCULATION

8.5.1　The 'conventional' approach

The 'conventional' approach is to be found in the case of *Harris v Empress Motors*,[3] but there is some debate as to whether this is always appropriate. This provides a rough and ready approach to a dependency claim in circumstances where partners were married or living as husband and wife. In following this approach, it is

---

[1]　[1993] PIQR Q24.
[2]　(Unreported) 11 February 2000 (summary available on Lawtel).
[3]　[1983] 3 All ER 561.

necessary to consider the amount the deceased would be likely to have spent on himself and the balance remaining.

In taking account of the money the deceased would have spent on himself:

(1)   33$\frac{1}{3}$ per cent is deducted if the deceased left only a dependent spouse; and

(2)   25 per cent is deducted if there are dependent children as well as a spouse.

The percentage multiplier will often have to be approached carefully, because part of the multiplier will be attributed to the period when the children are dependent and the balance to the period when they cease to be dependent.

The conventional approach is not always applicable. In *Coward v Comex Houlder Diving Ltd*,[1] an increased percentage for dependency was allowed by the Court of Appeal because the husband worked as a diver in the North Sea for long periods and was considered to have been likely to have spent less money on himself as a result.

8.5.2   If a spouse is earning

If a spouse is earning before the death and continues earning after death, then the calculation is slightly more complex.

(1)   The dependency is assessed by calculating two-thirds of the *joint* income and deducting from that figure the amount of the survivor's earnings.

(2)   So, for example, if husband and wife with no children are each earning £25,000 per year net:
    (a)   the joint income is £50,000;
    (b)   two-thirds of the joint income is approximately £33,300;
    (c)   deduct the surviving partner's earnings of £25,000;
    (d)   the annual loss is approximately £8,300.

This can give rise to some disappointing and surprising results; however, it is not open to the court to ignore the surviving spouse's income: see *Crabtree v Wilson*.[2]

---

[1]   (Unreported 1998). Cited in *Kemp & Kemp*, vol 3, paras M2-024 and M2-232.
[2]   [1993] PIQR Q24.

8.5.3   A practical approach

Care must be taken to ensure that the approach taken in terms of the dependency calculation is one that is most beneficial for the client. It is surprising how many clients are willing to accept the 'rough and ready' *Harris* approach.[1] If, after consideration of the issues, this is what the client wishes it is useful to ask the defendant, at the outset, whether he is willing to accept this as a proper approach. This should be done under the ambit of, or at least the spirit of, the Pre-action Protocol. If the parties can agree the principle of calculation at the outset, then this would have numerous advantages:

(1)   costs will be reduced;
(2)   there will be less need for detailed examination of the family lifestyle prior to death;
(3)   requirements for disclosure and inspection are reduced.

However, the use of the *Harris* approach should not be taken as an excuse not to consider the claim thoroughly. It should only be used after consideration of the issues with the client.

8.6   STEP 3: THE MULTIPLIER[2]

8.6.1   The current difficulty

The difficulty with the multiplier at present is as follows.

(1)   The assessment takes place given factors up to the date of trial. The court awards:
      (a) damages for past loss;
      (b) damages for future loss of earning, on the basis of the earnings that the deceased would have had at the date of trial.
(2)   The multiplier runs from the date of death.
      In *Cookson v Knowles*,[3] the House of Lords held that the multiplier should be calculated from the date of death. The court then divides the multiplier between the pre-trial period

---

[1] See para **8.5.1**.
[2] For a detailed explanation of how to apply the Actuarial Tables to fatal accident cases, see 'How to use Multipliers in Assessing Damages under Fatal Accidents, Using the "Revised Ogden Tables"', by David Kemp QC and Rowland Hogg [2000] JPIL 142.
[3] [1979] AC 556.

and post-trial period. That part of the multiplier which remains after trial is applied to assess the post-trial losses.

In cases where there has been some delay between the death and trial the multiplier could, therefore, be 'used up'. In these circumstances the Court of Appeal has held that the calculation can be more flexible to reflect the fact that the length of time has reduced the element of uncertainty: *Corbett v Barking, Havering and Brentwood Health Authority*.[1]

This approach was criticised by the Law Commission in *Claims for Wrongful Death* (Law Com No 263) where it was advocated that the multiplier should be calculated from the date of trial. It has been suggested that this proposal can be put in place without legislation. However, in *White v ESAB Group (UK) Ltd*,[2] Nelson J held that the proper method of calculation of the multiplier was from the date of death.

8.6.2 Factors affecting the multiplier

(1) Expectation of life of deceased and dependants.
     The defendants will be particularly keen to examine the medical records of the deceased. They are entitled to do this. However, the defendant is not normally entitled to demand that the survivor(s) undergo a medical examination in relation to their own life expectancy.

(2) Expectation of dependency of child dependants.
     This will affect how the 'dependency percentage' is apportioned.

(3) Expectation of divorce or separation of deceased and dependant.
     In *Owen v Martin*,[3] the marriage was regarded as fragile and the multiplier reduced from 15 to 11 by the Court of Appeal. The Law Commission was critical of this approach which is defined further at Chapter 25.

(4) The prospects of remarriage of a widow (and her actual remarriage) are ignored (Fatal Accidents Act 1976, s 3(3)). (As we shall see at para **9.3.4**, it is arguable that this also applies to remarriage of a widower.) The prospects of marriage of a widow or the actual remarriage cannot, therefore, be used to reduce the multiplier.

---

[1] [1991] 2 QB 408.
[2] [2002] PIQR P26.
[3] [1992] PIQR Q151.

(5)   The fact that a couple are not married is taken into account (Fatal Accidents Act 1976, s 3(4)). In practice, this usually leads to a reduced multiplier.

8.7 PRACTICAL POINTS

(1)   Although fatal accident dependency involves considerable calculations, the approach can require lateral thinking.

(2)   In looking at the loss of income and services provided by the deceased:

    (a)   consider future income and prospects;

    (b)   consider fringe benefits;

    (c)   consider loss of services;

    (d)   the test is reasonable expectation of benefit, which can include loss of a right of action;

    (e)   there is a conventional approach to loss of dependency; however, check whether it is necessarily appropriate.

(3)   When looking at the multiplier, always consider the argument that the multiplier should run from the date of trial rather than the date of death.

(4)   Remember to look carefully at the deceased's state of health. If the deceased had a lower life expectancy, then the value of the claim will be reduced.

(5)   If the dependant was a cohabitee, then the court must take this into account. Further, in the case of a female dependant, the prospects of remarriage can arguably be taken into account.

CHAPTER 9

SECTION 4 OF THE
FATAL ACCIDENTS ACT 1976 –
MATTERS WHICH SHOULD BE DISREGARDED

9.1   INTRODUCTION

An understanding of s 4 of the Fatal Accidents Act 1976 is central to an understanding of dependency claims. In practical terms, any positive benefits to the dependants that arise out of the death are ignored in calculating their claim against the defendant.

There is an ongoing debate in relation to s 4. In essence, the Law Commission feels that this section has been interpreted too widely. In response, the editors of *Kemp & Kemp* have replied, robustly, that the section is meant to be given a wide construction. However, in the absence of specific legislative intervention, it appears clear that the wider construction prevails.

Section 4 states:

> 'In assessing damages in respect of a person's death in an action under this Act, benefits which have accrued or will or may accrue to any person from his estate or otherwise as a result of his death shall be disregarded.'

This amendment was introduced because of recommendations by the Law Commission and the Pearson Commission. It replaced the 'list' of items to be disregarded that was in the previous fatal accident legislation and gave rise to some anomalies.

9.2   CONSTRUING SECTION 4

The width of s 4 has been criticised by the Law Commission. However, even the Law Commission observed that:

> 'Nevertheless, a natural reading of the section suggests that all benefits accruing as a result of death should be disregarded.'[1]

In *McGreggor on Damages*,[2] it is observed that 'the immense range of this omnibus provision needs to be appreciated'.

The word 'benefits' has been given a wide construction, as the examples below demonstrate. It goes beyond financial benefits and covers care, services and, possibly, even remarriage.

9.3   EXAMPLES OF SECTION 4 IN ACTION

It is helpful to look at some examples.

9.3.1   *Auty v National Coal Board*[3]

A widow received a pension after the death of her husband. She claimed that she should recover damages for the post-retirement widow's pension that she would have received. Section 4 should be applied and the widow's pension that she had received since her husband' s death should be ignored. The court held that:

(1)   as against her claim for the loss of her husband's (pre-retirement) support, the pension she received was ignored; and

(2)   as against that part of her loss she had suffered no loss as she was in receipt of a widow's pension.

9.3.2   *Stanley v Siddique*[4]

A child claimed damages under the Act following the death of his mother. After the accident his father met and married another woman. It was found that the child was receiving better care from his father's wife than he would have expected from his mother. The court held that this was a benefit resulting from the death within s 4

---

1   Law Commission Report No 263 *Claims for Wrongful Death*, at para 2.39.
2   At p 1820.
3   [1985] 1 WLR 784.
4   [1991] 2 WLR 459.

and so should not be taken into account in assessing the child's damages.

9.3.3   Hayden v Hayden[1]

A child lost her mother in a driving accident caused by her father's negligence. The father gave up work to look after his daughter. The Court of Appeal decided that the plaintiff's damages should be reduced to the extent that her father remedied the loss of her mother's services.

9.3.4   Topp v London Country Bus South West Ltd[2]

The issue here concerned the prospect of remarriage of a widower. In Topp, both parties had agreed that the court was bound to ignore the prospects of remarriage as a result of the decision in Stanley v Siddique.[3] However, the defendant reserved the right to argue a different position in a different court. (The Law Commission does not appear to agree with this.)

9.3.5   Insurance policies

Section 4 was designed to ensure that matters such as insurance policies, life insurance and similar types of policy were not deducted.

9.3.6   Watson v Wilmott[4]

In Watson v Wilmott, a young child's parents were both killed because of the defendant's negligence. He was subsequently adopted by his uncle and aunt. It was held that the adoption replaced the loss of dependency. As a result of the wide interpretation of s 4, it is unlikely that the decision in Watson v Wilmott is sustainable.

9.4   PRACTICAL POINTS

(1)   Be aware that the benefits covered by s 4 have a wide construction.

---

[1]   [1992] 1 WLR 986.
[2]   [1992] PIQR 206.
[3]   [1991] 2 WLR 459.
[4]   [1991] 1 QB 140.

(2)   Look carefully at the claimants' position after the death and
      the way their life has changed or ways in which they have
      benefited. Be prepared to argue that, if there is a positive
      benefit, then this should be ignored.
(3)   Be wary of any argument from the defendant (which often
      arises) that claims or losses should be discounted or ignored
      because of services provided after the death.

CHAPTER 10

LOSS OF AN INCOME EARNER

10.1   INTRODUCTION

We have looked in detail already at the appropriate approach to
assessing income and the loss, including the need to take account of
promotion prospects and fringe benefits. In this chapter we look at
a pragmatic approach to loss of earnings.

10.2   YOUR LOSS OF INCOME CHECKLIST

Look in detail at Chapter 6. As much documentation as possible
needs to be obtained in relation to the deceased's income, see the
checklist at Appendix 1.

Remember that fringe benefits and promotion prospects are all
factors the court should take into account. Remember also the
difficulties that arise out of business benefits.

Two recent decisions illustrate the difficulties that can arise in the
calculation of financial dependency and the pragmatic approach
that the courts can take.

10.3   WHEN THE DECEASED MADE HIS LIVING OFF CAPITAL

10.3.1   *Cape Distribution v O'Loughlin*[1]

The Court of Appeal considered a case where Mr O'Loughlin made
his living from property development, which thus formed the sole

---

[1]   [2001] PIQR Q8.

basis of the family's finances. He and his family had built up a property portfolio of some seven investment properties. After his death Mrs O'Loughlin did not suffer any immediate financial disadvantage, as she received the full capital value of the property. However, she could not manage the properties with the skill shown by her husband. Three of the properties were sold and there was a decreasing income from the properties.

The trial judge awarded damages on the basis that the family had lost the flair, experience and entrepreneurial skills of Mr O'Loughlin. He assessed how much it would cost to replace Mr O'Loughlin's skills with those of another person and applied an appropriate multiplier to this figure.

10.3.2   The defendant's arguments

The defendant's argument was that the dependants had lost little. The full value of the capital assets were available to them and they had the benefit of the rental income. In the period immediately following the death the family had lost nothing. It was also argued that there was no proper evidence before the court to enable the court to come to a proper conclusion as to the true value of the dependency.

10.3.3   The Court of Appeal's decision

This case is important because of the pragmatic way in which the Court approached this issue. Latham LJ stated:

> 'the court's task in any case is to examine the particular facts of the case to determine whether or not any loss in money or in monies worth has been occasioned to the dependants and if it determines that it has, it must then use whatever material appears best to fit the facts of the particular case in order to determine the extent of that loss.'

In Mrs O'Loughlin's case, the judge came to the conclusion that the dependants had lost the flair and business acumen which would have resulted in a successful development of the property portfolio which represented the family's assets. The judge was, therefore, clearly correct in concluding that the dependants had suffered a loss capable of being measured in money terms.

The judge could have embarked upon complex evaluation of the extent to which the property portfolio would have been more valuable had it been managed by Mr O'Loughlin. However, this approach would be riddled with uncertainty and speculation.

However, it was certain that the family would have required professional advice in order to manage the family assets properly and effectively. The cost of such advice therefore represented the most secure basis from which to attempt to place a pecuniary value on the loss to the dependants.

10.3.4   The primacy of common sense

Judge LJ responded to the argument that no loss had been sustained by the widow by citing the trenchant observations of Holroyd Pearce LJ in *Daniels v Jones*:[1]

> 'If ... arithmetically the conclusion must be that there is no loss in this case, arithmetic has failed to provide the answer which common sense demands. It must be remembered that this is a question of fact expressly left to the jury ... Since the question is of one actual material loss, some arithmetical calculations are necessarily involved in an assessment of the injury. But they do not provide a substitute for common sense. Much of the calculation must be in the realms of hypothesis, and in that region arithmetic is a good servant, but a bad master.'

10.3.5   Lessons to be learnt

The observations of the Court of Appeal are, without doubt, of considerable assistance in those unusual and difficult cases where the dependency calculation cannot be based on an average weekly or annual earning figure. Remember:

(1)   the courts are highly suspicious of an argument that the loss of dependency is nil;

(2)   the fact that the dependant's income arises from capital assets does not prevent a claim for financial loss being made;

(3)   ultimately the issue of loss of dependency is a 'jury' issue (ie a decision of fact for the judge). While calculations assist, the court is entitled to apply common sense.

(4)   in these cases it clearly helps for the claimant to put forward a pragmatic argument which the court can grasp.

---

[1]   [1961] 1 WLR 1103.

10.4   CAREER PROSPECTS NOT AS POOR AS DEFENDANT CONTENDED

10.4.1   *Dalziel v Donald*[1]

This is a case where the deceased husband was a soldier who had recently been demoted. It was further complicated because the deceased husband had a mistress. Indeed, the mistress was a pillion passenger on the motorcycle that the husband was riding when he was killed.

What is remarkable about this case is the way that the claimant's case largely stood up against the defendant's furious attempts to decrease the dependency claim. The defendant had a lot of material to assist in these attempts. Not only did the deceased have a mistress, but the couple were heavily in debt and there was a danger that the family home would be repossessed. The deceased had been demoted and there were several adverse comments about him in the Army records.

10.4.2   The defendant's arguments

(1)   The existence of a mistress was used to argue that the marriage would have soon broken up and there was, therefore, only a minor claim by the widow.

This argument was considered by the judge. He found that the mistress did not know the deceased was married and would have ended the relationship if she did. Matters could not have continued for long. The judge found that the marriage was vulnerable to failure but was likely to have survived. To reflect the fact that the marriage was vulnerable the judge reduced the multiplier to 11 (in a case where the claimant contended for a multiplier of 20).

(2)   The defendant was also highly critical of the deceased's Army record and argued that because of a history of disciplinary problems (including demotion) he would not have been promoted and might well have been discharged from military service altogether.

The court rejected this argument. The court preferred the evidence of Army officers called by the claimant to give

---

[1]   [2001] PIQR Q44.

evidence of Mr Dalziel's Army career and his prospects. It found that there was a principle of 'retention' in an underfunded and undermanned Army and that Mr Dalziel would have received pro-active help from the Army and had a substantial chance of promotion to Lance-Corporal.

Although the widow was, understandably, disappointed with the reduction of the multiplier it is notable how, again, the application of common sense prevails here. The court did not take the defendant's assertions at face value and was willing to go into a detailed investigation of the facts.

The reported case does not do full justice to the facts. Although the claimant failed to beat the payment into court, she was awarded costs up to the date when the defendant disclosed a statement from the deceased's mistress – a date considerably later than the date of payment into court. The claimant was attempting to argue that the issue relating to breakdown of the marriage should be wholly ignored in accordance with Law Commission recommendations.[1]

10.5 LOSS OF INCOME: PRACTICAL POINTS

(1)   Take careful account not only of actual income but also of future prospects and loss of benefits.

(2)   Do not assume that because the family were living on capital there is no loss.

(3)   The fact that the defendant can point to problems in the deceased's career pattern does not inevitably mean that the court will accept that the claimant had no prospect of success nor any future loss of income.

---

[1]   See para **25.5**.

CHAPTER 11

DAMAGES FOR DEATH OF A MOTHER OR CARER

'The quantification of the services provided by a mother is particularly difficult.'[1]

11.1 INTRODUCTION

Because of the absence of statutory guidance, and the numerous different factual situations that the court has to consider, the valuation of the loss of caring services provided by a parent (usually, but not invariably, the mother) is extremely problematic. The difficulties and complications in this area were recognised by the Law Commission; however, no recommendations for reform were made. Claimants have to work on constructing a case based on very few governing principles.

At the outset it should be said that addressing the issue of 'loss of a mother' is often a misnomer. What we are concerned with here is the issue of loss of a person who provides services rather than income. Further individuals, including fathers, are not just economic units. Claims for loss of services can be made in cases where there are claims for loss of income.

11.2 THE JUDICIAL APPROACH

The courts have never approached the issue of valuation of loss of a mother's or carer's services on a strict mathematical basis. There are a number of variables. In particular the benefit received by a child

---

[1] Law Commission Report No 263 *Claims for Wrongful Death*, at para 2.27.

from its mother varies with the age of a child. In *Regan v Williamson*,[1] Watkins J considered a strictly arithmetical approach to the issue of loss of a mother, based on the hiring of a housekeeper. He observed that:

> 'The simplicity of such an exercise would, in my opinion, work an injustice upon the deceased's dependants which I think the average member of the public would describe as quite monstrous.'

He observed, at p 309, that:

> 'the word "services" has been too narrowly construed. It should, at least, include an acknowledgment that a wife and mother does not work to set hours and, still less, to rule. She is in constant attendance, save for those hours when she is, if that is the fact, at work. During some of those hours she may well give the children instruction on essential matters to do with their upbringing and, possibly, with such things as their homework. This sort of attention seems to be as much of a service, and probably more valuable to them, than the other kinds of service conventionally so described.'

11.3   GENERAL PRINCIPLES

A few general principles can be ascertained.

11.3.1   Hiring of relatives

The courts tend to look kindly on the hiring of relatives even if this is more expensive than other alternatives. In *Morris v Rigby*,[2] the widower employed his wife's sister to care for his children. The Court of Appeal held this to be entirely reasonable, even though it was more costly than market rates. Similarly, in *Regan*, it was held entirely reasonable for the plaintiff to bring into his home someone whom he knew, who knew the children and who had an attachment to them.

11.3.2   Loss of mother's services

The courts will make a separate, distinct, award for the financial value of the loss of a mother's services. This is often done on the basis of the cost of a third party providing the same services, such as a housekeeper or nanny.[3]

---

[1]   [1976] 1 WLR 305.

[2]   (1966) 110 SJ 834.

[3]   *Clay v Pooler* [1982] 3 All ER 570; *Regan v Williamson* [1976] 1 WLR 305.

11.3.3 Separate award for 'intangible' loss

There is a growing trend for a 'separate' award to be made for the 'intangible' loss of a mother's services. This arises, primarily, out of arguments in *McGreggor on Damages* (op cit) where it was observed, at p 1805, that:

> 'it may be argued that the benefit of a mother's personal attention to a child's upbringing, morals, education and psychology, which the services of a housekeeper, nurse or governess could never provide, is in the long run a financial value for the child, difficult as this is to assess.'

This was approved and a modest award made in *Regan v Williamson*[1] and *Mehmet v Perry*.[2]

This head of damages – an 'intangible' loss – is a common feature of claims brought by children when their mother is killed. The sums appear to be relatively modest. In *Corbett v Barking, Havering and Brentwood Health Authority*,[3] £3,000 was awarded. In *Johnson v British Midland Airways Ltd*,[4] a 13-year-old son was awarded £3,500. However, damages were not awarded when the deceased mother was not actually providing care, *Stanley v Siddique*.[5] In *ATH v MS* [2002] EWCA Civ 792,[6] the Court of Appeal reduced awards of £5,000 and £7,000, to children aged 11 and 8 at their mother's death, to £3,500 and £4,500.

11.4 LOSS OF MOTHER: THE PRACTICAL APPROACH

It is necessary to ensure that the details of the care provided by the mother are considered in some detail.

(1) Look at the reality of the situation – who is caring for the children? Is this a satisfactory situation? Is it likely to be permanent?

(2) Consider the commercial costs argument. Obtain quotations from local agencies in relation to the costs of a nanny/housekeeper.

---

[1] [1976] 1 WLR 305.
[2] [1977] 2 All ER 529.
[3] [1991] 2 QB 408.
[4] [1996] PIQR Q8.
[5] [1991] 2 WLR 459, CA.
[6] (Unreported).

(3) Consider the period of dependency – the dependency will decrease as the children get older. If there is more than one child, account must be taken of the fact that dependency will decrease as children 'leave the nest', although a mother's services often continue until long after her children reach the age of 18.

(4) Finally, remember the 'intangible loss' argument and the willingness of the courts to make awards, albeit modest, under this head.

11.5 QUALITY OF MOTHER'S CARE

If the quality of the mother's care is poor, then damages may be reduced. However, the fact that the children now get better care from a step-mother is ignored as a benefit arising under s 4.

11.6 LOSS OF HOUSEKEEPING SERVICES

There are surprisingly few cases in relation to the loss of services provided by a housewife, or househusband, to the surviving spouse alone. However, it is logical to put these cases forward on the basis of the provision of alternative, commercial, care. Thus, if the deceased was providing housekeeping services, then the commercial costs of these services should be quantified and a claim made in that respect.

Any gratuitous services provided by relatives or friends should be ignored under s 4 – as benefits arising out of the death.

There are some useful examples relating, in particular, to loss of a carer.

(1) In *Feay v Barnwell*,[1] the husband was blind and cared for entirely by his wife. The court allowed the cost of a housekeeper.

(2) In *W v H*,[2] a 44-year-old man was awarded £446,084 for loss of dependency suffered as a result of his wife's death. The claimant suffered from multiple sclerosis and his wife had provided care for him at home prior to her death. The

---

[1] [1938] 1 All ER 31.
[2] (Unreported) 11 February 2000 (summary available on Lawtel).

claimant moved into a nursing home. The cost of the claimant's nursing care was found to be recoverable from the defendant.

It may help considerably to give, here, three recent examples of awards for loss of a mother. These judgments help practitioners to get a 'feel' for the subject and both are good examples of a well-considered approach to such a loss.

11.7   *L (A CHILD) v BARRY MAY HAULAGE*[1]

11.7.1   The facts

The infant claimant was born on 6 September 1985. At the time of his mother's death he was living with her at home. His father, the litigation friend, had separated from the deceased some 4 years earlier. They were not married. Upon the deceased's death, the claimant went to live with his father and his 'new' family (his partner and their three young daughters all aged under 10 years).

11.7.2   The case

Somewhat surprisingly, no witness evidence at all was put in to support the claimant's case. The approach of the claimant was to ask the court to perform a conventional calculation on the basis that the deceased had been the sole source of financial and other services to the claimant. The judge, with the consent of the parties, permitted the claimant's father to give evidence.

The father's family were, in the main, wholly dependent on State benefits. The claimant moved into a three-bedroomed house so that all three step-sisters had to share a room. His new step-mother was welcoming but expected him to 'fend for himself to a very large extent'. This contrasted with his former life with his mother who was in reasonably well-paid work. They lived in a spacious three-bedroomed property, they enjoyed occasional holidays abroad and the nature of his mother's work allowed him to accompany her on regular weekends away to sporting activities.

---

[1]   [2002] PIQR Q35.

11.7.3   The issues

The judge identified several issues.

(1)   The mother's actual level of income.

(2)   How long any dependency would exist, ie whether to the age of 18 or if there were prospects of the claimant going on into higher education.

(3)   How the two elements should be assessed and whether it was appropriate to take any, and if so what, conventional percentage as reflecting likely dependency.

(4)   What regard, if any, should be had to the substitute arrangements whereby the litigation friend and his partner had taken over the responsibility for meeting the claimant's financial and other needs.

(5)   As a separate matter, the claimant was in the car at the time of the accident. He suffered no physical injury, but it was necessary to assess a sum for the psychological effects on him, not for the loss of his mother, but consequent upon his own presence at the scene.

11.7.4   Dependency

The judge found that the claimant was likely to go onto higher education and would have been dependent on his mother to the age of 21.

11.7.5   The effect of the natural father taking over care of the claimant

The defendant argued that the legal position was different where a natural father had taken over care of the child. The father had never taken any financial responsibility for the claimant (he was never in the financial position to do so). However, the defendant argued that the position in relation to s 4 was different and the most that could be recovered was the 'difference' between the two situations.

The judge considered the Law Commission's report and recommendations, and *Stanley v Saddique*,[1] *Hayden v Hayden*[2] and *R v Criminal Injuries Compensation Board*.[3] There was, it has to be said, some confusion as to the position when someone who had a duty to

---

[1]   [1991] 2 WLR 459.

[2]   [1992] 1 WLR 986.

[3]   [1999] 2 WLR 948.

care for a minor took over that duty after the death of another carer. The judge found that *Stanley* was the case preferred by authority, academic opinion and the Law Commission.

11.7.6 The nature of the loss

The judge came to the conclusion that, on the facts of the case, a real and substantial loss had been demonstrated and that the provision of substitute services must, in the case before him, be disregarded. This was because:

(1) prior to the death no significant support or services were, in fact, being provided;

(2) there was no real likelihood that any such services would have been provided;

(3) as a matter of fact the services and support provided had arisen as a result of the death;

(4) although the father was under a potential legal obligation to maintain the claimant, there was no likelihood that this obligation would be realised; and

(5) the obligation to maintain arose only because the father accepted the obligations arising under the testamentary guardianship which came into effect as a result of the death.

The judge observed that:

'The matter would have been entirely different if, as in *Hayden*, the parents had been living together before the death or if, as in *Martin v Grey* there had been a financial order or actual support in place, again before the death. If there had, at the time of death, been a real prospect of the father providing future support that would, in my view, be a matter properly to be brought into account.'

11.7.7 A jury award

The judge observed that he had been reminded a number of times that the assessment of damages was a jury point. He dealt with this in this matter by stating:

'I confess that, left to their own devices many juries might well say that no (or only the most minimal) award should be made where, as it were, the infant claimant has simply swapped one loving parent (and her home) for another loving parent (and their home). However I must remind myself that, just as in criminal trials, a jury would require direction as to the law and, having directed myself as to the law, as I perceive it, I have concluded that if, as a matter of fact, the father's support and services arise (and only arise) as a result of the death then, as a matter of law, first they must be disregarded and second having disregarded them there is a true loss.'

11.7.8   Assessment of the loss

The judge took the multiplier from the date of death. He observed that the Law Commission had recommended that the multiplier run from the trial but felt that this was not a matter for him. He applied a multiplier of 8.07 (the 2½ per cent discount table for a period of 9 months certain).

The services claim was put at £25,000 – nearly £3,000 per annum. This was described as well in line with previous awards and, given the finding as to the law, need not be discounted further. The judge observed that:

> 'That figure, as it seems to me, already encompasses the necessary "last lingering look" at the injury to check it is appropriate in amount.'

The judge also observed that had he been bound to take the father's services into account he would have awarded £17,500.

So far as the issue of financial dependency was concerned, the judge adopted the principles in *Owen v Martin*.[1] The substitute home was to be disregarded until the claimant reached the age of 18. After that age, a dependency figure of 50 per cent remained appropriate.

11.7.9   Psychological injury

The medical evidence was that the psychological effects of the injury were short lived. There had not been any significant effects of the diagnosed condition of post-traumatic stress disorder. The award of £2,000 included a modest element for enhanced vulnerability and a further figure of £1,500 for possible future psychological counselling.

11.7.10   The overall award

The overall award was:

Pain, suffering, loss and amenity	£2,000
Future counselling	£1,500
Past services (dependency)	£15,000
Future services (dependency)	£10,000
Past financial dependency	£54,000
Future financial dependency:	
to 18 years	£29,000
thereafter	£29,000

---

[1]   [1992] PIQR Q151.

The figures were rounded to the nearest £1,000. The judge observed that 'the exercise is not one capable of precision on the scale attempted'. Subject to interest, the total award was £140,500.

11.8 *BORDIN v ST MARY'S NHS TRUST*[1]

This was a decision of Crane J given on 26 January 2000. This case was somewhat unusual in that the first claimant (the husband of the deceased) did not attend the trial. The case concerned the second claimant, who was the deceased's son. The deceased had died as the result of treatment by the defendant in the course of giving birth to the second claimant.

11.8.1 Damages for loss of a mother's services

The judge considered the issue of damages for loss of the mother's services. He considered the case of *Corbett v Barking, Havering and Brentwood Health Authority*,[2] where the Court of Appeal approved an award of £3,000. That sum had a contemporary value of £4,500 and the judge awarded £5,000 under this head.[3]

11.8.2 Rejection of the broad brush approach

The judge undertook an exhaustive examination of authorities on the matter, including the Law Commission's discussion and recommendations. He stated that:

'First of all, in my judgment the words of the Act are important. The reference to juries, as I have noted, no longer appears, although in *Spittle v Bunney* and indeed in *Stanley v Saddique* the Court of Appeal indicated that the judge should direct himself on the principles which a jury would properly adopt. But, unlike a jury, a judge must deliver a reasoned judgment and it seems to me that it would be inappropriate for a judge to shelter behind the proposition that he should act like a jury and decline a reasoned approach, if one is available on the evidence.'

The judge was suspicious of the 'broad brush' approach.

'In so far as there is a reasoned basis which can be found for the assessment, it seems to me to be appropriate for the judge to use that basis, checking at each stage the reasonableness of the claim and standing back at the end of the calculation to check that there has been no over-compensation. It would be

---

[1] [2000] Lloyd's Rep Med 287.
[2] [1991] 2 QB 408.
[3] See para **11.3.3**.

inappropriate to use a "broad brush" artificially to the total, or to do so artificially.'

11.8.3   The appropriate approach

A nanny had not been employed in the *Bordin* case throughout the entire period. However, the judge held that there was authority for using the costs of employing, even when no nanny had been retained. This provided the starting point and the judge proposed to 'perform the necessary calculations and then to stand back to check whether there has been any over-compensation'.

11.8.4   The 'care claim'

From May 1995 to January 1996 the second claimant was cared for by his grandparents, first in London and then in Madrid. The claim was made on the basis of 15 hours a day, 7 days a week. This was conceded as appropriate care for a very young baby. An hourly rate of £4.50, less 35 per cent to take account of the fact that this was non-paid care, was permitted.

For the later period to trial, a claim was made on the basis of the employment of a nanny for 20 hours a week, a domestic for 10 hours a week and voluntary care at £35.00 a week. The defendant argued that the evidence was that a nanny would have been employed in any event and that only the 'additional' costs should be recoverable. This was accepted by the judge.

For future dependency it was accepted that the need for a nanny would reduce and, further, that a nanny would have been employed in any event. The defendant successfully argued that there should be a gradual reduction of the voluntary care as the second claimant gets older.

11.8.5   The income claim

The claim for loss of income was agreed between the parties.

11.8.6   The overall award

The overall award was approximately £85,000. The judge found these to be real losses. Further, he observed that:

'It seems to me that so far as dependency is concerned in relation to the mother's services, there is no overlap with the sum of £5,000 for her special care, nor is there any over-recovery.'

11.8.7   No 'rounding down'

The judge considered the issue of whether the figures should be revised, since the award was a jury award, but stated:

> 'It does not seem to me that, having made those calculations and made those reductions where, in my view, appropriate, that I should simply produce some round figures because a jury might, if a jury was still to hear such a case, be likely to produce a round figure in the end. If one looks at *Kemp & Kemp*, there are some examples of judges making calculations. I accept the submissions of counsel for the second claimant that I should not simply reduce the final figure arbitrarily to make it look, as it were, more like a jury award. Provided there has been careful attention to the need to avoid overcompensation along the way, I see no reason not to award the final figure at which I have arrived by this process. There is in the end some difficulty in seeing why one has to be more arbitrary in a Fatal Accidents Act case, bearing in mind the terms of s.3 of the Act, that one does in other kinds of tortious recovery. That seems to me to some extent to be a matter of convention.'

11.9   *ATH v MS* [2002] EWCA Civ 792[1]

This is an important Court of Appeal decision. There were four children, three of whom brought the claim. After their mother's death, two of the children went to live with their father, who was divorced from their mother. The Court of Appeal reviewed the authorities and made it clear that:

> 'in the light of the authorities, the position is reasonably clear. Where, as here, infant children are living with and are dependent on one parent, with no support being provided by the other parent, in circumstances where the provision of such support in the future seems unlikely, and the parent with whom they are living is killed, in circumstances giving rise to liability under the Fatal Accidents Act, after which the other parent (who is not the tortfeasor) houses and takes responsibility for the children, the support which they enjoy after the accident is a benefit which has accrued as a result of the death and, pursuant to section 4 of the 1975 Act, it must be disregarded, both in the assessment of loss and the calculation of damages.'

However, it was made clear that '... such damages can only be awarded on the basis that they are used to reimburse the voluntary carer for services already rendered, and are available to pay for such services in the future'.

---

[1]   (Unreported).

11.10 SUMMARY: CASES FOR LOSS OF CARER

These cases illustrate three responses to a claim for loss of a mother who was also working. They show the pragmatic way in which the courts approach these issues. They also illustrate the difficulties that litigators can face. In *L (A Child) v Barry May Haulage*[1] the claimant had not put in any witness evidence, but the father was allowed to give evidence at trial. In *Bordin*,[2] the father did put in evidence but did not appear at trial and the claim for dependency was struck out. Despite these difficulties the court still managed to make awards which were 'fair' to the dependent children.

11.11 PRACTICAL POINTS

(1)   Consider the commercial cost of hiring a nanny/housekeeper.
(2)   Remember the 'intangible' loss element which is often awarded for loss of a mother.
(3)   The financial claim for loss of a carer can be substantial. The courts tend to be sympathetic when the deceased was providing special care to a disabled dependant.

---

[1]   See para **11.7**.
[2]   See para **11.8**.

CHAPTER 12

DEPENDENCY CASES: PARENTS OF ADULT CHILDREN; LOSS OF A CHILD

12.1 INTRODUCTION

We are considering here a claim for financial losses. Even in cases where there is is no financial loss, there can be a bereavement award (see Chapter 15). However, there can be no bereavement award for the loss of a parent or loss of an adult child.

12.2 ADULT CHILDREN WHERE A PARENT HAS BEEN KILLED

A claim for financial loss by adult children presents unique difficulties.

(1)   Remember that the claim is one for loss of reasonable expectation of benefit.

(2)   If regular financial contributions are being made, for instance a student is being supported through his studies, then the loss is clear.

(3)   There can be losses outside normal financial dependency, so in *Betney v Rowland and Mallard*[1] one of the claimant daughters recovered the loss of the contribution expected from her parents to their daughter's wedding. Further, one of the daughters had discussed with her mother the possibility of the mother providing childcare services. It was agreed that whenever that daughter had a child the mother would give up her part-time job to look after the child. The value of the services was discounted because of the rather speculative

---

[1]   [1992] CLY 1786.

nature of the claim. The daughters were successful in claiming the loss of DIY, car maintenance and gardening services which their father had provided prior to his death.

(4)   There can also be a claim if gifts that had been made to the dependants become subject to taxes as a result of the premature death of the deceased.

12.3   PARENTS' CLAIM FOLLOWING THE DEATH OF A CHILD

The primary issue here is establishing a loss of a reasonable expectation of benefit. There is long established case-law where damages have been awarded to parents following the death of an adult child (see Chapter M5 of *Kemp & Kemp*). However, the old cases rely on previous social values; it may be less common now for parents to expect to be dependent upon their children.

(1)   In the case of a very young child it may well be that the loss is now regarded as too speculative. The claim of a 13-year-old child succeeded in *Buckland v Guildford Gas Light and Coke Company*.[1] However, in *Barnett v Cohen*,[2] a claim for a very young child, aged 4, was rejected because it was not possible to show a reasonable probability of reasonable financial support to the parents.

In these cases the kindest, and usually the most accurate, advice is that the bereavement payment plus the funeral expenses is the only feasible claim.

(2)   In the case of older children some care should be taken. In these circumstances there is no bereavement payment if the child died after the age of 18. If a reasonable expectation of benefit can be shown, then a claim could succeed, albeit contained within modest limits.

12.4   EXAMPLES OF CLAIMS SUCCEEDING IN RELATION TO THE DEATH OF A MINOR CHILD

In *Wathen v Vernon*,[3] the deceased was 17½ years of age and an apprentice. The sum of £500 was awarded under the

---

[1]   [1949] 1 KB 410.

[2]   [1921] 2 KB 461.

[3]   [1970] RTR 471.

Fatal Accidents Act 1976. The court held that the deceased would have helped his parents, particularly if their position worsened, but he had his own life to lead and the prospect of his marrying and having to look after a family of his own had to be taken into account when calculating a multiplier. It is important to note that the court was clear on the point that it was entitled to give damages for loss of *potential* support in cases where no support had yet been forthcoming and the possibility of support being necessary in the future or being provided was rather remote.

However, it must be emphasised that claims for loss of dependency following the death of a minor child are extremely problematic. Unless there are specific cultural or family features which demonstrate a likelihood of dependence, these cases will rarely succeed and the awards made are likely to be minimal.

12.5 EXAMPLES OF CLAIMS SUCCEEDING FOLLOWING THE DEATH OF AN ADULT CHILD

The case of *Davis v Bonner*[1] is of some interest. The deceased was aged 29 when he died. He had special educational needs. He was in full-time employment and lived in a flat provided by a college that provided for his needs. The dependency claim was brought by his parents, who argued that the deceased's father planned to retire in 1995 and the deceased would have then lived with them and have been a wage earner who contributed to their household.

The trial judge rejected the dependency claim. He found that the parents were not dependent upon the deceased at the time of his death. The Court of Appeal, applying *Davies v Taylor*[2] held that the test was not whether a dependency claim was established on the balance of probabilities, but whether the chance of such a claim being established was substantial, that is beyond a mere possibility or speculation.[3]

The Court rejected a strictly arithmetical approach to the issue of dependency and awarded £5,000 by way of damages.

---

[1]   (Unreported), 6 April 1995. Cited in *Kemp & Kemp*, paras M5-017/2 and M5-103.

[2]   [1974] AC 207.

[3]   See para **6.4.**

Neill LJ observed:

> 'Counsel for both parties accepted that the test to be applied was that explained in the speeches in the House of Lords in *Davies v Taylor* [1974] AC 207, particularly in the speech of Lord Reid. The dividing line is between a substantial prospect and a speculative prospect. It is not a test on the balance of probabilities.
>
> One should be very careful not to examine a judgment as though it were a statute. But for my part, I am not convinced that the learned judge asked himself the right question in this case: was there a substantial prospect that the deceased would have contributed to the support of his parents if he had survived? If that question is posed on the facts of this case ... the answer is "yes", though the uncertainties to which the judge drew attention in his very careful judgment, must mean that the prospect is certainly not near the top of the scale. The Court must look at the matter broadly and consider all the facts. I agree with Mr Justice Cazalet's assessment that £5,000 fairly represents the injury suffered by the two dependants jointly.'

This 'overview' approach, rather than a strictly mathematical approach, is supported in several other cases. In *Doleman & Doleman v Deakin*,[1] the Court of Appeal upheld an award of £1,500 by Potts J to the parents of a an 18-year-old man. Potts J stated:

> 'This is not a case for a multiplicand or a multiplier ... This is a case which the court must on the evidence do its best to decide what a reasonable figure is in all the circumstances, giving full weight to the many uncertainties of life to which counsel referred me, and not overlooking the fact that any award is an award in respect of items of dependency that would not necessarily arise for some years to come.'

12.6 SUMMARY: CLAIMS FOR AN ADULT CHILD

It is clear that a claim can be made following the death of an adult child.

(1)   The appropriate test in assessing the possibility of any loss is that set out in *Davis v Bonner* (above). It is *not* a test on the balance of probabilities, but the court has to consider whether the chance of a dependency relationship being established is 'substantial', ie beyond a mere possibility or speculation.

(2)   Once a dependency relationship is established the court is unlikely to take a wholly mathematical approach. It is certain that discounts will be given for the contingencies involved and,

---

[1]   (Unreported) 24 January 1990.

more often than not, the court will decide upon a 'reasonable figure in all the circumstances' as in *Doleman*.

12.7 CULTURAL FACTORS

Reference has been made above to the fact that certain cultural or family features could be used to demonstrate that children were likely to support their parents. In *Kandella v British European Airways Corporation*,[1] two daughters were killed in a car crash. They practised as doctors in England; however, their parents were Iraqi. It was shown that the parents were likely to have to leave Baghdad and live in exile. They would have been reliant upon their daughters' support. A figure equivalent to one-quarter of the daughters' net earnings was awarded.

In this respect, evidence of the practice within the particular community or of that particular family is extremely useful.

12.8 PRACTICAL POINTS

(1)   It is possible for an adult child to bring a claim following the death of a parent if the child can show a loss of reasonable expectation of benefit. The benefit need not be wholly financial.

(2)   Claims for loss of financial dependency following the death of a minor child are possible, but extremely difficult to establish.

(3)   Claims for loss of financial dependency following the death of an adult child are possible. Care must be taken to establish the loss of a reasonable chance of benefit. The burden of proof is extremely important in this respect.

(4)   It may be that certain cultural or family features can be used to show that the child was likely to have maintained or supported his parents.

---

[1]   [1980] 1 All ER 341.

CHAPTER 13

DIFFICULT ISSUES IN DEPENDENCY CLAIMS

13.1 INTRODUCTION

This book is designed to be an introductory guide to fatal accidents. However, it is surprising how often difficult issues arise – in relation to dependency claims in particular. This chapter examines some of those difficult issues.

13.2 ILLEGAL MEANS OF SUPPORT

There is some controversy surrounding less legitimate, or totally illegitimate, means of earning an income.

(1) In *Burns v Edman*[1] the deceased's life had been 'devoted to crime' and it was highly unlikely that he would have reformed. His dependants were held not to be entitled to damages for their loss of dependency because the support came directly from the proceeds of criminal offences.

(2) In *Hunter v Butler*[2] an argument that there was a dependency based on the deceased having worked 'on the side' while still claiming social security benefits was rejected on the basis that this amounted to fraud. However, on the facts, the Court of Appeal did find that the deceased would have found legitimate work and awarded damages on that basis.

Note that these decisions are heavily criticised in *Kemp & Kemp*.[3]

---

[1] [1970] 2 QB 541.
[2] [1996] RTR 396.
[3] Volume 1, paras 25-006–25-008.

The issue may be different if work is being done legally, but the proceeds not declared to the Inland Revenue.[1]

13.3   SOCIAL SECURITY IS THE MAIN SOURCE OF INCOME

In *Hunter v Butler*,[2] the court considered an argument that a loss of social security was a recoverable loss. The widow had received both widow's allowance and widowed mother's allowance which were higher than supplementary benefit would be. Waite LJ observed:

> 'The argument that the appellant in these circumstances suffered "injury" within the terms of section 3 as a result of the deceased's death appears to me to be wholly untenable. In respect of Supplementary Benefit, she no less than he, was dependent in that regard upon the state.'

In *Cox v Hockenhull*,[3] a husband was denied recovery for the loss of the invalid care allowance which he had been paid as carer of his severely disabled wife. This was not a benefit derived from the relationship of husband and wife. The husband had been employed by the State to care for a severely disabled person.

However, the husband's loss of financial dependency *was* measured by a proportion of the State benefits received, in the form of disability living allowance, disablement allowance and – to an extent – income support. It was held to be immaterial that the source of income, both before and after the death, was the State and it made no difference at all that the benefits had been non-contributory. *Hunter v Butler* was distinguished because the State benefits to the wife in that case were to continue after the husband's death. For this reason there was no recovery in respect of housing benefit and council tax benefit.

The husband also recovered for his loss of his wife's services, although her disability and deteriorating health meant that the Court of Appeal reduced the award substantially.

---

[1]   See *Duller v South East Lincs Engineers* (unreported). Cited in *Kemp & Kemp*, para 25-008/1.

[2]   [1996] RTR 396.

[3]   [2000] 1 WLR 750.

13.4 WHERE A DEPENDANT IS ALSO THE TORTFEASOR

There has been considerable discussion as to what the results should be if the tortfeasor is also a dependant.[1] It is far from clear how the House of Lords' decision in *Hunt v Severs*[2] affects fatal accident claims. However, it is clear that:

(1) the negligent dependant cannot claim against himself for his own losses;
(2) it is unlikely that any expenditure, including care, provided by the negligent party will be recoverable, even as another dependant's loss or damage. In *Hayden v Hayden*,[3] a child lost her mother in a driving accident caused by her father's negligence. The father gave up work to look after his daughter. The Court of Appeal decided that the plaintiff's damages should be reduced to the extent that her father remedied the loss of her mother's services.

13.5 WERE THERE ALLEGATIONS THAT THE RELATIONSHIP BETWEEN THE DECEASED AND THE CLAIMANTS HAD BROKEN DOWN, OR WAS ABOUT TO DO SO?

In *Owen v Martin*,[4] the marriage was regarded as fragile and the multiplier reduced from 15 to 11 by the Court of Appeal.

13.6 FAMILY LIVING ON CAPITAL

In *Cape Distribution v O'Loughlin*,[5] the Court of Appeal considered a case where the family made its living from property development. For further details of this case, see para **10.3**.

---

[1] See Law Commission Report No 263 *Claims for Wrongful Death*, at para 5.54.
[2] [1994] 2 AC 350.
[3] [1992] 1 WLR 986.
[4] [1992] PIQR Q151. See para **8.6.2**.
[5] [2001] PIQR Q8.

13.7   A PRAGMATIC APPROACH TO DIFFICULT ISSUES

The above cases give some indication of the difficult issues that can arise. The examples given show that the courts retain considerable flexibility in their approach to these issues. It may pay to be suspicious of arguments that the dependency is 'nil'.

PART 4

NON-DEPENDENCY CLAIMS

In this section we look at those aspects of fatal accident damages that do not require a dependency relationship.

(1) Funeral expenses.
(2) Bereavement damages.
(3) Pain and suffering by the deceased prior to death.
(4) Damages for psychiatric injuries to others following a death.

CHAPTER 14

FUNERAL EXPENSES

14.1 CLAIMS WHERE THERE IS NO GRANT OF PROBATE

The dependants can recover the expenses of the deceased's funeral even if there is no grant of probate. Section 3(5) of the Fatal Accidents Act 1976 states:

'If the dependants have incurred funeral expenses in respect of the deceased, damages may be awarded in respect of those expenses.'

Such expenses are recoverable even where there is no dependency (ie loss of pecuniary benefit). They are also recoverable by the estate under s 1(2) of the Law Reform (Miscellaneous Provisions) Act 1934.

One advantage of the estate claiming the funeral expenses is that no reduction will be made for any contributory negligence on the part of the dependant.[1]

14.2 THE NATURE OF THE RECOVERABLE FUNERAL EXPENSES

The expenses recoverable must be reasonable in all the circumstances, including the deceased's station in life, creed and racial origin.[2] Claims for a tombstone have succeeded.[3] Embalming costs have also been allowed.[4] The court also approved a claim for

---

[1]   *Mullholland v McCrea* [1981] NI 135.
[2]   *Gammell v Wilson* [1982] AC 27.
[3]   *Goldstein v Salvation Army Assurance Society* [1917] 2 KB 291.
[4]   *Hart v Griffiths-Jones* [1948] 2 All ER 729.

expenses of friends who helped a widow after her husband was killed in France and arranged for the return of the body.[1]

The cost of a wake and a memorial or monument to the deceased failed in *Gammell v Wilson*, but succeeded in *Kegworth v British Midland Airways*.[2] It can be difficult, however, to distinguish between a tombstone and a memorial. In *Gammell v Wilson*, Mr BA Hytner QC (sitting as a deputy judge of the High Court) stated that 'there is a distinction between a headstone finishing off, describing and marking the grave, which is part of the funeral service, and a memorial which is not'.

14.3   AN UNUSUAL EXAMPLE

In *Quainoo v Brent & Harrow Health Authority*,[3] the deceased was a member of the Ghanaian Royal Family.

(1)   Items recovered included three air fares from London to Accra; air freight of the coffin; the charges of a London funeral director and the cost of hiring cars for the funeral procession of 80 miles from Accra to Kumasi.

(2)   Items disallowed included printing and stationery for the funeral announcements; wreaths and other decorations; photographer's fees; telephone calls before and after the funeral; hire of a hall in London for a reception before the funeral for 500 people and funeral clothes.

14.4   A CLAIM IN RESPECT OF A LIVING CLAIMANT WHO IS SHORTLY TO DIE

In *Bateman v Hydro Agri (UK) Ltd*,[4] the plaintiff was suffering from mesothelioma and was likely to die within 3 months of the date of the trial. Mr Anthony Temple QC allowed the cost of the future funeral expenses. The editors of *Kemp & Kemp* observe that this was a bold decision, but that they believe it to be right in principle.

---

[1]   *Schneider v Eisovitch* [1960] 2 QB 430.
[2]   (Unreported). Cited in *Kemp & Kemp*, para 20-022.
[3]   (1982) 132 NLJ 1000.
[4]   (Unreported). Cited in *Kemp & Kemp*, para 20-024.

14.5 PRACTICAL POINTS

(1) In practice the funeral expenses are rarely problematic. However, care should be taken in relation to expenses incurred in relation to a 'wake' or a headstone. It cannot be guaranteed that these expenses will be recoverable.

(2) However, do remember to ask the dependants to keep copies of all the receipts and expenses incurred.

(3) Note also the date on which payments for funeral expenses were made. Interest should be claimed at *the full rate* from the date of payment.

(4) Many insurers are, however, amenable to making an immediate interim payment in relation to the funeral expenses and associated losses. This is often a prudent move on the defendant's behalf since it serves to relieve the dependants of some of the immediate expenses. It also prevents interest accruing at the full rate.

(5) If an interim payment in relation to funeral expenses is not forthcoming, there is no harm, once proceedings have been issued, in making an immediate application for such an interim payment and, if appropriate, for the bereavement payment.

CHAPTER 15

BEREAVEMENT DAMAGES

15.1 INTRODUCTION

Section 3 of the Administration of Justice Act 1982 inserted s 1A into the Fatal Accidents Act 1976 and introduced a statutory claim for damages for bereavement in respect of the death of a limited class of close relatives.

The sum currently stands at £10,000 for deaths after 1 April 2002.

15.2 A VERY LIMITED CLASS OF CLAIMANTS

There is a very limited class of relatives entitled to the bereavement payment. Section 1A(2) of the Fatal Accidents Act 1976 states:

'(2) A claim for damages for bereavement shall only be for the benefit –
    (a)   of the wife or husband, or the deceased; and
    (b)   where the deceased was a minor who was never married –
         (i)   of his parents, if he was legitimate, and
        (ii)   of his mother, if he was illegitimate.'

15.3 THE EXCLUDED CATEGORIES

(1)   The former husband or wife is excluded from recovery. However, this section tends to be construed strictly. If, at the date of death, the *decree nisi* has been made but not the *decree absolute*, then the spouse is entitled to recover.

(2)   Cohabitees cannot recover.

(3)   The father of an illegitimate child cannot claim under the section.

(4)   Where both parents claim bereavement damages, the damages
       are divided equally between them.[1] There is some dispute as
       to what should happen if one of the parents is responsible for
       the death and is thus unable to recover damages. Judicial
       authority suggests that the parent not at fault recovers half of
       the payment.[2]

(5)   The crucial date is the date of the death. In *Doleman &*
       Doleman v Deakin,[3] the Court of Appeal upheld a decision not
       to award bereavement damages to parents when their son was
       injured shortly before his eighteenth birthday, was in a coma
       for 6 weeks and died shortly after his eighteenth birthday.

Interest runs at the full rate from the date of death.[4]

15.4   PRACTICAL POINTS

(1)   It is rare for problems to occur in relation to the statutory
       bereavement payment once entitlement is established. Indeed,
       many insurers make such payments even when, strictly, there
       is no entitlement.

(2)   The fact that interest runs at the full rate means that insurers
       are often keen to make these payments promptly. If this suits
       the claimants there is no harm in asking for, or if necessary
       applying for, an interim payment.

---

[1]   Fatal Accidents Act 1976, s 1A(4).
[2]   *Navaei v Navaei* (unreported). Cited in *Kemp & Kemp*, para 4-007/2.
[3]   (Unreported) 24 January 1990. Cited in *Kemp & Kemp*, para M5-018.
[4]   *Prior v Hastie* [1987] CLY 1219.

CHAPTER 16

INJURIES AND LOSSES OF THE DECEASED PRIOR TO DEATH

16.1 ACTION BROUGHT BY THE ESTATE

An important practical point is that a claim for injuries and losses prior to the death can only be made by the deceased's estate, not the dependants. In these circumstances it is necessary for a grant of probate to be taken out.

16.2 PAIN AND SUFFERING PRIOR TO DEATH

(1) If the death was instantaneous, or almost instantaneous, then there is no award. In *Hicks v Chief Constable of South Yorkshire*,[1] the Court of Appeal held that where unconsciousness and death occur in such a short period after the injury which causes death no damages are payable. The last few moments of mental agony and pain are in reality part of the death itself.

(2) If there is pain and suffering prior to death then an award can be made to the *estate*. In theory, general damages in these cases are assessed in a similar way to general damages in other cases.

   (a) In *Roughead v Railway Executive*,[2] the deceased underwent terrible suffering for one day. An award of £250 was made. (This is the equivalent of over £4,000 at contemporary values.)

   (b) In *Watson v Willmott*,[3] the husband was in the same accident in which his wife was killed. He suffered nervous

---

[1] [1992] 1 All ER 690.
[2] (1949) 65 TLR 435.
[3] [1991] 1 QB 140.

shock on seeing her body immediately afterwards, followed by clinical depression for 4 months, before committing suicide. The suicide was attributed to the defendant in the original accident. An award of £4,000 was awarded to the husband's estate.

(c) In *Robertson v Lestrange,*[1] an award of £150 was made for 4 days' pain and suffering between injury and death.

(d) In *Fallon v Beaumont,*[2] a 22-year-old male was a passenger in the front seat of a car involved in a high-speed collision. Upon impact the car exploded and burst into flames. Two further explosions occurred after the car came to a halt. The deceased was trapped in the burning car until the emergency services arrived. There was no evidence that he lost consciousness during that period. He would have had significant insight into the gravity of his situation and died 30 days after the accident. An award of £10,000 was made for pain and suffering.

There are relatively few cases on this issue. A selection can be found in *Kemp & Kemp* at para L7-023. The approach adopted is that the court isolates the 'pain and suffering' element of the claim for personal injury and awards damages for that element. In *Fallon*, for instance, it was common ground that if the deceased had lived he would have received damages in the region of £70,000–£75,000.

16.3 LOSSES AND EXPENSES PRIOR TO DEATH

The estate can also claim losses and expenses incurred by the deceased prior to his death. In cases where there is a considerable lapse of time between the event which caused the death and the death itself, this can be a matter of considerable practical importance.

(1) A claim for loss of income will be on the basis of the *full* loss of earnings rather than on *Owen v Martin*[3] principles.

(2) There could be a considerable claim for nursing expenses, including the cost of hospital visits and gratuitous care provided.

---

[1] [1985] 1 All ER 950.
[2] (Unreported), 16 December 1993. Cited in *Kemp & Kemp*, para L7-023.
[3] [1992] PIQR Q151.

(3)   It is highly arguable that interest on these losses should run at the *full* rate after the death.

16.4   PRACTICAL POINTS

(1)   In cases where death is instantaneous or almost instantaneous, then it is improbable that damages will be awarded for pain and suffering prior to death.

(2)   If there is a claim for pain and suffering prior to death, the court is, in essence, called upon to isolate the pain and suffering element of the claim.

(3)   If there is a delay between the incident that led to the death and the death itself, the estate can, and should, make a claim for the financial losses involved. This can have considerable financial advantages in terms of the amount recovered.

CHAPTER 17

DAMAGES FOR INJURY TO ANOTHER ARISING OUT OF THE DEATH

17.1 CLAIMS FOR GRIEF AND STRESS

A lawyer involved in advising dependants and family after a death will often be asked whether there is any claim that the relatives can make because of the grief and stress they have suffered. It is not intended, here, to give a detailed account on the law relating to psychiatric injury.[1] Instead, we will look, in particular, at cases relating to psychiatric injury to relatives and dependants following a fatality. There are a number of hurdles that such a claimant has to jump.

(1) The claimant must have suffered a recognised psychiatric illness. 'Shock' or upset or grief is not sufficient.
(2) The claimant must then bring the action within one of the recognised categories for a claim.

17.2 ESTABLISHING PSYCHIATRIC INJURY

Damages for grief and shock are not recoverable. In practical terms it is often difficult to distinguish between grief arising from the death and the psychiatric injuries arising from the incident. In *Hinchcliffe v British Schoolboys Association & East Anglian Schoolboys Scrambling Club*,[2] the claimants were a family who saw their 8-year-old child die in a motorcycling accident on a scrambling course. The judge recognised that the claimants had suffered considerable grief following the accident. However, it was held that this was a natural

---

[1] See Napier and Wheat *Recovering Damages for Psychiatric Injury* 2nd edn (OUP, 2002).

[2] (Unreported) 12 April 2000 (cited in Lawtel).

consequence of the death rather than being due to witnessing the accident. Their feelings were not abnormal and did not give rise to a separate claim.

17.3   THE DISTINCTION BETWEEN PRIMARY AND SECONDARY VICTIMS

If the claimant's reaction does give rise to a recognised psychiatric injury, the claimant still has to come within one of the recognised categories of victims.

In *Page v Smith*,[1] the court distinguished between primary and secondary victims, defining the latter as someone in the vicinity of an accident scene, who is not physically injured but who suffers psychiatric injury.[2]

(1)   A 'primary victim' is someone who could anticipate physical injury to himself by virtue of being within the range of foreseeable injury, the test being whether the defendant could reasonably foresee that his conduct would expose the claimant to a risk of personal injury, either physical or psychiatric.

(2)   A 'secondary' victim is one who could not anticipate actual physical injury to himself. The issue of the 'secondary victim' was considered in *McLoughlin v O'Brien*[3] and *Alcock v Chief Constable of South Yorkshire.*[4] It was held that a non-injured party could only recover damages for psychiatric injury following a fatality if:
    (a)   the relation between the injured person and the deceased was sufficiently proximate; and
    (b)   the injured person was sufficiently close in time and space to the incident or its immediate aftermath.

17.4   ESTABLISHING PROXIMITY

An example of the difficulties in establishing proximity is *Tranmore v TE Scudder Limited* [1998] EWCA 1895.[5] In that case an accident

---

[1]   [1996] AC 155.
[2]   For a useful discussion of these issues, see S Allen, 'Post Traumatic Stress Disorder: the Claims of Primary and Secondary Victims' [2000] JPIL 108.
[3]   [1983] 1 AC 410.
[4]   [1992] 1 AC 310.
[5]   (Unreported).

occurred at 6 pm when a building collapsed on a site on which the plaintiff's son was working. The plaintiff was told of the collapse at 7.30 pm when he arrived home from work and he arrived at the site about 8 pm. On arrival at the site he was told that his son was in the building but was not allowed to enter the site. He watched the site from an office for 2 hours, knowing that his son was in the collapsed building. At 10 pm the emergency services were able to get into the building, after which the plaintiff was told that his son had been killed instantly when the accident occurred.

The Court of Appeal held that it should apply the *McLoughlin v O'Brien* test, ie 'a strict test of proximity by sight or hearing'.

The Court held that, since in this case the plaintiff was not present at the scene of the accident, he did not witness the death of his son, nor the extreme danger to his son. Also, 2 hours had passed between the collapse of the building and the plaintiff's arrival at the site, this deprived the plaintiff's case of the immediacy required before the necessary proximity could be said to exist.

17.5 CASES WHERE CLAIMS HAVE SUCCEEDED

There are a number of cases where the claimant has successfully recovered damages. In *Marshall v Lionel Enterprises Inc*,[1] a wife came upon the badly injured body of her husband shortly after he was involved in an accident.

In *McLoughlin v O'Brien*,[2] Mrs McLoughlin was not present at the scene of the accident, but attended hospital 2½ hours afterwards. She saw her husband and her surviving children in great pain and distress, in exactly the same blood-spattered state as if they had been at the accident scene. She also heard that her youngest child had been killed. The House of Lords held that she could recover. However, it has been observed that this decision was on the margin of what the process of logical progression should allow.

In *Alcock v Chief Constable of South Yorkshire*,[3] it was observed that the striking feature of the *McLoughlin* case was that the victims were

---

[1]   [1972] OR 177.
[2]   [1983] 1 AC 410.
[3]   [1992] 1 AC 310.

very much in the same state as they would have been if Mrs McLoughlin had found them at the scene of the accident.

17.6   NO AWARD FOR SURVIVORS' GUILT

In *Hunter v British Coal Corporation Cementation Mining Company* [1998] EWCA 644,[1] the Court of Appeal considered the issue of whether an award could be made for 'survivors' guilt'. The claimant had damaged a hydrant at the workplace. While he was away from the scene attempting to find a hose to channel the water, a 'freak accident' occurred which led to the death of a colleague. The plaintiff did not witness the accident, he was not a rescuer was not in physical danger and was not allowed back to witness the scene. However, the plaintiff did develop a nervous illness due to his involvement in the incident. The Court of Appeal refused to extend the law to cover survivors' guilt.

17.7   NOT TO BE CONFUSED WITH BEREAVEMENT AWARD

In Law Commission Report No 263 *Claims for Wrongful Death*, the Commission recommended (although legislation was not necessary) that a clear distinction be kept between the bereavement award and damages for a recognised psychiatric loss. There is a clear distinction between 'normal bereavement' and psychiatric illness. It recommended that:

(1)   a claimant should not be barred from recovering both damages for bereavement and, if liability is established, damages for a recognised psychiatric illness;

(2)   the quantum of bereavement damages should not be affected by the quantum of damages recoverable for a recognised psychiatric illness;

(3)   the quantum of damages for psychiatric injuries should not be affected by the quantum of damages for bereavement.

The Commission also rejected the idea that a claim for grief counselling should be available as a head of damages under the Fatal Accidents Act 1976.[2] There are no cases that support the view

---

[1]   (Unreported).

[2]   Law Commission Report No 263 *Claims for Wrongful Death*, at para 3.59.

that grief counselling is recoverable as a head of damages. (The situation is different where the claimant comes within one of the recognised categories of claimant and claims damages for psychiatric treatment.)

17.8 PRACTICAL POINTS

(1)   Grief alone does not give rise to a claim for damages, the claimant must suffer from a recognised psychiatric injury.

(2)   A claimant can claim damages for psychiatric injury if:

    (a)   he was sufficiently proximate in time and space to the accident scene; and

    (b)   he had a sufficiently close relationship to the deceased.

(3)   There is no award for 'survivors' guilt'.

(4)   A claim for psychiatric injury does not affect or decrease the statutory bereavement payment.

PART 5

PROCEDURE

In this section we consider the procedure involved in pursuing a fatal accident claim, looking in particular at:

(1)   fatal accidents and the Pre-action Protocol;
(2)   procedural matters during the course of proceedings;
(3)   drafting witness statements;
(4)   drafting Schedules of Damages;
(5)   apportionment.

Chapter 24 on Coroner's Courts is also highly relevant to issues relating to investigating the claim.

CHAPTER 18

PRE-ACTION PROTOCOLS

18.1 THE PROTOCOLS

The only prudent approach to pre-action matters is to assume that the Pre-Action Protocols apply in fatal accident claims. Although the Notes of Guidance to the Personal Injury Protocol state that it is primarily intended for lower value claims there is no doubt that the principle and 'spirit' of the protocol permeates the judiciary's approach to all litigation. A failure by either the claimant's or defendant's lawyer to follow the principles, suitably adapted, could lead to severe criticism of the lawyers involved and also to adverse costs consequences.

18.2 THE PERSONAL INJURY PROTOCOL: AN OVERVIEW

There are four essential elements to the Personal Injury Protocol.

(1) A standard letter of claim.
(2) Early disclosure of documents.
(3) The joint selection of, and instructions to, experts.
(4) Parties are encouraged to consider entering into discussions and/or negotiations and, in appropriate cases, attempting mediation or alternative dispute resolution (ADR) ('parties should bear in mind that the courts increasingly take the view that litigation should be a last resort').

18.2.1 The letter of claim

The claimant is enjoined to send *two* copies of the letter of claim to the defendant as soon as sufficient information is available to substantiate a realistic claim and before issues of quantum are addressed in detail.

The letter must contain *a clear summary of the facts* on which the claim is based together with the *nature of any injuries* suffered and of *any financial loss incurred*. In a fatal case it may be important to set out the injuries sustained if a claim is to be made for the pain and suffering of the deceased prior to death. The letter should ask for *details of the insurer*; if the insurer is known it should be sent directly to the insurer. *Sufficient information* must be given in order to enable the defendant to commence investigations and, at least, to put a broad valuation on the 'risk'.

18.2.2   Practical consequences

It is clear that detailed information will need to be obtained at the outset. In one sense the Protocol may be unrealistic in that, in some cases of moderate severity, the claimant may not be in a position to give full instructions. However, the defendant may benefit from being told, at a very early stage, that a claim is being contemplated. In these circumstances it is difficult to see any objection to a 'non-Protocol' letter, written merely to inform the defendant that the solicitor has been instructed and that a full letter of claim will be written as soon as possible.

18.2.3   No express sanctions if the case subsequently differs

It should be noted that the Protocol expressly states:

> 'letters of claim are *not* intended to have the same formal status as a *pleading* or any sanctions to apply if the letter of claim and any subsequent statement of claim if the proceedings differ.'

However, claimants' lawyers will be particularly wary of the problems caused when the client's case differs from the letter of claim. Such differences can cause evidential difficulties and fruitful cross-examination material for the defendant if the matter proceeds to trial. Pre-action letters must be considered with some care.

18.2.4   The defendant's response

The defendant should reply within 21 days, giving the identity of his insurers (if applicable). If there is no reply, then the claimant can issue proceedings and there will be no further sanction for proceeding with the action. If the defendant does acknowledge receipt of the letter, he then has a maximum of 3 months (inclusive of the 21 days) to investigate the claim. At the end of this period, the defendant should reply stating whether or not liability is denied and, if so, giving reasons for the denial of liability.

18.2.5   An admission of liability

If the defendant subsequently admits liability, there is a presumption that the defendant is bound by this admission for all claims with a value of up to £15,000.

18.2.6   Steps to be taken on a denial of liability

If the defendant denies liability, he should enclose with the formal letter of reply any documents in his possession which are clearly relevant to the issues between the parties and which are likely to be ordered to be disclosed by the court, either on an application for pre-action disclosure, or on disclosure during any proceedings.

In the Protocol there are specimen, *but non-exhaustive*, lists of documents likely to be relevant in different types of claim.

18.2.7   Contributory negligence

Where the defendant admits liability, but alleges contributory negligence, he should still disclose those documents that are relevant to the issues in dispute.

18.2.8   Special damages

A schedule of special damages, with supporting documents, must be submitted as soon as possible.

18.2.9   Instructing experts

It is unusual for an expert to be instructed at an early stage in a claim unrelated to clinical negligence. However, if there are disputes as to the cause of death or life expectancy, or a claim for pain and suffering prior to death, then the claimant may wish to instruct doctors. In these circumstances:

(1)   before any prospective party to the action instructs an expert he should give the other party a list of the names of one or

more experts in the relevant speciality who (in his opinion) are suitable to instruct;

(2)   within 14 days, the other party may indicate an objection to one or more of the experts. The first party should then instruct a mutually acceptable expert;

(3)   if none of the experts is mutually acceptable, the parties may instruct experts of their own. It would be for the court to decide, if proceedings are issued, whether either party had acted unreasonably;

(4)   if the second party does not object to a nominated expert, he will not be entitled to rely on his own expert within that particular speciality unless:

(a)   the first party agrees;

(b)   the court directs; or

(c)   the first party's report has been amended and the first party is not prepared to disclose the original report.

Either party may send to the expert written questions on the report, relevant to the issues, via the first party's solicitors. The expert should send answers to the questions separately and directly to each party.

18.2.10 Medical experts

The above provisions also apply to medical experts. In addition:

(1)   when a medical expert is instructed, the claimant's solicitor should organise access to the relevant medical records; and

(2)   a recommended letter of instructions to a medical expert is annexed to the Protocol. This is unlikely to be of much assistance in a fatal accident case.

18.3   THE CLINICAL NEGLIGENCE PROTOCOL

If the death arises out of alleged clinical negligence, the Clinical Negligence Protocol (its full title being 'Pre-action Protocol for the Resolution of Clinical Negligence Disputes') should be followed closely.

18.3.1   The foreword to the Protocol

Unusually, this Protocol has a lengthy explanatory text, in three parts, before the text of the Protocol proper begins. This introductory text should not be ignored. The preamble to the Protocol is, probably, as important as the text itself since it gives a full explanation of the aims and purpose of the Protocol. If any dispute occurs in relation to construction of the protocol the courts will undoubtedly refer to the introductory text.

18.3.2 The 'Executive Summary'

The Executive Summary is the first part of the text. This explains the background to the Protocol and provides a useful overview of its aims. Paragraph 3 states:

> 'The protocol –
>
> – encourages a climate of openness when something has "gone wrong" with a patient's treatment or the patient is dissatisfied with that treatment and/or the outcome. This reflects the new and developing requirements for clinical guidance within healthcare;
> – provides *general guidance* on how this more open culture might be achieved when disputes arise;
> – recommends a *timed sequence* of steps for patients and healthcare providers, and their advisers to follow when a dispute arises. This should facilitate and speed up exchanging information and increase the prospects that disputes can be resolved without resort to legal action.'

18.3.3 Why this Protocol?

Chapter 1 of the Protocol documents the fact that complaints against healthcare providers are increasing and identifies the need for complaints to be resolved as quickly and professionally as possible. It goes on to identify the growth of a culture of mistrust on both sides which impedes the resolution of disputes.

The Protocol is clear that this mistrust needs to be removed and a more co-operative culture needs to develop. It states that healthcare professionals and providers need to adopt a constructive approach to complaints and claims. In particular, aggrieved patients are entitled to an explanation and an apology, if warranted, and to appropriate redress in the event of negligence. An overly defensive approach is not in the long-term interest of patient care. Patients must recognise that unintended or unfortunate consequences of medical treatment can only be rectified if they are brought to the attention of the healthcare provider as soon as possible.

18.3.4   The aims of the Protocol

Chapter 2 of the Protocol sets out the aims of the Protocol. The *general* aims are:

(1)   to maintain/restore the patient/healthcare provider relationship; and
(2)   to resolve as many disputes as possible without litigation.

The specific objectives are as follows.

(1)   *Openness*: in particular, the need to encourage early communication of any perceived problem; to encourage patients to voice concerns as soon as possible; to encourage healthcare providers to develop systems of early reporting and investigation for problems and to provide full and prompt explanations to dissatisfied patients; and to ensure that both parties disclose sufficient information to enable each to understand the other's perspective.
(2)   *Timeliness*: this includes encouragement for health providers to identify cases where investigation is required, to provide records within a reasonable time and:

    (a)   'where a resolution is not achievable to lay the ground to enable litigation to proceed on a reasonable timetable, at a reasonable and proportionate cost and to limit the matters in contention'; and

    (b)   'to discourage the prolonged pursuit of unmeritorious claims and the prolonged defence of meritorious claims'.

18.3.5   Awareness of options

The final aim set out is 'to ensure that patients and healthcare providers are made aware of the available options to pursue and resolve disputes and what each might involve'.

18.3.6   The Protocol in outline

Chapter 3 of the Protocol makes it clear that 'This protocol is not a comprehensive code governing all the steps in clinical disputes. Rather it attempts to set out a *code of good practice* which parties should follow when litigation might be a possibility'.

The 'working' part of the Protocol is in two parts:

(1)   the *commitments* section; and
(2)   the *steps* section.

18.3.7   Commitments of healthcare providers

There are a large number of commitments made by healthcare providers. These include ensuring that key staff are trained appropriately and have some knowledge of healthcare law; the development of an approach to clinical governance that ensures consistent performance and a system of clinical audit; the setting up of adverse outcome reporting systems; using the results of adverse incidents and complaints positively; ensuring that patients receive clear and comprehensible information in an accessible form about how to raise complaints; the establishment of effective and efficient systems of recording and storing patient records; and finally, advising patients of a serious adverse outcome and providing an explanation of what happened.

18.3.8   Commitments of patients

There are a number of commitments by patients: first, to report any concerns and dissatisfaction as soon as is reasonable; secondly, to consider the full range of options available, including appropriate dispute resolution methods; and finally, and of some importance to litigators, to inform the healthcare provider when the patient is satisfied that the matter has been concluded.

This final commitment also imposes a specific obligation on legal advisers to notify the provider when they are no longer acting for the patient, particularly if the proceedings have not started. This is useful, and helpful, to providers who, otherwise, may have to keep files open for considerable periods. It should also provide some relief to medical practitioners who would, otherwise, be faced with an open-ended concern about whether or not proceedings would be issued.

18.4   THE PROTOCOL STEPS

18.4.1   An outline

In essence, the Protocol provides three essential steps.

(1)   A procedure and timetable for obtaining the medical records.
(2)   Recommended contents of a letter of claim.
(3)   A timetable and template for a letter of response.

18.4.2   Obtaining the medical records

The request for medical records should provide sufficient information to alert the healthcare provider that it refers to a situation where an adverse outcome has had serious consequences. It should be as specific as possible about the records which are requested. Requests should be made using The Law Society and DOH standard forms, adapted as necessary. Copies of the form are at Annex B of the Protocol.

The copy records should be provided within 40 days of the request and for a cost not exceeding the charges permissible under the Access to Health Records Act 1990 (currently a maximum of £10) plus photocopying and postage. Any difficulty in complying with this time-limit should be explained promptly.

A failure to provide health records within the time-limit can lead to an application for pre-action disclosure and the court can, where appropriate, impose costs sanctions for unreasonable delay in providing records.

18.4.3   The letter of claim

There is a template letter of claim at Annex C1 of the Protocol. The essential elements that the letter should contain are:

(1)   a clear summary of the facts on which the claim is based;
(2)   the main allegations of negligence;
(3)   a description of the patient's injuries, including prognosis;
(4)   details of the financial loss incurred by the claimant;
(5)   reference to any relevant documentation, together with copies of those which are not already in the defendant's possession.

In more complex cases, it is recommended that a chronology of relevant events be included, particularly if a number of different healthcare providers have been involved.

Overall, it is recommended that sufficient information be given 'to enable the healthcare provider defendant to commence investigations and to put an initial valuation on the claim'.

18.4.4 The issue of proceedings and an offer to settle

It is recommended that proceedings not be issued until at least 3 months have passed since the letter of claim. However, there is an important and realistic caveat, in that it is recognised that proceedings may be issued if 'there is a limitation problem and/or the patient's position needs to be protected by early issue'.

The Protocol also points out that, at this stage, the claimant could make an offer to settle. In these circumstances it would be usual for the letter of claim to be accompanied by a medical report as to the injuries, condition and prognosis.

18.4.5 The response

There is a template for a letter of response. The healthcare provider must acknowledge receipt within 14 days and identify the person who is dealing with the matter. Within 3 months of the letter of claim the provider should provide a *reasoned* answer:

(1) stating, in clear terms, whether the claim is admitted; or
(2) if part of the claim is admitted, stating which parts are admitted or denied; and
(3) stating whether it is intended any admissions will be binding.

If the claim is denied, the denial should include specific comments on the allegations of negligence and, if the version of events put forward by the claimant is disputed, the provider's version of those events. If additional documents are relied upon, copies should be provided.

If the patient has made an offer to settle, the healthcare provider should respond to that offer in the response letter. The provider may even make its own offer to settle at this stage, either as a counter-offer or of its own accord. However, any offer should be accompanied by supporting medical evidence and any other evidence in relation to the value of the claim which is in the provider's possession.

If the parties reach agreement on liability, but time is needed to resolve the value of the claim, the parties should agree a reasonable period.

18.4.6   Experts

The Protocol appears to be less dogmatic on the issue of joint experts than the Personal Injury Protocol or the Civil Procedure Rules 1998 (CPR 1998). It recommends economy in the use of experts and a less adversarial expert culture. However:

> 'It is recognised that in clinical negligence disputes, the parties and their advisers will require flexibility in their approach to expert evidence. Decisions on whether experts might be instructed jointly, and on whether reports might be disclosed sequentially or by exchange, should rest with the parties and their advisers. Sharing expert evidence may be appropriate on issues relating to the value of the claim. However, this protocol does not attempt to be prescriptive on issues in relation to expert evidence.'

18.5   THE CLINICAL NEGLIGENCE PROTOCOL AND FATAL ACCIDENTS

The Clinical Negligence Protocol is easier to adapt to fatal accident claims than the Personal Injury Protocol. The need for a comprehensive statement, access to the medical records and the need for expert evidence on causation and liability make the initial issues in a fatal accident case similar to the issues in most clinical negligence cases.

18.6   PRACTICAL POINTS

(1)   The protocols set out specific guidance for:
    (a)   standard means of obtaining medical records;
    (b)   a comprehensive letter of claim; and
    (c)   a comprehensive letter of response.
(2)   The 'spirit' of the Protocols is as important as the specific guidance. Both parties are best advised to endeavour to comply with the overall aims of the relevant Protocol as closely as possible.
(3)   The Clinical Negligence Protocol is not at all prescriptive on the issue of experts. In this respect the parties have to work out the most appropriate strategy bearing in mind the aims of the Protocol and the overriding objective set out in the CPR 1998.

CHAPTER 19

PROCEDURAL MATTERS UPON ISSUE OF PROCEEDINGS

19.1 REQUIREMENTS UNDER THE CIVIL PROCEDURE RULES 1998

19.1.1 Specific requirements

Fatal accident claims as a specific issue do not figure highly in the CPR 1998.

Paragraph 5.1 of the Practice Direction to Part 16 states that a claimant in a personal injury case must, in the Particulars of Claim, state:

(1)   that it is brought under the Fatal Accidents Act 1976;
(2)   the dependants on whose behalf the claim is made;
(3)   the date of birth of each dependant; and
(4)   details of the nature of the dependency claim.

The Practice Direction also states that the fatal accident claim may also include a claim for damages for bereavement and a claim under the Law Reform (Miscellaneous Provisions) Act 1934.

Rule 37.4 of the CPR 1998 states that where a claim is made under the Fatal Accidents Act 1976 and the Law Reform (Miscellaneous Provisions) Act 1934, a single sum of money is paid into court, and the money is accepted, then the court should apportion the money between the different claims.

19.1.2 General requirements

Apart from these requirements, the normal procedural requirements of the CPR 1998 in personal injury cases apply.

(1)   If the claim has a value of less than £50,000 it should be issued in the county court.

(2)   The rules as to pleadings, service and requests for information are similar. It is not proposed to give these in detail here.[1]

19.2   ALLOCATION

It is possible for a fatal accident claim to be issued to the small claims track or fast track if it is of low value. However, value is only one of the factors that a court takes into account in the allocation of a case.[2] There are powerful arguments against a fatal accident case being allocated to the small claims or fast track. This could be viewed as insensitive, and the need for the court to consider the issues and take a 'jury' approach could make it particularly unsuitable for these tracks. However, there is no authority on the point, so if the claim is of modest value the consequences of reference to these tracks should be considered and, if necessary, the arguments against reference should be set out in detail in the Allocation Questionnaire.

19.3   PART 36 PAYMENTS AND APPORTIONMENT

There are specific rules governing Part 36 payments and apportionment which are considered in Chapter 22.

---

[1]   For detailed information see, for example, *Butterworths' Personal Injury Litigation Service* or Hendy, Day and Buchan and Kennedy *Personal Injury Practice* (Butterworths, 3rd edn, 2000).

[2]   See CPR 1998, r 26.8(1).

CHAPTER 20

DRAFTING WITNESS STATEMENTS

20.1 INTRODUCTION

The drafting of witness statements in fatal accident cases requires skill, judgment and diplomacy. Although the final decision is made by a judge, many issues are decided on a 'jury' basis. We have to consider how the witness statement is going to come across at trial and the effect it will have on the judge's approach to the issues. In other words, the drafting of the witness statement is an essential part of the advocacy process.

(1)   It is extremely difficult, at trial, to repair the damage caused by bad witness statements.

(2)   Witness statements can create insurmountable problems and *lose* a case or, at least, lose certain issues in the case.

(3)   Effective witness statements can serve to *win* the case.

The drafting of witness statements is a neglected craft. It is a craft that requires enormous skill and calls upon knowledge of both law and a degree of 'psychology'. In essence, what is required is a large degree of common sense. However, it must be remembered that we are not involved in the manipulation of evidence, rather in the effective presentation of the evidence to put the case forward in the most favourable light. This is an important distinction, indeed a crucial distinction.

Because of the overwhelming importance of witness statements in fatal accident cases, it is worthwhile spending a little time looking at the background to the rules and the skills now required.

20.2   THE BACKGROUND

In the *Final Report on Access to Justice*[1] ('the Report'), Lord Woolf generally approved of the use of witness statements. However, this approval was subject to some major caveats:

> 'Witness statements have ceased to be the authentic account of the lay witness; instead they have become an elaborate, costly branch of legal drafting.'[2]

20.2.1   An end to 'over-drafting'

The problem identified by Lord Woolf was the fear that a witness will not be allowed to depart from the statement or amplify parts of it. The natural consequence is that lawyers 'over-draft' to ensure that the statement is totally comprehensive. The suggested solution was that:

> 'The new rules will provide that the court can allow evidence which has not been foreshadowed by a witness statement to be given at trial where admitting the evidence will not cause any party injustice ... additional expense to a party caused by a late, unjustified change of tack by his opponent can be regarded as a potential aspect of injustice. Departing from the present assumptions, however, this type of prejudice should not be regarded as remediable simply by an order for costs. There may accordingly be cases where the court has to refuse to allow the additional evidence to be given.'

Because of the increased flexibility of the new system, the legal profession should be less concerned with the need to draft wholly comprehensive statements:

> 'This is not to be taken as encouragement deliberately to omit relevant material, but simply to rein back the excessive effort now devoted to gilding the lily.'

20.2.2   The threat of wasted costs

As a result trial judges are encouraged to scrutinise witness statements rigorously, this being the only way to identity repetition, legal argument or analysis of documents:

> 'This is a fault which must in the main be attributed to the legal profession and not to its clients; wasted costs orders may therefore be appropriate in some instances of grossly overdone drafting.'[3]

---

[1]   HMSO, 1996.
[2]   Ibid, at para 55.
[3]   Ibid, at para 58.

20.2.3 The recommendation

The Report makes the following specific witness recommendations about witness statements:

'witness statements should:
(a)   so far as possible, be in the witness's own words;
(b)   not discuss legal propositions;
(c)   not comment on documents;
(d)   conclude with a signed statement by the witness that the evidence is a true statement and that it is in his own words.'[1]

20.2.4 The 'merging' of witness statements and affidavits

Finally, the Report concludes that, since the Civil Evidence Act 1995 is now in force, hearsay evidence is admissible with only a minimum of formality needed to identify it. It will be unnecessary for lawyers to edit hearsay; however, the statement must indicate the source of knowledge, belief or information on which the witness himself is relying. 'In this respect the difference between witness statements and affidavits will diminish.'[2]

20.3   THE NEW SKILLS

It is clear that the collection and collation of evidence, together with the drafting of a witness statement, is now a skilled task. This skill will be to ensure that the statement has proper lucidity, authenticity and relevance, as opposed to drafting one which attempts to argue the case with reference to legal principles and extensive documentation.

It must also be noted that the proposal is that a witness cannot 'comment' on documents. This is not a blanket ban on referral to documents, as it is clear that in many cases it is *essential* that a witness refer to documents if they are relevant to his or her evidence. What is to be avoided is any attempt to comment on the documents in detail.

---

[1]   *Final Report on Access to Justice* (HMSO, 1996), Recommendations, para 149.
[2]   Ibid, chapter 12, para 60.

20.4   THE RULES

The rules relating to witness statements are at Part 32 of the CPR 1998 and supplemented by a very important draft Practice Direction. The salient part of the rule (from a drafting viewpoint) is that:

'**32.8   Form of witness statement**

A witness statement must comply with the requirements set out in the relevant practice direction.

(Part 22 requires that a witness statement be verified by a statement of truth.)'

20.5   WITNESS STATEMENTS AND 'THE ART OF ADVOCACY'

20.5.1   The aim of this section

We will now examine the science and the 'art' of drafting witness statements in fatal accident cases. As well as looking at the technicalities, it is important to emphasise that witness statements are an 'art', in that they represent the most important part of the case and now replace the important part of evidence-in-chief.

20.5.2   Practical consequences

In addition to ensuring the service of statements of *all* the witnesses upon whom a party intends to rely, it is important that the *contents* of the statements deal with every essential issue in the action.

It is important to ensure that a witness statement covers *everything*, but in the appropriate amount of detail.

20.5.3   Use of precedents

Individual styles of drafting vary; however, it is important that:

(1)   the statements are in a logical order with numbered paragraphs;
(2)   all the matters that the party needs to establish (or disprove) are dealt with; and
(3)   you should consider:
    (a)   proving dependency (if in issue);
    (b)   setting up and establishing the heads of claim;
    (c)   dealing with issues such as the multiplier.

Finally, remember that the witness statement is the evidence of the witness. It is the lawyer's task to help the witness put forward his or her evidence in a logical format and in a way that assists the court. It may be important to edit out aspects of the evidence that are not relevant; however, you must be careful to avoid doctoring the evidence.

One useful strategy is to compare the witness statement with the schedule of damages and to ensure that the witness evidence proves, so far as it can, all the items in the schedule.

CHAPTER 21

THE SCHEDULE OF DAMAGES

21.1 INTRODUCTION

It cannot be emphasised strongly enough that this is a crucial document. The way in which the schedule is prepared and presented can make a tremendous difference to the way that the matter is treated at trial, and to the defendant's response. The schedule must be:

(1)   comprehensive;
(2)   clear; and
(3)   credible.

The rules as to the format of a schedule are extremely brief. Paragraph 4.1 of PD 16 to the CPR 1998 states:

> 'The claimant must attach to his particulars of claim a schedule of details of any past and future expenses and losses which he claims.'

There are no absolute rules for drafting a schedule. However, consider clarity, in particular:

(1)   each head of damages should be on a new page;
(2)   detailed calculations should be carried out in 'schedules' to the schedule.

21.2 THE SCHEDULE OF DAMAGES: PRESENTATION AND ADVOCACY

Rather than set out here a series of general rules for the preparation of schedules, there are several examples at Appendix 2. The important point is to set out the damages claim in a comprehensive, lucid and credible manner.

The role of the schedule of damages is, like that of the witness statement, an important one. Many schedules are, frankly, incomprehensible (sometimes this is a deliberate policy on the part of the claimant's lawyer in an attempt to bamboozle the defendant or the court). It is submitted that such tactics are mistaken. The claimant's interests are best served by putting forward the case for damages in a careful and comprehensible manner. Similar principles apply to the quantification of the claim in the schedule. While the claimant's case can properly be put at its most favourable, care must be taken not to exaggerate the claim or to claim for items that are clearly not recoverable. Again, such tactics are often adopted deliberately on the grounds that the defendant, or the court, will cut out items in any event. However, such an approach is often misguided since it damages the credibility of the claimant's case and, in many instances, leads to exaggerated expectations on the claimant's part. It can also lead to penalties in costs.

It is emphasised again that it is no part of the lawyer's task to edit out those parts of the claim which are debatable or which may not succeed. The schedule can properly represent the claimant's *best* case; it should not, however, include any items which the claimant could not reasonably expect to recover or for which there is no evidence to support the loss.

CHAPTER 22

APPORTIONMENT

22.1 THE LAW

It is difficult to find any definitive principles concerning apportionment, particularly in relation to the awards made to children where there is a surviving parent. The reported cases demonstrate considerable differences between the proportion given to children in the case where there is a surviving parent. The best summary of the pragmatic approach of the court can be found in *R v Criminal Injuries Compensation Board, ex parte Barrett.*[1] Latham J observed that the practice has developed in relation to the valuation of the dependency, where there has been the loss of a father or a mother, whereby an overall figure is calculated. However:

> 'The approach to the apportionment of the overall figure has essentially been pragmatic; the courts have sought to provide as much money in free cash terms for the parent who is caring for the child as is sensible in all the circumstances, so that there can be ready access for that parent to the fund representing the lost dependency. The bulk has therefore been apportioned to the parent. That was and is a fiction, because in most cases, when analysed, it is plain the children were in fact the parties, or the dependants, for whom the substantial proportion, where care was concerned, of the value of the claim was intended. It was for their benefit. And it is right to say that this has never been reduced to any coherent or sensible principle. It has essentially been an approach which has the attraction which I have already indicated to the parent who needs the cash; and there is no doubt that it could be said to be founded on good common sense.'

The principle is that each person who can be described as a dependant is entitled to the value of his or her dependency. The value of that dependency depends, so far as the children are concerned, on their ages and the financial circumstances of the family.

---
[1] [1994] PIQR Q44.

However, Latham J observed:

> 'In normal circumstances it would clearly not be wrong or unreasonable to follow the normal practice of apportioning damages in the way I have indicated the courts have done in the past, even if a strict analysis suggests that this does not give proper effect to the child's separate right to claim the full value of his or her dependency.'

22.2   DEPARTING FROM THE NORMAL PRACTICE

In the *Barrett* case, the effect of apportioning the damages in the normal way reduced the damages payable by the Criminal Injuries Compensation Board (as it was then known) because of the effect of an insurance policy. For this reason the court overturned the Criminal Injuries Compensation Board's decision on apportionment and awarded the loss of damages for the mother's services wholly to the children. The children had made a claim in their own right under the Scheme, they had no insurance money to make up their loss and, therefore, they were awarded the full claim for future care.

22.3   APPORTIONMENT IN NON-CHILDREN CASES

In non-children cases it is a matter of resolving the entitlement of each dependant. In cases of serious dispute between dependants it may be that the court has to make an order that each dependant is separately represented.

22.4   APPORTIONMENT AND PROCEDURE

Rule 37.4 of the CPR 1998 states:

'(1)   Where –
  (a)   a claim includes claims arising under –
     (i)   the Fatal Accidents Act 1976; and
     (ii)   the Law Reform (Miscellaneous Provisions) Act 1934;
  (b)   a single sum of money is paid into court in satisfaction of those claims; and
  (c)   the money is accepted,
  the court shall apportion the money between the different claims.
(2)   The court shall apportion money under paragraph (1) –
  (a)   when it gives directions under rule 21.11 (control of money received by a child or patient); or

(b) if rule 21.11 does not apply, when it gives permission for the money to be paid out of court.

(3) Where, in an action in which a claim under the Fatal Accidents Act 1976 is made by or on behalf of more than one person –

(a) a sum in respect of damages is ordered or agreed to be paid in satisfaction of the claim; or

(b) a sum of money is accepted in satisfaction of the claim,

the court shall apportion it between the persons entitled to it unless it has already been apportioned by the court, a jury, or agreement between the parties.'

22.5 PRACTICAL SIGNIFICANCE

The practical significance of this is that whenever there is more than one claimant under the Fatal Accidents Act 1976 the court must apportion the damages.

(1) If one or more of the claimants is under a disability (ie a minor or a patient) then this will be considered at the approval application.

(2) Even if the claimants are not under a disability, the court still needs to apportion the damages.

(3) If one of the claimants is under a disability, then an offer or payment into court can only be accepted with the permission of the court.

(4) Even if the claimants are not under a disability, permission of the court is needed.

The Practice Direction to the CPR 1998, Part 36 states at para 7.8:

'Where:

(1) the court's approval, or

(2) an order for payment of money out of court, or

(3) an order for payment of money in court –

(a) between the Fatal Accidents Act 1976 and the Law Reform (Miscellaneous Provisions) Act 1934, or

(b) between the persons entitled to it under the Fatal Accidents Act 1976, is required for acceptance of a Part 36 offer or Part 36 payment, application for the approval or the order should be made in accordance with Part 23.'

PART 6

MATTERS REQUIRING SPECIAL CARE

(1) Fatal accidents and the Criminal Injuries Compensation Authority (CICA).
(2) Coroner's court.
(3) Dealing with the bereaved client.

CHAPTER 23

CRIMINAL INJURIES AND FATAL ACCIDENTS

23.1 INTRODUCTION

Where the death is due to a criminal act, it is often the case that there is no defendant worth pursuing and a claim must be made to the CICA. All deaths after 1 April 2001 are covered by the 2001 Criminal Injuries Compensation Scheme. The sections of the scheme relevant to fatal accidents are sections 37–44. The central points of the scheme, so far as fatal accidents are concerned, are dealt with here. It is important to remember that this is a statutory scheme and that common law principles do not, generally, apply. The terms of the scheme must be studied carefully when making the claim and when explaining the likely award to dependants.

It is important to remember that, unlike the situation at common law, an application for compensation can be made by the dependants, even if a payment was made to the deceased before his death.

Generally, the claim to the CICA must be made within 2 years after the incident of which complaint is made. This time-limit can be extended if there is good reason for the delay and it is in the interests of justice to do so.

23.2 NO PAYMENT TO THE ESTATE

Where the victim has died in consequence of the injury, the only payment which can be made to the estate is for the funeral expenses. These expenses will be payable 'up to an amount considered reasonable by a claims officer', even where the person who pays for the funeral is otherwise ineligible to claim under the scheme.

23.3   THOSE ELIGIBLE TO MAKE A CLAIM

To make a claim to the CICA, the applicant must be a 'qualifying claimant'. One important point about the scheme is that, unlike the common law position to date, it recognises homosexual relationships. An applicant can be:

(1)   the partner of the deceased. This is defined as:

> 'a person who was living with the deceased as husband and wife or as a same sex partner in the same household immediately before the date of death and who, if not formally married to him, had been so living throughout the two years before that date.'[1]

(2)   a spouse or former spouse of the deceased, who was financially supported by him immediately before the date of the death;

(3)   a parent of the deceased, whether or not the natural parent, provided that he was accepted by the deceased as a parent of his family; or

(4)   a child of the deceased, whether or not a natural child, provided that he was accepted by the deceased as a child of his family or was dependent on him.

A person who was responsible for the death of a victim cannot be a qualifying claimant.

23.4   DID THE CRIMINAL INJURY CAUSE THE DEATH?

A distinction is drawn between cases where the victim has died in consequence of the injury and where the victim has died otherwise than in consequence of the injury.

(1)   Where the victim has died in consequence of the injury, compensation is paid to the claimant under the terms of sections 39–42 of the scheme: see paras **23.5** *et seq*.

---

[1]   Criminal Injuries Compensation Scheme, para 38(a)(i).

(2)   Where the victim has died otherwise than in consequence of the injury, compensation may be paid in accordance with section 44 of the scheme (see para **23.10**).

23.5 'BEREAVEMENT DAMAGES' AWARD

Paragraph 39 of the scheme provides standard compensation, which appears to be akin to the bereavement award.

(1)   When there is one qualifying claimant, an amount of compensation equivalent to level 13 of the tariff is payable. Currently this is £11,000.
(2)   Where there is more than one qualifying claimant, the standard amount for each claimant is on level 10 of the tariff, currently £5,500.

However, a former spouse is not entitled to this type of award.

23.6 LOSS OF DEPENDENCY CLAIMS

In addition to the 'bereavement award' under section 39 of the scheme, additional compensation can be paid where a claims officer is satisfied that the claimant was financially dependent on the deceased.

However, dependency will not be established where the deceased's only normal income was from UK social security benefits, or other benefits paid by another country.

23.7 CALCULATION OF THE LOSS OF DEPENDENCY

The amount of compensation is calculated on the basis of net loss of earnings.

23.7.1 Upper limit on loss of earnings

The Rules refer to the calculation as similar to that carried out for the loss of income of a living claimant under sections 31–34 of the scheme. This puts a maximum on the earnings that will be paid. Section 34 states:

'Any rate of net loss of earning capacity (before any reduction in accordance with this Scheme) which is to be taken into account in calculating any compensation payable under paragraphs 30–33 must not exceed one and a half times the gross average industrial earnings at the time of assessment according to the latest figures published by the Department of Education and Employment.'

23.7.2 Period of calculation

The period of loss begins at the date of the deceased's death and continues for such period as the claims officer may determine 'with no account being taken, where the qualifying claimant was formally married to the deceased, of the prospects of remarriage or prospects of remarriage'.

23.7.3 Dependant's income taken into account

The CICA will take into account the qualifying claimant's income and emoluments.

23.7.4 Reduction because of deceased's expenses

Where the deceased had been living in the same household as the claimant, the CICA will, in calculating the multiplicand, make a proportional reduction to take account of the deceased's own personal and living expenses.

23.8 LOSS OF PARENTS' SERVICES

Where a qualifying claimant was under 18 years of age at the time of the deceased's death and was dependent upon him (or her) for parental services, the following additional compensation may also be payable:

(1)   a payment for loss of that parent's services at an annual rate of Level 5 of the Tariff (ie £2,000 per annum);
(2)   such other payments as a claims officer considers reasonable to meet other resultant losses.

Each of these payments will be multiplied by an appropriate multiplier selected by the CICA. Account is taken of the period remaining before the claimant reaches the age of 18 and any other factors and contingencies which appear to the claims officer to be relevant.

It appears to be clear that the £2,000 per annum is designed to represent the 'intangible' loss of services and, thereafter, the CICA is only concerned with direct financial dependency.

23.9   A SECOND AWARD CAN BE MADE

Section 43 of the scheme states that an application can be made in a fatal case even where an award has been made to the victim in respect of that injury before his death. It is necessary to reopen the case in accordance with the scheme and the compensation paid (except for the funeral expenses and standard 'bereavement' compensation) will be reduced by the amount paid to the victim. The amounts paid to the victim and the qualifying claimants will not exceed £500,000 in total.

23.10   VICTIM DIES BEFORE AWARD BUT NOT AS A CONSEQUENCE OF THE CRIMINAL ACT

Where a victim who would have qualified for a claim for loss of earnings and special expenses dies otherwise than in consequence of the relevant criminal attack, but before a payment is made, then a claim can be made or continued. This claim can be made even if the deceased had not made such a claim prior to his death. Payment is made for the victim/deceased's loss of earnings (except for the first 28 weeks of such loss) and for any special expenses (damage to property or equipment, medical treatment, special equipment and appliances needed). The total amount payable to the victim and qualifying claimant will not exceed £500,000.

23.11   PENSIONS TAKEN INTO ACCOUNT

Section 47 states that where the victim has died in consequence of the criminal injury, the dependency payment will be 'reduced to take account of any pension payable, as a result of the victim's death for the benefit of the applicant'. Where such pensions are taxable, one half of their value is deducted; otherwise, they will be deducted in full, for instance where a lump sum payment not subject to income tax is made. Pension means:

> 'any payment payable as a result of the injury or death in pursuance of pension or any other rights connected with the victim's employment, and includes any

gratuity of that kind and similar benefits payable under insurance policies paid for by the victim's employers. Pension rights accruing solely as a result of payments by the victim or a dependant will be disregarded.'

The final point is important. A pension paid for solely by the victim or a dependant is *not* deducted.

23.12 OTHER CICA MATTERS

Payments can be reduced or refused if the deceased or the claimant had a criminal record. A form of application can be obtained from: the Criminal Injuries Compensation Authority, Tay House, 300 Bath Street, Glasgow G2 4JR. Tel: 0800 359 3601, Fax: 0141 331 2287. Website: www.cica.gov.uk.

CHAPTER 24

AN INTRODUCTION TO CORONERS' INQUESTS

24.1 HISTORICAL ORIGINS OF THE ROLE OF CORONER

The office of coroner dates back to 1194, when officers were appointed by King Richard I to help him administer justice and raise money. The coroner was a revenue collector; one of his most important duties was the investigation of deaths, which were a profitable source of revenue for the Crown.

As a judicial officer, the coroner administered justice and raised revenues for the Crown by fining criminal offenders. It was also the coroner who supervised the practice of trial by ordeal: if a suspected criminal was unharmed, then he was innocent. The coroner would record the event and preserve forfeited property for the Crown.

Over time, the coroner's role evolved to include making enquiries and taking evidence. At the outset, coroners were principally involved in recording criminal events. From the sixteenth century onwards, they were almost exclusively concerned with the investigation of sudden death.

24.2 PRESENT ROLE OF THE CORONER

The coroner still retains his independence as an independent judicial officer under the Crown, but is appointed and paid for by the local council. To qualify for the office of coroner the candidate must be a qualified lawyer or doctor with 5 years' or more experience. There are approximately 146 coroners in England and Wales, 26 of them full-time officers.

In 1836, the coroner became responsible for registering all deaths and for arranging medical witnesses to examine bodies in cases of sudden death. Coroners' Acts were passed between 1987 and 1980 setting out the rules and regulations governing the coroner's jurisdiction. These were eventually consolidated in the Coroners Act 1988. The Coroners Rules 1984 are unaffected by the consolidation Act.

Section 8(1) of the Coroners Act 1988 sets out the jurisdiction for the holding of an inquest. The coroner has compulsory jurisdiction in cases of:

(a)   violent or unnatural death;
(b)   sudden death whose cause is unknown; and
(c)   death in prison.

An unnatural death is described as one 'involving a wholly unexpected death from natural causes which would not have occurred but for some culpable human failure'.[1] In this case, death resulting from inadequate monitoring of the deceased's blood pressure after giving birth was an unnatural death for the purposes of s 8(1):

> '... an inquest should be held whenever a wholly unexpected death, albeit from natural causes, resulted from some culpable human failure? (Or, more strictly, whenever the Coroner had reasonable grounds to suspect that such is the case.)' (*per* Simon Brown LJ at para 43).

When a coroner accepts jurisdiction over a body he can insist on a post-mortem being carried out.[2]

In such an event, the coroner has a duty to notify any relative who has informed the coroner of his or her interest; the deceased's regular medical practitioner and hospital doctor; the Pneumoconiosis Panel in a suspected pneumoconiosis case; an enforcing panel or government department in any relevant case; and the chief of police for the area in which the death occurred. Any of these interested parties can be represented at the post-mortem by a qualified medical practitioner but that medical practitioner must not interfere in the post-mortem. He or she is there merely as an observer.[3]

---

[1]   *R v HM Coroner for Inner London, ex parte Touche* [2001] EWCA Civ 383.
[2]   *R v HM Coroner for Greater Manchester, ex parte Worch* 1987 QV 627.
[3]   Coroners Rules 1984, SI 1984/552, r 8.

It is the coroner who appoints the pathologist and acts as his employer. The pathologist will be independent (and relatives can insist on this); he must have suitable facilities for the conduct of a post-mortem; and he must be of an appropriate discipline. A paediatric pathologist would therefore be appropriate in the case of the death of a child. It is also the custom and practice that if a death has occurred in a hospital in which failure of treatment is suspected, the coroner will select a pathologist from another hospital or area.

The coroner's control over a body arises as soon as he decides to hold an inquest and lasts at common law until the inquest itself is determined.[1] If organs are to be retained, the coroner is notified, although as a matter of good practice the coroner would usually provide the relevant information to relatives.

While relatives cannot refuse a coroner's decision to hold a post-mortem, they are in turn entitled, as of right, to a second post-mortem.[2] Because the coroner's pathologist is supposed to have appropriate specialist knowledge and to be independent, it is rare that a second post-mortem can be justified; once the independence of the coronial system and the coroner's pathologist is explained, most relatives no longer desire a second post-mortem.

The post-mortem report itself is a confidential document which is supplied by the pathologist to the coroner alone.[3] Any person can apply to the coroner for a copy of the post-mortem report which can be inspected free[4] or a copy can be supplied for a fee.[5] Practice differs between coroners as to whether a post-mortem report will be released prior to the inquest being held. The modern and more acceptable practice is that a copy of the post-mortem report will be released before the inquest to interested parties, on payment of the appropriate fee.

The form of the post-mortem report will generally follow the form recommended by the World Health Organisation with an analysis of the body as seen on dissection followed by a conclusion. Part One of the conclusion sets out the sequence of disease or conditions leading

---

1   *R v HM Coroner for Bristol, ex parte Kerr* [1974] 2 All ER 719.
2   *R v HM Coroner for Greater London, ex parte Ridley* [1985] 1 WLR 1347.
3   Coroners Rules 1984, r 10.
4   Ibid, r 57(2).
5   Ibid, r 57(1).

to death and Part Two lists other disease processes contributing to death but not directly involved.

A typical format for a cause of death is illustrated below.

Cause of death
1(a) Broncho-pneumonia
1(b) Altzheimer's disease
2   Fractured femur (operated)

24.3 THE INQUEST

24.3.1 Remit

There are only four questions for the coroner to consider at an inquest.

(1)   Who was the deceased?
(2)   How did the deceased come by his death?
(3)   When did the deceased come by his death?
(4)   Where did the deceased come by his death?

The inquest is a fact-finding, non-adversarial enquiry. The coroner is expressly forbidden to consider criminal liability[1] or civil responsibility[2] on the part of a named individual.

The coroner has the option to decide whether or not to hold the inquest with a jury. A jury is mandatory in cases of death in prison or police custody; or in cases where allegations of a breach of s 19 of the Health and Safety at Work etc Act 1974 are considered, or where the events which led to this death or their possible recurrence are prejudicial to the safety of the public. In all other cases, the coroner need only appoint a jury where he considers it is in the public interest to do so.[3] In the vast majority of cases, the coroner will sit without a jury.

The inquest falls into two parts. At the opening of the inquest, which normally takes place a few days after the death, formal evidence of identification is given (often through the coroner's officer), and an interim certificate of death is issued. The coroner can then give an

---

[1]   Coroners Rules 1984, r 42a.
[2]   Ibid, r 42b.
[3]   Coroners Act 1988, s 8(4).

order for disposal of the body, authorising cremation or burial as appropriate, although that might take place some days or weeks later.

During the resumption of the inquest, the evidence is entirely within the control of the coroner. He decides which experts to call and which lay witnesses to call. He chooses the pathologist and decides whether or not his evidence should be called; decides whether or not to admit statements and accepts evidence whether it is hearsay or not. The identification of child witnesses is banned under the s 39(1) of the Children and Young Persons Act 1933. Otherwise, any witness called by a Coroner is bound to attend and give evidence. The witness can only refuse to give evidence by attending and electing not to give evidence on the grounds of self-incrimination. In order to do so, there must be a real and appreciable risk of criminal offences and penalties.[1] There is, however, no complete immunity against questioning. The ability to refuse to give evidence relates only to those questions which would reflect the risk of criminal offences.

24.3.2   Documentation

Documentation for the inquest is likewise controlled entirely by the coroner. It is his decision whether or not documentary evidence should be admitted. Such evidence should be read aloud[2] unless the coroner otherwise directs. The coroner will frequently admit a suicide note, for example, but – in the interests of the relatives – direct that it not be read out. The full version of the post-mortem report is seldom read out. In any event, should an advocate be representing relatives at an inquest, it is recommended practice to suggest to the relatives that they may wish to leave the room while the pathologist's evidence is being given. However, documentation used at the inquest must be shown to interested parties who wish to see it at the time.[3]

Historically, coroners have not been willing to disclose documentation to interested parties prior to the inquest. In these more enlightened days under the influence of the Human Rights Act 1998, it is generally considered better practice that documentation should be made available to interested parties. The

---

[1]   Coroners Rules 1984, r 22(1).
[2]   Ibid, r 37(6).
[3]   *R v HM Coroner for Southwark, ex parte Hicks* [1987] 1 WLR 1624.

court's view is that it will not fetter the discretion of coroners by being prescriptive but judges have indicated that it would be helpful if at least a list of witnesses accompanied by a short summary of the gist of the witnesses' evidence, should be provided to interested parties, even if the actual statements themselves are (for one reason or another) withheld.[1]

24.3.3 Requirements of an effective enquiry

It is, however, essential that the coroner should conduct a full and effective enquiry, otherwise the deceased's relatives may have remedies to demand a full enquiry.[2]

The case of *Jordan v UK*[3] sets out the criteria for an investigation to be acceptable. It must:

(1) be independent;
(2) be effective;
(3) be prompt;
(4) involve a sufficient element of public scrutiny; and
(5) involve the next of kin

As Jackson J reminded everyone:

> 'steps should be taken to ensure that in every case where Article 2 of the Convention may be engaged, the Coroner's Inquest complies with the procedural obligations arising under that article.'

It is essential that relatives attending an inquest are briefed by the advocate concerned as to what to expect. An inquest is an enquiry not an adversarial proceeding. As seen above, the evidence is entirely within the control of the coroner. After the coroner has produced a witness and relevant document(s) and asked his own questions, interested parties may ask questions by way of examination (but not by way of cross-examination).

Sometimes, advocates have witness or documentary evidence which they may feel would assist the coroner in his enquiry. However, it is not possible for interested parties to call their own evidence.

---

[1] *R v HM Coroner for Lincolnshire, ex parte Hay* 2000 MLC 190.
[2] See Arts 2 and 3 of the European Convention on Human Rights; *McCann v UK* (1996) 21 EHRR 97; *Wright v Secretary of State for Home Department* [2001] EWHC Admin 520 (unreported).
[3] 11 BHRC 1.

Instead, such evidence should be supplied to the Coroner who can decide whether a particular witness or a particular item of evidence should be called during the course of the enquiry itself. It is now accepted that medical records should be supplied in advance of an inquest.[1]

The questioning of witnesses during the coroner's inquiry is entirely controlled by the coroner who will bear in mind the four questions he must consider. In many inquests, the interested parties have a much wider agenda than the coroner. Only if the coroner believes that it is in the public interest that the enquiry be widened is he likely to allow detailed examination of witnesses outside the strict limits of the four questions he has to answer. It is entirely his discretion whether to admit those questions and the enquiry will be stopped if the coroner considers that the question is not relevant or that it is a cross-examination rather than an examination.[2]

Questions can only be asked by an interested party.[3] The relatives of a passenger in a car in which the deceased was travelling would not be an interested party for this purpose.[4]

24.3.4   The verdict

At the conclusion of the evidence, the coroner has to decide on the verdict. Before doing so, it is open to the representatives of interested parties to make submissions. Those submissions, however, can only relate to the verdict. They can only be made by an interested party; they must be made to the coroner in the absence of the jury, and not to the jury; and they must be made prior to the summing up. Of greatest importance is that the submissions must be of law and not as to the facts of the enquiry.

As seen above, the coroner cannot be involved in determining criminal or civil liability. His verdict therefore cannot be framed to determine criminal liability on the part of a named person or civil liability on behalf of any person or organisation. The usual verdicts are likely to be as follows:

---

[1]   *Stobart v NHA* [1992] 3 MEDLR 284.
[2]   *R v HM Coroner for South London, ex parte Thompson* (1982) 126 SJ 625.
[3]   Coroners Rules 1984, r 20.
[4]   *R v Coroner of the Queens Household, ex parte Al Fayed* 58 BMLR 205.

- natural causes;
- industrial disease;
- want of attention at birth;
- suicide;
- accidental or misadventure;
- unlawful killing;
- open verdict; or
- still birth.

A verdict of unlawful killing is unlikely unless criminal proceedings are out of the question; for example, because the perpetrator is already dead. Such a verdict can cover murder, reckless manslaughter or gross negligence manslaughter. The most difficult area is probably in relation to the latter. In gross negligence manslaughter, the evidence must demonstrate the existence of a duty of care; a breach of that duty; and gross negligence such as inattention or failure to advert to a serious risk whether beyond mere inadvertence in relation to the obvious and important matter which the duty demanded the individual should address.[1]

Accidental death and misadventure are the same verdict. Sometimes, accidental death is used to denote the activities of the deceased, while misadventure is used where the death was caused by a third party.

There can be no objection to a verdict which incorporates a brief neutral and factual statement. Many coroners would prefer to have the ability to return a verdict which simply states the facts causing the death without characterising it with a description and some already do so.

Verdicts of natural causes, industrial disease and want of attention at birth can all carry the rider 'aggravated by lack of care'. This rider does not describe carelessness or negligence. Lack of care denotes neglect; the opposite of self-neglect. If an advocate is considering representing parties at an Inquest, he should read *R v HM Coroner for North Humberside, ex parte Jamieson*[2] which contains a comprehensive review of the verdicts open to a coroner, with specific reference to the use of the verdict of lack of care or neglect.

---

[1]   *R v Adomako* [1995] AC 171; *R v Adomako, Prentice and Sulman* [1994] QB 302.
[2]   [1994] 3 All ER 972.

A coroner's inquest can be an extremely useful part of the evidence-gathering exercise prior to presentation of a claim. It is, however, a mediaeval system struggling to exist in the twenty-first century and all parties agree that the system is in need of reform. A Home Office working party is looking at the future of the coronial system. One possibility is that the coroner will take overall charge of all deaths, with the registrar of deaths working under him and the coroner deciding which deaths should be investigated; the investigation being conducted under much more Woolfian principles than the current Coroners Rules 1984.

PART 7

FUTURE DEVELOPMENTS IN THE LAW RELATING TO FATAL ACCIDENTS

In this Part we consider the Law Commission Report of 1999 which recommended a number of changes to the current regime, and the implications of the Human Rights Act 1998 for this area of law.

CHAPTER 25

THE LAW COMMISSION RECOMMENDATIONS

25.1 INTRODUCTION

The observations in the Law Commission Report[1] produced on 1 November 1999 remain a useful guide on many points relating to fatal accidents. The Law Commission made the point that many of the recommendations it makes can be implemented by the courts without recourse to legislation. This chapter concentrates on those points where the Law Commission recommended reform. The recommendations are important, since the Law Commission's view is often given considerable weight by the courts. The areas where statutory change is needed are also set out below.

25.2 EXTENSION OF THE CLASS OF PEOPLE ENTITLED TO CLAIM

The Law Commission recommended that the present list of those able to make a claim should be maintained. However, it suggested the addition to the list of a generally worded class of claimant whereby any other individual who 'was being wholly or partly maintained by the deceased immediately or who would, but for the death, have been so maintained at a time beginning after the death', would be able to bring a claim after the death.[2] (Statutory change would probably be needed, but see the discussion at Chapter 26.)

---

[1]   Law Commission Report No 263 *Claims for Wrongful Death.*
[2]   Ibid, at para 3.46.

25.3   THE MULTIPLIER CALCULATED FROM DEATH

The Law Commission recommended that the Ogden Working Party should consider and explain how the actuarial tables should be used to produce accurate assessments in fatal accident cases (as opposed to personal injury cases). The preferred view of the Law Commission was that a multiplier which has been discounted for the early receipt of damages should only be used in the calculation of post-trial losses.[1]

25.4   PROSPECTS OF REMARRIAGE OF A WIDOW

The Law Commission recommended that s 3(3) of the Fatal Accidents Act 1976 be repealed (ie ignoring the actual or chance of remarriage of a widow). However, unless a person has remarried or is engaged to be married at the time of trial, the prospect that he or she will marry, remarry or enter into financially supportive cohabitation with a new partner should not be taken into account when assessing any claim for damages under the Fatal Accidents Act 1976. The fact of a marriage or of financially supportive cohabitation should be taken into account wherever relevant.[2]

25.5   PROSPECTS OF BREAKDOWN OF A MARRIAGE

The prospect of divorce or breakdown of a relationship between the deceased and his or her spouse should not be taken into account when assessing damages for the purpose of any claim under the Fatal Accidents Act 1976, unless the couple were no longer living together at the time of death, or one of the couple had petitioned for divorce, judicial separation or nullity.[3]

25.6   PROSPECTS OF BREAKDOWN OF A COHABITEE RELATIONSHIP

Section 3(4) of the Fatal Accidents Act 1976 (ie the fact that a couple were cohabiting and not married should be taken into account) should be abolished. The prospect of breakdown in the relationship

---

[1]   Law Commission Report No 263 *Claims for Wrongful Death*, at para 4.23.
[2]   Ibid, at para 4.53.
[3]   Ibid, at para 4.66.

between the deceased and his partner should not be taken into account when assessing damages under the Act.[1]

25.7   ABOLITION OF SECTION 4

The Law Commission recommended that s 4 be abolished. The law should be made consistent with other personal injury claims and list charity, insurance, survivors' pensions and inheritance as non-deductible.[2] This, too, would require legislation.

25.8   GRATUITOUS CARE

The dependant would be under a legal obligation to account for damages awarded for past services of gratuitous care to the person who provided such care. However, there should be no obligation in relation to future care.[3]

25.9   RECOUPMENT OF BENEFITS

The Social Security (Recovery of Benefits) Act 1997 should be extended so as to apply to benefits received by a claimant under the Fatal Accidents Act 1976.[4] This would require new legislation.

25.10   EXTENSION OF THOSE WHO CAN CLAIM BEREAVEMENT DAMAGES

The role of bereavement damages should be clarified so as to make it clear that their function is to compensate (insofar as a standardised award of money can do so) for grief, sorrow and the loss of non-pecuniary benefits of the deceased's care, guidance and society.

Bereavement damages should be recoverable by:[5]

---

[1]   Law Commission Report No 263 *Claims for Wrongful Death*, at para 4.71.
[2]   Ibid, at para 7.21.
[3]   Ibid, at para 5.5.
[4]   Ibid, at para 7.24.
[5]   Ibid, at para 6.31; see Chapter 15.

(1)   a spouse of the deceased;
(2)   a parent of the deceased, including adoptive parents;
(3)   a child of the deceased, including adoptive children;
(4)   a brother or sister of the deceased, including an adoptive brother or sister;
(5)   a person who was engaged to be married to the deceased;
(6)   a person who, although not married to the deceased, had lived with the deceased as man and wife (or if of the same gender, in the equivalent relationship) for not less than 2 years prior to the accident. This change, too, would require legislation.

25.11   INCREASE IN THE LEVEL OF BEREAVEMENT DAMAGES

The Commission recommended that bereavement damages be increased to £10,000 and that they should be linked to the Retail Prices Index. (This has now been done.) The defendant's liability to pay bereavement damages should be limited to a maximum sum of £30,000.[1] This recommendation would also require new legislation.

25.12   CLAIMANT ABLE TO CLAIM DAMAGES FOR BEREAVEMENT AND DAMAGES FOR A RECOGNISED PSYCHIATRIC ILLNESS

The Law Commission did not think statutory intervention was needed, but recommended that:

(1)   a claimant should not be barred from recovering damages both for bereavement and, if liability is established, for a recognised psychiatric injury;
(2)   the quantum of bereavement damages should not be affected by the quantum of damages recoverable for a recognised psychiatric illness; and
(3)   the quantum of damages for psychiatric illness should not be affected by the quantum of damages for bereavement.[2]

---

[1]   Law Commission Report No 263 *Claims for Wrongful Death*, at para 6.51. See Chapter 15.
[2]   Ibid, at para 6.57.

CHAPTER 26

HUMAN RIGHTS AND FATAL ACCIDENT CLAIMS

26.1 INTRODUCTION

Given the wide-ranging effect of the Human Rights Act 1998 (HRA 1998), there is an argument that human rights issues should be dealt with throughout the text and, in places, this has been attempted. However, the provisions of the HRA 1998 have not yet been fully considered by the courts and advice on this point is speculative. There is no doubt that every litigator needs to be aware of the potential advantages of the HRA 1998.

This chapter sets out the opportunities that the HRA 1998 accords, by discussing some decided cases and by relating the HRA 1998 and the European Convention on Human Rights to each relevant chapter of this book.

The HRA 1998 came into force on 2 October 2000. It has the effect of incorporating the European Convention on Human Rights into UK law. It is not proposed to deal with the detailed provisions of the HRA 1998 or the European Convention here, but rather to look at those matters which may impact upon fatal accident litigation.

26.2 IMPORTANT PARTS OF THE HRA 1998

The HRA 1998 states that all legislation must be read and given effect to in a way which is compatible with the Convention rights. Particularly important to the Fatal Accidents Act 1976 are:

(1) Art 2 – the right to life;
(2) Art 6 – the right to a fair hearing;

(3)   Art 8 – the right to respect private and family life; and
(4)   Art 14 – prohibition of discrimination.

Article 14, in particular, is worth setting out in full:

> 'The enjoyment of the rights and freedom set forth in this convention shall be secured without discrimination on any ground such as sex, race, colour, language, religion, political or other opinion, national or social origin, association with a national minority, property, birth or other status.'

26.3   THE POTENTIAL EFFECT ON FATAL ACCIDENT CASES

26.3.1   Chapter 1: The legal background

Chapter 1 observes that this is an area full of ambiguity and uncertainty. The HRA 1998 probably adds to this but, on the whole, it provides positive benefits for the claimant. As we shall see below, the general observation that fatal accident damages are a 'jury point', coupled with a failure to carry out a proper assessment, is arguably a breach of Art 6; with a failure to provide a reasoned judgment for a decision being a breach of the European Convention on Human Rights.

26.3.2   Chapter 2: Funding fatal accident cases

There are arguments that failure to provide a proper system of funding and representation is a breach of Art 6, particularly in the case of coroners' hearings.

26.3.3   Chapter 4: The type of incident that can give rise to a claim

It is possible that Art 2 gives rise to a new cause of action, particularly against a local authority.

26.3.4   Chapter 5: Is your client a dependant?

The limited definition of dependant in the Fatal Accidents Act 1976 is arguably a breach of Art 14. There are no logical grounds for discriminating against persons who are not married, or against illegitimate children.

26.3.5   Chapter 6: Limitation

The effects of the HRA 1998 are discussed in detail in this chapter.

26.3.6   Chapter 8: Basic principles of dependency calculation

The Act and Convention could be important in arguments concerning the prospects of remarriage, particularly of a widower. There are no proper grounds for taking into account the prospects of remarriage (or actual remarriage) of a widower.

26.3.7   Chapter 11: Damages for death of a mother or carer

It is likely that the general damages award made for loss of general maternal services should be extended to award damages also for loss of paternal services.

26.3.8   Chapter 14: Funeral expenses

Given Arts 8 and 14, it may be possible to argue that a court cannot discriminate against the funeral expenses of certain groups from certain national or ethnic origins. If these expenses are a part of the normal private and family life of the deceased, then they must be paid.

26.3.9   Chapter 15: Bereavement damages

The very limited aspect of this award is arguably a breach of Art 14. In particular, the fact that the father of an illegitimate child cannot recover.

26.3.10   Chapter 19: Procedural matters upon the issue of proceedings

A good example of the HRA 1998 having a direct effect on a personal injury case can be found in *Goode v Martin*.[1] The court considered the issue of amendment of pleadings.

(1)   The facts
The case concerned a yachting accident in which the claimant suffered catastrophic injury when struck by a piece of equipment while the yacht was jibbing. A defence was filed claiming that the claimant had leaned over into the path of the boom and was

---

[1]   [2002] PIQR P23.

knocked to the deck. This was contrary to the claimant's case that she had been struck by a car. Leave to amend was sought in order to plead, in the alternative, that if the claimant had been struck by the boom, this was due to the negligence of the defendant.

The defendant's solicitors opposed the application to amend, despite the fact that the alternative allegation was based on the defendant's account of what happened. Both the master and the judge refused to allow the application to amend. This was because the CPR 1998, r 17.4(2) states that where a party seeks to amend his statement of case and that period of limitation has expired:

> '(2) The court may allow an amendment whose effect will be to add or substitute a new claim, but only if the new claim arises out of the same facts or substantially the same facts as a claim in respect of which the party applying for permission has already claimed a remedy in the proceedings.'

The master and judge refused the application to amend on the grounds that the alternative version did not arise from the same facts, or even substantially the same facts, as the claim as originally formulated.

(2) The human rights argument before the Court of Appeal

At the Court of Appeal the claimant put forward a new argument based on Art 6 of the European Convention on Human Rights. It was argued that if the amendments were not allowed on the basis of a conventional construction of the rules, then the court should adopt a more unconventional approach. In the absence of a conventional construction, the claimant's right to access to the court would be impaired by a restriction which impaired the essence of that right and which did not have a legitimate aim. Even if a legitimate aim could be shown, the restriction employed means which were not reasonably proportionate to that aim.

Brooke LJ held that the Court possessed more tools than had previously been available, saying that:

– under the CPR 1998 the court must seek to give effect to the overriding objective of dealing with cases justly when any rule is interpreted;[1] and
– under the HRA 1998 the court must read and give effect to subordinate legislation, so far as it is possible to do so, in a way

---

[1] CPR 1998, r 1.2(b).

which is compatible with the Convention rights set out in Sch 1 to the Act.[1]

In *Goode*, all the claimant sought to state was that, if the accident happened the way the defendant said it happened, it was due to the negligence of the defendant. She did not seek to introduce any facts which would not flow naturally from the way that the defendant put its defence.

(3)   The effect of the HRA 1998

Brooke LJ stated that if it was not for the HRA 1998 he would have been of the view that the correct argument was that a narrow construction of the rule should be adopted.

> 'Without the encouragement of section 3(1) of the 1998 Act, I could see no way of interpreting the language of the rule so as to produce a just result.'

However:

> 'The 1998 Act, however, does in my judgment alter the position. I can detect no sound policy reason why the claimant should not add to her claim in the present action the alternative plea which she now proposes. No new facts are being introduced: she merely wants to say that if the defendant succeeds in establishing his version of the facts, she will still win because those facts, too, show that he was negligent and should pay her compensation.'

To prevent the claimant amending her case would impose an impediment on her access to the court which would require justification. There was no reasonable justification. The construction of the rule adopted by the master and judge had no legitimate aim. Further, even if it had a legitimate aim the means used were not reasonably proportionate to that aim. The Court referred to the House of Lords' judgment in *R v A* [2001] UKHL 251 at para [44],[2] in particular the speech of Lord Steyn:

> 'In accordance with the will of Parliament as reflected in section 3 it will sometimes be necessary to adopt an interpretation which linguistically may appear strained. The techniques to be used will not only involve the reading down of express language in a statute but also the implication of provisions.'

The construction of the rule in such a way as to allow the claimant to plead facts that are already in issue enabled the rule to be construed in a manner that did not violate the claimant's rights under Art 6(1).

---

[1]   HRA 1998, s 3(1).
[2]   [2001] 2 WLR 1568.

26.3.11 Final note: consider the HRA 1998 at all times

As the *Goode* case shows, the HRA 1998 can have a major and direct effect on the construction of legislation It cannot be ignored.

APPENDICES

APPENDIX 1

EXAMPLE CLIENT QUESTIONNAIRE

[This is an example of the type of questionnaire that can be adapted to suit the individual case. In a fatal accident case it is more appropriate to adapt a standard form and to 'personalise' it rather than use an impersonal form. With the use of word-processing each questionnaire should take only 10–15 minutes to personalise. The psychological advantages of having a personalised form should not be underestimated.]

This questionnaire is designed to help us to get the information we need to conduct your case properly. We understand that filling in some of the answers could be difficult. You may prefer to fill in some of the answers alone in your own time. If you prefer to go through the questionnaire in an interview with us then please contact [, the relevant fee earner] and we will be pleased to arrange an appointment. If you find any of these questions difficult to answer, for instance because they are upsetting, please leave them. We may need time to deal with these matters later but we will choose an appropriate time.

In many cases you may have provided the information to us already. In these circumstances it is often helpful to us to have the information again and we would prefer it if the form were completed in as much detail as possible. However, if you find repeating the information to be too much hard work please leave these sections.

If you have difficulty in answering any of these questions it is helpful to fill in as much as you can and the arrange to see [*fee earner's name*] to discuss the whole form.

INFORMATION ABOUT YOU

1. Your full name and address.
2. Do you have a mobile telephone number? If so, what is it?
3. Tell us the way you prefer to be contacted.
4. Tell us ways in which you would prefer us **not** to contact you, for instance if you do not wish to be contacted at work.
5. Your date of birth.
6. Did you see the accident?
7. Do you work now?

8.   If you do work what is your job and the name and address of your employer?
9.   Did you work before ... [the deceased] was killed?
10.   If so:
      (a)   Where did you work?
      (b)   How much did you earn?
11.   What was your relationship with ... ?
12.   Is there anything further about you that you can think may be relevant to this claim? (Do not spend too much time worrying about this question. The courts may think it important, eg if you have been married before, or have particular health problems.)

...'s Death

We need a lot of information about ...

13.   Can you give us ...'s full name?
14.   ...'s date of birth?
15.   The date ... died?
16.   The date of the incident that caused ...'s death?
17.   Can you state what caused ...'s death?
18.   Where was ... when he suffered the injury that caused his death?
19.   Who do you think is to blame for ...'s death?
20.   Do you know if anyone witnessed ...'s death?
21.   If someone was a witness can you give us their name(s) and address(es)?

...'s Life

22.   What was the name and address of ...'s employer?
23.   What was ...'s job?
24.   Can you tell us what you know about ...'s education and employment history. We do not need a great deal of detail at this stage, however, it helps if we know:
      (a)   What qualifications ... obtained (both at school and afterwards, eg City and Guilds).
      (b)   What education ... had.
      (c)   What jobs ... had before his previous job.
25.   Do you know how much ... was earning?
26.   Did ... have any 'fringe benefits' in addition to the money he earned? For instance a company car, health insurance.
27.   Did ... have a pension?
28.   Did you expect ... to change jobs, obtain promotion or earn more in the future? If you can, tell us what you expected to happen.
29.   Can you tell us the name and address of ...'s GP?
30.   Had ... been to hospital or received treatment from his GP in the year before he was killed?
31.   Did ... do any work around the home, eg DIY, housework, gardening?
32.   Can you estimate how many hours ... spent doing this work?
33.   Who does the work now?
      (a)   How long does it take them?
      (b)   Have you had to pay anyone to do these jobs?
      (c)   How much have you paid?

YOUR LOSSES

34. What was your relationship with ... ?
35. How long had you been in that relationship?
36. Do you or ... have any children? (This includes children who are adopted or who are step-children.)
   (a) What are their dates of birth and current ages?
37. Are there any children still at school?
   (a) What school are they at?
   (b) How is the school funded?
38. Can you tell us what the usual weekly budget was?
   (a) Before ... was killed?
   (b) Now.
   We will discuss this with you in some detail. It may help if you obtain the documents listed below.
39. Have you received any payments following ...'s death?
40. Do you know of anyone else who was dependent upon ... ? (This means anyone that ... supported financially or provided free services to.) If so, can you give us their name(s) and address(es)?
41. We will need a large number of documents from you. If you have any doubts as to whether the documents you have are important or relevant please bring them to us. The kind of documents we are looking for are:
   (a) **Insurance policies.** Please bring us all the insurance policies you can find. We need to know about house and car insurance and also life insurance. We need to know this because some insurance policies may provide you with life and legal insurance.
   (b) **Marriage and birth certificates.** It would be helpful if you could let us have any certificates you can find.
   (c) **Earnings documents.** It would help if you could provide us with any wage slips you have (both your own and ...'s). If you have any income tax returns or documents from accountants then this would help.
   (d) **Documents relating to ...'s education.** Do you have any of ...'s education certificates, details of training courses attended and professional qualifications?
   (e) **Documents relating to pensions.**
   (f) **Documents relating to funeral expenses.**
   (g) **Documents relating to your children's education.** It often helps if we have any certificates and school reports.
   (h) **Household bills and other expenses you have incurred as a result of ... being killed.** For instance if you have had to employ someone to do jobs that ... would have done.

OTHER INFORMATION

42. Please use this section to write down anything at all that you think is important or relevant and that you think we should know in relation to both ...'s death and your losses afterwards.

APPENDIX 2

PRECEDENTS

This section includes examples of various documents including:

(a)   Particulars of claim.
(b)   Schedule of damages.
(c)   Skeleton argument.

The above documents all relate to one case so you can follow it through (results will be shown at the end). This is based on a real case that went to trial during the writing of this book and was successful. Some details have been changed to protect confidentiality.

(d)   Skeleton argument on liability.
(e)   Further schedule of damages.

IN THE YORK COUNTY COURT   CASE No.

BETWEEN:

MARK HENRY
The Widower and Administrator of the estate of Sheila Henry deceased

Claimant

and

ANTHONY BERNARD CROMWELL

Defendant

PARTICULARS OF CLAIM

---

1.   The Claimant is the widower and the administrator of the estate of Sheila Henry having been granted Letters of Administration out of the Probate Registry at York on the 5th September 1998. He brings this action for the benefit of the dependants of the deceased, under the Fatal Accidents Act 1976, as amended and for the benefit of the estate of the deceased under the Law Reform (Miscellaneous Provisions) Act 1934.

THE FACTS

2.   On the 9th April 1997 the deceased was a pedestrian crossing Meanwood Road, Leeds as she crossed the road she was struck by a motor car, registration H543 UWU, driven by the Defendant.

3.   As a result of the said collision the deceased was killed.

LIABILITY FOR THE ACCIDENT

4.   The said incident was caused by the negligence of the Defendant.

PARTICULARS OF NEGLIGENCE

(1)   Stealing and driving a motor car with which he was not familiar and could not control.
(2)   Driving too fast.
(3)   Driving in a dangerous and reckless manner.
(4)   Losing control of the motor car.
(5)   Failing to stop, slow down, swerve or so to manage or control the Defendant's car so as to avoid the accident.
(6)   Failed to warn the deceased adequately in time or at all of the movements of the Defendant's car.
(7)   Failing to observe or heed in time, adequately or at all the deceased the signs and markings and layout of the road.

(8) The Claimant will further rely upon the happening of the said accident as evidence in itself of the negligence of the Defendant.

(9) The Claimant will further rely on the Defendant's convictions of:
  (a) Causing death by reckless driving.
  (b) Taking a vehicle without consent.

at the York Crown Court on 20th September 1997. The said convictions are relevant to the issues of liability and damage herein as they arise because the Defendant's driving killed the deceased.

LOSSES ARISING OUT OF THE DEFENDANT'S NEGLIGENCE

5. By reason of above matters, the deceased was killed and her widower, the Claimant has suffered bereavement and the dependants and estate of the deceased have suffered loss and damage.

PARTICULARS PURSUANT TO THE FATAL ACCIDENTS ACT 1976 AS AMENDED

(1) The deceased was born on 01.03.1936 and was aged 60 at the date of her death.

(2) The names of the persons for whose benefit this action is brought:
  (a) The Claimant Mark Henry, the deceased's husband, who was born on the 1st July 1937.

(3) The nature of the claim in respect of which damages are sought:

At the time of her death the deceased was a healthy and happy 60 year old. She was an astute and enterprising business woman. She would make fancy goods and sell them door to door. She would make baby cot sets, curtains, cushion covers and napkins. She would also buy fancy goods such as teddy bears from factory warehouses and sell these also.

The deceased would work Monday to Friday and sometimes Saturdays. During the winter she should would also visit pubs and working men's clubs selling her wares, particularly in the pre-Christmas period. She would sit up to 2.00pm–3.00pm in the morning sewing.

The deceased was a family woman who doted upon her grandchildren. She also did most of the household tasks, shopping, cleaning and cooking.

The deceased was responsible for all the family finances and was the primary breadwinner. She paid for family holidays abroad and spent lavishly on her grandchildren both on presents and buying and keeping horses.

6. Further, the Claimant claims damages for bereavement.

7. Further, on behalf of the estate of the deceased, the Plaintiff claims funeral expenses:

(1) Funeral expenses £1,815.91.
(2) Headstone £1,953.25.
(3) Flowers £545.00.

The Claimant's claim is further particularised in the Schedule served herewith.

8. The Claimant is entitled to and claims interest pursuant to section 69 of the County Courts Act 1984 upon any damages which may be recovered at such a rate and for such a period as the Court thinks fit.

AND the Claimant claims:-

(1) **DAMAGES** under the Fatal Accidents Act 1976, as amended, for himself and the dependant of the deceased.
(2) **DAMAGES** for bereavement under the Fatal Accidents Act 1976, as amended.
(3) On behalf of the estate of the deceased, under the Law Reform (Miscellaneous Provisions) Act 1934, damages.
(4) **INTEREST** pursuant to section 69 of the County Courts Act 1984. The Plaintiff claims damages at the full rate on all expenses incurred soon after the death of the deceased.

IN THE YORK COUNTY COURT   CASE No.

BETWEEN:

The Widower and Administrator of the Estate of Sheila Henry deceased.

Claimant

and

ANTHONY BERNARD CROMWELL

Defendant

SCHEDULE OF DAMAGES

---

9.   Date of birth of the deceased.   The deceased was born on 01.03.1936 and was aged 60 at the date of her death.

10. Claimant's date of birth.   1st July 1937.

11. Date of accident   9th April 1997.

12. Date of issue   December 2000. (Interest calculations are to the 1st January 2001)

LOSSES IMMEDIATELY UPON DEATH

13. Funeral expenses.

(1)   Funeral expenses   £1,815.91.
(2)   Headstone   £1,953.25.
(3)   Flowers   £545.00.

                          £4,314.16

14. Interest
Interest is claimed at the full rate from the date of death to 1st January 2001 (and thereafter).

BEREAVEMENT DAMAGES

15. The Claimant is entitled to £7,500 statutory bereavement damages.

16. INTEREST The Claimant is entitled to interest at the **full** rate from the date of death. Interest is calculated to the 1st January 2001.

£519.45

The nature of the claim in respect of which damages are sought

17. The Court is referred to the Particulars of Claim. At the time of her death the deceased was a healthy and happy 60 year old. She was an astute and enterprising business woman. She would make fancy goods and sell them door to door. She would make baby cot sets, curtains, cushion covers and napkins. She would also buy fancy goods such as teddy bears from factory warehouses and sell these also.

The deceased would work Monday to Friday and sometimes Saturdays. During the winter she would also visit pubs and working men's clubs selling her wares, particularly in the pre-Christmas period. She would sit up to 2.00pm–3.00pm in the morning sewing.

The deceased was a family woman who doted upon her grandchildren. She also did most of the household tasks, shopping, cleaning and cooking.

The deceased was responsible for all the family finances and was the primary breadwinner. The Claimant is illiterate and was highly reliant upon the deceased. She paid for family holidays abroad and spent lavishly on her grandchildren both on presents and buying and keeping horses.

SERVICES AROUND THE HOME

18. Apart from the hoovering the deceased used to carry out all the housework and cooking. Mr. Henry has now had to carry out these alone, and has received assistance from the family.

19. To replace the deceased's services, in relation to housework and cooking, Mr. Henry needs domestic assistance for some 3 hours a day.
     (1)   The appropriate hourly rate is £5.55 per hour during the week and £6.66 at the weekend. (British Nursing Association rates for home helps and companions.)
           (a)   Daily cost (weekdays)   £16.65.
           (b)   Daily cost (weekends)   £19.98.
           Weekly cost: £123.21.
     (2)   Annual costs   £6,406.92.

PAST COST OF CARE

20. From the 9th April 1997 to 1st January 1999. When services were provided by family, some 87 weeks at £124.21 per week.

£10,806.27.

21. Interest is accepted at half rate and calculated to 1st January 2001.

£772.11

FUTURE COST OF CARE

22. The multiplier (using the Claimant's life expectancy since the deceased could be expected to outlive him) is 18.02.

23. The multiplier 18.02 × the annual cost of £6,406.92 totals £115,452.69.

LOSS OF FINANCIAL DEPENDENCY

24. The deceased was a successful entrepreneur. Her style of life and expenditure indicated an income of at least £40,000 per year. Whilst all her dealings were lawful it is conceded that she never paid tax or national insurance and that credit must be given for this. The deceased never intended to stop working and would have worked far beyond the normal retirement age. She had a successful business with no overheads and made substantial profits.

    (1) The appropriate figure for loss of earnings is £29,294 (being the sum of £40,000 reduced to take account of tax and national insurance).

    (2) The Claimant earned some £60.00 per week which he retained solely for his own use. This should not be taken into account in calculating his loss of dependency.

    (3) The deceased did spend money on herself, particularly on jewellery and her entertainments, it is conceded that 25% of the earnings should be taken as the deceased's own expenditure. However, a higher sum is not justified.

    (a) The deceased had a grandchild living in her home at the date of her death and treated him as her own child.

    (b) The deceased spent lavishly on her grandchildren.

25. The annual figure for loss of earnings (taking into account the concession for tax and insurance and a reduction for the deceased's own expenditure) is £21,970.50.

PAST LOSS OF DEPENDENCY

26. Past loss of issue up to issue £36,617.50.

27. **INTEREST** on past loss of earnings £2,536.17.

FUTURE LOSS OF FINANCIAL DEPENDENCY

28. The appropriate multiplier in this case is 18.02.

The loss totals: 18.02 × £21,970.50.

£395,908.41

SUMMARY OF CLAIM

29.　Summary

(1)	Funeral expenses	4,314.16
(2)	Interest	£616.49
(3)	Bereavement damages	£7,500
(4)	Interest	£519.45
(5)	Past loss of services	£10,806.27
(6)	Future loss of services	£115,452.69
(7)	Interest	£772.11
(8)	Past loss of financial dependency	£36,167.60
(9)	Interest	£2,536.17
(10)	Future loss of financial dependency	£395,908.4

Total:　　　　　　　　　　　　　　　£574,593,35

IN THE YORK COUNTY COURT

CASE No.Y07007

BETWEEN:

MARK HENRY

Widower and Administrator of the Estate of Sheila Henry Deceased

Claimant

and

ANTHONY BERNARD CROMWELL

Defendant

CLAIMANT'S SUBMISSIONS

---

30. Mrs. Henry was killed on 9 April 1997 by the driving of Mr. Cromwell a (inaptly named) 'joy rider' who was subsequently convicted of Causing Death by Reckless Driving. Unsurprisingly the hearing today is only concerned with the issue of damages.

THE 'UNCONTROVERSIAL' ASPECTS OF THE CLAIM

31. There is an amended schedule at pp. xx–xx and counter-schedule at pp. xx–xx.
    (1) The funeral expenses of £1,815.91 is agreed.
    (2) The flowers of £545.00 are agreed.
    (3) The bereavement award of £7,500 is agreed.

32. **INTEREST** The Claimant agrees that interest on (1) and (2) should be from date of payment rather than from date of death. However, interest on all these items are at the **full** rate.
    (1) Interest on £1,815.91 from 23.06.1997   £533.00
        (aggregate rate of 29.34%).
    (2) Interest on £545.00 from 23.06.1997   £160.00.
    (3) Interest on bereavement award from 9 April 1997   £2,324.00.

THE HEADSTONE

33. The Defendant agrees that a headstone was necessary but disputes the cost, and reasonableness.

This is an allegation of failure to mitigate loss. The burden is on the Defendant to show it was unreasonable. It is not apparent that any evidence is being produced as to the 'reasonableness' of the costs of headstones.
    (1) Claimant's figure   £1,953.25
    (2) Defendant's figure   £1,000.00

34. **INTEREST**. From 14.05.98 (date contended for by the Defendant).
     (1)   On Claimant's figure   215.00
     (2)   On Defendant's figure   £111.00.

LOSS OF HOUSEKEEPING AND 'MOTHERLY' SERVICES

35. The Claimant's case is summarised at pp. xx–xx. The Defendant's comments are at p. xx.

36. **THE DEFENDANT'S COMMENTS**. Unfortunately, and regrettably, the Defendant's observations at p. xxx are, in the large part, errant nonsense. The Court is concerned here with compensating Mr. Henry for loss of services he did in fact suffer:-
     (1)   The argument that the Claimant should have done a **'fair share'** is non-sensical in the context of a fatal accident case. The Court is concerned to look at the reality as what went on. The Defendant cannot impose on Mr. Henry an argument that he should have done a 'fair share'. Relationships differ enormously and the Court is concerned with compensating Mr. Henry for the loss he suffered as a result of the loss of his wife and **this** relationship.
     (2)   **Discount for gratuitous nature of care given**. The care given afterwards is an absolute irrelevance. This is a benefit that falls to be disregarded as a benefit arising out of the death. Section 4 of the Fatal Accidents Act. (See the observations of the Court of Appeal at p. xx of the bundle – an authority supplied by the defendant).
     (3)   **Discount to reflect joint benefit**. This is another piece of nonsense. The Court is concerned with the loss to Mr. Henry. If Mrs. Henry does not perform those tasks for him then he is entitled to compensation for his loss. Mrs. Henry cannot be there to benefit or not to benefit from them.
     (4)   **Claimant's duty to mitigate**. At this point it is worth considering whether the Defendant appreciates the nature of a Fatal Accidents Act claim at all. Mrs. Henry **would** have performed these tasks had she not been killed. The fact that Mr. Henry may now have to carry out these tasks himself is his very complaint (or is failing to carry them out and thus living in squalor) is the very nature of his complaint and claim for damages.
     (5)   **Putting the Claimant to proof of the level of assistance**. This is the one aspect of the counter-schedule of some substance. However, the Claimant's evidence is clear. Mrs. Henry was sprightly and able to get about and she did all the work around the home, see p. xx.

The truth is that the Court is faced with the unenviable task of putting a value of Mrs. Henry's services. This is a 'jury' issue. However, the observations at para 21-006 of *Kemp* may assist.

–   A wife and mother provides services where she is in virtual constant attendance and which cannot be replaced by another.
–   Some judges have assessed the dependency on the basis of the cost of employing a residential housekeeper, or a daily help.

It is submitted that the cost of commercial help is a realistic approach to this 'jury' issue. The Defendants are confusing different elements of damages when they state that a discount should be given for 'gratuitous' care.

The sum of £6,406.92 for a period of five years is a reasonable and proper assessment of the value of the housekeeping, and motherly, services provided.

£6,406.92 × 5 =   £32,034.60.

37. **INTEREST**. Interest at half rate from the date of death on past element of loss is £4,020.97.

LOSS OF FINANCIAL DEPENDENCY

38. There is no agreement here. It is clear that Mrs. Henry enjoyed a considerable income. It is conceded that a discount must be given for tax and national insurance that should have been paid. It is pointed out that:-
     (1) The money was not obtained illegally.
     (2) The Defendant is put to strict proof that the benefit that Mrs. Henry received precluded her from working.

IN THE YORK COUNTY COURT   CASE No.BD807424

BETWEEN:

ADRIAN BROWN

Claimant

and

(1) GREEN LIMITED
(2) BLUE LIMITED

Defendants

CLAIMANT'S SUBMISSIONS AS TO LIABILITY

---

1. **THE FACTS**. There may be little dispute as to the basic facts of this matter:-
    (1) Mr. Brown was employed as an electrician by the Second Defendant.
    (2) On 2 July 1995 he was working on an overhead crane at the First Defendant's premises. Mr. Brown worked regularly at the premises.
    (3) Whilst working on the crane Mr. Brown was electrocuted. This electrocution led to his death.

    (A diagram of the cab in which Mr. Brown was working is at p. xx and photographs at pp. xx–xx.)

2. **THE CAUSE OF THE ELECTROCUTION**. The power supply to the cab was switched on when Mr. Brown went to work in it.
    (1) There was a 415 volt three phase supply to the cab.
    (2) The main isolation switch for the electricity to the crane is located at ground level in the centre of the warehouse.
    (3) At the time he was electrocuted no tools were out of Mr. Brown's toolbag.
    (4) The hoist control had its protective cover removed. This could be removed using clips (see the evidence of Mr. White to the Coroner at p. xx).
    (5) There was a fault with the isolator switch which may have given an inaccurate impression as to whether the power was on or off.
    (6) In any event it is clear that Mr Brown's body (most probably his hands – see the evidence of Dr. Purple at p. xx and the diagrams of charring at p. xx) touched a live electrical cable and this led to his death.

3. **THE CLAIMANT'S CASE AS TO LIABILITY**. The Claimant's main arguments relate to the failure to provide a safe system and safe place of work together with a failure to provide proper equipment.

4. **THE CLAIMANT'S EVIDENCE**. Clearly there is little the Claimant, personally, can say in relation to the facts of the accident. So far as liability is concerned the Claimant relies on the evidence of:
    (1) Mr. Azure.
    (2) Mr. Violet (the expert witness).

The Transcript of the Evidence at the Coroner's Court has been rendered admissible without the need to call evidence by order of the District Judge and Mrs. Brown relies upon that evidence as setting out the basic facts surrounding the death.

THE FIRST DEFENDANT

5. The First Defendant was the occupier of the premises. The duties owed are three-fold:-
    (1) The duty of care owed to workers involved in employer's activities (see *Munkman* pp. 70 onwards).
    (2) The duty as occupier.
    (3) The duty under section 29 of the Factories Act 1961.

6. **SECTION 29 OF THE FACTORIES ACT: STILL IN FORCE AT THE DATE OF THE ACCIDENT**. It is alleged in the First Defendant's expert report that this Section has been repealed, this error is repeated in the joint report of the experts (however this is a matter of **law** and not of expert opinion). The experts' view is inaccurate since **at the time of the accident** the section was in force so far as this workplace was concerned:-
    (1) The section was repealed by Regulation 27 of and Schedule 2 to the Workplace (Health, Safety and Welfare) Regulations 1992.
    (2) However, there was a transitional period for existing workplaces. Regulation 1(3) of those Regulations stated that Regulations 5 to 27 and the Schedules shall only come into force on 1 January 1996 in relation to any workplace which was not a **'new workplace'**.
    (3) Therefore workplaces which were in use as a workplace prior to 1st January 1993 were subject to the Factories Act until 1 January 1996.
    (4) This accident occurred in July 1995. **The Factories Act <u>still</u> applied at that date.**

7. **SECTION 29 AND THE FIRST DEFENDANT**. Section 29 imposes a duty to **'make and keep safe'** every place at which a person is required to work. In construing these Regulations the following matters may assist the Court:-
    (1) The House of Lords has held **'any person'** means a person working for the purposes of the factory *Wigley v British Vinegars* [1964] AC 307. It does not apply only to an employee–employer relationship.
    (2) The Court of Appeal in *Larner v British Steel plc* [1993] 1 All ER 103, held that the issue of 'reasonable foreseeability' did not arise in construing the issue of whether the premises were safe under section 29. Section 29 contains no reference to foreseeability.
    (3) Peter Gibson J pointed out the very real difference between a case based on negligence and a case based on statutory duty:-

    '... the issue of negligence requires a very different approach from the issue of breach of statutory duty. To make good a claim in negligence the onus is on the plaintiff to establish matters such as the foreseeability of the damage resulting from a breach of duty of care. To make good a claim for breach of statutory duty under section 29(1) of the Factories Act 1961 the plaintiff has to allege and prove injury while and in consequence of working at a place at which he has to work and that such place was not made or kept safe for him.'

(4)   The section does provide a defence of reasonable practicability. However, this has to be both pleaded and proven by the Defendant (this is clear from the *Larner* decision). The First Defendant (against whom this section is aimed in the current case) does not plead the issue of 'reasonable practicability' at all in its Defence (see pp. xx–xx of the trial bundle). The Court need not consider this Defence in relation to this section. (The Second Defendant does plead that it relies upon **the limits of reasonable practicability**, however the allegation in section 29 is only made or maintainable against the First Defendant and the other statutes relies upon have no such defence available).

8.   **THE WORKPLACE WAS NOT SAFE**. It is submitted that the workplace was not 'safe' as envisaged by the statute since, at a time when an electrician was going to work on it, an electric current, at an obviously fatal level, was being supplied to the cab. To be a safe place at which Mr. Brown had to work the electricity supply to the cab had to be cut off. It was the Defendant's statutory duty to provide a safe place of work. It is not fulfilment of their statutory duty to argue that this was left to Mr. Brown as is stated in *Munkman* at p. xx:-

'The proper approach in each case is: what is the danger contemplated by the statute? A thing will then be "safe" if the danger in contemplation is removed, but not otherwise.'

And at p. xx:-

'It has long been established that in deciding on danger or safety, the careless or inadvertent worker as well as the prudent must be taken into account eg *Keenan v Rolls Royce Ltd* 1970 SLT 90.'

9.   **THE PROVISION AND USE OF WORK EQUIPMENT REGULATIONS 1992**. At the date of the accident only Regulation 5 of these Regulations were in force:
(1)   These apply to both the First and Second Defendant (see the provisions at Regulation 4(2)(b) and (c). The reference to 'employer' also applies to the occupier of a factory.
(2)   These impose **absolute** obligations, there is no defence of 'reasonable practicability'. The Court is referred to the recent decision in *Stark v the Post Office* [2000] PIQR P105.
(3)   The Claimant submits that both Regulation 5(1) and (2) were breached. However, Regulation 5(3) imposes upon both defendants an **absolute** obligation:

'Every employer shall ensure that work equipment is used only for operations for which, and under conditions for which, it is suitable.'

It is submitting that in allowing the work equipment to be used, for repair work, when the electricity was not isolated is a clear breach of the Regulations.

THE SECOND DEFENDANT

10. **THE ELECTRICITY AT WORK REGULATIONS**. These impose duties on the **employer** and also duties on the **employee**, see Regulation 3(1) and (2).

There is no doubt that:-
(1) Regulation 4 of these Regulations was breached. At very least Regulation 4(3) was breached.
(2) Regulation 14 was breached. This is one of the items agreed by all the experts.

11. **RESPONSIBILITY FOR THE BREACH**. It is clearly a large part of the Defendant's case that since Mr. Brown was a workman working alone then he was solely responsible for the breaches. It is argued that Mr. Brown breached the statute. However, this is an issue of contributory negligence rather than absolution:-
(1) Obviously, as in contributory negligence, regard must be had to all the features of the case, see *Munkman* at p. 516.
(2) The duty was on the Second Defendant to establish a safe system of work. There is no evidence of training in the requirements of these Regulations (there is only a very vague reference to 'on the job' training.
(3) Even if the Second Defendant argues that the breach was brought about by Mr. Brown alone this does not end the matter. The law is summarised in *Munkman* at p. 519:

'prima facie where a breach of statutory duty has caused an accident there is liability; *it is for the defendant to show* that it took *all* necessary steps but in spite of these the plaintiff himself caused the breach.'

Earlier in the text it is emphasised that this occurs when the incident happened **'solely'** because of the claimant's conduct, without any failure on the part of the defendant or on any other person for whom he is responsible:-

'The emphasis is on the word "solely". If there is any failure to provide necessary equipment, or to give instructions (including instructions as to safety regulations), the defendant is not exonerated: it must have done everything in its power to meet the duty. In both the above cases the defendant did not succeed in showing this, and it was irrelevant that his failure was not negligent.'

ALLEGATIONS OF NEGLIGENCE

12. Mrs. Brown does not abandon her allegations of negligence against the Defendants.
(1) A system of work permits should have been introduced. Further work should not have started until the First Defendant's supervisor had discussed with Mr. Brown the most appropriate means of avoiding injury (see the First Defendant's document at p. xx). Without doubt such a discussion would have prompted the turning off of the electricity supply.

(2)   A system should have been in place where the electricity was isolated from the gantry crane prior to any contractor being allowed upon it.

CONTRIBUTORY NEGLIGENCE

13.   It is clear that both Defendants attempted to put the whole of the blame upon Mr. Brown. However, Mr. Brown was not responsible for a large part of the Defendants' breaches of statutory duty or negligence (if these are established). Further, the Claimant submits in assessing any allegation of contributory negligence the Court has to take into account:-

(1)   The speeches of the House of Lords in *Caswell v Powell Duffryn Associated Collieries Ltd* (summarised and cited in *Munkman* at p. xx).

(2)   'Inadvertence' by an employee in these circumstances is not negligence:

> 'The point is that the employee's responsibility for statutory duties should not be reduced by throwing the blame on a person injured by a risk the duty was intended to prevent; and if the worker's carelessness oversteps the boundary between inadvertence and negligence, the point is taken into account.'

(3)   The Court may be assisted by the following pages of the text in *Munkman*, in particular at p. 512:

> 'Inadvertence has been excused even in the case of skilled metal workers carrying out their skilled work without any special hurry or fatigue ... Lord Keith, in his speech in *Frost's* case, indicated that "momentary inadvertence" is not enough, and something like "disobedience to orders", or "reckless disregard by a workman of his own safety", must be proved before he can be held negligent.'

(4)   In the present case the Defendant's case as to contributory negligence is, perhaps inevitably, speculative. However, it is submitted that it is more likely that Mr. Brown's actions were due to momentary inadvertence rather than reckless disregard of his safety.

(5)   Further, even if there was reckless disregard the death only came about because of the Defendants' breaches and this is a relevant factor in assessing the proportion of contributory negligence.

The Defendants allege, in essence, that the Claimant was an experienced electrician (which is true) and that his error was the sole cause of the incident that led to his death. However, this ignores the fundamental duty of care placed on both the employer and occupier and the fact that the Regulations that the Claimant relies upon are in place for the very reason that workmen, going about their work, are sometimes engrossed with other matters and make mistakes. It was incumbent upon the Defendants to provide Mr. Hughes with both a **safe place**, safe system of work and safe equipment. None of this happened. As a result Mr. Brown is dead.

IN THE HIGH COURT OF JUSTICE   No. _____
QUEEN'S BENCH DIVISION
YORK DISTRICT REGISTRY

BETWEEN:

PETER GREEN

Claimant

and

LINDA TAWNY

Defendant

SCHEDULE OF DAMAGES

---

14. Mrs. Green's date of death   20 May 1998

15. Mrs. Green's date of birth   1 March 1946

16. Mr. Green's date of birth   1 May 1946.

(All calculations are to the 19th January 2001)

BEREAVEMENT DAMAGES

17. The statutory payment is   £7,500.

18. **INTEREST**. Interest is claimed at the full rate from the date of death.

(550 days with an aggregate rate of 10.58%)

£794.00

FUNERAL EXPENSES

19. The funeral expenses totalled   £2,150.86

20. **INTEREST**. Interest is claimed at the full rate from the 13th August 1999.

£228.88

BEREAVEMENT COUNSELLING

21. Mr. Green received bereavement counselling from April 2000 to May 2000 at the Mid Yorkshire Nuffield Hospital. The total cost was

£160.00

22. **INTEREST**. Interest is claimed at the full rate from the 18 May 2000.
(Aggregate rate 4.72%)

                                                                £8.00

PAST LOSS OF FINANCIAL DEPENDENCY

23   At the date of Mrs. Green's death:-
     (1) Mr. Green was receiving £1,461.69 net, a total of £17,540.28 per annum
          net.
     (2) Mrs. Green was on an annual salary of £32,952 gross. In addition she
          earned large bonuses. In the year ending April 1998 she received a
          bonus of approximately £35,000 gross. Her future earnings were likely
          to include large bonuses.

          A working assumption of £50,000 per annum gross is made. Amounting
          to £34,014.00 net.

24. **THE APPROPRIATE DEPENDENCY CALCULATION**

     (1) The joint income of Mr. and Mrs. Green would be £34,104.00 +
          £17,540.20 = £51,644.20.
     (2) £51,644.20 × 75% = £38,733.15.
     (3) Mr. Green worked for this period and it is appropriate to deduct his
          earnings of £17,540.20

          Total dependency   £21,192.00 per annum.

25. **LOSSES TO DATE**. For an 18-month period

     £21,192.00 × 1.5. = £31,789.42.

26. **INTEREST**. Interest is accepted at half rate from the date of death.
     Aggregate rate 5.29%

                                                                £1,681.66

NON-FINANCIAL LOSSES

27. (1) Mr. Green now uses:-
          (a) Ironing services at £9.00 per week.
          (b) Two cleaners at a cost of £20.00 per week.

          The annual cost is £29.00 × 52 = £1,508.00

          The loss to assumed date (18 months).

          £1,508.00 × 1.5 =   £2,262.00

(2) In addition Mrs. Green did most of the cooking, and she did a lot of the
     housework. She used her lunchtimes to do the shopping. Around 8 hours a
     week was spent in cooking, housework and shopping (in addition to the
     cleaning now done by the cleaners and the ironing). Mrs. Green gardened
     for around 2 hours a week.

(a)   10 hours a week × £5.00 per hour = £50.00
(b)   The annual loss is £2,600
    £2,600 × 1.5   £3,900

Total   £6,162.00

28.   **INTEREST**. Interest at half rate from the date of death is accepted.

£326.00

FUTURE LOSSES

FUTURE LOSS OF FINANCIAL DEPENDENCY: EARNINGS

29. (1)   The appropriate annual loss is £38,733.15.
    (2)   The appropriate multiplier is 5.42

£38,733.15 × 5.42 = £209,933.67

The annual figure is put forward on the basis that Mr. Green has ceased working. He has found the strain of working, after the death of his wife, to be immense. His case is that he ceased working as a result of the death. If Mrs. Green had not been killed he would have remained in work.

In these circumstances it would be unjust to penalise him by deducting his (now non-existent) earnings from the dependency calculation.

FUTURE LOSS OF FINANCIAL DEPENDENCY: PENSION

30. Mr. and Mrs. Green planned to retire at the same time at the age of 60. Mrs. Green continued to make payments of £400 per month into her pension and her employers paid £155.00 per month. The Claimant puts the claim in two ways:-
    (1)   Mr. Green has suffered the loss of £80,947.00 of the potential pension fund.

                                                                                £80,947.00
    (2)   If Mrs. Green had worked to the full retirement age she would have had continued to receive a monthly payment from her employer of £155.00 gross into her pension.
    £155.00 × 12 × 6 =   £11,160.00

FUTURE NON-FINANCIAL DEPENDENCY

31. (1)   **Ironing and cleaning costs**. Assuming the costs continue at £29.00 per week
    £29.00 × 52 = £1,508.00
    £1,508 × multiplier of 19.37 = £29,209.96
    (2)   **Future housekeeping costs**. Assuming future housekeeping costs of:
        (a)   The current BNA Home Help and Companion rate is £7.10 per hour at weekdays and £7.81 per hour at weekends.
        (b)   10 hours a week:
            (i)   8 at £7.10 = £56.80
            (ii)   2 at £7.81 = £15.62

                                                                                £72.42
        Annual loss of £3,765.84.
    (3)   £3,765.84 × 19.37 = £72,944.32.

TOTAL: £102, 154.28

SUMMARY

32.

(1)	Bereavement damages	£7,500
(2)	Interest	£794.00
(3)	Funeral expenses	£2,150.86
(4)	Interest	£228.88
(5)	Bereavement Counselling	£160.00
(6)	Interest	£8.00
(7)	Past loss of financial dependency	£31,789.42
(8)	Interest	£1,681.66
(9)	Past dependency	£6,162.00
(10)	Interest	£326.00
(11)	Future loss of financial dependency	£209,933.67
(12)	Pension	£80,947.00
(13)	Non-financial dependency	£102,154.28.

APPENDIX 3

STATUTORY MATERIALS

Law Reform (Miscellaneous Provisions) Act 1934
i[1]

1 **Effect of death on certain causes of action**

(1) Subject to the provisions of this section, on the death of any person after the commencement of this Act all causes of action subsisting against or vested in him shall survive against, or, as the case may be, for the benefit of, his estate. Provided that this subsection shall not apply to causes of action for defamation ...[2].

[(1A) The right of a person to claim under section 1A of the Fatal Accidents Act 1976 (bereavement) shall not survive for the benefit of his estate on his death.][3]

(2) Where a cause of action survives as aforesaid for the benefit of the estate of a deceased person, the damages recoverable for the benefit of the estate of that person –

[(a) shall not include –
   (i) any exemplary damages;
   (ii) any damages for loss of income in respect of any period after that person's death;][4]

(b) ...[5]

(c) where the death of that person has been caused by the act or omission which give rise to the cause of action, shall be calculated without reference to any loss or gain to his estate consequent on his death, except that a sum in respect of funeral expenses may be included.

---

[1] Act reference: 1934 c 41.
Royal assent: 25 July 1934.
Long title: An Act to amend the law as to the effect of death in relation to causes of action and as to the awarding of interest in civil proceedings.

[2] Amendment: Words repealed: Law Reform (Miscellaneous Provisions) Act 1970, s 7, Sch; Administration of Justice Act 1982, ss 4(2), 75, Sch 9, Pt I, with effect from 1 January 1983 (Administration of Justice Act 1982, s 76(11)).

[3] Amendment: Subsection inserted: Administration of Justice Act 1982, ss 4(1), 73(1), with effect from 1 January 1983 (Administration of Justice Act 1982, s 76(11)).

[4] Amendment: Paragraph substituted: Administration of Justice Act 1982, ss 4(2), 73(3), (4), with effect from 1 January 1983 (Administration of Justice Act 1982, s 76(11)).

[5] Amendment: Paragraph repealed: Law Reform (Miscellaneous Provisions) Act 1970, s 7, Sch.

(3)   ...[1]

(4)   Where damage has been suffered by reason of any act or omission in respect
         of which a cause of action would have subsisted against any person if that
         person had not died before or at the same time as the damage was suffered,
         there shall be deemed, for the purposes of this Act, to have been subsisting
         against him before his death such cause of action in respect of that act or
         omission as would have subsisted if he had died after the damage was
         suffered.

(5)   The rights conferred by this Act for the benefit of the estates of deceased
         persons shall be in addition to and not in derogation of any rights conferred
         on the dependants of deceased persons by the Fatal Accidents Acts 1846 to
         1908 ...[2] and so much of this Act as relates to causes of action against the
         estates of deceased persons shall apply in relation to causes of action under
         the said Acts as it applies in relation to other causes of action not expressly
         excepted from the operation of subsection (1) of this section.

(6)   In the event of the insolvency of an estate against which proceedings are
         maintainable by virtue of this section, any liability in respect of the cause of
         action in respect of which the proceedings are maintainable shall be deemed
         to be a debt provable in the administration of the estate, notwithstanding
         that it is a demand in the nature of unliquidated damages arising otherwise
         than by a contract, promise or breach of trust.

(7)   ...[3]

2
...[4]

3   **Power of courts of record to award interest on debts and damages**
(1)   *In any proceedings tried in any court of record for the recovery of any debt or*
           damages, the court may, if it thinks fit, order that there shall be included in the sum
           for which judgment is given interest at such rate as it thinks fit on the whole or any
           part of the debt or damages for the whole or any part of the period between the date
           when the cause of action arose and the date of the judgment:
           Providing that nothing in this section –
           (a)   shall authorise the giving of interest upon interest; or
           (b)   shall apply in relation to any debt upon which interest is payable as of right
                 whether by virtue of any agreement or otherwise; or
           (c)   shall affect the damages recoverable for the dishonour of a bill of exchange.
[(1A)   *Where in any such proceedings as are mentioned in subsection (1) of this section*
           judgment is given for a sum which (apart from interest on damages) exceeds £200
           and represents or includes damages in respect of personal injuries to the plaintiff or
           any other person, or in respect of a person's death, then (without prejudice to the
           exercise of the power conferred by that subsection in relation to any part of that sum
           which does not represent such damages) the court shall exercise that power so as to
           include in that sum interest on those damages or on such part of them as the court
           considers appropriate, unless the court is satisfied that there are special reasons why no
           interest should be given in respect of those damages.

---

[1]   Amendment: Subsection repealed: Proceedings Against Estates Act 1970, s 1.
[2]   Amendment: Words repealed: Carriage by Air Act 1961, s 14(3), Sch 2.
[3]   Amendment: Subsection repealed: Statute Law Revision Act 1950.
[4]   Amendment: Section repealed: Fatal Accidents Act 1976, s 6(2), Sch 2.

(1B)　*Any order under this section may provide for interest to be calculated at different rates in respect of different parts of the period for which interest is given, whether that period is the whole or part of the period mentioned in subsection (1) of this section.*

(1C)　...[1]

(1D)　*In this section 'personal injuries' includes any disease and any impairment of a person's physical or mental condition, ...[2]][3]*

(2)　...[4]
　　...[5]

4　Short title and extent

(1)　This Act may be cited as the Law Reform (Miscellaneous Provisions) Act 1934.

(2)　This Act shall not extend to Scotland or Northern Ireland.

---

[1]　Amendment: Subsection ceased to have effect following repeal of section in its application to county courts: Administration of Justice Act 1982, s 15(4), (5), with effect from 1 April 1983 (Administration of Justice Act 1982 (Commencement No 1) Order 1983, SI 1983/236).

[2]　Amendment: Words ceased to have effect following repeal of section in its application to county courts: Administration of Justice Act 1982, s 15(4), (5), with effect from 1 April 1983 (Administration of Justice Act 1982 (Commencement No 1) Order 1983, SI 1983/236).

[3]　Amendment: Subsections inserted: Administration of Justice Act 1969.

[4]　Amendment: Subsection repealed: Statute Law Revision Act 1950.

[5]　Amendment: Section repealed in its application to the High Court and county courts: Administration of Justice Act 1982, s 15(4), (5), with effect from 1 April 1983 (Administration of Justice Act 1982 (Commencement No 1) Order 1983, SI 1983/236).

Fatal Accidents Act 1976
i[1]

[1 **Right of action for wrongful act causing death**

(1)   If death is caused by any wrongful act, neglect or default which is such as would (if death had not ensued) have entitled the person injured to maintain an action and recover damages in respect thereof, the person who would have been liable if death had not ensued shall be liable to an action for damages, notwithstanding the death of the person injured.

(2)   Subject to section 1A(2) below, every such action shall be for the benefit of the dependants of the person ('the deceased') whose death has been so caused.

(3)   In this Act 'dependant' means –

(a)   the wife or husband or former wife or husband of the deceased;

(b)   any person who –

(i)   was living with the deceased in the same household immediately before the date of the death; and

(ii)   had been living with the deceased in the same household for at least two years before that date; and

(iii)   was living during the whole of that period as the husband or wife of the deceased;

(c)   any parent or other ascendant of the deceased;

(d)   any person who was treated by the deceased as his parent;

(e)   any child or other descendant of the deceased;

(f)   any person (not being a child of the deceased) who, in the case of any marriage to which the deceased was at any time a party, was treated by the deceased as a child of the family in relation to that marriage;

(g)   any person who is, or is the issue of, a brother, sister, uncle or aunt of the deceased.

(4)   The reference to the former wife or husband of the deceased in subsection (3)(a) above includes a reference to a person whose marriage to the deceased has been annulled or declared void as well as a person whose marriage to the deceased has been dissolved.

(5)   In deducing any relationship for the purposes of subsection (3) above –

(a)   any relationship of affinity shall be treated as a relationship by consanguinity, any relationship of the half blood as a relationship of the whole blood, and the stepchild of any person as his child, and

(b)   an illegitimate person shall be treated as the legitimate child of his mother and reputed father.

(6)   Any reference in this Act to injury includes any disease and any impairment of a person's physical or mental condition.][2]

[1A **Bereavement**

(1)   An action under this Act may consist of or include a claim for damages for bereavement.

(2)   A claim for damages for bereavement shall only be for the benefit –

(a)   of the wife or husband of the deceased; and

---

[1]   Act reference: 1976 c 30.
Royal assent: 22 July 1976.
Long title: An Act to consolidate the Fatal Accidents Acts.

[2]   Amendment: Section substituted: Administration of Justice Act 1982, s 3, with effect from 1 January 1983 (Administration of Justice Act 1982, s 76(11)).

　　(b)　where the deceased was a minor who was never married –
　　　　(i)　of his parents, if he was legitimate; and
　　　　(ii)　of his mother, if he was illegitimate.

(3)　Subject to subsection (5) below, the sum to be awarded as damages under this section shall be [£10,000][1].

(4)　Where there is a claim for damages under this section for the benefit of both the parents of the deceased, the sum awarded shall be divided equally between them (subject to any deduction falling to be made in respect of costs not recovered from the defendant).

(5)　The Lord Chancellor may by order made by statutory instrument, subject to annulment in pursuance of a resolution of either House of Parliament, amend this section by varying the sum for the time being specified in subsection (3) above.][2]

[2　Persons entitled to bring the action

(1)　The action shall be brought by and in the name of the executor or administrator of the deceased.

(2)　If –
　　(a)　there is no executor or administrator of the deceased, or
　　(b)　no action is brought within six months after the death by and in the name of an executor or administrator of the deceased.
　　the action may be brought by and in the name of all or any of the persons for whose benefit an executor or administrator could have brought it.

(3)　Not more than one action shall lie for and in respect of the same subject matter of complaint.

(4)　The plaintiff in the action shall be required to deliver to the defendant or his solicitor full particulars of the persons for whom and on whose behalf the action is brought and of the nature of the claim in respect of which damages are sought to be recovered.

3　Assessment of damages

(1)　In the action such damages, other than damages for bereavement, may be awarded as are proportioned to the injury resulting from the death to the dependants respectively.

(2)　After deducting the costs not recovered from the defendant any amount recovered otherwise than as damages for bereavement shall be divided among the dependants in such shares as may be directed.

(3)　In an action under this Act where there fall to be assessed damages payable to a widow in respect of the death of her husband there shall not be taken account the re-marriage of the widow or her prospects of re-marriage.

(4)　In an action under this Act where there fall to be assessed damages payable to a person who is a dependant by virtue of section 1(3)(b) above in respect of the death of the person with whom the dependant was living as husband or wife there shall be taken into account (together with any other matter that appears to the court to be relevant to the action) the fact that the dependant had no enforceable right to financial support by the deceased as a result of their living together.

---

[1]　Amendment: Sum substituted: Damages for Bereavement (Variation of Sum) (England and Wales) Order 2002, SI 2002/644, with effect from 1 April 2002.

[2]　Amendment: Section inserted: Administration of Justice Act 1982, s 3, with effect from 1 January 1983 (Administration of Justice Act 1982, s 76(11)).

(5)   If the dependants have incurred funeral expenses in respect of the deceased, damages may be awarded in respect of those expenses.

(6)   Money paid into court in satisfaction of a cause of action under this Act may be in one sum without specifying any person's share.

4   Assessment of damages: disregard of benefits
In assessing damages in respect of a person's death in an action under this Act, benefits which have accrued or will or may accrue to any person from his estate or otherwise as a result of his death shall be disregarded.][1]

5[2]   Contributory negligence
Where any person dies as the result partly of his own fault and partly of the fault of any other person or persons, and accordingly if an action were brought for the benefit of the estate under the Law Reform (Miscellaneous Provisions) Act 1934 the damages recoverable would be reduced under section 1(1) of the Law Reform (Contributory Negligence) Act 1945, any damages recoverable in an action ...[3] under this Act shall be reduced to a proportionate extent.

6[4]   Consequential amendments and repeals
(1)   Schedule 1 to this Act contains consequential amendments.

(2)   The enactments in Schedule 2 to this Act are repealed to the extent specified in the third column of that Schedule.

7[5]   Short title, etc
(1)   This Act may be cited as the Fatal Accidents Act 1976.

(2)   This Act shall come into force on 1st September 1976, but shall not apply to any cause of action arising on a death before it comes into force.

(3)   This Act shall not extend to Scotland or Northern Ireland.

Schedule 1[6]
Consequential Amendments
General
1
(1)   Any enactment or other document whatsoever referring to any enactment repealed by this Act shall, unless the contrary intention appears, be construed as referring (or as including a reference) to the corresponding enactment in this Act.

(2)   This paragraph applies whether or not the enactment or other document was enacted, made, served or issued before the passing of this Act.

(3)   This paragraph is without prejudice to section 38 of the Interpretation Act 1889 (effect of repeals), and the following provisions of this Schedule are without prejudice to the generality of this paragraph.

---

[1]   Amendment: Sections 2–4 substituted: Administration of Justice Act 1982, s 3, with effect from 1 January 1983 (Administration of Justice Act 1982, s 76(11)).

[2]   Information: Commencement: 1 September 1976 (s 7(2)).

[3]   Amendment: Words repealed: Administration of Justice Act 1982, s 3, s 75, Sch 9, Pt I, with effect from 1 January 1983 (Administration of Justice Act 1982, s 76(11)).

[4]   Information: Commencement: 1 September 1976 (s 7(2)).

[5]   Information: Commencement: 1 September 1976 (s 7(2)).

[6]   Information: Commencement: 1 September 1976 (s 7(2)).

2

(1)   In the following enactments references to the Fatal Accidents Acts, or to the Fatal Accidents Act 1846, or to section 1 of that Act, include references to this Act.

(2)   The said enactments are –

section 1(5) of the Law Reform (Miscellaneous Provisions) Act 1934 (cause of action surviving death),

...¹

section 3 of the Carriage by Air Act 1961 (civil liability under Convention implemented by that Act),

section 14(2) of the Gas Act 1965 (civil liability under that Act),

section 10 of the Animals Act 1971 (civil liability under that Act),

section 11(2) of the Mineral Workings (Offshore Installations) Act 1971 (civil liability under that Act),

...²

section 88(4)(a) of the Control of Pollution Act 1974 (civil liability under that Act),

section 6(1)(d) of the Industrial Injuries and Diseases (Old Cases) Act 1975,

...³

Limitation Act 1939

3

...⁴

Carriage by Railway Act 1972

4

...⁵

Schedule 2⁶
Repeals

Chapter	Short title	Extent of Repeal
9 & 10 Vict c 93	Fatal Accidents Act 1846	The whole Act.
27 & 28 Vict c 95	Fatal Accidents Act 1864	The whole Act.
24 & 25 Geo 5 c 41	Law Reform (Miscellaneous Provisions) Act 1934	Section 2.
8 & 9 Geo 6 c 28	Law Reform (Contributory Negligence) Act 1945	Section 1(4).
		In section 4 the definition of 'dependant'.

---

¹   Amendment: Words repealed: Coal Mining Subsidence Act 1991, s 53(2), Sch 8, with effect from 30 November 1991 (Coal Mining Subsidence Act 1991 (Commencement) Order 1991, SI 1991/2508).

²   Amendment: Words repealed: Administration of Justice Act 1982, s 75, Sch 9, Pt I, with effect from 1 January 1983 (Administration of Justice Act 1982, s 76(11)).

³   Amendment: Words repealed: Petroleum Act 1998, s 51, Sch 5, Pt I, with effect from 15 February 1999 (Petroleum Act 1998 (Commencement No 1) Order 1999, SI 1999/161).

⁴   Amendment: Paragraph repealed: Limitation Act 1980, s 40(3), Sch 4, with effect from 1 May 1981 (Limitation Act 1980, s 41(2)).

⁵   Amendment: Paragraph repealed: International Transport Conventions Act 1983, s 11(2), Sch 3, with effect from 1 May 1985 (International Transport Conventions Act 1983 (Certification of Commencement of Convention) Order 1985, SI 1985/612).

⁶   Information: Commencement: 1 September 1976 (s 7(2)).

7 & 8 Eliz 2 c 65	Fatal Accidents Act 1959	The whole of section 1 except for subsection (4).
		Section 2.
1971 c 43	Law Reform (Miscellaneous Provisions) Act 1971	Part II, but not so as to affect a right to make an application under section 5(2).
1973 c 38	Social Security Act 1973	In Schedule 27 paragraph 20.
1975 c 54	Limitation Act 1975	In Schedule 1 paragraph 1.

Limitation Act 1980
(ss 11, 11A, 12, 13 and 33)
i[1]

Part I
Ordinary Time Limits for Different Classes of Action

****[2]

Actions in respect of wrongs causing personal injuries or death

11[3]   Special time limit for actions in respect of personal injuries

(1)   This section applies to any action for damages for negligence, nuisance or breach of duty (whether the duty exists by virtue of a contract or of provision made by or under a statute or independently of any contract or any such provision) where the damages claimed by the plaintiff for the negligence, nuisance or breach of duty consist of or include damages in respect of personal injuries to the plaintiff or any other person.

[(1A)   This section does not apply to any action brought for damages under section 3 of the Protection from Harassment Act 1997.][4]

(2)   None of the time limits given in the preceding provisions of this Act shall apply to an action to which this section applies.

(3)   An action to which this section applies shall not be brought after the expiration of the period applicable in accordance with subsection (4) or (5) below.

(4)   Except where subsection (5) below applies, the period applicable is three years from –
(a)   the date on which the cause of action accrued; or
(b)   the date of knowledge (if later) of the person injured.

(5)   If the person injured dies before the expiration of the period mentioned in subsection (4) above, the period applicable as respects the cause of action surviving for the benefit of his estate by virtue of section 1 of the Law Reform (Miscellaneous Provisions) Act 1934 shall be three years from –
(a)   the date of death; or
(b)   the date of the personal representative's knowledge;
whichever is the later.

(6)   For the purposes of this section 'personal representative' includes any person who is or has been a personal representative of the deceased, including an executor who has not proved the will (whether or not he has renounced probate) but not anyone appointed only as a special personal representative in relation to settled land; and regard shall be had to any knowledge acquired by any such person while a personal representative or previously.

---

[1]   Act reference: 1980 c 58.
  Royal assent: 13 November 1980.
  Long title: An Act to consolidate the Limitation Acts 1939 to 1980.
[2]   Omission: Sections not reproduced.
[3]   Information: Commencement: 1 May 1981 (s 41(2)).
[4]   Amendment: Subsection inserted: Protection from Harassment Act 1997, s 6, with effect from 16 June 1997 (Protection from Harassment Act 1997 (Commencement) (No 2) Order 1997, SI 1997/1498).

(7)   If there is more than one personal representative, and their dates of knowledge are different, subsection (5)(b) above shall be read as referring to the earliest of those dates.

[11A   Actions in respect of defective products
(1)   This section shall apply to an action for damages by virtue of any provision of Part I of the Consumer Protection Act 1987.
(2)   None of the time limits given in the preceding provisions of this Act shall apply to an action to which this section applies.
(3)   An action to which this section applies shall not be brought after the expiration of the period of ten years from the relevant time, within the meaning of section 4 of the said act of 1987; and this subsection shall operate to extinguish a right of action and shall do so whether or not that right of action had accrued, or time under the following provisions of this Act had begun to run, at the end of the said period of ten years.
(4)   Subject to subsection (4) below, an action to which this section applies in which the damages claimed by the plaintiff consist of or include damages in respect of personal injuries to the plaintiff or any other person or loss of or damage to any property, shall not be brought after the expiration of the period of three years from whichever is the later of –
        (a)   the date on which the cause of action accrued; and
        (b)   the date of knowledge of the injured person or, in the case of loss of damage to property, the date of knowledge of the plaintiff or (if earlier) of any person in whom his cause of action was previously vested.
(5)   If in a case where the damages claimed by the plaintiff consist of or include damages in respect of personal injuries to the plaintiff or any other person the injured person died before the expiration of the period mentioned in subsection (4) above, that subsection shall have effect as respects the cause of action surviving for the benefit of his estate by virtue of section 1 of the Law Reform (Miscellaneous Provisions) Act 1934 as if for the reference to that period there were substituted a reference to the period of three years from whichever is the later of –
        (a)   the date of death; and
        (b)   the date of the personal representative's knowledge.
(6)   For the purposes of this section 'personal representative' includes any person who is or has been a personal representative of the deceased, including an executor who has not proved the will (whether or not he has renounced probate) but not anyone appointed only as a special personal representative in relation to settled land; and regard shall be had to any knowledge acquired by any such person while a personal representative or previously.
(7)   If there is more than one personal representative and their dates of knowledge are different, subsection (5)(b) above shall be read as referring to the earliest of those dates.
(8)   Expressions used in this section or section 14 of this Act and in Part I of the Consumer Protection Act 1987 have the same meanings in this section or that section as in that Part; and section 1(1) of that Act (Part I to be construed as enacted for the purpose of complying with the product liability Directive) shall apply for the purpose of construing this section and the following provisions of this Act so far as they relate to an action by virtue of

any provision of that Part as it applies for the purpose of construing that Part.][1]

12[2]   Special time limit for actions under Fatal Accidents legislation

(1)   An action under the Fatal Accidents Act 1976 shall not be brought if the death occurred when the person injured could no longer maintain an action and recover damages in respect of the injury (whether because of a time limit in this Act or in any other Act, or for any other reason).

Where any such action by the injured person would have been barred by the time limit in section 11 [or 11A][3] of this Act, no account shall be taken of the possibility of that time limit being overridden under section 33 of this Act.

(2)   None of the time limits given in the preceding provisions of this Act shall apply to an action under the Fatal Accidents Act 1976, but no such action shall be brought after the expiration of three years from –

(a)   the date of death; or

(b)   the date of knowledge of the person for whose benefit the action is brought;

whichever is the later.

(3)   An action under the Fatal Accidents Act 1976 shall be one to which sections 28, 33 and 35 of this Act apply, and the application to any such action of the time limit under subsection (2) above shall be subject to section 39; but otherwise Parts II and III of this Act shall not apply to any such action.

13[4]   Operation of time limit under section 12 in relation to different dependants

(1)   Where there is more than one person for whose benefit an action under the Fatal Accidents Act 1976 is brought, section 12(2)(b) of this Act shall be applied separately to each of them.

(2)   Subject to subsection (3) below, if by virtue of subsection (1) above the action would be outside the time limit given by section 12(2) as regards one or more, but not all, of the persons for whose benefit it is brought, the court shall direct that any person as regards whom the action would be outside that limit shall be excluded from those for whom the action is brought.

(3)   The court shall not give such a direction if it is shown that if the action were brought exclusively for the benefit of the person in question it would not be defeated by a defence of limitation (whether in consequence of section 28 of this Act or an agreement between the parties not to raise the defence, or otherwise).

****[5]

---

1   Amendment: Section inserted: Consumer Protection Act 1987, s 6, Sch 1, Pt I, para 1, with effect from 1 March 1988 (Consumer Protection Act 1987 (Commencement No 1) Order 1987, SI 1987/1680).

2   Information: Commencement: 1 May 1981 (s 41(2)).

3   Amendment: Words inserted: Consumer Protection Act 1987, s 6, Sch 1, Pt I, para 2, with effect from 1 March 1988 (Consumer Protection Act 1987 (Commencement No 1) Order 1987, SI 1987/1680).

4   Information: Commencement: 1 May 1981 (s 41(2)).

5   Omission: Sections not reproduced.

Part II
Extension or Exclusion of Ordinary Time Limits

****[1]

Discretionary exclusion of time limit for actions in respect of personal injuries or death

33[2] **Discretionary exclusion of time limit for actions in respect of personal injuries or death**

(1)   If it appears to the court that it would be equitable to allow an action to proceed having regard to the degree to which –

(a)   the provisions of section 11 [or 11A][3] or 12 of this Act prejudice the plaintiff or any person whom he represents; and

(b)   any decision of the court under this subsection would prejudice the defendant or any person whom he represents;

the court may direct that those provisions shall not apply to the action, or shall not apply to any specified cause of action to which the action relates.

[(1A)   The court shall not under this section disapply –

(a)   subsection (3) of section 11A; or

(b)   where the damages claimed by the plaintiff are confined to damages for loss of or damage to any property, any other provision in its application to an action by virtue of Part I of the Consumer Protection Act 1987.][4]

(2)   The court shall not under this section disapply section 12(1) except where the reason why the person injured could no longer maintain an action was because of the time limit in section 11 [or subsection (4) of section 11A][5].

If, for example, the person injured could at his death no longer maintain an action under the Fatal Accidents Act 1976 because of the time limit in Article 29 in Schedule 1 to the Carriage by Air Act 1961, the court has no power to direct that section 12(1) shall not apply.

(3)   In acting under this section the court shall have regard to all the circumstances of the case and in particular to –

(a)   the length of, and the reasons for, the delay on the part of the plaintiff;

(b)   the extent to which, having regard to the delay, the evidence adduced or likely to be adduced by the plaintiff or the defendant is or is likely to be less cogent than if the action had been brought within the time allowed by section 11 [, by section 11A][6] or (as the case may be) by section 12;

---

[1]   Omission: Sections not reproduced.

[2]   Information: Commencement: 1 May 1981 (s 41(2)).

[3]   Amendment: Words inserted: Consumer Protection Act 1987, s 6, Sch 1, Pt I, para 6, with effect from 1 March 1988 (Consumer Protection Act 1987 (Commencement No 1) Order 1987, SI 1987/1680).

[4]   Amendment: Subsection inserted: Consumer Protection Act 1987, s 6, Sch 1, Pt I, para 6, with effect from 1 March 1988 (Consumer Protection Act 1987 (Commencement No 1) Order 1987, SI 1987/1680).

[5]   Amendment: Words inserted: Consumer Protection Act 1987, s 6, Sch 1, Pt I, para 6, with effect from 1 March 1988 (Consumer Protection Act 1987 (Commencement No 1) Order 1987, SI 1987/1680).

[6]   Amendment: Words inserted: Consumer Protection Act 1987, s 6, Sch 1, Pt I, para 6, with effect from 1 March 1988 (Consumer Protection Act 1987 (Commencement No 1) Order 1987, SI 1987/1680).

(c) the conduct of the defendant after the cause of action arose, including the extent (if any) to which he responded to requests reasonably made by the plaintiff for information or inspection for the purpose of ascertaining facts which were or might be relevant to the plaintiff's cause of action against the defendant;

(d) the duration of any disability of the plaintiff arising after the date of the accrual of the cause of action;

(e) the extent to which the plaintiff acted promptly and reasonably once he knew whether or not the act or omission of the defendant, to which the injury was attributable, might be capable at that time of giving rise to an action for damages;

(f) the steps, if any, taken by the plaintiff to obtain medical, legal or other expert advice and the nature of any such advice he may have received.

(4) In a case where the person injured died when, because of section 11 [or subsection (4) of section 11A][1], he could no longer maintain an action and recover damages in respect of the injury, the court shall have regard in particular to the length of, and the reasons for, the delay on the part of the deceased.

(5) In a case under subsection (4) above, or any other case where the time limit, or one of the time limits, depends on the date of knowledge of a person other than the plaintiff, subsection (3) above shall have effect with appropriate modifications, and shall have effect in particular as if references to the plaintiff included references to any person whose date of knowledge is or was relevant in determining a time limit.

(6) A direction by the court disapplying the provisions of section 12(1) shall operate to disapply the provisions to the same effect in section 1(1) of the Fatal Accidents Act 1976.

(7) In this section 'the court' means the court in which the action has been brought.

(8) References in this section to section 11 [or 11A][2] include references to that section as extended by any of the preceding provisions of this Part of this Act or by any provision of Part III of this Act.

****[3]

---

[1] Amendment: Words inserted: Consumer Protection Act 1987, s 6, Sch 1, Pt I, para 6, with effect from 1 March 1988 (Consumer Protection Act 1987 (Commencement No 1) Order 1987, SI 1987/1680).

[2] Amendment: Words inserted: Consumer Protection Act 1987, s 6, Sch 1, Pt I, para 6, with effect from 1 March 1988 (Consumer Protection Act 1987 (Commencement No 1) Order 1987, SI 1987/1680).

[3] Omission: Sections & Schedules not reproduced.

Human Rights Act 1998

i[1]

Introduction

1[2]   **The Convention Rights**

(1)   In this Act 'the Convention rights' means the rights and fundamental freedoms set out in –

(a)   Articles 2 to 12 and 14 of the Convention,

(b)   Articles 1 to 3 of the First Protocol, and

(c)   Articles 1 and 2 of the Sixth Protocol,

as read with Articles 16 to 18 of the Convention.

(2)   Those Articles are to have effect for the purposes of this Act subject to any designated derogation or reservation (as to which see sections 14 and 15).

(3)   The Articles are set out in Schedule 1.

(4)   The [Lord Chancellor][3] may by order make such amendments to this Act as he considers appropriate to reflect the effect, in relation to the United Kingdom, of a protocol.

(5)   In subsection (4) 'protocol' means a protocol to the Convention –

(a)   which the United Kingdom has ratified; or

(b)   which the United Kingdom has signed with a view to ratification.

(6)   No amendment may be made by an order under subsection (4) so as to come into force before the protocol concerned is in force in relation to the United Kingdom.

2[4]   **Interpretation of Convention rights**

(1)   A court or tribunal determining a question which has arisen in connection with a Convention right must take into account any –

(a)   judgment, decision, declaration or advisory opinion of the European Court of Human Rights,

(b)   opinion of the Commission given in a report adopted under Article 31 of the Convention,

(c)   decision of the Commission in connection with Article 26 or 27(2) of the Convention, or

(d)   decision of the Committee of Ministers taken under Article 46 of the Convention,

whenever made or given, so far as, in the opinion of the court or tribunal, it is relevant to the proceedings in which that question has arisen.

(2)   Evidence of any judgment, decision, declaration or opinion of which account may have to be taken under this section is to be given in

---

[1]   Act reference: 1998 c 42.

Royal assent: 9 November 1998.

Long title: An Act to give further effect to rights and freedoms guaranteed under the European Convention on Human Rights; to make provision with respect to holders of certain judicial offices who become judges of the European Court of Human Rights; and for connected purposes.

[2]   Information: Commencement: 2 October 2000, SI 2000/1851.

[3]   Amendment: Words substituted: Transfer of Functions (Miscellaneous) Order 2001, SI 2001/3500, with effect from 26 November 2001.

[4]   Information: Commencement: 2 October 2000, SI 2000/1851.

proceedings before any court or tribunal in such manner as may be provided by rules.

(3)   In this section 'rules' means rules of court or, in the case of proceedings before a tribunal, rules made for the purposes of this section –

(a)   by the Lord Chancellor or the Secretary of State, in relation to any proceedings outside Scotland;

(b)   by the Secretary of State, in relation to proceedings in Scotland; or

(c)   by a Northern Ireland department, in relation to proceedings before a tribunal in Northern Ireland –

(i)   which deals with transferred matters; and

(ii)   for which no rules made under paragraph (a) are in force.

Legislation

3[1]   Interpretation of legislation

(1)   So far as it is possible to do so, primary legislation and subordinate legislation must be read and given effect in a way which is compatible with the Convention rights.

(2)   This section –

(a)   applies to primary legislation and subordinate legislation whenever enacted;

(b)   does not affect the validity, continuing operation or enforcement of any incompatible primary legislation; and

(c)   does not affect the validity, continuing operation or enforcement of any incompatible subordinate legislation if (disregarding any possibility of revocation) primary legislation prevents removal of the incompatibility.

4[2]   Declaration of incompatibility

(1)   Subsection (2) applies in any proceedings in which a court determines whether a provision of primary legislation is compatible with a Convention right.

(2)   If the court is satisfied that the provision is incompatible with a Convention right, it may make a declaration of that incompatibility.

(3)   Subsection (4) applies in any proceedings in which a court determines whether a provision of subordinate legislation, made in the exercise of a power conferred by primary legislation, is compatible with a Convention right.

(4)   If the court is satisfied –

(a)   that the provision is incompatible with a Convention right, and

(b)   that (disregarding any possibility of revocation) the primary legislation concerned prevents removal of the incompatibility,

it may make a declaration of that incompatibility.

(5)   In this section 'court' means –

(a)   the House of Lords;

(b)   the Judicial Committee of the Privy Council;

(c)   the Courts-Martial Appeal Court;

(d)   in Scotland, the High Court of Justiciary sitting otherwise than as a trial court or the Court of Session;

---

[1]   Information: Commencement: 2 October 2000, SI 2000/1851.

[2]   Information: Commencement: 2 October 2000, SI 2000/1851.

(e)   in England and Wales or Northern Ireland, the High Court or the
      Court of Appeal.

(6)   A declaration under this section ('a declaration of incompatibility') –
      (a)   does not affect the validity, continuing operation or enforcement of the
            provision in respect of which it is given; and
      (b)   is not binding on the parties to the proceedings in which it is made.

5[1]   Right of Crown to intervene

(1)   Where a court is considering whether to make a declaration of
      incompatibility, the Crown is entitled to notice in accordance with rules of
      court.

(2)   In any case to which subsection (1) applies –
      (a)   a Minister of the Crown (or a person nominated by him),
      (b)   a member of the Scottish Executive,
      (c)   a Northern Ireland Minister
      (d)   a Northern Ireland department,
      is entitled, on giving notice in accordance with rules of court, to be joined as
      a party to the proceedings.

(3)   Notice under subsection (2) may be given at any time during the
      proceedings.

(4)   A person who has been made a party to criminal proceedings (other than in
      Scotland) as the result of a notice under subsection (2) may, with leave,
      appeal to the House of Lords against any declaration of incompatibility
      made in the proceedings.

(5)   In subsection (4) –
      'criminal proceedings' includes all proceedings before the Courts-Martial
            Appeal Court; and
      'leave' means leave granted by the court making the declaration of
            incompatibility or by the House of Lords.

Public authorities

6[2]   Acts of public authorities

(1)   It is unlawful for a public authority to act in a way which is incompatible
      with a Convention right.

(2)   Subsection (1) does not apply to an act if –
      (a)   as the result of one or more provisions of primary legislation, the
            authority could not have acted differently; or
      (b)   in the case of one or more provisions of, or made under, primary
            legislation which cannot be read or given effect in a way which is
            compatible with the Convention rights, the authority was acting so as to
            give effect to or enforce those provisions.

(3)   In this section 'public authority' includes –
      (a)   a court or tribunal, and
      (b)   any person certain of whose functions are functions of a public nature,
            but does not include either House of Parliament or a person exercising
            functions in connection with proceedings in Parliament.

(4)   In subsection (3) 'Parliament' does not include the House of Lords in its
      judicial capacity.

---

[1]   Information: Commencement: 2 October 2000, SI 2000/1851.
[2]   Information: Commencement: 2 October 2000, SI 2000/1851.

(5)   In relation to a particular act, a person is not a public authority by virtue only of subsection (3)(b) if the nature of the act is private.

(6)   'An act' includes a failure to act but does not include a failure to –
   (a)   introduce in, or lay before, Parliament a proposal for legislation; or
   (b)   make any primary legislation or remedial order.

7[1]   Proceedings

(1)   A person who claims that a public authority has acted (or proposes to act) in a way which is made unlawful by section 6(1) may –
   (a)   bring proceedings against the authority under this Act in the appropriate court or tribunal, or
   (b)   rely on the Convention right or rights concerned in any legal proceedings,
   but only if he is (or would be) a victim of the unlawful act.

(2)   In subsection (1)(a) 'appropriate court or tribunal' means such court or tribunal as may be determined in accordance with rules; and proceedings against an authority include a counterclaim or similar proceeding.

(3)   If the proceedings are brought on an application for judicial review, the applicant is to be taken to have a sufficient interest in relation to the unlawful act only if he is, or would be, a victim of that act.

(4)   If the proceedings are made by way of a petition for judicial review in Scotland, the applicant shall be taken to have title and interest to sue in relation to the unlawful act only if he is, or would be, a victim of that act.

(5)   Proceedings under subsection (1)(a) must be brought before the end of –
   (a)   the period of one year beginning with the date on which the act complained of took place; or
   (b)   such longer period as the court or tribunal considers equitable having regard to all the circumstances,
   but that is subject to any rule imposing a stricter time limit in relation to the procedure in question.

(6)   In subsection (1)(b) 'legal proceedings' includes –
   (a)   proceedings brought by or at the instigation of a public authority; and
   (b)   an appeal against the decision of a court or tribunal.

(7)   For the purposes of this section, a person is a victim of an unlawful act only if he would be a victim for the purposes of Article 34 of the Convention if proceedings were brought in the European Court of Human Rights in respect of that act.

(8)   Nothing in this Act creates a criminal offence.

(9)   In this section 'rules' means –
   (a)   in relation to proceedings before a court or tribunal outside Scotland, rules made by the Lord Chancellor or the Secretary of State for the purposes of this section or rules of court,
   (b)   in relation to proceedings before a court or tribunal in Scotland, rules made by the Secretary of State for those purposes,
   (c)   in relation to proceedings before a tribunal in Northern Ireland –
      (i)   which deals with transferred matters; and
      (ii)   for which no rules made under paragraph (a) are in force,
         rules made by a Northern Ireland department for those purposes,
   and includes provision made by order under section 1 of the Courts and Legal Services Act 1990.

---

[1]   Information: Commencement: 2 October 2000, SI 2000/1851.

(10)   In making rules, regard must be had to section 9.

(11)   The Minister who has power to make rules in relation to a particular tribunal may, to the extent he considers it necessary to ensure that the tribunal can provide an appropriate remedy in relation to an act (or proposed act) of a public authority which is (or would be) unlawful as a result of section 6(1), by order add to –
(a)   the relief or remedies which the tribunal may grant; or
(b)   the grounds on which it may grant any of them.

(12)   An order made under subsection (11) may contain such incidental, supplemental, consequential or transitional provision as the Minister making it considers appropriate.

(13)   'The Minister' includes the Northern Ireland department concerned.

8[1]   Judicial remedies

(1)   In relation to any act (or proposed act) of a public authority which the court finds is (or would be) unlawful, it may grant such relief or remedy, or make such order, within its powers as it considers just and appropriate.

(2)   But damages may be awarded only by a court which has power to award damages, or to order the payment of compensation, in civil proceedings.

(3)   No award of damages is to be made unless, taking account of all the circumstances of the case, including –
(a)   any other relief or remedy granted, or order made, in relation to the act in question (by that or any other court), and
(b)   the consequences of any decision (of that or any other court) in respect of that act,
the court is satisfied that the award is necessary to afford just satisfaction to the person in whose favour it is made.

(4)   In determining –
(a)   whether to award damages, or
(b)   the amount of an award,
the court must take into account the principles applied by the European Court of Human Rights in relation to the award of compensation under Article 41 of the Convention.

(5)   A public authority against which damages are awarded is to be treated –
(a)   in Scotland, for the purposes of section 3 of the Law Reform (Miscellaneous Provisions) (Scotland) Act 1940 as if the award were made in an action of damages in which the authority has been found liable in respect of loss or damage to the person to whom the award is made;
(b)   for the purposes of the Civil Liability (Contribution) Act 1978 as liable in respect of damage suffered by the person to whom the award is made.

(6)   In this section –
'court' includes a tribunal;
'damages' means damages for an unlawful act of a public authority; and
'unlawful' means unlawful under section 6(1).

---

[1]   Information: Commencement: 2 October 2000, SI 2000/1851.

9[1]   Judicial acts

(1)   Proceedings under section 7(1)(a) in respect of a judicial act may be brought only –

(a)   by exercising a right of appeal;

(b)   on an application (in Scotland a petition) for judicial review; or

(c)   in such other forum as may be prescribed by rules.

(2)   That does not affect any rule of law which prevents a court from being the subject of judicial review.

(3)   In proceedings under this Act in respect of a judicial act done in good faith, damages may not be awarded otherwise than to compensate a person to the extent required by Article 5(5) of the Convention.

(4)   An award of damages permitted by subsection (3) is to be made against the Crown; but no award may be made unless the appropriate person, if not a party to the proceedings, is joined.

(5)   In this section –

'appropriate person' means the Minister responsible for the court concerned, or a person or government department nominated by him;

'court' includes a tribunal;

'judge' includes a member of a tribunal, a justice of the peace and a clerk or other officer entitled to exercise the jurisdiction of a court;

'judicial act' means a judicial act of a court and includes an act done on the instructions, or on behalf, of a judge; and

'rules' has the same meaning as in section 7(9).

Remedial action

10[2]   Power to take remedial action

(1)   This section applies if –

(a)   a provision of legislation has been declared under section 4 to be incompatible with a Convention right and, if an appeal lies –

(i)   all persons who may appeal have stated in writing that they do not intend to do so;

(ii)   the time for bringing an appeal has expired and no appeal has been brought within that time; or

(iii)   an appeal brought within that time has been determined or abandoned; or

(b)   it appears to a Minister of the Crown or Her Majesty in Council that, having regard to a finding of the European Court of Human Rights made after the coming into force of this section in proceedings against the United Kingdom, a provision of legislation is incompatible with an obligation of the United Kingdom arising from the Convention.

(2)   If a Minister of the Crown considers that there are compelling reasons for proceeding under this section, he may by order make such amendments to the legislation as he considers necessary to remove the incompatibility.

(3)   If, in the case of subordinate legislation, a Minister of the Crown considers –

(a)   that it is necessary to amend the primary legislation under which the subordinate legislation in question was made, in order to enable the incompatibility to be removed, and

(b)   that there are compelling reasons for proceeding under this section,

---

[1]   Information: Commencement: 2 October 2000, SI 2000/1851.

[2]   Information: Commencement: 2 October 2000, SI 2000/1851.

he may by order make such amendments to the primary legislation as he considers necessary.

(4) This section also applies where the provision in question is in subordinate legislation and has been quashed, or declared invalid, by reason of incompatibility with a Convention right and the Minister proposes to proceed under paragraph 2(b) of Schedule 2.

(5) If the legislation is an Order in Council, the power conferred by subsection (2) or (3) is exercisable by Her Majesty in Council.

(6) In this section 'legislation' does not include a Measure of the Church Assembly or of the General Synod of the Church of England.

(7) Schedule 2 makes further provision about remedial orders.

Other rights and proceedings

11[1] Safeguard for existing human rights

A person's reliance on a Convention right does not restrict –

(a) any other right or freedom conferred on him by or under any law having effect in any part of the United Kingdom; or

(b) his right to make any claim or bring any proceedings which he could make or bring apart from sections 7 to 9.

12[2] Freedom of expression

(1) This section applies if a court is considering whether to grant any relief which, if granted, might affect the exercise of the Convention right to freedom of expression.

(2) If the person against whom the application for relief is made ('the respondent') is neither present nor represented, no such relief is to be granted unless the court is satisfied –

(a) that the applicant has taken all practicable steps to notify the respondent; or

(b) that there are compelling reasons why the respondent should not be notified.

(3) No such relief is to be granted so as to restrain publication before trial unless the court is satisfied that the applicant is likely to establish that publication should not be allowed.

(4) The court must have particular regard to the importance of the Convention right to freedom of expression and, where the proceedings relate to material which the respondent claims, or which appears to the court, to be journalistic, literary or artistic material (or to conduct connected with such material), to –

(a) the extent to which –

(i) the material has, or is about to, become available to the public; or

(ii) it is, or would be, in the public interest for the material to be published;

(b) any relevant privacy code.

(5) In this section –

'court' includes a tribunal; and

'relief' includes any remedy or order (other than in criminal proceedings).

---

[1]   Information: Commencement: 2 October 2000, SI 2000/1851.

[2]   Information: Commencement: 2 October 2000, SI 2000/1851.

13[1]   **Freedom of thought, conscience and religion**

(1)   If a court's determination of any question arising under this Act might affect the exercise by a religious organisation (itself or its members collectively) of the Convention right to freedom of thought, conscience and religion, it must have particular regard to the importance of that right.

(2)   In this section 'court' includes a tribunal.

Derogations and reservations

14[2]   **Derogations**

(1)   In this Act 'designated derogation' means –

...[3]

any derogation by the United Kingdom from an Article of the Convention, or of any protocol to the Convention, which is designated for the purposes of this Act in an order made by the [Lord Chancellor][4].

(2)   ...[5]

(3)   If a designated derogation is amended or replaced it ceases to be a designated derogation.

(4)   But subsection (3) does not prevent the [Lord Chancellor][6] from exercising his power under subsection (1)...[7] to make a fresh designation order in respect of the Article concerned.

(5)   The [Lord Chancellor][8] must by order make such amendments to Schedule 3 as he considers appropriate to reflect –
(a)   any designation order; or
(b)   the effect of subsection (3).

(6)   A designation order may be made in anticipation of the making by the United Kingdom of a proposed derogation.

15[9]   **Reservations**

(1)   In this Act 'designated reservation' means –
(a)   the United Kingdom's reservation to Article 2 of the First Protocol to the Convention; and
(b)   any other reservation by the United Kingdom to an Article of the Convention, or of any protocol to the Convention, which is designated

---

[1]   Information: Commencement: 2 October 2000, SI 2000/1851.
[2]   Information: Commencement: 2 October 2000, SI 2000/1851.
[3]   Amendment: Words repealed: Human Rights Act (Amendment) Order 2001, SI 2001/1216, with effect from 1 April 2001.
[4]   Amendment: Words substituted: Transfer of Functions (Miscellaneous) Order 2001, SI 2001/3500, with effect from 26 November 2001.
[5]   Amendment: Subsection repealed: Human Rights Act (Amendment) Order 2001, SI 2001/1216, with effect from 1 April 2001.
[6]   Amendment: Words substituted: Transfer of Functions (Miscellaneous) Order 2001, SI 2001/3500, with effect from 26 November 2001.
[7]   Amendment: Paragraph reference repealed: Human Rights Act (Amendment) Order 2001, SI 2001/1216, with effect from 1 April 2001.
[8]   Amendment: Words substituted: Transfer of Functions (Miscellaneous) Order 2001, SI 2001/3500, with effect from 26 November 2001.
[9]   Information: Commencement: 2 October 2000, SI 2000/1851.

for the purposes of this Act in an order made by the [Lord Chancellor][1].

(2)   The text of the reservation referred to in subsection (1)(a) is set out in Part II of Schedule 3.

(3)   If a designated reservation is withdrawn wholly or in part it ceases to be a designated reservation.

(4)   But subsection (3) does not prevent the [Lord Chancellor][2] from exercising his power under subsection (1)(b) to make a fresh designation order in respect of the Article concerned.

(5)   The [Lord Chancellor][3] must by order make such amendments to this Act as he considers appropriate to reflect –
(a)   any designation order; or
(b)   the effect of subsection (3).

16[4]   Period for which designated derogations have effect

(1)   If it has not already been withdrawn by the United Kingdom, a designated derogation ceases to have effect for the purposes of this Act –
...[5]
at the end of the period of five years beginning with the date on which the order designating it was made.

(2)   At any time before the period –
(a)   fixed by subsection (1)...[6], or
(b)   extended by an order under this subsection,
comes to an end, the [Lord Chancellor][7] may by order extend it by a further period of five years.

(3)   An order under section 14(1)...[8] ceases to have effect at the end of the period for consideration, unless a resolution has been passed by each House approving the order.

(4)   Subsection (3) does not affect –
(a)   anything done in reliance on the order; or
(b)   the power to make a fresh order under section 14(1)...[9].

(5)   In subsection (3) 'period for consideration' means the period of forty days beginning with the day on which the order was made.

(6)   In calculating the period for consideration, no account is to be taken of any time during which –

---

[1]   Amendment: Words substituted: Transfer of Functions (Miscellaneous) Order 2001, SI 2001/3500, with effect from 26 November 2001.

[2]   Amendment: Words substituted: Transfer of Functions (Miscellaneous) Order 2001, SI 2001/3500, with effect from 26 November 2001.

[3]   Amendment: Words substituted: Transfer of Functions (Miscellaneous) Order 2001, SI 2001/3500, with effect from 26 November 2001.

[4]   Information: Commencement: 2 October 2000 (SI 2000/1851).

[5]   Amendment: Words repealed: Human Rights Act (Amendment) Order 2001, SI 2001/1216, with effect from 1 April 2001.

[6]   Amendment: Words repealed: Human Rights Act (Amendment) Order 2001, SI 2001/1216, with effect from 1 April 2001.

[7]   Amendment: Words substituted: Transfer of Functions (Miscellaneous) Order 2001, SI 2001/3500, with effect from 26 November 2001.

[8]   Amendment: Paragraph reference repealed: Human Rights Act (Amendment) Order 2001, SI 2001/1216, with effect from 1 April 2001.

[9]   Amendment: Paragraph reference repealed: Human Rights Act (Amendment) Order 2001, SI 2001/1216, with effect from 1 April 2001.

(a) Parliament is dissolved or prorogued; or

(b) both Houses are adjourned for more than four days.

(7) If a designated derogation is withdrawn by the United Kingdom, the [Lord Chancellor][1] must by order make such amendments to this Act as he considers are required to reflect that withdrawal.

17[2] Periodic review of designated reservations

(1) The appropriate Minister must review the designated reservation referred to in section 15(1)(a) –

(a) before the end of the period of five years beginning with the date on which section 1(2) came into force; and

(b) if that designation is still in force, before the end of the period of five years beginning with the date on which the last report relating to it was laid under subsection (3).

(2) The appropriate Minister must review each of the other designated reservations (if any) –

(a) before the end of the period of five years beginning with the date on which the order designating the reservation first came into force; and

(b) if the designation is still in force, before the end of the period of five years beginning with the date on which the last report relating to it was laid under subsection (3).

(3) The Minister conducting a review under this section must prepare a report on the result of the review and lay a copy of it before each House of Parliament.

Judges of the European Court of Human Rights

18[3] Appointment to European Court of Human Rights

(1) In this section 'judicial office' means the office of –

(a) Lord Justice of Appeal, Justice of the High Court or Circuit judge, in England and Wales;

(b) judge of the Court of Session or sheriff, in Scotland;

(c) Lord Justice of Appeal, judge of the High Court or county court judge, in Northern Ireland.

(2) The holder of a judicial office may become a judge of the European Court of Human Rights ('the Court') without being required to relinquish his office.

(3) But he is not required to perform the duties of his judicial office while he is a judge of the Court.

(4) In respect of any period during which he is a judge of the Court –

(a) a Lord Justice of Appeal or Justice of the High Court is not to count as a judge of the relevant court for the purposes of section 2(1) or 4(1) of the Supreme Court Act 1981 (maximum number of judges) nor as a judge of the Supreme Court for the purposes of section 12(1) to (6) of that Act (salaries etc);

(b) a judge of the Court of Session is not to count as a judge of that court for the purposes of section 1(1) of the Court of Session Act 1988 (maximum number of judges) or of section 9(1)(c) of the Administration of Justice Act 1973 ('the 1973 Act') (salaries etc);

---

[1] Amendment: Words substituted: Transfer of Functions (Miscellaneous) Order 2001, SI 2001/3500, with effect from 26 November 2001.

[2] Information: Commencement: 2 October 2000, SI 2000/1851.

[3] Information: Commencement: 9 November 1998 (s 22(2)).

(c)   a Lord Justice of Appeal or judge of the High Court in Northern
      Ireland is not to count as a judge of the relevant court for the purposes
      of section 2(1) or 3(1) of the Judicature (Northern Ireland) Act 1978
      (maximum number of judges) nor as a judge of the Supreme Court of
      Northern Ireland for the purposes of section 9(1)(d) of the 1973 Act
      (salaries etc);

(d)   a Circuit judge is not to count as such for the purposes of section 18 of
      the Courts Act 1971 (salaries etc);

(e)   a sheriff is not to count as such for the purposes of section 14 of the
      Sheriff Courts (Scotland) Act 1907 (salaries etc);

(f)   a county court judge of Northern Ireland is not to count as such for
      the purposes of section 106 of the County Courts Act Northern
      Ireland) 1959 (salaries etc).

(5)   If a sheriff principal is appointed a judge of the Court, section 11(1) of the
      Sheriff Courts (Scotland) Act 1971 (temporary appointment of sheriff
      principal) applies, while he holds that appointment, as if his office is vacant.

(6)   Schedule 4 makes provision about judicial pensions in relation to the holder
      of a judicial office who serves as a judge of the Court.

(7)   The Lord Chancellor or the Secretary of State may by order make such
      transitional provision (including, in particular, provision for a temporary
      increase in the maximum number of judges) as he considers appropriate in
      relation to any holder of a judicial office who has completed his service as a
      judge of the Court.

Parliamentary procedure

19[1] Statements of compatibility

(1)   A Minister of the Crown in charge of a Bill in either House of Parliament
      must, before Second Reading of the Bill –

      (a)   make a statement to the effect that in his view the provisions of the Bill
            are compatible with the Convention rights ('a statement of
            compatibility'); or

      (b)   make a statement to the effect that although he is unable to make a
            statement of compatibility the government nevertheless wishes the
            House to proceed with the Bill.

(2)   The statement must be in writing and be published in such manner as the
      Minister making it considers appropriate.

Supplemental

20[2] Orders etc under this Act

(1)   Any power of a Minister of the Crown to make an order under this Act is
      exercisable by statutory instrument.

(2)   The power of the Lord Chancellor or the Secretary of State to make rules
      (other than rules of court) under section 2(3) or 7(9) is exercisable by
      statutory instrument.

(3)   Any statutory instrument made under section 14, 15 or 16(7) must be laid
      before Parliament.

---

[1]   Information: Commencement: 24 November 1998, SI 1998/2882.
[2]   Information: Commencement: 9 November 1998 (s 22(2)).

(4)   No order may be made by the Lord Chancellor or the Secretary of State under section 1(4), 7(11) or 16(2) unless a draft of the order has been laid before, and approved by, each House of Parliament.

(5)   Any statutory instrument made under section 18(7) or Schedule 4, or to which subsection (2) applies, shall be subject to annulment in pursuance of a resolution of either House of Parliament.

(6)   The power of a Northern Ireland department to make –
      (a)   rules under section 2(3)(c) or 7(9)(c), or
      (b)   an order under section 7(11),
      is exercisable by statutory rule for the purposes of the Statutory Rules (Northern Ireland) Order 1979.

(7)   Any rules made under section 2(3)(c) or 7(9)(c) shall be subject to negative resolution; and section 41(6) of the Interpretation Act Northern Ireland) 1954 (meaning of 'subject to negative resolution') shall apply as if the power to make the rules were conferred by an Act of the Northern Ireland Assembly.

(8)   No order may be made by a Northern Ireland department under section 7(11) unless a draft of the order has been laid before, and approved by, the Northern Ireland Assembly.

21¹   Interpretation,

(1)   In this Act –
      'amend' includes repeal and apply (with or without modifications);
      'the appropriate Minister' means the Minister of the Crown having charge of the appropriate authorised government department (within the meaning of the Crown Proceedings Act 1947);
      'the Commission' means the European Commission of Human Rights;
      'the Convention' means the Convention for the Protection of Human Rights and Fundamental Freedoms, agreed by the Council of Europe at Rome on 4th November 1950 as it has effect for the time being in relation to the United Kingdom;
      'declaration of incompatibility' means a declaration under section 4;
      'Minister of the Crown' has the same meaning as in the Ministers of the Crown Act 1975;
      'Northern Ireland Minister' includes the First Minister and the deputy First Minister in Northern Ireland;
      'primary legislation' means any –
      (a)   public general Act;
      (b)   local and personal Act;
      (c)   private Act;
      (d)   Measure of the Church Assembly;
      (e)   Measure of the General Synod of the Church of England;
      (f)   Order in Council –
            (i)   made in exercise of Her Majesty's Royal Prerogative;
            (ii)   made under section 38(1)(a) of the Northern Ireland Constitution Act 1973 or the corresponding provision of the Northern Ireland Act 1998; or
            (iii) amending an Act of a kind mentioned in paragraph (a), (b) or (c);

---

¹   Information: Commencement: Subss (1)–(4): 2 October 2000, SI 2000/1851; Subs (5): 9 November 1998 (s 22(2)).

and includes an order or other instrument made under primary legislation (otherwise than by the National Assembly for Wales, a member of the Scottish Executive, a Northern Ireland Minister or a Northern Ireland department) to the extent to which it operates to bring one or more provisions of that legislation into force or amends any primary legislation;

'the First Protocol' means the protocol to the Convention agreed at Paris on 20th March 1952;

'the Sixth Protocol' means the protocol to the Convention agreed at Strasbourg on 28th April 1983;

'the Eleventh Protocol' means the protocol to the Convention (restructuring the control machinery established by the Convention) agreed at Strasbourg on 11th May 1994;

'remedial order' means an order under section 10;

'subordinate legislation' means any –

(a) Order in Council other than one –
   (i) made in exercise of Her Majesty's Royal Prerogative;
   (ii) made under section 38(1)(a) of the Northern Ireland Constitution Act 1973 or the corresponding provision of the Northern Ireland Act 1998; or
   (iii) amending an Act of a kind mentioned in the definition of primary legislation;

(b) Act of the Scottish Parliament;

(c) Act of the Parliament of Northern Ireland;

(d) Measure of the Assembly established under section 1 of the Northern Ireland Assembly Act 1973;

(e) Act of the Northern Ireland Assembly;

(f) order, rules, regulations, scheme, warrant, byelaw or other instrument made under primary legislation (except to the extent to which it operates to bring one or more provisions of that legislation into force or amends any primary legislation);

(g) order, rules, regulations, scheme, warrant, byelaw or other instrument made under legislation mentioned in paragraph (b), (c), (d) or (e) or made under an Order in Council applying only to Northern Ireland;

(h) order, rules, regulations, scheme, warrant, byelaw or other instrument made by a member of the Scottish Executive, a Northern Ireland Minister or a Northern Ireland department in exercise of prerogative or other executive functions of Her Majesty which are exercisable by such a person on behalf of Her Majesty;

'transferred matters' has the same meaning as in the Northern Ireland Act 1998; and

'tribunal' means any tribunal in which legal proceedings may be brought.

(2) The references in paragraphs (b) and (c) of section 2(1) to Articles are to Articles of the Convention as they had effect immediately before the coming into force of the Eleventh Protocol.

(3) The reference in paragraph (d) of section 2(1) to Article 46 includes a reference to Articles 32 and 54 of the Convention as they had effect immediately before the coming into force of the Eleventh Protocol.

(4) The references in section 2(1) to a report or decision of the Commission or a decision of the Committee of Ministers include references to a report or decision made as provided by paragraphs 3, 4 and 6 of Article 5 of the Eleventh Protocol (transitional provisions).

(5)   Any liability under the Army Act 1955, the Air Force Act 1955 or the Naval Discipline Act 1957 to suffer death for an offence is replaced by a liability to imprisonment for life or any less punishment authorised by those Acts; and those Acts shall accordingly have effect with the necessary modifications.

22[1]   Short title, commencement, application and extent
(1)   This Act may be cited as the Human Rights Act 1998.
(2)   Sections 18, 20 and 21(5) and this section come into force on the passing of this Act.
(3)   The other provisions of this Act come into force on such day as the Secretary of State may by order appoint; and different days may be appointed for different purposes.
(4)   Paragraph (b) of subsection (1) of section 7 applies to proceedings brought by or at the instigation of a public authority whenever the act in question took place; but otherwise that subsection does not apply to an act taking place before the coming into force of that section.
(5)   This Act binds the Crown.
(6)   This Act extends to Northern Ireland.
(7)   Section 21(5), so far as it relates to any provision contained in the Army Act 1955, the Air Force Act 1955 or the Naval Discipline Act 1957, extends to any place to which that provision extends.

SCHEDULES

Schedule 1[2]
The Articles

Part I
The Convention

Rights and Freedoms

Article 2   Right to Life

1.   Everyone's right to life shall be protected by law. No one shall be deprived of his life intentionally save in the execution of a sentence of a court following his conviction of a crime for which this penalty is provided by law.

2.   Deprivation of life shall not be regarded as inflicted in contravention of this Article when it results from the use of force which is no more than absolutely necessary:
(a)   in defence of any person from unlawful violence;
(b)   in order to effect a lawful arrest or to prevent the escape of a person lawfully detained;
(c)   in action lawfully taken for the purpose of quelling a riot or insurrection.

****[3]

---

[1]   Information: Commencement: 9 November 1998 (s 22(2)).
[2]   Information: Commencement: 2 October 2000, SI 2000/1851.
[3]   Omission: Article 3 not reproduced.

Article 4   Prohibition of Slavery and Forced Labour

1.   No one shall be held in slavery or servitude.

2.   No one shall be required to perform forced or compulsory labour.

3.   For the purpose of this Article the term 'forced or compulsory labour' shall not include:

(a)   any work required to be done in the ordinary course of detention imposed according to the provisions of Article 5 of this Convention or during conditional release from such detention;

(b)   any service of a military character or, in case of conscientious objectors in countries where they are recognised, service exacted instead of compulsory military service;

(c)   any service exacted in case of an emergency or calamity threatening the life or well-being of the community;

(d)   any work or service which forms part of normal civic obligations.

****[1]

Article 6   Right to a Fair Trial

1.   In the determination of his civil rights and obligations or of any criminal charge against him, everyone is entitled to a fair and public hearing within a reasonable time by an independent and impartial tribunal established by law. Judgment shall be pronounced publicly but the press and public may be excluded from all or part of the trial in the interest of morals, public order or national security in a democratic society, where the interests of juveniles or the protection of the private life of the parties so require, or to the extent strictly necessary in the opinion of the court in special circumstances where publicity would prejudice the interests of justice.

2.   Everyone charged with a criminal offence shall be presumed innocent until proved guilty according to law.

3.   Everyone charged with a criminal offence has the following minimum rights:

(a)   to be informed promptly, in a language which he understands and in detail, of the nature and cause of the accusation against him;

(b)   to have adequate time and facilities for the preparation of his defence;

(c)   to defend himself in person or through legal assistance of his own choosing or, if he has not sufficient means to pay for legal assistance, to be given it free when the interests of justice so require;

(d)   to examine or have examined witnesses against him and to obtain the attendance and examination of witnesses on his behalf under the same conditions as witnesses against him;

(e)   to have the free assistance of an interpreter if he cannot understand or speak the language used in court.

****[2]

---

[1]   Omission: Article 5 not reproduced.
[2]   Omission: Articles 7–12 not reproduced.

Article 14   Prohibition of Discrimination

The enjoyment of the rights and freedoms set forth in this Convention shall be secured without discrimination on any ground such as sex, race, colour, language, religion, political or other opinion, national or social origin, association with a national minority, property, birth or other status.

****[1]

Part II
The First Protocol

Article 1   Protection of Property

Every natural or legal person is entitled to the peaceful enjoyment of his possessions. No one shall be deprived of his possessions except in the public interest and subject to the conditions provided for by law and by the general principles of international law.

The preceding provisions shall not, however, in any way impair the right of a State to enforce such laws as it deems necessary to control the use of property in accordance with the general interest or to secure the payment of taxes or other contributions or penalties.

Article 2   Right to Education

No person shall be denied the right to education. In the exercise of any functions which it assumes in relation to education and to teaching, the State shall respect the right of parents to ensure such education and teaching in conformity with their own religious and philosophical convictions.

Article 3   Right to Free Elections

The High Contracting Parties undertake to hold free elections at reasonable intervals by secret ballot, under conditions which will ensure the free expression of the opinion of the people in the choice of the legislature.

Part III
The Sixth Protocol

Article 1   Abolition of the Death Penalty

The death penalty shall be abolished. No one shall be condemned to such penalty or executed.

Article 2   Death Penalty in Time of War

A State may make provision in its law for the death penalty in respect of acts committed in time of war or of imminent threat of war; such penalty shall be

---

[1]   Omission: Articles 16–18 not reproduced.

applied only in the instances laid down in the law and in accordance with its provisions. The State shall communicate to the Secretary General of the Council of Europe the relevant provisions of that law.

Civil Procedure Rules 1998, rule 37.4
(SI 1998/3132)

37.4[1] Proceedings under Fatal Accidents Act 1976 and Law Reform (Miscellaneous Provisions) Act 1934 – apportionment by court

(1) Where –
   (a) a claim includes claims arising under –
      (i)   the Fatal Accidents Act 1976; and
      (ii) the Law Reform (Miscellaneous Provisions) Act 1934;
   (b) a single sum of money is paid into court in satisfaction of those claims; and
   (c) the money is accepted,
   the court shall apportion the money between the different claims.

(2) The court shall apportion money under paragraph (1) –
   (a) when it gives directions under rule 21.11 (control of money received by a child or patient); or
   (b) if rule 21.11 does not apply, when it gives permission for the money to be paid out of court.

(3) Where, in an action in which a claim under the Fatal Accidents Act 1976 is made by or on behalf of more than one person –
   (a) a sum in respect of damages is ordered or agreed to be paid in satisfaction of the claim; or
   (b) a sum of money is accepted in satisfaction of the claim,
   the court shall apportion it between the persons entitled to it unless it has already been apportioned by the court, a jury, or agreement between the parties.

(Other rules about payments into court can be found –

   (a) in Schedule 1, in the following RSC – Ord 49 (garnishee proceedings); Ord 50 (stop orders in funds in court); ...[2] Ord 92 (payments into court in particular circumstances); and
   (b) in Schedule 2, in the following CCR – Ord 30 (garnishee proceedings); Ord 49 (payment in under various statutes).)

---

[1] Information: Commencement: 26 April 1999.
[2] Amendment: Words deleted: Supplement 13 (issued 29 March 2000), with effect from 2 May 2000. Previous text = "Ord 82 (defamation claims);".

Practice Direction –
Statements of Case[1]

This Practice Direction supplements the Civil Procedure Rules 1998, Part 16 (PD16).

FATAL ACCIDENT CLAIMS

5.1   In a fatal accident claim the claimant must state in his particulars of claim:

(1)   that it is brought under the Fatal Accidents Act 1976,
(2)   the dependants on whose behalf the claim is made,
(3)   the date of birth of each dependant, and
(4)   details of the nature of the dependency claim.

---

[1]   Information: Commencement: 26 April 1999 (issued January 1999).

APPENDIX 4

OGDEN TABLES
(NARRATIVE (SECTION D) AND TABLES

SECTION D: APPLICATION OF TABLES TO FATAL ACCIDENT CASES

50.   Whereas in personal injury cases the problem to be solved is that of setting a value on an income stream during the potential life of one person (the claimant), the situation is generally more complicated in fatal accident cases. Here the compensation is intended to reflect the value of an income stream during the lifetime of one or more dependants of the deceased (or the expected period for which the dependants would have expected to receive the dependency, if shorter) but limited according to the expectation of how long the deceased would have been able to provide the financial support, had he or she not been involved in the fatal accident.

51.   In principle, therefore, the compensation for post-trial dependency should be based on the present value at the date of the trial of the dependency during the expected future joint lifetime of the deceased and the dependant or claimant (had the deceased survived naturally to the date of the trial), subject to any limitations on the period of dependency and any expected future changes in the level of dependency, for example, on attaining retirement age. In addition there should be compensation for the period between the date of accident and the date of trial.

52.   A set of actuarial tables to make such calculations accurately would require tables similar to Tables 1 to 36 but for each combination of ages as at the date of the trial of the deceased and the dependant to whom compensation is to be paid. The Working Party concluded that this would not meet the criterion of simplicity of application which was a central objective of these tables and recommends that, in complex cases, or cases where the accuracy of the multiplier is thought by the parties to be of critical importance and material to the resulting amount of compensation (for example in cases potentially involving very large claims where the level of the multiplicand is unambiguously established), the advice of a professionally qualified actuary should be sought. However, for the majority of cases, a certain amount of approximation will be appropriate, bearing in mind the need for a simple and streamlined process, and taking into consideration the other uncertainties in the determination of an appropriate level of compensation. The following paragraphs describe a methodology using Tables 1 to 36 which can be expected to yield satisfactory answers.

Damages for the period from the fatal accident to the date of trial

53. The period of pre-trial dependency will normally be equal to the period between the date of the fatal accident and the date of the trial, substituting where appropriate the lower figure of the expected period for which the deceased would have provided the dependency, had he or she not been killed in the accident, or if the period of dependency would have been limited in some way, for example if the dependant is a child.

54. A deduction may be made for the risk that the deceased might have died anyway, in the period between the date of the fatal accident and the date at which the trial takes place. In many cases this deduction will be small and could usually be regarded as de minimis. The need for a deduction becomes more necessary the longer the period from the date of accident to the date of trial and the older the deceased at the date of death. As an illustration of the order of magnitude of the deduction, Table D shows some examples of factors by which the multiplier should be multiplied for different ages of the deceased and for different periods from the date of accident to the date of the trial.

TABLE D
Factor by which pre-trial damages should be multiplied to allow for the likelihood that the deceased would not in any case have survived to provide the dependency for the full period to the date of trial.

Age of deceased at date of accident	Period from date of accident to date of trial or date of cessation of dependency, if earlier (years)					
	Male deceased			Female deceased		
	3	6	9	3	6	9
10	1.00	1.00	1.00	1.00	1.00	1.00
20	1.00	1.00	1.00	1.00	1.00	1.00
30	1.00	1.00	1.00	1.00	1.00	1.00
40	1.00	0.99	0.99	1.00	1.00	0.99
50	0.99	0.99	0.98	1.00	0.99	0.99
60	0.98	0.96	0.94	0.99	0.98	0.96
70	0.95	0.90	0.85	0.97	0.94	0.90
80	0.88	0.76	0.65	0.92	0.83	0.73

Note: The factor is clearly one for a period of zero years. Factors for other ages and periods not shown in the table may be obtained approximately by interpolation.

55. The resultant multiplier, after application of any discount for the possibility of early death of the deceased before the date of trial, even had the accident not taken place, is to be applied to the multiplicand, which is determined in the usual way. Interest will then be added up to the date of trial on the basis of special damages.

Damages from the date of trial to retirement age

56. The assessment of the multiplier involves the following steps:

(1) Determine the expected period for which the deceased would have been able to provide the dependency (see paragraph 57).

(2)　Determine the expected period for which the dependant would have been able to receive the dependency (see paragraph 57).

(3)　Take the lesser of the two periods.

(4)　Treat the resulting period as a term certain for which the multiplier is to be determined and look up the figure in Table 38 for this period at the appropriate rate of interest.

(5)　Apply any adjustment for contingencies other than mortality in accordance with Section B.

(6)　If necessary, make an allowance for the risk that the deceased might have died anyway before the date of the trial (see paragraph 59).

57.　The expected periods at (1) and (2) of paragraph 56 may be obtained from the 0% column of the appropriate table at the back of this booklet. For (1), if historical mortality is to be used, Tables 3 to 10 will be relevant, according to the sex of the deceased and the expected age of retirement, or Tables 21 to 28 if the Court agrees with the recommendation of the Working Party that projected mortality is more appropriate. The age at which the table should be entered is the age which the deceased would have been at the date of the trial. For (2) Tables 1 and 2 or 19 and 20 can be used, according to the sex of the dependant and looking up the table at the age of the dependant at the date of the trial.

58.　If the period for which the dependency would have continued is a short fixed period, as in the case of a child, the figure at (2) would be the outstanding period at the date of the trial.

59.　A deduction may be made for the risk that the deceased might have died anyway before the date of trial. The need for such a deduction becomes more necessary the longer the period from the date of accident to the date of trial and the older the deceased at the date of death. As an illustration of the order of magnitude of the deduction, Table E shows some examples of the factor by which the multiplier, determined as above, should be multiplied for different ages of the deceased and for different periods from the date of accident to the date of the trial.

60.　The resulting multiplier, after application of any discount for the possibility of early death of the deceased before the date of trial, even had the accident not taken place, is to be applied to the appropriate multiplicand, determined in relation to dependency as assessed for the period up to retirement age.

61.　If there are several dependants, to whom damages are to be paid in respect of their own particular lifetime (or for a fixed period of dependency), separate multipliers should be determined for each and multiplied by the appropriate multiplicand using the procedure in paragraphs 56 to 60. The total amount of damages is then obtained by adding the separate components. If a single multiplicand is determined, but the damages are to be shared among two or more dependants so long as they are each alive, or during a period of common dependency, then the multiplier will be calculated using the procedure in paragraphs 56 to 60. However, at step (2) of paragraph 56 the expected period will be the longest of the expected periods for which the dependency might last.

TABLE E
Factor by which post-trial damages should be multiplied to allow for the likelihood that the deceased would not in any case have survived to the date of trial in order to provide any post-trial dependency.

Age of deceased at date of accident	Period from date of accident to date of trial					
	Male deceased			Female deceased		
	3	6	9	3	6	9
10	1.00	1.00	1.00	1.00	1.00	1.00
20	1.00	0.99	0.99	1.00	1.00	1.00
30	1.00	0.99	0.99	1.00	1.00	0.99
40	0.99	0.99	0.98	1.00	0.99	0.99
50	0.99	0.97	0.95	0.99	0.98	0.97
60	0.97	0.92	0.87	0.98	0.95	0.92
70	0.90	0.80	0.68	0.94	0.87	0.78
80	0.75	0.53	0.33	0.83	0.64	0.45

Note: The factor is clearly one for a period of zero years. Factors for other ages and periods not shown in the table may be obtained approximately by interpolation.

Damages for the period of dependency after retirement age

62. The method described in paragraphs 56 to 61 for pre-retirement age dependency cannot satisfactorily be applied directly to post-retirement age dependency with a sufficient degree of accuracy. We therefore propose a method which involves determining the multiplier by looking at dependency for the rest of life from the date of trial and then subtracting the multiplier for dependency up to retirement age.

63. The assessment of the multiplier for whole of life dependency involves the following steps:

(1)   Determine the expectation of life which the deceased would have had as at the date of trial, or such lesser period for which the deceased would have been able to provide the dependency (see paragraph 64).

(2)   Determine the expected period for which the dependant would have been able to receive the dependency (see paragraph 64).

(3)   Take the lesser of the two periods.

(4)   Treat the resulting period as a term certain for which the multiplier is to be determined and look up the figure in Table 38 for this period at the appropriate rate of interest.

64. The expected periods at (1) and (2) of paragraph 63 may be obtained from the 0% column of the appropriate table at the back of this booklet. For (1), if historical mortality is to be used, Tables 1 or 2 will be relevant, according to the sex of the deceased, or Tables 19 or 20 if the Court agrees with the recommendation of the Working Party that projected mortality is more appropriate. The age at which the table should be entered is the age which the deceased would have attained at the date of the trial. For (2) Tables 1 and 2 or 19 and 20 can be used, according to

the sex of the dependant and looking up the table at the age of the dependant at the date of the trial.

65. Deduct the corresponding multiplier for post-trial pre-retirement dependency, as determined in paragraphs 56 to 61, but without any adjustment for contingencies other than mortality, or that the deceased may have died anyway before the date of trial. The result is the multiplier for post-retirement dependency, which must then be applied to the appropriate multiplicand, assessed in relation to dependency after retirement age. The adjustment for contingencies other than mortality in respect of the damages for the period of dependency after retirement age will often be less than that required for pre-retirement age damages (see paragraph 34).

66. A deduction may finally be made for the risk that the deceased might have died anyway before the date of trial. The need for such a deduction becomes more necessary the longer the period from the date of accident to the date of trial and the older the deceased at the date of death. As an illustration of the order of magnitude of the deduction, Table E shows some examples of the factor by which the multiplier, determined as above, should be multiplied for different ages of the deceased and for different periods from the date of accident to the date of the trial. The factors for this purpose are exactly the same deductions as used in the calculation at paragraphs 56 to 61.

Cases where dependency is not related to employment

67. The layout of paragraphs 56 to 66 is based on the assumption that the dependency provided by the deceased would have changed at retirement age. This may not be appropriate in some cases, particularly in the important case of the deceased wife and mother whose contribution has been solely in the home or in the case of an adult child caring for an elderly parent or parents. In cases like this, where the deceased might have provided the dependency throughout their lifetime, paragraphs 62 to 66 should be ignored and paragraphs 56 to 61 used, with the difference that the expected period required at step (1) of paragraph 56 should be a whole of life expectancy, taken from Tables 1 and 2 or 19 and 20. This is also the approach to use when the deceased was already a pensioner.

Example 3

68. The dependant is female, aged 38 at the date of the trial, which is taking place 6 years after the date of the fatal accident which killed the male deceased, at that time aged 37, on whom the dependant was financially dependent. The Court has determined a multiplicand, up to the deceased's normal retirement age of 65, of £30,000 and has decided that no post-retirement damages are payable. The damages are to be calculated as follows:

Pre-trial damages:
(1)   Period between fatal accident and trial: 6 years.
(2)   Factor for possible early death (Table D for male aged 37 and 6 years): 0.99
(3)   therefore Pre-trial damages   = 6 × 0.99 × £30,000
                                     = £178,200 (plus interest as special damages)

Post-trial damages:
(1) Expected period for which the deceased would have provided the dependency (Table 25 at 0% for male aged 43, the age as at the date of trial): 21.14
(2) Expected period for which the dependant would have been able to receive the dependency (Table 20 at 0% for female aged 38): 46.36
(3) Lesser of two periods at (1) and (2) = 21.14
(4) Multiplier for term certain of 21.14 years at 3% rate of return (interpolating between the values for 21 and 22 years in Table 38)
$$= (22 - 21.14) \times 15.65 + (21.14 - 21) \times 16.17$$
$$= 15.72$$
(5) Adjustment factor for contingencies other than mortality (in accordance with Section B). Assume medium economic activity. Factor from Table A: 0.96
(6) Adjustment factor for the risk that the deceased might have died anyway before the date of trial (Table E for male aged 37 and 6 years): 0.99
(7) Post-trial damages $= 15.72 \times 0.96 \times 0.99 \times £30,000$
$$= £448,209 \text{ or } £450,000 \text{ say.}$$

Example 4

69.   The dependant is female, aged 50 at the date of the trial, which is taking place 4 years after the date of the fatal accident which killed the man, at that time aged 47, on whom she was financially dependent. The Court has determined a multiplicand, up to the deceased's normal retirement age of 60, of £50,000 and has decided that post-retirement damages should be payable based on a multiplicand of £30,000. The damages are to be calculated as follows:

Pre-trial damages:
(1) Period between fatal accident and trial: 4 years
(2) Factor for possible early death (Table D for male aged 47 and 4 years): 0.99
(3) therefore Pre-trial damages $= 4 \times 0.99 \times £50,000$
$$= £198,000 \text{ (plus interest as special damages)}$$

Post-trial pre-retirement damages:
(1) Expected period for which the deceased would have provided the dependency (Table 23 at 0% for male aged 51, the age as at the date of trial): 8.80
(2) Expected period for which the dependant would have been able to receive the dependency (Table 20 at 0% for female aged 50): 34.49
(3) Lesser of two periods at (1) and (2) = 8.80
(4) Multiplier for term certain of 8.80 years at 3% rate of return (interpolating between the values for 8 and 9 in Table 38)
$$= (9 - 8.80) \times 7.12 + (8.80 - 8) \times 7.90$$
$$= 7.74$$
(5) Adjustment factor for contingencies other than mortality (in accordance with Section B). Assume medium economic activity. Factor from Table B: 0.94
(6) Adjustment factor for the risk that the deceased might have died anyway before the date of trial (Table E for male aged 47 and 4 years): 0.98
(7) Post-trial pre-retirement damages $= 7.74 \times 0.94 \times 0.98 \times £50,000$
$$= £356,504$$

Post-retirement damages:
(1) Expectation of life of deceased at date of trial (Table 19 at 0% for male aged 51): 29.91
(2) Expected period for which the dependant would have been able to receive the dependency (Table 20 at 0% for female aged 50): 34.49
(3) Lesser of two periods at (1) and (2) = 29.91
(4) Multiplier for time certain of 29.91 years at 3% rate of return (interpolating between the values for 29 and 30 in Table 38)
    = (30 – 29.91) × 19.47 + (29.91 – 29) × 19.89 = 19.85
(5) Deduct multiplier for post-trial pre-retirement damages before application of adjustment factors for contingencies other than mortality and for the risk that the deceased might have died anyway before the date of trial:
    19.85 – 7.74 = 12.11
(6) Adjustment factor for the risk that the deceased might have died anyway before the date of trial (Table E for male aged 47 and 4 years): 0.98
(7) Post-retirement damages = 12.11 × 0.98 × £30,000 = £356,034

Example 5

70. There are two dependants, respectively a child aged 10 and a male aged 41 at the date of the trial, which is taking place 3 years after the date of the fatal accident which killed the woman, at that time aged 35, on whom both were financially dependent. She worked in London for a computer company and future economic activity is deemed by the Court to be high. The Court has determined a multiplicand, up to the deceased's normal retirement age of 62, of £50,000 for the male dependant and £10,000 for the child, up to the age of 21, and has decided that post-retirement damages should be payable based on a multiplicand of £20,000. The damages are to be calculated as follows:

Pre-trial damages:
(1) Period between fatal accident and trial: 3 years
(2) Factor for possible early death (Table D for female aged 35 and 3 years): 1.00
(3) therefore Pre-trial damages = 3 × 1.00 × (£50,000 + £10,000)
    = £180,000 (plus interest as special damages)

Post-trial pre-retirement damages:
(1) Expected period for which the deceased would have provided the dependency should be based on female aged 38 at the date of trial with retirement age of 62. First calculate as though deceased were aged 36 and had retirement age of 60 (Table 24 at 0% for female aged 36): 23.57
    Then calculate as though deceased were aged 41 and had retirement age of 65 (Table 26 at 0% for female aged 41): 23.34
    Interpolate for age 38 with retirement age of 62
    = (3 × 23.57 + 2 × 23.34)/5 = 23.48
(2) Expected period for which the male dependant would have been able to receive the dependency (Table 19 at 0% for male aged 41): 39.71
    Expected period for which child would have been able to receive the dependency = 11.00
(3) Lesser of two periods at (1) and (2) = 11.00 (in case of child)
                                           = 23.48 (in case of man).
(4) Multiplier for term certain of 11 years at 3% (Table 38): 9.39

Multiplier for term certain of 23.48 years at 3% rate of return (interpolating between the values for 23 and 24 in Table 38)
= (24 – 23.48) × 16.69 + (23.48 – 23) × 17.19
= 16.93

(5) Adjustment factor for contingencies other than mortality (in accordance with Section B). Factor from Table C, allowing for occupation and geographical area: 0.96 (does not apply to child)

(6) Adjustment factor for the risk that the deceased might have died anyway before the date of trial (Table E for female aged 35 and 3 years): 1.00

(7) Pre-retirement damages
= 9.39 × 1.00 × £10,000 + 16.93 × 0.96 × 1.00 × £50,000
= £93,900 + £812,640
= £906,540

Post-retirement damages:

(1) Expectation of life of deceased at date of trial (Table 20 at 0% for female aged 38): 46.36

(2) Expected period for which the dependant would have been able to receive the dependency (Table 19 at 0% for male aged 41): 39.71 (no post-retirement dependency for child)

(3) Lesser of two periods at (1) and (2) = 39.71

(4) Multiplier for time certain of 39.71 years at 3% rate of return (interpolating between the values for 39 and 40 in Table 38)
= (40 – 39.71) × 23.15 + (39.71 – 39) × 23.46 = 23.37

(5) Deduct multiplier for post-trial pre-retirement damages before application of adjustment factors for contingencies other than mortality and for the risk that the deceased might have died anyway before the date of trial:
23.37 – 16.93 = 6.44

(6) Adjustment factor for the risk that the deceased might have died anyway before the date of trial (Table E for female aged 35 and 3 years) = 1.00

(7) Post-retirement damages   =   6.44 × 1.00 × £20,000
=   £128,800

Table 1   Multipliers for pecuniary loss of life (males)

Age at date of trial	Multiplier calculated with allowance for population mortality and rate of return of											Age at date of trial
	0.0%	0.5%	1.0%	1.5%	2.0%	2.5%	3.0%	£3.5%	4.0%	4.5%	5.0%	
0	73.42	61.05	51.47	43.97	38.02	33.25	29.38	26.22	23.60	21.41	19.57	0
1	73.02	60.86	51.41	43.98	38.08	33.34	29.49	26.34	23.72	21.53	19.68	1
2	72.06	60.20	50.95	43.66	37.86	33.18	29.38	26.26	23.67	21.49	19.66	2
3	71.09	59.52	50.47	43.32	37.62	33.01	29.26	26.17	23.60	21.45	19.62	3
4	70.11	58.83	49.99	42.98	37.37	32.84	29.13	26.08	23.53	21.40	19.58	4
5	69.13	58.14	49.49	42.63	37.12	32.65	29.00	25.98	23.46	21.34	19.54	5
6	68.14	57.44	48.99	42.27	36.86	32.47	28.86	25.88	23.39	21.28	19.50	6
7	67.16	56.73	48.49	41.90	36.59	32.27	28.72	25.77	23.31	21.22	19.45	7
8	66.17	56.02	47.98	41.53	36.32	32.07	28.57	25.66	23.22	21.16	19.41	8
9	65.18	55.31	47.46	41.16	36.05	31.87	28.42	25.55	23.14	21.10	19.35	9
10	64.19	54.60	46.94	40.77	35.76	31.66	28.26	25.43	23.05	21.03	19.30	10
11	63.21	53.88	46.41	40.38	35.48	31.44	28.10	25.31	22.95	20.95	19.24	11
12	62.22	53.15	45.88	39.99	35.18	31.22	27.93	25.18	22.85	20.88	19.19	12
13	61.23	52.43	45.34	39.59	34.88	30.99	27.76	25.05	22.75	20.80	19.12	13
14	60.24	51.70	44.80	39.19	34.58	30.76	27.58	24.91	22.65	20.72	19.06	14
15	59.26	50.97	44.26	38.78	34.27	30.53	27.41	24.77	22.54	20.63	18.99	15
16	58.28	50.24	43.71	38.37	33.96	30.29	27.22	24.63	22.43	20.55	18.93	16
17	57.31	49.52	43.17	37.96	33.65	30.05	27.04	24.49	22.32	20.46	18.86	17
18	56.36	48.80	42.63	37.55	33.33	29.82	26.86	24.35	22.21	20.38	18.79	18
19	55.41	48.08	42.08	37.13	33.02	29.57	26.67	24.21	22.10	20.29	18.72	19
20	54.45	47.36	41.54	36.71	32.70	29.33	26.48	24.06	21.98	20.20	18.65	20
21	53.50	46.63	40.98	36.29	32.37	29.07	26.28	23.90	21.86	20.10	18.57	21
22	52.54	45.91	40.42	35.86	32.03	28.81	26.08	23.74	21.74	20.00	18.49	22
23	51.59	45.17	39.86	35.42	31.69	28.55	25.87	23.58	21.60	19.90	18.41	23
24	50.63	44.44	39.28	34.97	31.35	28.27	25.65	23.41	21.47	19.79	18.32	24
25	49.68	43.70	38.71	34.52	30.99	27.99	25.43	23.23	21.33	19.67	18.23	25
26	48.72	42.95	38.12	34.06	30.63	27.70	25.20	23.04	21.18	19.55	18.13	26
27	47.76	42.20	37.53	33.59	30.26	27.41	24.96	22.85	21.02	19.43	18.03	27
28	46.80	41.44	36.93	33.12	29.88	27.10	24.72	22.66	20.86	19.30	17.92	28
29	45.84	40.68	36.33	32.64	29.49	26.79	24.47	22.45	20.70	19.16	17.81	29
30	44.88	39.92	35.72	32.15	29.10	26.47	24.21	22.24	20.52	19.02	17.69	30
31	43.92	39.15	35.10	31.65	28.70	26.15	23.94	22.02	20.34	18.87	17.57	31
32	42.96	38.38	34.48	31.15	28.29	25.81	23.67	21.80	20.16	18.71	17.44	32
33	42.01	37.61	33.86	30.64	27.87	25.47	23.38	21.56	19.96	18.55	17.30	33
34	41.05	36.83	33.22	30.12	27.44	25.12	23.09	21.32	19.76	18.38	17.16	34
35	40.09	36.05	32.59	29.60	27.01	24.76	22.80	21.07	19.55	18.21	17.01	35
36	39.14	35.27	31.94	29.07	26.57	24.40	22.49	20.82	19.34	18.03	16.86	36
37	38.18	34.49	31.30	28.54	26.13	24.03	22.18	20.56	19.12	17.84	16.70	37
38	37.24	33.71	30.65	28.00	25.68	23.65	21.86	20.29	18.89	17.64	16.53	38
39	36.29	32.92	30.00	27.45	25.22	23.26	21.54	20.01	18.65	17.44	16.36	39
40	35.35	32.14	29.34	26.90	24.76	22.87	21.20	19.73	18.41	17.23	16.18	40
41	34.41	31.35	28.68	26.34	24.28	22.47	20.86	19.43	18.16	17.02	15.99	41
42	33.47	30.56	28.01	25.78	23.80	22.06	20.51	19.13	17.90	16.79	15.80	42
43	32.54	29.77	27.34	25.21	23.32	21.64	20.15	18.82	17.63	16.56	15.60	43
44	31.61	28.98	26.67	24.63	22.83	21.22	19.79	18.51	17.36	16.32	15.39	44
45	30.68	28.19	26.00	24.05	22.33	20.79	19.41	18.18	17.07	16.07	15.17	45
46	29.76	27.41	25.32	23.47	21.82	20.35	19.03	17.85	16.78	15.82	14.94	46
47	28.85	26.62	24.64	22.89	21.31	19.91	18.65	17.51	16.48	15.55	14.71	47
48	27.95	25.84	23.97	22.30	20.80	19.46	18.25	17.16	16.18	15.28	14.47	48
49	27.05	25.06	23.29	21.71	20.28	19.01	17.85	16.81	15.87	15.01	14.22	49
50	26.16	24.29	22.61	21.11	19.76	18.55	17.45	16.45	15.55	14.72	13.97	50
51	25.28	23.52	21.94	20.52	19.24	18.09	17.04	16.09	15.22	14.43	13.71	51
52	24.41	22.75	21.27	19.93	18.72	17.62	16.62	15.72	14.89	14.14	13.44	52
53	23.55	21.99	20.60	19.33	18.19	17.15	16.20	15.34	14.55	13.83	13.17	53
54	22.70	21.24	19.93	18.74	17.66	16.68	15.78	14.96	14.21	13.52	12.89	54
55	21.86	20.50	19.26	18.15	17.13	16.20	15.35	14.57	13.86	13.21	12.60	55
56	21.03	19.76	18.60	17.55	16.60	15.72	14.92	14.18	13.51	12.88	12.31	56
57	20.21	19.03	17.95	16.97	16.07	15.24	14.49	13.79	13.15	12.56	12.01	57
58	19.41	18.31	17.30	16.38	15.54	14.76	14.05	13.39	12.79	12.23	11.71	58
59	18.62	17.60	16.66	15.80	15.01	14.28	13.61	13.00	12.42	11.89	11.40	59
60	17.85	16.90	16.03	15.22	14.49	13.81	13.18	12.60	12.06	11.56	11.09	60
61	17.09	16.21	15.40	14.66	13.97	13.33	12.74	12.20	11.69	11.22	10.78	61
62	16.36	15.54	14.79	14.10	13.45	12.86	12.31	11.80	11.32	10.88	10.46	62
63	15.64	14.89	14.19	13.55	12.95	12.40	11.88	11.40	10.95	10.54	10.15	63
64	14.94	14.25	13.60	13.01	12.45	11.94	11.46	11.01	10.59	10.20	9.83	64

Table 1 *continued*

65	14.27	13.63	13.03	12.48	11.97	11.49	11.04	10.62	10.23	9.86	9.52	65
66	13.61	13.02	12.47	11.96	11.49	11.04	10.63	10.24	9.87	9.53	9.21	66
67	12.98	12.44	11.93	11.46	11.02	10.61	10.22	9.86	9.52	9.20	8.90	67
68	12.36	11.87	11.40	10.97	10.56	10.18	9.82	9.49	9.17	8.87	8.59	68
69	11.77	11.31	10.89	10.49	10.11	9.76	9.43	9.12	8.82	8.55	8.28	69
70	11.19	10.77	10.38	10.02	9.67	9.35	9.04	8.75	8.48	8.22	7.98	70
71	10.62	10.25	9.89	9.55	9.24	8.94	8.66	8.39	8.14	7.90	7.68	71
72	10.08	9.73	9.41	9.10	8.81	8.54	8.28	8.04	7.80	7.58	7.37	72
73	9.56	9.24	8.95	8.67	8.40	8.15	7.91	7.69	7.47	7.27	7.08	73
74	9.06	8.77	8.50	8.25	8.00	7.77	7.56	7.35	7.15	6.97	6.79	74
75	8.57	8.31	8.07	7.84	7.62	7.41	7.21	7.02	6.84	6.67	6.50	75
76	8.11	7.87	7.65	7.44	7.24	7.05	6.87	6.69	6.53	6.37	6.22	76
77	7.66	7.45	7.25	7.05	6.87	6.70	6.53	6.37	6.22	6.08	5.94	77
78	7.23	7.04	6.86	6.69	6.52	6.36	6.21	6.07	5.93	5.80	5.67	78
79	6.83	6.65	6.49	6.33	6.18	6.04	5.90	5.77	5.65	5.53	5.41	79
80	6.44	6.28	6.14	5.99	5.86	5.73	5.61	5.49	5.37	5.26	5.16	80
81	6.07	5.93	5.80	5.67	5.55	5.43	5.32	5.21	5.11	5.01	4.91	81
82	5.72	5.59	5.47	5.36	5.25	5.14	5.04	4.94	4.85	4.76	4.67	82
83	5.38	5.27	5.16	5.06	4.96	4.86	4.77	4.68	4.60	4.52	4.44	83
84	5.06	4.96	4.87	4.77	4.68	4.60	4.52	4.44	4.36	4.28	4.21	84
85	4.76	4.67	4.59	4.50	4.42	4.35	4.27	4.20	4.13	4.06	4.00	85
86	4.48	4.40	4.32	4.25	4.17	4.10	4.04	3.97	3.91	3.85	3.79	86
87	4.21	4.14	4.07	4.01	3.94	3.88	3.82	3.76	3.70	3.65	3.59	87
88	3.97	3.90	3.84	3.78	3.72	3.67	3.61	3.56	3.51	3.46	3.41	88
89	3.73	3.68	3.62	3.57	3.52	3.47	3.42	3.37	3.32	3.28	3.24	89
90	3.51	3.46	3.41	3.36	3.31	3.27	3.23	3.18	3.14	3.10	3.06	90
91	3.29	3.24	3.20	3.15	3.11	3.07	3.03	3.00	2.96	2.92	2.89	91
92	3.07	3.03	2.99	2.95	2.92	2.88	2.85	2.81	2.78	2.75	2.72	92
93	2.87	2.84	2.80	2.77	2.74	2.70	2.67	2.64	2.61	2.59	2.56	93
94	2.69	2.66	2.63	2.60	2.57	2.54	2.52	2.49	2.46	2.44	2.41	94
95	2.53	2.50	2.48	2.45	2.42	2.40	2.37	2.35	2.33	2.30	2.28	95
96	2.38	2.36	2.33	2.31	2.29	2.26	2.24	2.22	2.20	2.18	2.16	96
97	2.24	2.22	2.20	2.18	2.16	2.14	2.12	2.10	2.08	2.06	2.04	97
98	2.11	2.09	2.07	2.06	2.04	2.02	2.00	1.98	1.97	1.95	1.93	98
99	1.99	1.97	1.96	1.94	1.92	1.91	1.89	1.87	1.86	1.84	1.83	99
100	1.87	1.86	1.84	1.83	1.81	1.80	1.78	1.77	1.76	1.74	1.73	100

Table 2   Multipliers for pecuniary loss of life (females)

Age at date of trial	Multiplier calculated with allowance for population mortality and rate of return of											Age at date of trial
	0.0%	0.5%	1.0%	1.5%	2.0%	2.5%	3.0%	£3.5%	4.0%	4.5%	5.0%	
0	78.96	64.89	54.15	45.85	39.35	34.21	30.08	26.73	23.99	21.70	19.79	0
1	78.46	64.62	54.03	45.82	39.38	34.27	30.16	26.83	24.08	21.80	19.88	1
2	77.50	63.98	53.59	45.52	39.18	34.13	30.07	26.76	24.04	21.77	19.86	2
3	76.53	63.31	53.14	45.21	38.97	33.99	29.97	26.69	23.99	21.73	19.84	3
4	75.55	62.64	52.68	44.89	38.75	33.83	29.86	26.61	23.93	21.69	19.81	4
5	74.56	61.96	52.21	44.57	38.52	33.67	29.74	26.53	23.87	21.65	19.78	5
6	73.57	61.28	51.73	44.24	38.28	33.51	29.63	26.45	23.81	21.61	19.75	6
7	72.58	60.59	51.25	43.90	38.05	33.34	29.51	26.36	23.75	21.56	19.71	7
8	71.59	59.90	50.77	43.56	37.80	33.16	29.38	26.27	23.68	21.51	19.68	8
9	70.60	59.21	50.28	43.21	37.55	32.98	29.25	26.17	23.61	21.46	19.64	9
10	69.61	58.51	49.78	42.86	37.30	32.80	29.12	26.08	23.54	21.41	19.60	10
11	68.62	57.81	49.28	42.50	37.04	32.61	28.98	25.97	23.47	21.35	19.56	11
12	67.63	57.10	48.78	42.13	36.78	32.42	28.84	25.87	23.39	21.29	19.51	12
13	66.64	56.39	48.27	41.76	36.51	32.22	28.69	25.76	23.31	21.23	19.46	13
14	65.65	55.68	47.75	41.39	36.23	32.02	28.54	25.65	23.22	21.17	19.42	14
15	64.66	54.97	47.23	41.01	35.95	31.81	28.39	25.54	23.14	21.10	19.37	15
16	63.67	54.25	46.71	40.63	35.67	31.60	28.23	25.42	23.05	21.03	19.31	16
17	62.69	53.53	46.18	40.24	35.38	31.39	28.07	25.30	22.95	20.96	19.26	17
18	61.71	52.81	45.66	39.85	35.09	31.17	27.91	25.17	22.86	20.89	19.20	18
19	60.73	52.09	45.12	39.45	34.80	30.95	27.74	25.04	22.76	20.82	19.15	19
20	59.75	51.37	44.58	39.05	34.49	30.72	27.57	24.91	22.66	20.74	19.08	20
21	58.77	50.64	44.04	38.64	34.18	30.48	27.39	24.77	22.55	20.65	19.02	21
22	57.79	49.90	43.49	38.22	33.87	30.24	27.20	24.63	22.44	20.57	18.95	22
23	56.80	49.17	42.93	37.80	33.55	30.00	27.01	24.48	22.33	20.48	18.88	23
24	55.82	48.43	42.37	37.37	33.22	29.74	26.82	24.33	22.21	20.38	18.81	24
25	54.84	47.68	41.80	36.94	32.88	29.49	26.61	24.17	22.09	20.29	18.73	25
26	53.86	46.93	41.23	36.50	32.54	29.22	26.41	24.01	21.96	20.18	18.65	26
27	52.88	46.18	40.65	36.05	32.20	28.95	26.19	23.84	21.82	20.08	18.56	27
28	51.90	45.43	40.07	35.59	31.84	28.67	25.97	23.67	21.68	19.97	18.47	28
29	50.92	44.67	39.48	35.13	31.48	28.39	25.75	23.49	21.54	19.85	18.38	29
30	49.94	43.91	38.88	34.67	31.11	28.09	25.52	23.30	21.39	19.73	18.28	30
31	48.96	43.14	38.28	34.20	30.74	27.80	25.28	23.11	21.23	19.60	18.18	31
32	47.98	42.38	37.68	33.72	30.36	27.49	25.03	22.91	21.07	19.47	18.07	32
33	47.01	41.61	37.07	33.23	29.97	27.18	24.78	22.71	20.91	19.34	17.96	33
34	46.03	40.84	36.46	32.74	29.58	26.86	24.53	22.50	20.74	19.20	17.84	34
35	45.06	40.06	35.84	32.25	29.18	26.54	24.26	22.28	20.56	19.05	17.72	35
36	44.09	39.29	35.22	31.75	28.77	26.21	23.99	22.06	20.38	18.90	17.59	36
37	43.12	38.51	34.59	31.24	28.36	25.87	23.71	21.83	20.19	18.74	17.46	37
38	42.16	37.73	33.96	30.73	27.94	25.53	23.43	21.60	19.99	18.58	17.32	38
39	41.20	36.95	33.33	30.21	27.51	25.18	23.14	21.36	19.79	18.41	17.18	39
40	40.24	36.17	32.69	29.68	27.08	24.82	22.84	21.11	19.58	18.23	17.03	40
41	39.28	35.39	32.04	29.15	26.64	24.45	22.54	20.85	19.37	18.05	16.88	41
42	38.32	34.60	31.40	28.61	26.19	24.08	22.22	20.59	19.14	17.86	16.72	42
43	37.37	33.82	30.74	28.07	25.74	23.70	21.91	20.32	18.92	17.67	16.55	43
44	36.43	33.03	30.09	27.53	25.28	23.31	21.58	20.04	18.68	17.46	16.38	44
45	35.48	32.25	29.43	26.98	24.82	22.92	21.25	19.76	18.44	17.25	16.20	45
46	34.54	31.46	28.77	26.42	24.35	22.52	20.91	19.47	18.19	17.04	16.01	46
47	33.61	30.68	28.11	25.86	23.88	22.12	20.56	19.17	17.93	16.82	15.82	47
48	32.68	29.90	27.45	25.30	23.40	21.71	20.21	18.87	17.67	16.59	15.62	48
49	31.76	29.12	26.79	24.73	22.91	21.29	19.85	18.56	17.40	16.36	15.41	49
50	30.85	28.34	26.12	24.16	22.42	20.87	19.48	18.24	17.12	16.11	15.20	50
51	29.94	27.56	25.45	23.59	21.92	20.44	19.11	17.91	16.84	15.86	14.98	51
52	29.03	26.78	24.79	23.01	21.42	20.00	18.73	17.58	16.55	15.61	14.76	52
53	28.13	26.01	24.12	22.43	20.92	19.56	18.34	17.24	16.25	15.35	14.52	53
54	27.24	25.24	23.45	21.84	20.41	19.12	17.95	16.90	15.94	15.07	14.28	54
55	26.36	24.47	22.77	21.26	19.89	18.66	17.55	16.55	15.63	14.80	14.03	55
56	25.48	23.70	22.10	20.67	19.38	18.21	17.15	16.19	15.31	14.51	13.78	56
57	24.61	22.94	21.44	20.08	18.86	17.75	16.74	15.82	14.98	14.22	13.52	57
58	23.76	22.19	20.77	19.49	18.33	17.28	16.33	15.45	14.65	13.92	13.25	58
59	22.91	21.44	20.11	18.91	17.82	16.82	15.91	15.08	14.32	13.62	12.98	59
60	22.08	20.70	19.45	18.32	17.29	16.35	15.49	14.70	13.98	13.31	12.70	60
61	21.26	19.97	18.80	17.74	16.77	15.88	15.07	14.32	13.63	13.00	12.42	61
62	20.45	19.25	18.16	17.16	16.25	15.41	14.64	13.94	13.29	12.69	12.13	62
63	19.66	18.54	17.52	16.58	15.73	14.94	14.22	13.55	12.93	12.36	11.84	63
64	18.88	17.84	16.89	16.01	15.21	14.47	13.79	13.16	12.58	12.04	11.54	64

Table 2 *continued*

65	18.11	17.15	16.26	15.45	14.70	14.01	13.37	12.77	12.22	11.71	11.24	65
66	17.36	16.47	15.64	14.89	14.19	13.54	12.94	12.38	11.87	11.38	10.94	66
67	16.62	15.79	15.03	14.33	13.68	13.07	12.51	11.99	11.50	11.05	10.63	67
68	15.90	15.13	14.43	13.77	13.17	12.61	12.08	11.59	11.14	10.71	10.32	68
69	15.19	14.48	13.83	13.23	12.66	12.14	11.65	11.20	10.77	10.37	10.00	69
70	14.49	13.84	13.24	12.68	12.16	11.68	11.22	10.80	10.40	10.03	9.68	70
71	13.80	13.21	12.66	12.14	11.66	11.21	10.79	10.40	10.03	9.68	9.36	71
72	13.13	12.59	12.08	11.61	11.17	10.75	10.36	10.00	9.66	9.33	9.03	72
73	12.48	11.98	11.52	11.09	10.68	10.30	9.94	9.60	9.29	8.99	8.70	73
74	11.85	11.40	10.98	10.58	10.21	9.86	9.53	9.21	8.92	8.64	8.38	74
75	11.23	10.82	10.44	10.08	9.74	9.42	9.11	8.83	8.55	8.30	8.06	75
76	10.63	10.26	9.91	9.58	9.27	8.98	8.70	8.44	8.19	7.95	7.73	76
77	10.04	9.71	9.39	9.09	8.81	8.54	8.29	8.05	7.82	7.60	7.40	77
78	9.48	9.18	8.89	8.62	8.36	8.12	7.89	7.67	7.46	7.26	7.07	78
79	8.93	8.66	8.40	8.16	7.93	7.71	7.50	7.30	7.11	6.93	6.75	79
80	8.41	8.17	7.94	7.72	7.51	7.31	7.12	6.94	6.76	6.60	6.44	80
81	7.91	7.70	7.49	7.29	7.10	6.92	6.75	6.58	6.43	6.28	6.13	81
82	7.43	7.24	7.05	6.87	6.70	6.54	6.39	6.24	6.10	5.96	5.83	82
83	6.97	6.80	6.63	6.47	6.32	6.18	6.04	5.90	5.77	5.65	5.53	83
84	6.53	6.38	6.23	6.09	5.95	5.82	5.69	5.57	5.46	5.35	5.24	84
85	6.11	5.97	5.84	5.71	5.59	5.48	5.36	5.26	5.15	5.05	4.96	85
86	5.72	5.59	5.48	5.36	5.25	5.15	5.05	4.95	4.86	4.77	4.68	86
87	5.35	5.24	5.14	5.04	4.94	4.85	4.76	4.67	4.59	4.51	4.43	87
88	5.00	4.91	4.81	4.72	4.64	4.55	4.47	4.40	4.32	4.25	4.18	88
89	4.67	4.58	4.50	4.42	4.34	4.27	4.20	4.13	4.06	4.00	3.94	89
90	4.35	4.28	4.21	4.14	4.07	4.00	3.94	3.88	3.82	3.76	3.71	90
91	4.06	4.00	3.93	3.87	3.81	3.75	3.70	3.64	3.59	3.54	3.49	91
92	3.80	3.74	3.68	3.63	3.57	3.52	3.47	3.42	3.37	3.33	3.28	92
93	3.55	3.50	3.45	3.40	3.35	3.31	3.26	3.22	3.18	3.13	3.09	93
94	3.32	3.28	3.23	3.19	3.15	3.11	3.07	3.03	2.99	2.95	2.92	94
95	3.11	3.07	3.03	2.99	2.96	2.92	2.88	2.85	2.81	2.78	2.75	95
96	2.92	2.89	2.85	2.82	2.78	2.75	2.72	2.69	2.66	2.63	2.60	96
97	2.75	2.72	2.69	2.66	2.63	2.60	2.57	2.54	2.52	2.49	2.46	97
98	2.59	2.56	2.53	2.50	2.48	2.45	2.42	2.40	2.38	2.35	2.33	98
99	2.42	2.40	2.37	2.35	2.32	2.30	2.28	2.26	2.23	2.21	2.19	99
100	2.27	2.25	2.22	2.20	2.18	2.16	2.14	2.12	2.10	2.08	2.06	100

Table 3 Multipliers for loss of earnings to pension age 55 (males)

Age at date of trial	Multiplier calculated with allowance for population mortality and rate of return of											Age at date of trial
	0.0%	0.5%	1.0%	1.5%	2.0%	2.5%	3.0%	£3.5%	4.0%	4.5%	5.0%	
16	38.10	34.66	31.65	28.99	26.65	24.58	22.75	21.12	19.66	18.36	17.19	16
17	37.12	33.85	30.97	28.44	26.19	24.20	22.43	20.85	19.44	18.17	17.04	17
18	36.15	33.04	30.30	27.88	25.72	23.81	22.10	20.58	19.21	17.98	16.88	18
19	35.18	32.24	29.63	27.31	25.25	23.41	21.77	20.30	18.98	17.78	16.71	19
20	34.21	31.42	28.94	26.73	24.77	23.00	21.43	20.01	18.73	17.58	16.53	20
21	33.24	30.60	28.25	26.15	24.27	22.59	21.07	19.71	18.48	17.36	16.35	21
22	32.27	29.78	27.55	25.56	23.77	22.16	20.71	19.40	18.21	17.13	16.16	22
23	31.30	28.95	26.85	24.96	23.25	21.72	20.33	19.08	17.94	16.90	15.95	23
24	30.32	28.12	26.13	24.35	22.73	21.27	19.95	18.74	17.65	16.65	15.74	24
25	29.35	27.28	25.41	23.72	22.20	20.81	19.55	18.40	17.35	16.39	15.52	25
26	28.37	26.44	24.68	23.09	21.65	20.33	19.14	18.04	17.04	16.12	15.28	26
27	27.40	25.59	23.95	22.45	21.09	19.85	18.71	17.67	16.72	15.84	15.04	27
28	26.42	24.74	23.20	21.80	20.52	19.35	18.27	17.29	16.38	15.55	14.78	28
29	25.44	23.88	22.45	21.14	19.94	18.84	17.82	16.89	16.03	15.24	14.50	29
30	24.47	23.02	21.69	20.47	19.34	18.31	17.36	16.48	15.67	14.91	14.22	30
31	23.49	22.15	20.92	19.78	18.74	17.77	16.88	16.05	15.29	14.58	13.92	31
32	22.51	21.28	20.14	19.09	18.12	17.22	16.39	15.61	14.89	14.22	13.60	32
33	21.53	20.40	19.36	18.39	17.49	16.66	15.88	15.16	14.48	13.85	13.27	33
34	20.55	19.52	18.57	17.68	16.85	16.08	15.36	14.68	14.06	13.47	12.92	34
35	19.57	18.64	17.77	16.95	16.19	15.48	14.82	14.20	13.61	13.07	12.55	35
36	18.60	17.75	16.96	16.22	15.52	14.87	14.27	13.69	13.15	12.65	12.17	36
37	17.62	16.86	16.14	15.47	14.84	14.25	13.70	13.17	12.68	12.21	11.77	37
38	16.64	15.96	15.32	14.72	14.15	13.62	13.11	12.63	12.18	11.76	11.35	38
39	15.67	15.06	14.49	13.95	13.45	12.96	12.51	12.08	11.67	11.28	10.91	39
40	14.69	14.16	13.66	13.18	12.73	12.30	11.89	11.50	11.13	10.78	10.45	40
41	13.71	13.25	12.81	12.39	11.99	11.61	11.25	10.91	10.58	10.27	9.97	41
42	12.74	12.34	11.96	11.59	11.24	10.91	10.59	10.29	10.00	9.72	9.46	42
43	11.76	11.42	11.09	10.78	10.48	10.19	9.92	9.65	9.40	9.16	8.93	43
44	10.79	10.50	10.22	9.96	9.70	9.46	9.22	9.00	8.78	8.57	8.37	44
45	9.81	9.57	9.34	9.12	8.91	8.70	8.51	8.31	8.13	7.95	7.78	45
46	8.84	8.64	8.46	8.28	8.10	7.93	7.77	7.61	7.46	7.31	7.16	46
47	7.86	7.71	7.56	7.42	7.28	7.14	7.01	6.88	6.76	6.64	6.52	47
48	6.89	6.77	6.65	6.54	6.43	6.33	6.23	6.13	6.03	5.93	5.84	48
49	5.91	5.82	5.74	5.66	5.58	5.50	5.42	5.34	5.27	5.20	5.13	49
50	4.93	4.87	4.81	4.76	4.70	4.64	4.59	4.53	4.48	4.43	4.38	50
51	3.95	3.92	3.88	3.84	3.80	3.77	3.73	3.70	3.66	3.63	3.59	51
52	2.97	2.95	2.93	2.91	2.89	2.87	2.85	2.82	2.80	2.79	2.77	52
53	1.99	1.98	1.97	1.96	1.95	1.94	1.93	1.92	1.91	1.90	1.89	53
54	1.00	0.99	0.99	0.99	0.99	0.98	0.98	0.98	0.98	0.97	0.97	54

Table 4 Multipliers for loss of earnings to pension age 55 (females)

Age at date of trial	Multiplier calculated with allowance for population mortality and rate of return of											Age at date of trial
	0.0%	0.5%	1.0%	1.5%	2.0%	2.5%	3.0%	£3.5%	4.0%	4.5%	5.0%	
16	38.53	35.03	31.97	29.28	26.90	24.80	22.94	21.29	19.82	18.50	17.32	16
17	37.54	34.21	31.29	28.72	26.44	24.42	22.62	21.02	19.59	18.31	17.16	17
18	36.55	33.39	30.61	28.15	25.97	24.02	22.29	20.75	19.36	18.12	17.00	18
19	35.56	32.57	29.92	27.57	25.48	23.62	21.96	20.46	19.12	17.92	16.83	19
20	34.57	31.74	29.22	26.99	24.99	23.21	21.61	20.17	18.88	17.71	16.65	20
21	33.58	30.90	28.52	26.39	24.49	22.78	21.25	19.86	18.62	17.49	16.47	21
22	32.59	30.07	27.81	25.79	23.98	22.35	20.88	19.55	18.35	17.26	16.27	22
23	31.60	29.22	27.09	25.18	23.45	21.90	20.49	19.22	18.07	17.02	16.06	23
24	30.61	28.38	26.37	24.56	22.92	21.44	20.10	18.88	17.78	16.77	15.85	24
25	29.62	27.53	25.63	23.92	22.38	20.97	19.70	18.53	17.47	16.51	15.62	25
26	28.63	26.67	24.89	23.28	21.82	20.49	19.28	18.17	17.16	16.23	15.38	26
27	27.64	25.81	24.15	22.63	21.26	20.00	18.85	17.80	16.83	15.95	15.13	27
28	26.65	24.95	23.39	21.97	20.68	19.49	18.41	17.41	16.49	15.65	14.87	28
29	25.66	24.08	22.63	21.30	20.09	18.97	17.95	17.01	16.14	15.34	14.59	29
30	24.67	23.20	21.86	20.62	19.49	18.44	17.48	16.59	15.77	15.01	14.31	30
31	23.68	22.33	21.08	19.94	18.88	17.90	17.00	16.16	15.39	14.67	14.00	31
32	22.69	21.45	20.30	19.24	18.25	17.34	16.50	15.72	14.99	14.31	13.68	32
33	21.70	20.56	19.51	18.53	17.62	16.77	15.99	15.26	14.58	13.94	13.35	33
34	20.72	19.67	18.71	17.81	16.97	16.19	15.46	14.78	14.15	13.56	13.00	34
35	19.73	18.78	17.90	17.08	16.31	15.59	14.92	14.29	13.70	13.15	12.63	35
36	18.74	17.89	17.09	16.34	15.64	14.98	14.36	13.79	13.24	12.73	12.25	36
37	17.76	16.99	16.27	15.59	14.95	14.35	13.79	13.26	12.76	12.29	11.85	37
38	16.77	16.08	15.44	14.83	14.25	13.71	13.20	12.72	12.26	11.83	11.42	38
39	15.78	15.18	14.60	14.06	13.54	13.05	12.59	12.16	11.75	11.35	10.98	39
40	14.80	14.26	13.75	13.27	12.82	12.38	11.97	11.58	11.21	10.85	10.52	40
41	13.82	13.35	12.90	12.48	12.07	11.69	11.33	10.98	10.65	10.33	10.03	41
42	12.83	12.43	12.04	11.67	11.32	10.98	10.66	10.36	10.07	9.79	9.52	42
43	11.85	11.50	11.17	10.85	10.55	10.26	9.98	9.72	9.46	9.22	8.98	43
44	10.86	10.57	10.29	10.02	9.77	9.52	9.28	9.05	8.83	8.62	8.42	44
45	9.88	9.64	9.41	9.18	8.97	8.76	8.56	8.37	8.18	8.00	7.83	45
46	8.90	8.70	8.51	8.33	8.15	7.98	7.82	7.66	7.50	7.35	7.21	46
47	7.91	7.76	7.61	7.46	7.32	7.18	7.05	6.92	6.80	6.67	6.56	47
48	6.93	6.81	6.69	6.58	6.47	6.37	6.26	6.16	6.06	5.97	5.87	48
49	5.94	5.86	5.77	5.69	5.61	5.53	5.45	5.37	5.30	5.23	5.16	49
50	4.96	4.90	4.84	4.78	4.72	4.67	4.61	4.56	4.50	4.45	4.40	50
51	3.97	3.93	3.89	3.86	3.82	3.78	3.75	3.71	3.68	3.64	3.61	51
52	2.98	2.96	2.94	2.92	2.90	2.88	2.86	2.83	2.81	2.79	2.78	52
53	1.99	1.98	1.97	1.96	1.95	1.94	1.93	1.93	1.92	1.91	1.90	53
54	1.00	1.00	0.99	0.99	0.99	0.99	0.98	0.98	0.98	0.98	0.97	54

Table 5 Multipliers for loss of earnings to pension age 60 (males)

Age at date of trial	Multiplier calculated with allowance for population mortality and rate of return of											Age at date of trial
	0.0%	0.5%	1.0%	1.5%	2.0%	2.5%	3.0%	£3.5%	4.0%	4.5%	5.0%	
16	42.62	38.33	34.63	31.43	28.64	26.20	24.07	22.20	20.55	19.09	17.79	16
17	41.64	37.54	33.99	30.91	28.22	25.86	23.79	21.97	20.36	18.93	17.66	17
18	40.67	36.76	33.35	30.39	27.79	25.51	23.51	21.74	20.17	18.78	17.54	18
19	39.70	35.97	32.71	29.86	27.36	25.16	23.22	21.50	19.98	18.62	17.40	19
20	38.74	35.17	32.06	29.33	26.92	24.80	22.92	21.26	19.77	18.45	17.26	20
21	37.77	34.38	31.40	28.78	26.47	24.43	22.61	21.00	19.56	18.27	17.12	21
22	36.80	33.58	30.74	28.23	26.01	24.05	22.30	20.74	19.34	18.09	16.96	22
23	35.83	32.77	30.07	27.67	25.55	23.66	21.97	20.46	19.11	17.90	16.80	23
24	34.87	31.96	29.39	27.11	25.07	23.26	21.64	20.18	18.87	17.69	16.63	24
25	33.90	31.15	28.70	26.53	24.59	22.85	21.29	19.89	18.62	17.48	16.45	25
26	32.92	30.33	28.01	25.94	24.09	22.43	20.93	19.58	18.37	17.26	16.26	26
27	31.95	29.50	27.31	25.34	23.58	21.99	20.56	19.27	18.10	17.03	16.07	27
28	30.98	28.67	26.60	24.74	23.06	21.55	20.18	18.94	17.82	16.79	15.86	28
29	30.00	27.84	25.88	24.12	22.53	21.09	19.79	18.60	17.52	16.54	15.64	29
30	29.03	27.00	25.16	23.50	21.99	20.63	19.39	18.25	17.22	16.28	15.41	30
31	28.06	26.15	24.43	22.87	21.44	20.15	18.97	17.89	16.91	16.00	15.17	31
32	27.08	25.31	23.69	22.22	20.88	19.66	18.54	17.52	16.58	15.72	14.92	32
33	26.11	24.45	22.95	21.57	20.31	19.16	18.10	17.13	16.24	15.42	14.66	33
34	25.13	23.60	22.19	20.91	19.73	18.64	17.65	16.73	15.88	15.10	14.38	34
35	24.16	22.74	21.43	20.24	19.13	18.12	17.18	16.32	15.52	14.78	14.09	35
36	23.19	21.88	20.67	19.55	18.53	17.58	16.70	15.89	15.14	14.44	13.79	36
37	22.22	21.01	19.90	18.87	17.91	17.03	16.21	15.45	14.74	14.08	13.47	37
38	21.25	20.14	19.12	18.17	17.28	16.47	15.70	14.99	14.33	13.71	13.14	38
39	20.28	19.27	18.33	17.46	16.65	15.89	15.18	14.52	13.91	13.33	12.79	39
40	19.31	18.39	17.54	16.74	16.00	15.30	14.65	14.04	13.46	12.93	12.42	40
41	18.34	17.51	16.74	16.01	15.33	14.70	14.10	13.53	13.01	12.51	12.04	41
42	17.38	16.63	15.93	15.27	14.66	14.08	13.53	13.02	12.53	12.07	11.64	42
43	16.41	15.74	15.12	14.53	13.97	13.44	12.95	12.48	12.04	11.62	11.22	43
44	15.44	14.85	14.30	13.77	13.27	12.80	12.35	11.93	11.53	11.15	10.78	44
45	14.48	13.96	13.47	13.00	12.56	12.14	11.74	11.36	10.99	10.65	10.32	45
46	13.52	13.06	12.63	12.22	11.83	11.46	11.10	10.77	10.44	10.14	9.84	46
47	12.56	12.16	11.79	11.43	11.09	10.77	10.45	10.16	9.87	9.60	9.34	47
48	11.60	11.26	10.94	10.63	10.34	10.06	9.79	9.53	9.28	9.04	8.81	48
49	10.64	10.36	10.08	9.82	9.57	9.33	9.10	8.88	8.67	8.46	8.26	49
50	9.68	9.45	9.22	9.00	8.79	8.59	8.40	8.21	8.03	7.85	7.68	50
51	8.72	8.53	8.35	8.17	8.00	7.83	7.67	7.52	7.37	7.22	7.08	51
52	7.77	7.61	7.47	7.33	7.19	7.05	6.93	6.80	6.68	6.56	6.44	52
53	6.81	6.69	6.58	6.47	6.36	6.26	6.16	6.06	5.96	5.87	5.78	53
54	5.85	5.76	5.68	5.60	5.52	5.44	5.36	5.29	5.22	5.15	5.08	54
55	4.89	4.83	4.77	4.71	4.65	4.60	4.55	4.49	4.44	4.39	4.34	55
56	3.92	3.88	3.85	3.81	3.77	3.74	3.70	3.67	3.63	3.60	3.57	56
57	2.95	2.93	2.91	2.89	2.87	2.85	2.83	2.81	2.79	2.77	2.75	57
58	1.98	1.97	1.96	1.95	1.94	1.93	1.92	1.91	1.90	1.89	1.88	58
59	0.99	0.99	0.99	0.99	0.98	0.98	0.98	0.98	0.97	0.97	0.97	59

Table 6   Multipliers for pecuniary loss of life (females)

Age at date of trial	Multiplier calculated with allowance for population mortality and rate of return of											Age at date of trial
	0.0%	0.5%	1.0%	1.5%	2.0%	2.5%	3.0%	£3.5%	4.0%	4.5%	5.0%	
16	43.23	38.86	35.08	31.81	28.97	26.50	24.33	22.42	20.74	19.26	17.94	16
17	42.24	38.06	34.44	31.29	28.55	26.15	24.05	22.19	20.56	19.11	17.82	17
18	41.26	37.26	33.79	30.76	28.12	25.80	23.76	21.96	20.37	18.95	17.69	18
19	40.27	36.46	33.13	30.23	27.68	25.44	23.47	21.72	20.17	18.79	17.55	19
20	39.28	35.65	32.47	29.68	27.23	25.07	23.16	21.47	19.96	18.62	17.41	20
21	38.29	34.83	31.80	29.13	26.78	24.70	22.85	21.21	19.75	18.44	17.26	21
22	37.31	34.02	31.12	28.57	26.31	24.31	22.53	20.94	19.52	18.25	17.11	22
23	36.32	33.19	30.44	28.00	25.84	23.91	22.20	20.66	19.29	18.06	16.94	23
24	35.33	32.37	29.75	27.42	25.35	23.51	21.86	20.38	19.05	17.85	16.77	24
25	34.34	31.54	29.05	26.83	24.86	23.09	21.50	20.08	18.80	17.64	16.59	25
26	33.35	30.70	28.35	26.24	24.35	22.66	21.14	19.77	18.53	17.42	16.40	26
27	32.36	29.87	27.63	25.63	23.84	22.22	20.77	19.45	18.26	17.18	16.20	27
28	31.38	29.02	26.91	25.02	23.31	21.77	20.38	19.12	17.98	16.94	15.99	28
29	30.39	28.18	26.19	24.40	22.78	21.31	19.99	18.78	17.69	16.69	15.77	29
30	29.40	27.33	25.46	23.77	22.23	20.84	19.58	18.43	17.38	16.42	15.55	30
31	28.41	26.47	24.72	23.12	21.68	20.36	19.16	18.07	17.06	16.15	15.30	31
32	27.43	25.61	23.97	22.47	21.11	19.87	18.73	17.69	16.73	15.86	15.05	32
33	26.44	24.75	23.22	21.82	20.53	19.36	18.29	17.30	16.39	15.56	14.79	33
34	25.45	23.89	22.46	21.15	19.95	18.84	17.83	16.90	16.04	15.24	14.51	34
35	24.47	23.02	21.69	20.47	19.35	18.32	17.36	16.48	15.67	14.92	14.22	35
36	23.49	22.15	20.92	19.78	18.74	17.77	16.88	16.05	15.29	14.58	13.92	36
37	22.50	21.27	20.14	19.09	18.12	17.22	16.38	15.61	14.89	14.22	13.60	37
38	21.52	20.39	19.35	18.38	17.48	16.65	15.87	15.15	14.48	13.85	13.27	38
39	20.54	19.51	18.56	17.67	16.84	16.07	15.35	14.68	14.05	13.47	12.92	39
40	19.56	18.63	17.75	16.94	16.18	15.47	14.81	14.19	13.61	13.06	12.55	40
41	18.58	17.74	16.95	16.21	15.51	14.86	14.26	13.68	13.15	12.64	12.17	41
42	17.60	16.84	16.13	15.46	14.83	14.24	13.69	13.16	12.67	12.20	11.76	42
43	16.62	15.95	15.31	14.70	14.14	13.60	13.10	12.62	12.17	11.75	11.34	43
44	15.65	15.04	14.48	13.94	13.43	12.95	12.49	12.06	11.66	11.27	10.90	44
45	14.67	14.14	13.64	13.16	12.71	12.28	11.87	11.49	11.12	10.77	10.44	45
46	13.70	13.23	12.79	12.37	11.98	11.60	11.24	10.89	10.56	10.25	9.95	46
47	12.72	12.32	11.94	11.58	11.23	10.90	10.58	10.28	9.99	9.71	9.45	47
48	11.75	11.41	11.08	10.77	10.47	10.18	9.91	9.64	9.39	9.15	8.91	48
49	10.78	10.49	10.21	9.95	9.69	9.45	9.21	8.99	8.77	8.56	8.36	49
50	9.80	9.56	9.33	9.11	8.90	8.69	8.50	8.31	8.12	7.94	7.77	50
51	8.83	8.64	8.45	8.27	8.09	7.92	7.76	7.60	7.45	7.30	7.16	51
52	7.86	7.70	7.56	7.41	7.27	7.14	7.00	6.88	6.75	6.63	6.51	52
53	6.88	6.77	6.65	6.54	6.43	6.33	6.22	6.12	6.03	5.93	5.84	53
54	5.91	5.82	5.74	5.65	5.57	5.49	5.42	5.34	5.27	5.20	5.13	54
55	4.93	4.87	4.81	4.75	4.70	4.64	4.59	4.53	4.48	4.43	4.38	55
56	3.95	3.91	3.88	3.84	3.80	3.77	3.73	3.69	3.66	3.63	3.59	56
57	2.97	2.95	2.93	2.91	2.89	2.86	2.84	2.82	2.80	2.78	2.77	57
58	1.99	1.98	1.97	1.96	1.95	1.94	1.93	1.92	1.91	1.90	1.89	58
59	1.00	0.99	0.99	0.99	0.99	0.98	0.98	0.98	0.98	0.97	0.97	59

Table 7 Multipliers for loss of earnings to pension age 65 (males)

Age at date of trial	Multiplier calculated with allowance for population mortality and rate of return of											Age at date of trial
	0.0%	0.5%	1.0%	1.5%	2.0%	2.5%	3.0%	£3.5%	4.0%	4.5%	5.0%	
16	46.83	41.68	37.29	33.54	30.32	27.54	25.14	23.05	21.23	19.63	18.23	16
17	45.86	40.90	36.68	33.05	29.93	27.23	24.89	22.86	21.07	19.51	18.12	17
18	44.89	40.14	36.07	32.56	29.54	26.92	24.65	22.66	20.91	19.38	18.02	18
19	43.93	39.37	35.45	32.07	29.15	26.61	24.39	22.45	20.75	19.24	17.91	19
20	42.97	38.60	34.83	31.57	28.75	26.28	24.13	22.24	20.57	19.10	17.80	20
21	42.00	37.82	34.20	31.07	28.34	25.95	23.86	22.02	20.39	18.96	17.68	21
22	41.04	37.04	33.57	30.55	27.92	25.61	23.58	21.79	20.21	18.80	17.55	22
23	40.07	36.25	32.93	30.03	27.49	25.26	23.29	21.56	20.01	18.64	17.42	23
24	39.11	35.46	32.28	29.50	27.05	24.90	23.00	21.31	19.81	18.48	17.28	24
25	38.14	34.67	31.63	28.96	26.61	24.53	22.69	21.06	19.60	18.30	17.14	25
26	37.18	33.87	30.97	28.41	26.15	24.15	22.38	20.80	19.39	18.12	16.98	26
27	36.21	33.07	30.30	27.85	25.69	23.77	22.05	20.53	19.16	17.93	16.82	27
28	35.24	32.26	29.62	27.29	25.22	23.37	21.72	20.24	18.92	17.73	16.65	28
29	34.27	31.44	28.94	26.71	24.73	22.96	21.38	19.95	18.67	17.52	16.48	29
30	33.30	30.63	28.25	26.13	24.24	22.54	21.02	19.65	18.42	17.30	16.29	30
31	32.33	29.80	27.55	25.54	23.73	22.11	20.66	19.34	18.15	17.07	16.10	31
32	31.36	28.98	26.85	24.94	23.22	21.68	20.28	19.02	17.87	16.84	15.89	32
33	30.39	28.15	26.14	24.33	22.70	21.23	19.89	18.69	17.59	16.59	15.68	33
34	29.42	27.31	25.42	23.71	22.17	20.77	19.50	18.34	17.29	16.33	15.45	34
35	28.45	26.48	24.70	23.08	21.62	20.29	19.09	17.98	16.98	16.06	15.22	35
36	27.48	25.64	23.97	22.45	21.07	19.81	18.67	17.62	16.66	15.78	14.97	36
37	26.51	24.79	23.23	21.81	20.51	19.32	18.24	17.24	16.33	15.49	14.71	37
38	25.55	23.95	22.49	21.16	19.94	18.82	17.79	16.85	15.98	15.18	14.44	38
39	24.59	23.10	21.74	20.50	19.35	18.30	17.34	16.45	15.63	14.87	14.16	39
40	23.63	22.25	20.99	19.83	18.76	17.78	16.87	16.03	15.26	14.54	13.87	40
41	22.67	21.40	20.23	19.15	18.16	17.24	16.39	15.60	14.87	14.19	13.56	41
42	21.71	20.54	19.47	18.47	17.55	16.69	15.90	15.16	14.48	13.84	13.24	42
43	20.75	19.68	18.69	17.78	16.92	16.13	15.39	14.71	14.06	13.47	12.91	43
44	19.79	18.82	17.92	17.07	16.29	15.56	14.87	14.24	13.64	13.08	12.56	44
45	18.84	17.96	17.13	16.36	15.64	14.97	14.34	13.75	13.20	12.68	12.19	45
46	17.89	17.09	16.34	15.64	14.99	14.37	13.79	13.25	12.74	12.26	11.81	46
47	16.94	16.22	15.55	14.92	14.32	13.76	13.23	12.74	12.27	11.83	11.41	47
48	16.00	15.35	14.75	14.18	13.64	13.14	12.66	12.21	11.78	11.37	10.99	48
49	15.05	14.48	13.95	13.44	12.96	12.50	12.07	11.66	11.27	10.91	10.56	49
50	14.11	13.61	13.14	12.69	12.26	11.85	11.47	11.10	10.75	10.42	10.10	50
51	13.18	12.74	12.32	11.93	11.55	11.19	10.85	10.52	10.21	9.92	9.63	51
52	12.24	11.87	11.50	11.16	10.83	10.52	10.22	9.93	9.65	9.39	9.14	52
53	11.31	10.99	10.68	10.38	10.10	9.83	9.56	9.31	9.07	8.84	8.62	53
54	10.38	10.11	9.85	9.60	9.35	9.12	8.90	8.68	8.48	8.28	8.08	54
55	9.45	9.23	9.01	8.80	8.60	8.40	8.21	8.03	7.85	7.68	7.52	55
56	8.53	8.34	8.16	7.99	7.82	7.66	7.51	7.36	7.21	7.07	6.93	56
57	7.60	7.45	7.31	7.17	7.04	6.91	6.78	6.66	6.54	6.43	6.31	57
58	6.67	6.56	6.45	6.34	6.23	6.13	6.04	5.94	5.85	5.76	5.67	58
59	5.74	5.65	5.57	5.49	5.42	5.34	5.27	5.19	5.12	5.05	4.99	59
60	4.80	4.74	4.69	4.63	4.58	4.52	4.47	4.42	4.37	4.32	4.27	60
61	3.86	3.83	3.79	3.75	3.72	3.68	3.65	3.61	3.58	3.55	3.51	61
62	2.92	2.90	2.87	2.85	2.83	2.81	2.79	2.77	2.75	2.73	2.72	62
63	1.96	1.95	1.94	1.93	1.92	1.91	1.90	1.89	1.89	1.88	1.87	63
64	0.99	0.99	0.98	0.98	0.98	0.98	0.97	0.97	0.97	0.97	0.97	64

Table 8   Multipliers for loss of earnings to pension age 65 (females)

Age at date of trial	Multiplier calculated with allowance for population mortality and rate of return of											Age at date of trial
	0.0%	0.5%	1.0%	1.5%	2.0%	2.5%	3.0%	£3.5%	4.0%	4.5%	5.0%	
16	47.75	42.44	37.93	34.08	30.78	27.93	25.47	23.34	21.47	19.84	18.41	16
17	46.77	41.67	37.32	33.59	30.39	27.62	25.23	23.14	21.32	19.72	18.31	17
18	45.78	40.88	36.70	33.10	30.00	27.31	24.98	22.94	21.16	19.59	18.21	18
19	44.79	40.10	36.07	32.60	29.60	26.99	24.72	22.73	20.99	19.46	18.10	19
20	43.81	39.31	35.44	32.09	29.19	26.66	24.45	22.52	20.82	19.31	17.98	20
21	42.82	38.52	34.80	31.57	28.77	26.32	24.18	22.30	20.64	19.17	17.86	21
22	41.84	37.72	34.15	31.05	28.34	25.98	23.90	22.07	20.45	19.01	17.74	22
23	40.85	36.92	33.50	30.52	27.91	25.62	23.61	21.83	20.25	18.85	17.61	23
24	39.86	36.11	32.84	29.98	27.47	25.26	23.31	21.58	20.05	18.69	17.47	24
25	38.88	35.30	32.17	29.43	27.02	24.89	23.00	21.33	19.84	18.51	17.32	25
26	37.89	34.49	31.50	28.87	26.56	24.51	22.69	21.07	19.62	18.33	17.17	26
27	36.90	33.67	30.82	28.31	26.09	24.11	22.36	20.79	19.39	18.14	17.01	27
28	35.91	32.85	30.14	27.74	25.61	23.71	22.02	20.51	19.16	17.94	16.84	28
29	34.93	32.02	29.44	27.16	25.12	23.30	21.68	20.22	18.91	17.73	16.66	29
30	33.94	31.19	28.74	26.57	24.62	22.88	21.32	19.92	18.65	17.51	16.48	30
31	32.96	30.36	28.04	25.97	24.12	22.45	20.96	19.61	18.39	17.29	16.29	31
32	31.97	29.52	27.33	25.36	23.60	22.01	20.58	19.28	18.11	17.05	16.08	32
33	30.99	28.68	26.61	24.75	23.07	21.56	20.19	18.95	17.83	16.80	15.87	33
34	30.01	27.84	25.89	24.13	22.54	21.10	19.79	18.61	17.53	16.55	15.65	34
35	29.02	26.99	25.16	23.50	21.99	20.63	19.39	18.26	17.22	16.28	15.42	35
36	28.04	26.14	24.42	22.86	21.44	20.14	18.97	17.89	16.90	16.00	15.17	36
37	27.06	25.29	23.68	22.21	20.87	19.65	18.53	17.51	16.57	15.71	14.92	37
38	26.09	24.43	22.93	21.55	20.30	19.15	18.09	17.12	16.23	15.41	14.65	38
39	25.11	23.58	22.17	20.89	19.71	18.63	17.63	16.72	15.87	15.09	14.37	39
40	24.13	22.71	21.41	20.22	19.11	18.10	17.17	16.30	15.50	14.77	14.08	40
41	23.16	21.85	20.64	19.53	18.51	17.56	16.68	15.87	15.12	14.42	13.78	41
42	22.19	20.98	19.87	18.84	17.89	17.01	16.19	15.43	14.72	14.07	13.46	42
43	21.21	20.11	19.09	18.14	17.26	16.44	15.68	14.97	14.31	13.70	13.12	43
44	20.24	19.24	18.30	17.43	16.62	15.86	15.16	14.50	13.89	13.31	12.77	44
45	19.27	18.36	17.51	16.71	15.97	15.27	14.62	14.01	13.44	12.91	12.41	45
46	18.31	17.48	16.71	15.98	15.31	14.67	14.07	13.51	12.99	12.49	12.02	46
47	17.34	16.60	15.90	15.25	14.63	14.05	13.51	12.99	12.51	12.05	11.62	47
48	16.38	15.72	15.09	14.50	13.95	13.42	12.93	12.46	12.02	11.60	11.21	48
49	15.42	14.83	14.27	13.75	13.25	12.78	12.33	11.91	11.51	11.13	10.77	49
50	14.46	13.94	13.45	12.98	12.54	12.12	11.72	11.34	10.98	10.64	10.31	50
51	13.50	13.05	12.61	12.20	11.81	11.44	11.09	10.75	10.43	10.12	9.83	51
52	12.54	12.15	11.78	11.42	11.08	10.75	10.44	10.15	9.86	9.59	9.33	52
53	11.58	11.25	10.93	10.62	10.33	10.05	9.78	9.52	9.27	9.03	8.81	53
54	10.63	10.35	10.07	9.81	9.56	9.32	9.09	8.87	8.66	8.45	8.25	54
55	9.67	9.44	9.21	8.99	8.79	8.58	8.39	8.20	8.02	7.85	7.68	55
56	8.72	8.52	8.34	8.16	7.99	7.83	7.66	7.51	7.36	7.21	7.07	56
57	7.76	7.61	7.46	7.32	7.18	7.05	6.92	6.79	6.67	6.55	6.44	57
58	6.80	6.69	6.57	6.46	6.36	6.25	6.15	6.05	5.96	5.86	5.77	58
59	5.84	5.76	5.67	5.59	5.51	5.44	5.36	5.29	5.21	5.14	5.07	59
60	4.88	4.82	4.77	4.71	4.65	4.60	4.54	4.49	4.44	4.39	4.34	60
61	3.92	3.88	3.84	3.81	3.77	3.73	3.70	3.66	3.63	3.60	3.56	61
62	2.95	2.93	2.91	2.89	2.87	2.85	2.83	2.81	2.79	2.77	2.75	62
63	1.98	1.97	1.96	1.95	1.94	1.93	1.92	1.91	1.90	1.89	1.88	63
64	0.99	0.99	0.99	0.99	0.98	0.98	0.98	0.98	0.97	0.97	0.97	64

Table 9 Multipliers for loss of earnings to pension age 70 (males)

Age at date of trial	Multiplier calculated with allowance for population mortality and rate of return of											Age at date of trial
	0.0%	0.5%	1.0%	1.5%	2.0%	2.5%	3.0%	£3.5%	4.0%	4.5%	5.0%	
16	50.58	44.57	39.53	35.28	31.67	28.60	25.96	23.69	21.73	20.02	18.53	16
17	49.60	43.82	38.94	34.82	31.31	28.31	25.74	23.52	21.59	19.91	18.44	17
18	48.64	43.07	38.36	34.36	30.95	28.03	25.52	23.34	21.45	19.80	18.36	18
19	47.68	42.32	37.77	33.90	30.59	27.74	25.29	23.16	21.31	19.69	18.26	19
20	46.72	41.56	37.17	33.43	30.21	27.45	25.05	22.97	21.16	19.57	18.17	20
21	45.76	40.80	36.57	32.95	29.83	27.14	24.81	22.78	21.00	19.44	18.07	21
22	44.80	40.04	35.96	32.46	29.45	26.83	24.56	22.58	20.84	19.31	17.96	22
23	43.84	39.27	35.35	31.97	29.05	26.52	24.31	22.37	20.67	19.18	17.85	23
24	42.88	38.50	34.73	31.47	28.65	26.19	24.04	22.16	20.50	19.04	17.74	24
25	41.92	37.72	34.10	30.97	28.24	25.86	23.77	21.94	20.32	18.89	17.61	25
26	40.95	36.94	33.47	30.45	27.82	25.51	23.49	21.71	20.13	18.73	17.49	26
27	39.98	36.15	32.83	29.92	27.39	25.16	23.20	21.47	19.93	18.57	17.35	27
28	39.02	35.36	32.18	29.39	26.95	24.80	22.90	21.22	19.73	18.40	17.21	28
29	38.05	34.57	31.52	28.85	26.50	24.43	22.59	20.96	19.51	18.22	17.06	29
30	37.09	33.77	30.86	28.30	26.04	24.05	22.28	20.70	19.29	18.03	16.90	30
31	36.12	32.97	30.19	27.74	25.58	23.66	21.95	20.42	19.06	17.84	16.74	31
32	35.15	32.16	29.52	27.18	25.10	23.26	21.61	20.14	18.82	17.64	16.57	32
33	34.19	31.35	28.83	26.60	24.62	22.85	21.27	19.85	18.57	17.42	16.39	33
34	33.22	30.53	28.15	26.02	24.13	22.43	20.91	19.55	18.32	17.20	16.20	34
35	32.25	29.71	27.45	25.43	23.63	22.00	20.55	19.23	18.05	16.97	16.00	35
36	31.29	28.90	26.75	24.84	23.12	21.57	20.17	18.91	17.77	16.74	15.79	36
37	30.33	28.07	26.05	24.23	22.60	21.12	19.79	18.58	17.48	16.49	15.58	37
38	29.37	27.25	25.34	23.62	22.07	20.67	19.40	18.24	17.19	16.23	15.36	38
39	28.41	26.42	24.63	23.00	21.54	20.20	18.99	17.89	16.88	15.96	15.12	39
40	27.46	25.60	23.91	22.38	20.99	19.73	18.58	17.53	16.57	15.69	14.88	40
41	26.51	24.76	23.18	21.75	20.44	19.24	18.15	17.15	16.24	15.40	14.62	41
42	25.55	23.93	22.45	21.10	19.87	18.75	17.71	16.77	15.90	15.10	14.36	42
43	24.61	23.10	21.72	20.46	19.30	18.24	17.27	16.37	15.55	14.78	14.08	43
44	23.66	22.26	20.98	19.80	18.72	17.72	16.81	15.96	15.18	14.46	13.79	44
45	22.71	21.42	20.23	19.14	18.13	17.20	16.34	15.54	14.81	14.12	13.49	45
46	21.77	20.58	19.48	18.47	17.53	16.66	15.86	15.11	14.42	13.77	13.17	46
47	20.84	19.74	18.73	17.79	16.92	16.11	15.36	14.67	14.02	13.41	12.85	47
48	19.90	18.90	17.97	17.11	16.30	15.56	14.86	14.21	13.61	13.04	12.51	48
49	18.98	18.06	17.21	16.42	15.68	14.99	14.35	13.74	13.18	12.65	12.16	49
50	18.05	17.22	16.45	15.73	15.05	14.42	13.82	13.27	12.74	12.25	11.79	50
51	17.14	16.39	15.68	15.03	14.41	13.83	13.29	12.77	12.29	11.84	11.41	51
52	16.22	15.55	14.92	14.32	13.76	13.23	12.74	12.27	11.83	11.41	11.02	52
53	15.31	14.71	14.14	13.61	13.11	12.63	12.18	11.75	11.35	10.97	10.61	53
54	14.41	13.87	13.37	12.89	12.44	12.01	11.61	11.22	10.86	10.51	10.18	54
55	13.51	13.04	12.59	12.17	11.77	11.39	11.02	10.68	10.35	10.04	9.74	55
56	12.61	12.20	11.81	11.44	11.08	10.75	10.42	10.12	9.82	9.54	9.28	56
57	11.72	11.37	11.03	10.70	10.39	10.10	9.81	9.54	9.28	9.04	8.80	57
58	10.83	10.53	10.24	9.96	9.69	9.44	9.19	8.95	8.73	8.51	8.30	58
59	9.95	9.69	9.45	9.21	8.98	8.76	8.55	8.35	8.15	7.97	7.78	59
60	9.07	8.86	8.65	8.45	8.26	8.08	7.90	7.73	7.56	7.40	7.25	60
61	8.19	8.02	7.85	7.68	7.53	7.37	7.23	7.08	6.95	6.81	6.68	61
62	7.31	7.17	7.04	6.91	6.78	6.66	6.54	6.42	6.31	6.20	6.10	62
63	6.43	6.33	6.22	6.12	6.02	5.92	5.83	5.74	5.65	5.56	5.48	63
64	5.55	5.47	5.39	5.32	5.24	5.17	5.10	5.03	4.96	4.90	4.83	64
65	4.67	4.61	4.55	4.50	4.45	4.40	4.35	4.30	4.25	4.20	4.15	65
66	3.77	3.73	3.70	3.66	3.63	3.59	3.56	3.53	3.49	3.46	3.43	66
67	2.86	2.84	2.82	2.80	2.78	2.76	2.74	2.72	2.70	2.68	2.66	67
68	1.93	1.92	1.91	1.91	1.90	1.89	1.88	1.87	1.86	1.85	1.84	68
69	0.98	0.98	0.98	0.97	0.97	0.97	0.97	0.97	0.96	0.96	0.96	69

Table 10   Multipliers for loss of earnings to pension age 70 (females)

Age at date of trial	Multiplier calculated with allowance for population mortality and rate of return of											Age at date of trial
	0.0%	0.5%	1.0%	1.5%	2.0%	2.5%	3.0%	£3.5%	4.0%	4.5%	5.0%	
16	51.98	45.71	40.46	36.04	32.30	29.12	26.40	24.06	22.04	20.28	18.75	16
17	50.99	44.95	39.87	35.59	31.95	28.84	26.18	23.89	21.90	20.18	18.67	17
18	50.01	44.19	39.28	35.12	31.58	28.56	25.96	23.71	21.77	20.07	18.59	18
19	49.03	43.42	38.68	34.65	31.22	28.27	25.73	23.53	21.62	19.96	18.50	19
20	48.04	42.65	38.08	34.18	30.84	27.97	25.50	23.35	21.48	19.84	18.40	20
21	47.06	41.87	37.46	33.69	30.46	27.67	25.25	23.16	21.32	19.72	18.30	21
22	46.07	41.09	36.84	33.20	30.07	27.36	25.00	22.96	21.16	19.59	18.20	22
23	45.09	40.31	36.22	32.70	29.67	27.04	24.75	22.75	21.00	19.45	18.09	23
24	44.10	39.52	35.59	32.20	29.26	26.71	24.48	22.54	20.82	19.31	17.98	24
25	43.11	38.73	34.95	31.68	28.85	26.37	24.21	22.31	20.64	19.17	17.86	25
26	42.13	37.93	34.31	31.16	28.42	26.03	23.93	22.09	20.46	19.01	17.73	26
27	41.14	37.13	33.66	30.63	27.99	25.68	23.64	21.85	20.26	18.85	17.60	27
28	40.16	36.33	33.00	30.10	27.55	25.32	23.35	21.60	20.06	18.69	17.46	28
29	39.17	35.52	32.34	29.55	27.10	24.95	23.04	21.35	19.85	18.51	17.32	29
30	38.19	34.71	31.67	29.00	26.65	24.57	22.73	21.09	19.63	18.33	17.16	30
31	37.21	33.90	31.00	28.44	26.18	24.18	22.40	20.82	19.41	18.14	17.00	31
32	36.22	33.08	30.32	27.87	25.71	23.78	22.07	20.54	19.17	17.94	16.84	32
33	35.24	32.26	29.63	27.30	25.22	23.38	21.73	20.25	18.93	17.74	16.66	33
34	34.26	31.44	28.94	26.71	24.73	22.96	21.38	19.96	18.68	17.52	16.48	34
35	33.28	30.61	28.24	26.12	24.23	22.54	21.02	19.65	18.42	17.30	16.29	35
36	32.30	29.78	27.54	25.53	23.72	22.11	20.65	19.33	18.15	17.07	16.09	36
37	31.33	28.95	26.83	24.92	23.21	21.66	20.27	19.01	17.87	16.83	15.88	37
38	30.35	28.12	26.11	24.31	22.68	21.21	19.88	18.67	17.58	16.58	15.67	38
39	29.38	27.28	25.39	23.69	22.14	20.75	19.48	18.33	17.27	16.32	15.44	39
40	28.41	26.44	24.67	23.06	21.60	20.27	19.07	17.97	16.96	16.04	15.20	40
41	27.44	25.60	23.93	22.42	21.04	19.79	18.64	17.60	16.64	15.76	14.95	41
42	26.47	24.75	23.20	21.77	20.48	19.29	18.21	17.22	16.31	15.47	14.70	42
43	25.50	23.91	22.45	21.12	19.90	18.79	17.77	16.82	15.96	15.16	14.42	43
44	24.54	23.06	21.70	20.46	19.32	18.27	17.31	16.42	15.60	14.84	14.14	44
45	23.58	22.21	20.95	19.79	18.73	17.75	16.84	16.00	15.23	14.51	13.85	45
46	22.62	21.35	20.19	19.12	18.12	17.21	16.36	15.57	14.85	14.17	13.54	46
47	21.66	20.50	19.43	18.43	17.51	16.66	15.87	15.13	14.45	13.81	13.22	47
48	20.71	19.64	18.66	17.74	16.89	16.10	15.36	14.68	14.04	13.44	12.88	48
49	19.76	18.79	17.88	17.04	16.26	15.53	14.85	14.21	13.62	13.06	12.54	49
50	18.81	17.93	17.10	16.34	15.62	14.95	14.32	13.73	13.18	12.66	12.17	50
51	17.86	17.07	16.32	15.62	14.97	14.35	13.77	13.23	12.72	12.24	11.79	51
52	16.92	16.20	15.53	14.90	14.30	13.74	13.22	12.72	12.25	11.81	11.39	52
53	15.98	15.34	14.73	14.17	13.63	13.12	12.65	12.19	11.77	11.36	10.98	53
54	15.04	14.47	13.93	13.43	12.94	12.49	12.06	11.65	11.26	10.90	10.55	54
55	14.10	13.60	13.13	12.68	12.25	11.84	11.46	11.09	10.74	10.41	10.10	55
56	13.17	12.73	12.31	11.92	11.54	11.18	10.84	10.51	10.20	9.91	9.62	56
57	12.23	11.86	11.49	11.15	10.82	10.51	10.21	9.92	9.65	9.38	9.13	57
58	11.30	10.98	10.67	10.37	10.09	9.82	9.56	9.31	9.07	8.84	8.62	58
59	10.38	10.10	9.84	9.59	9.35	9.11	8.89	8.68	8.47	8.27	8.08	59
60	9.45	9.22	9.00	8.79	8.59	8.40	8.21	8.03	7.85	7.68	7.52	60
61	8.52	8.34	8.16	7.99	7.82	7.66	7.51	7.35	7.21	7.07	6.93	61
62	7.60	7.45	7.31	7.17	7.04	6.91	6.78	6.66	6.54	6.43	6.31	62
63	6.67	6.56	6.45	6.34	6.24	6.14	6.04	5.94	5.85	5.76	5.67	63
64	5.74	5.66	5.58	5.50	5.42	5.34	5.27	5.20	5.13	5.06	4.99	64
65	4.81	4.75	4.69	4.64	4.58	4.53	4.47	4.42	4.37	4.32	4.27	65
66	3.87	3.83	3.79	3.76	3.72	3.69	3.65	3.62	3.58	3.55	3.52	66
67	2.92	2.90	2.88	2.86	2.84	2.82	2.80	2.78	2.76	2.74	2.72	67
68	1.96	1.95	1.94	1.93	1.92	1.92	1.91	1.90	1.89	1.88	1.87	68
69	0.99	0.99	0.99	0.98	0.98	0.98	0.98	0.97	0.97	0.97	0.97	69

Table 11 Multipliers for loss of pension commencing age 55 (males)

Age at date of trial	Multiplier calculated with allowance for population mortality and rate of return of											Age at date of trial
	0.0%	0.5%	1.0%	1.5%	2.0%	2.5%	3.0%	£3.5%	4.0%	4.5%	5.0%	
0	19.94	14.21	10.17	7.30	5.26	3.80	2.76	2.00	1.46	1.07	0.79	0
1	20.10	14.40	10.35	7.47	5.41	3.93	2.86	2.09	1.53	1.13	0.83	1
2	20.11	14.48	10.46	7.59	5.52	4.03	2.95	2.17	1.60	1.18	0.87	2
3	20.12	14.56	10.57	7.70	5.63	4.13	3.04	2.24	1.66	1.23	0.92	3
4	20.13	14.63	10.68	7.82	5.74	4.23	3.13	2.32	1.73	1.29	0.96	4
5	20.13	14.71	10.79	7.94	5.86	4.34	3.23	2.40	1.80	1.35	1.01	5
6	20.14	14.79	10.90	8.06	5.98	4.45	3.32	2.49	1.87	1.41	1.06	6
7	20.14	14.87	11.01	8.18	6.10	4.56	3.42	2.58	1.94	1.47	1.12	7
8	20.14	14.94	11.12	8.31	6.22	4.68	3.53	2.67	2.02	1.54	1.17	8
9	20.15	15.02	11.24	8.43	6.35	4.80	3.63	2.76	2.10	1.61	1.23	9
10	20.15	15.10	11.35	8.56	6.48	4.92	3.74	2.86	2.19	1.68	1.29	10
11	20.15	15.18	11.47	8.69	6.61	5.04	3.86	2.96	2.28	1.76	1.36	11
12	20.16	15.25	11.58	8.82	6.74	5.17	3.97	3.06	2.37	1.84	1.43	12
13	20.16	15.33	11.70	8.96	6.88	5.30	4.09	3.17	2.46	1.92	1.50	13
14	20.17	15.41	11.82	9.09	7.02	5.43	4.22	3.28	2.56	2.00	1.57	14
15	20.17	15.50	11.94	9.23	7.16	5.57	4.34	3.40	2.66	2.10	1.65	15
16	20.18	15.58	12.07	9.37	7.31	5.71	4.48	3.52	2.77	2.19	1.74	16
17	20.19	15.67	12.19	9.52	7.46	5.86	4.61	3.64	2.88	2.29	1.82	17
18	20.21	15.76	12.32	9.67	7.61	6.01	4.75	3.77	3.00	2.40	1.92	18
19	20.22	15.85	12.46	9.82	7.77	6.16	4.90	3.91	3.13	2.51	2.01	19
20	20.24	15.94	12.59	9.98	7.93	6.32	5.05	4.05	3.25	2.62	2.12	20
21	20.26	16.03	12.73	10.14	8.10	6.49	5.21	4.19	3.39	2.74	2.22	21
22	20.27	16.13	12.87	10.30	8.27	6.65	5.37	4.34	3.52	2.87	2.34	22
23	20.29	16.22	13.01	10.46	8.44	6.83	5.54	4.50	3.67	3.00	2.46	23
24	20.31	16.32	13.15	10.63	8.62	7.00	5.71	4.66	3.82	3.14	2.58	24
25	20.33	16.41	13.29	10.80	8.80	7.18	5.88	4.83	3.98	3.28	2.71	25
26	20.35	16.51	13.44	10.97	8.98	7.37	6.06	5.00	4.14	3.43	2.85	26
27	20.36	16.61	13.58	11.14	9.17	7.56	6.25	5.18	4.31	3.59	3.00	27
28	20.38	16.70	13.73	11.32	9.36	7.76	6.44	5.37	4.48	3.75	3.15	28
29	20.40	16.80	13.88	11.50	9.55	7.96	6.64	5.56	4.67	3.92	3.31	29
30	20.42	16.90	14.03	11.68	9.75	8.16	6.85	5.76	4.86	4.10	3.48	30
31	20.44	17.00	14.19	11.87	9.96	8.37	7.06	5.97	5.06	4.29	3.65	31
32	20.45	17.10	14.34	12.06	10.17	8.59	7.28	6.18	5.26	4.49	3.84	32
33	20.47	17.21	14.50	12.25	10.38	8.82	7.51	6.41	5.48	4.70	4.04	33
34	20.49	17.31	14.66	12.45	10.60	9.04	7.74	6.64	5.70	4.91	4.24	34
35	20.52	17.41	14.82	12.65	10.82	9.28	7.98	6.88	5.94	5.14	4.46	35
36	20.54	17.52	14.99	12.85	11.05	9.52	8.23	7.13	6.18	5.38	4.69	36
37	20.57	17.63	15.16	13.06	11.29	9.77	8.49	7.38	6.44	5.63	4.93	37
38	20.60	17.74	15.33	13.28	11.53	10.03	8.75	7.65	6.71	5.89	5.18	38
39	20.63	17.86	15.50	13.49	11.77	10.30	9.03	7.93	6.98	6.16	5.45	39
40	20.66	17.98	15.68	13.72	12.03	10.57	9.31	8.22	7.28	6.45	5.73	40
41	20.69	18.10	15.87	13.95	12.29	10.86	9.61	8.53	7.58	6.75	6.03	41
42	20.73	18.22	16.06	14.18	12.56	11.15	9.92	8.84	7.90	7.07	6.34	42
43	20.78	18.35	16.25	14.43	12.84	11.45	10.24	9.17	8.23	7.40	6.67	43
44	20.82	18.48	16.45	14.67	13.12	11.76	10.57	9.51	8.58	7.75	7.02	44
45	20.87	18.62	16.65	14.93	13.42	12.09	10.91	9.87	8.94	8.12	7.39	45
46	20.93	18.76	16.87	15.20	13.72	12.42	11.27	10.24	9.33	8.51	7.78	46
47	20.99	18.91	17.08	15.47	14.04	12.77	11.64	10.63	9.73	8.92	8.19	47
48	21.06	19.07	17.31	15.75	14.37	13.13	12.03	11.04	10.15	9.35	8.63	48
49	21.14	19.24	17.55	16.05	14.71	13.51	12.43	11.47	10.60	9.81	9.09	49
50	21.23	19.41	17.80	16.36	15.07	13.91	12.86	11.92	11.06	10.29	9.59	50
51	21.32	19.60	18.06	16.68	15.44	14.32	13.31	12.39	11.56	10.80	10.12	51
52	21.44	19.80	18.34	17.02	15.83	14.75	13.78	12.89	12.09	11.35	10.68	52
53	21.56	20.02	18.63	17.38	16.24	15.21	14.27	13.42	12.64	11.93	11.28	53
54	21.70	20.25	18.94	17.75	16.67	15.69	14.80	13.98	13.23	12.55	11.92	54
55	21.86	20.50	19.26	18.15	17.13	16.20	15.35	14.57	13.86	13.21	12.60	55

Table 12 Multipliers for loss of pension commencing age 55 (females)

Age at date of trial	Multiplier calculated with allowance for population mortality and rate of return of											Age at date of trial
	0.0%	0.5%	1.0%	1.5%	2.0%	2.5%	3.0%	£3.5%	4.0%	4.5%	5.0%	
0	24.92	17.58	12.46	8.86	6.33	4.54	3.26	2.36	1.71	1.24	0.91	0
1	25.07	17.78	12.66	9.05	6.50	4.68	3.38	2.46	1.79	1.31	0.96	1
2	25.09	17.88	12.79	9.19	6.63	4.80	3.49	2.54	1.86	1.37	1.01	2
3	25.10	17.97	12.93	9.33	6.76	4.92	3.59	2.63	1.94	1.43	1.06	3
4	25.10	18.07	13.06	9.47	6.90	5.05	3.70	2.73	2.01	1.49	1.11	4
5	25.11	18.16	13.19	9.62	7.04	5.17	3.81	2.82	2.09	1.56	1.17	5
6	25.11	18.25	13.32	9.76	7.18	5.30	3.93	2.92	2.18	1.63	1.22	6
7	25.11	18.35	13.46	9.91	7.33	5.44	4.05	3.02	2.27	1.70	1.29	7
8	25.12	18.44	13.60	10.06	7.47	5.57	4.17	3.13	2.36	1.78	1.35	8
9	25.12	18.54	13.73	10.21	7.62	5.71	4.29	3.24	2.45	1.86	1.42	9
10	25.12	18.63	13.87	10.37	7.78	5.86	4.42	3.35	2.55	1.95	1.49	10
11	25.13	18.73	14.01	10.53	7.94	6.00	4.56	3.47	2.65	2.03	1.56	11
12	25.13	18.82	14.16	10.69	8.09	6.15	4.69	3.59	2.76	2.13	1.64	12
13	25.13	18.92	14.30	10.85	8.26	6.31	4.84	3.72	2.87	2.22	1.72	13
14	25.14	19.02	14.44	11.01	8.42	6.47	4.98	3.85	2.99	2.32	1.81	14
15	25.14	19.12	14.59	11.18	8.59	6.63	5.13	3.99	3.11	2.43	1.90	15
16	25.15	19.22	14.74	11.35	8.77	6.80	5.29	4.13	3.23	2.54	2.00	16
17	25.15	19.32	14.89	11.52	8.95	6.97	5.45	4.27	3.36	2.65	2.10	17
18	25.16	19.42	15.05	11.70	9.13	7.15	5.61	4.42	3.50	2.77	2.20	18
19	25.17	19.52	15.20	11.88	9.31	7.33	5.78	4.58	3.64	2.90	2.31	19
20	25.18	19.63	15.36	12.06	9.50	7.51	5.96	4.74	3.78	3.03	2.43	20
21	25.19	19.73	15.52	12.24	9.70	7.70	6.14	4.91	3.94	3.17	2.55	21
22	25.19	19.84	15.68	12.43	9.89	7.90	6.33	5.08	4.09	3.31	2.68	22
23	25.20	19.94	15.84	12.62	10.09	8.10	6.52	5.26	4.26	3.46	2.82	23
24	25.21	20.05	16.00	12.82	10.30	8.30	6.72	5.45	4.43	3.62	2.96	24
25	25.22	20.16	16.17	13.01	10.51	8.51	6.92	5.64	4.61	3.78	3.11	25
26	25.23	20.26	16.33	13.21	10.72	8.73	7.13	5.84	4.80	3.95	3.26	26
27	25.24	20.37	16.50	13.42	10.94	8.95	7.35	6.05	4.99	4.13	3.43	27
28	25.25	20.48	16.67	13.62	11.16	9.18	7.57	6.26	5.19	4.32	3.60	28
29	25.26	20.59	16.85	13.83	11.39	9.41	7.80	6.48	5.40	4.51	3.78	29
30	25.27	20.70	17.02	14.04	11.62	9.65	8.04	6.71	5.62	4.72	3.97	30
31	25.28	20.82	17.20	14.26	11.86	9.90	8.28	6.95	5.85	4.93	4.17	31
32	25.29	20.93	17.38	14.48	12.10	10.15	8.53	7.20	6.08	5.16	4.38	32
33	25.30	21.05	17.56	14.71	12.35	10.41	8.79	7.45	6.33	5.39	4.61	33
34	25.32	21.16	17.75	14.94	12.61	10.67	9.06	7.72	6.59	5.64	4.84	34
35	25.33	21.28	17.94	15.17	12.87	10.95	9.34	7.99	6.86	5.90	5.08	35
36	25.35	21.40	18.13	15.41	13.13	11.23	9.63	8.28	7.13	6.17	5.34	36
37	25.37	21.53	18.33	15.65	13.41	11.52	9.92	8.57	7.43	6.45	5.61	37
38	25.39	21.65	18.52	15.90	13.69	11.82	10.23	8.88	7.73	6.74	5.90	38
39	25.41	21.78	18.73	16.15	13.97	12.12	10.55	9.20	8.05	7.05	6.20	39
40	25.44	21.91	18.93	16.41	14.27	12.44	10.87	9.53	8.38	7.38	6.52	40
41	25.46	22.04	19.14	16.67	14.57	12.76	11.21	9.87	8.72	7.72	6.85	41
42	25.49	22.18	19.36	16.94	14.87	13.10	11.56	10.23	9.08	8.08	7.20	42
43	25.53	22.32	19.57	17.22	15.19	13.44	11.92	10.60	9.45	8.45	7.57	43
44	25.56	22.46	19.80	17.50	15.52	13.80	12.30	10.99	9.85	8.84	7.96	44
45	25.60	22.61	20.03	17.79	15.85	14.16	12.69	11.39	10.26	9.25	8.37	45
46	25.65	22.76	20.26	18.09	16.20	14.54	13.09	11.81	10.69	9.69	8.80	46
47	25.70	22.92	20.51	18.40	16.56	14.94	13.51	12.25	11.14	10.14	9.26	47
48	25.76	23.09	20.76	18.72	16.92	15.34	13.95	12.71	11.61	10.62	9.75	48
49	25.82	23.26	21.02	19.04	17.30	15.76	14.40	13.18	12.10	11.13	10.26	49
50	25.89	23.44	21.28	19.38	17.70	16.20	14.87	13.68	12.62	11.66	10.80	50
51	25.96	23.62	21.56	19.73	18.10	16.66	15.36	14.20	13.16	12.22	11.37	51
52	26.05	23.82	21.85	20.09	18.53	17.13	15.87	14.75	13.73	12.81	11.98	52
53	26.14	24.03	22.14	20.47	18.96	17.62	16.41	15.32	14.33	13.44	12.63	53
54	26.24	24.24	22.45	20.85	19.42	18.13	16.97	15.92	14.96	14.10	13.31	54
55	26.36	24.47	22.77	21.26	19.89	18.66	17.55	16.54	15.63	14.80	14.03	55

Table 13   Multipliers for loss of pension commencing age 60 (males)

Age at date of trial	Multiplier calculated with allowance for population mortality and rate of return of											Age at date of trial
	0.0%	0.5%	1.0%	1.5%	2.0%	2.5%	3.0%	£3.5%	4.0%	4.5%	5.0%	
0	15.48	10.86	7.65	5.40	3.83	2.72	1.94	1.39	0.99	0.71	0.51	0
1	15.61	11.01	7.79	5.53	3.94	2.81	2.01	1.45	1.04	0.75	0.55	1
2	15.61	11.07	7.87	5.62	4.02	2.88	2.08	1.50	1.08	0.79	0.57	2
3	15.62	11.13	7.95	5.70	4.10	2.96	2.14	1.55	1.13	0.82	0.60	3
4	15.63	11.19	8.04	5.79	4.18	3.03	2.20	1.61	1.17	0.86	0.63	4
5	15.63	11.25	8.12	5.88	4.27	3.11	2.27	1.66	1.22	0.90	0.66	5
6	15.63	11.31	8.20	5.97	4.35	3.19	2.34	1.72	1.27	0.94	0.70	6
7	15.64	11.36	8.28	6.06	4.44	3.27	2.41	1.78	1.32	0.98	0.73	7
8	15.64	11.42	8.37	6.15	4.53	3.35	2.48	1.84	1.37	1.03	0.77	8
9	15.64	11.48	8.45	6.24	4.62	3.43	2.56	1.91	1.43	1.07	0.81	9
10	15.64	11.54	8.54	6.34	4.72	3.52	2.63	1.98	1.49	1.12	0.85	10
11	15.65	11.60	8.63	6.43	4.81	3.61	2.71	2.05	1.55	1.17	0.89	11
12	15.65	11.66	8.72	6.53	4.91	3.70	2.80	2.12	1.61	1.22	0.93	12
13	15.65	11.72	8.80	6.63	5.01	3.79	2.88	2.19	1.67	1.28	0.98	13
14	15.66	11.78	8.89	6.73	5.11	3.89	2.97	2.27	1.74	1.34	1.03	14
15	15.66	11.85	8.99	6.84	5.21	3.99	3.06	2.35	1.81	1.40	1.08	15
16	15.67	11.91	9.08	6.94	5.32	4.09	3.15	2.43	1.88	1.46	1.14	16
17	15.68	11.98	9.18	7.05	5.43	4.19	3.25	2.52	1.96	1.53	1.20	17
18	15.69	12.04	9.27	7.16	5.54	4.30	3.35	2.61	2.04	1.60	1.26	18
19	15.70	12.12	9.37	7.27	5.66	4.41	3.45	2.70	2.12	1.67	1.32	19
20	15.71	12.19	9.48	7.39	5.78	4.53	3.56	2.80	2.21	1.75	1.39	20
21	15.73	12.26	9.58	7.51	5.90	4.64	3.67	2.90	2.30	1.83	1.46	21
22	15.74	12.33	9.68	7.63	6.02	4.76	3.78	3.01	2.40	1.91	1.53	22
23	15.76	12.40	9.79	7.75	6.15	4.89	3.90	3.11	2.49	2.00	1.61	23
24	15.77	12.48	9.90	7.87	6.27	5.01	4.02	3.23	2.60	2.09	1.69	24
25	15.78	12.55	10.00	7.99	6.41	5.14	4.14	3.34	2.70	2.19	1.78	25
26	15.80	12.62	10.11	8.12	6.54	5.28	4.27	3.46	2.81	2.29	1.87	26
27	15.81	12.70	10.22	8.25	6.68	5.41	4.40	3.59	2.93	2.39	1.96	27
28	15.82	12.77	10.33	8.38	6.81	5.55	4.54	3.71	3.05	2.50	2.06	28
29	15.84	12.85	10.45	8.51	6.96	5.70	4.68	3.85	3.17	2.62	2.17	29
30	15.85	12.92	10.56	8.65	7.10	5.85	4.82	3.99	3.30	2.74	2.28	30
31	15.87	13.00	10.67	8.79	7.25	6.00	4.97	4.13	3.44	2.87	2.39	31
32	15.88	13.07	10.79	8.93	7.40	6.15	5.12	4.28	3.58	3.00	2.52	32
33	15.90	13.15	10.91	9.07	7.56	6.31	5.28	4.43	3.72	3.14	2.65	33
34	15.91	13.23	11.03	9.22	7.72	6.48	5.45	4.59	3.88	3.28	2.78	34
35	15.93	13.31	11.15	9.36	7.88	6.65	5.62	4.76	4.04	3.43	2.92	35
36	15.95	13.39	11.28	9.52	8.05	6.82	5.79	4.93	4.20	3.59	3.07	36
37	15.97	13.48	11.40	9.67	8.22	7.00	5.97	5.11	4.38	3.76	3.23	37
38	15.99	13.56	11.53	9.83	8.39	7.18	6.16	5.29	4.56	3.93	3.40	38
39	16.01	13.65	11.67	9.99	8.57	7.37	6.36	5.49	4.75	4.11	3.57	39
40	16.04	13.74	11.80	10.16	8.76	7.57	6.56	5.69	4.94	4.31	3.76	40
41	16.07	13.84	11.94	10.33	8.95	7.77	6.76	5.90	5.15	4.51	3.95	41
42	16.10	13.93	12.08	10.50	9.15	7.98	6.98	6.12	5.37	4.72	4.16	42
43	16.13	14.03	12.23	10.68	9.35	8.20	7.20	6.34	5.59	4.94	4.37	43
44	16.17	14.13	12.38	10.87	9.56	8.42	7.44	6.58	5.83	5.17	4.60	44
45	16.20	14.23	12.53	11.05	9.77	8.65	7.68	6.83	6.08	5.42	4.84	45
46	16.25	14.34	12.69	11.25	9.99	8.89	7.93	7.08	6.34	5.68	5.10	46
47	16.30	14.46	12.86	11.45	10.22	9.14	8.19	7.35	6.61	5.95	5.37	47
48	16.35	14.58	13.03	11.66	10.46	9.40	8.47	7.64	6.90	6.24	5.66	48
49	16.41	14.71	13.21	11.88	10.71	9.67	8.75	7.93	7.20	6.55	5.96	49
50	16.48	14.84	13.39	12.11	10.97	9.96	9.05	8.24	7.52	6.87	6.29	50
51	16.56	14.99	13.59	12.35	11.24	10.25	9.37	8.57	7.86	7.21	6.63	51
52	16.64	15.14	13.80	12.60	11.53	10.56	9.70	8.92	8.21	7.58	7.00	52
53	16.74	15.30	14.02	12.86	11.83	10.89	10.05	9.28	8.59	7.96	7.39	53
54	16.85	15.48	14.25	13.14	12.14	11.24	10.42	9.67	8.99	8.38	7.81	54
55	16.97	15.67	14.50	13.43	12.47	11.60	10.81	10.08	9.42	8.82	8.26	55
56	17.10	15.87	14.76	13.75	12.82	11.99	11.22	10.52	9.88	9.29	8.74	56
57	17.26	16.10	15.04	14.08	13.20	12.40	11.66	10.98	10.36	9.79	9.26	57
58	17.43	16.34	15.34	14.43	13.60	12.83	12.13	11.48	10.89	10.33	9.82	58
59	17.63	16.61	15.67	14.81	14.03	13.30	12.63	12.02	11.45	10.92	10.43	59
60	17.85	16.90	16.03	15.22	14.49	13.81	13.18	12.60	12.06	11.56	11.09	60

Table 14 Multipliers for loss of pension commencing age 60 (females)

Age at date of trial	Multiplier calculated with allowance for population mortality and rate of return of											Age at date of trial
	0.0%	0.5%	1.0%	1.5%	2.0%	2.5%	3.0%	£3.5%	4.0%	4.5%	5.0%	
0	20.25	14.08	9.82	6.88	4.83	3.41	2.41	1.71	1.22	0.87	0.62	0
1	20.38	14.24	9.98	7.03	4.96	3.52	2.50	1.78	1.28	0.92	0.66	1
2	20.39	14.32	10.09	7.14	5.06	3.61	2.58	1.85	1.33	0.96	0.69	2
3	20.40	14.39	10.19	7.25	5.17	3.70	2.65	1.91	1.38	1.00	0.73	3
4	20.40	14.47	10.30	7.36	5.27	3.79	2.73	1.98	1.44	1.05	0.76	4
5	20.41	14.54	10.40	7.47	5.38	3.89	2.82	2.05	1.49	1.09	0.80	5
6	20.41	14.62	10.51	7.58	5.49	3.98	2.90	2.12	1.55	1.14	0.84	6
7	20.41	14.69	10.62	7.70	5.60	4.08	2.99	2.20	1.62	1.19	0.88	7
8	20.42	14.77	10.72	7.81	5.71	4.19	3.08	2.27	1.68	1.25	0.93	8
9	20.42	14.85	10.83	7.93	5.82	4.29	3.17	2.35	1.75	1.30	0.98	9
10	20.42	14.92	10.94	8.05	5.94	4.40	3.27	2.43	1.82	1.36	1.02	10
11	20.43	15.00	11.05	8.17	6.06	4.51	3.37	2.52	1.89	1.42	1.08	11
12	20.43	15.08	11.16	8.30	6.18	4.62	3.47	2.61	1.97	1.49	1.13	12
13	20.43	15.15	11.28	8.42	6.31	4.74	3.57	2.70	2.05	1.56	1.19	13
14	20.43	15.23	11.39	8.55	6.44	4.86	3.68	2.80	2.13	1.63	1.25	14
15	20.44	15.31	11.51	8.68	6.57	4.98	3.79	2.89	2.22	1.70	1.31	15
16	20.44	15.39	11.63	8.81	6.70	5.11	3.91	3.00	2.30	1.78	1.37	16
17	20.45	15.47	11.75	8.95	6.83	5.24	4.02	3.10	2.40	1.86	1.44	17
18	20.45	15.55	11.87	9.08	6.97	5.37	4.15	3.21	2.49	1.94	1.52	18
19	20.46	15.64	11.99	9.22	7.11	5.50	4.27	3.32	2.59	2.03	1.59	19
20	20.47	15.72	12.11	9.36	7.26	5.64	4.40	3.44	2.70	2.12	1.67	20
21	20.47	15.80	12.24	9.51	7.41	5.79	4.53	3.56	2.81	2.22	1.76	21
22	20.48	15.89	12.36	9.65	7.56	5.93	4.67	3.69	2.92	2.32	1.84	22
23	20.49	15.97	12.49	9.80	7.71	6.08	4.81	3.82	3.04	2.42	1.94	23
24	20.49	16.06	12.62	9.95	7.87	6.24	4.96	3.95	3.16	2.53	2.04	24
25	20.50	16.14	12.75	10.10	8.03	6.40	5.11	4.09	3.29	2.65	2.14	25
26	20.51	16.23	12.88	10.26	8.19	6.56	5.27	4.24	3.42	2.77	2.25	26
27	20.51	16.32	13.02	10.41	8.36	6.72	5.43	4.39	3.56	2.89	2.36	27
28	20.52	16.40	13.15	10.57	8.53	6.90	5.59	4.54	3.70	3.03	2.48	28
29	20.53	16.49	13.29	10.74	8.70	7.07	5.76	4.71	3.85	3.16	2.60	29
30	20.54	16.58	13.43	10.90	8.88	7.25	5.94	4.87	4.01	3.31	2.73	30
31	20.55	16.67	13.57	11.07	9.06	7.43	6.12	5.04	4.17	3.46	2.87	31
32	20.56	16.76	13.71	11.24	9.25	7.62	6.30	5.22	4.34	3.61	3.02	32
33	20.57	16.85	13.85	11.42	9.44	7.82	6.50	5.41	4.52	3.78	3.17	33
34	20.58	16.95	14.00	11.60	9.63	8.02	6.69	5.60	4.70	3.95	3.33	34
35	20.59	17.04	14.15	11.78	9.83	8.22	6.90	5.80	4.89	4.13	3.50	35
36	20.61	17.14	14.30	11.96	10.03	8.44	7.11	6.01	5.09	4.32	3.67	36
37	20.62	17.24	14.45	12.15	10.24	8.65	7.33	6.22	5.30	4.52	3.86	37
38	20.64	17.34	14.61	12.34	10.45	8.88	7.56	6.45	5.51	4.72	4.06	38
39	20.66	17.44	14.77	12.54	10.67	9.11	7.79	6.68	5.74	4.94	4.26	39
40	20.68	17.55	14.93	12.74	10.90	9.34	8.03	6.92	5.97	5.17	4.48	40
41	20.70	17.65	15.10	12.94	11.13	9.59	8.28	7.17	6.22	5.41	4.71	41
42	20.72	17.76	15.27	13.15	11.36	9.84	8.54	7.43	6.48	5.66	4.95	42
43	20.75	17.87	15.44	13.37	11.60	10.10	8.81	7.70	6.74	5.92	5.21	43
44	20.78	17.99	15.61	13.59	11.85	10.36	9.08	7.98	7.02	6.19	5.48	44
45	20.81	18.11	15.80	13.81	12.11	10.64	9.37	8.27	7.32	6.48	5.76	45
46	20.85	18.23	15.98	14.05	12.37	10.93	9.67	8.58	7.62	6.79	6.06	46
47	20.89	18.36	16.17	14.28	12.65	11.22	9.98	8.89	7.94	7.11	6.37	47
48	20.94	18.49	16.37	14.53	12.93	11.53	10.30	9.23	8.28	7.44	6.71	48
49	20.99	18.63	16.58	14.78	13.22	11.84	10.64	9.57	8.63	7.80	7.06	49
50	21.04	18.77	16.79	15.05	13.52	12.17	10.98	9.93	9.00	8.17	7.43	50
51	21.11	18.92	17.00	15.32	13.83	12.51	11.35	10.31	9.39	8.56	7.82	51
52	21.17	19.08	17.23	15.60	14.15	12.87	11.73	10.71	9.79	8.98	8.24	52
53	21.25	19.24	17.46	15.89	14.49	13.24	12.12	11.12	10.22	9.41	8.69	53
54	21.33	19.41	17.71	16.19	14.83	13.62	12.53	11.56	10.67	9.88	9.16	54
55	21.42	19.59	17.96	16.50	15.20	14.02	12.97	12.01	11.15	10.37	9.66	55
56	21.53	19.79	18.23	16.83	15.57	14.44	13.42	12.49	11.65	10.88	10.19	56
57	21.64	19.99	18.51	17.17	15.97	14.88	13.89	13.00	12.18	11.43	10.75	57
58	21.77	20.21	18.81	17.54	16.39	15.34	14.40	13.53	12.74	12.02	11.36	58
59	21.92	20.45	19.12	17.92	16.83	15.83	14.93	14.10	13.34	12.64	12.00	59
60	22.08	20.70	19.45	18.32	17.29	16.35	15.49	14.70	13.98	13.31	12.70	60

Table 15   Multipliers for loss of pension commencing age 65 (males)

Age at date of trial	Multiplier calculated with allowance for population mortality and rate of return of											Age at date of trial
	0.0%	0.5%	1.0%	1.5%	2.0%	2.5%	3.0%	£3.5%	4.0%	4.5%	5.0%	
0	11.31	7.81	5.41	3.76	2.62	1.83	1.28	0.90	0.63	0.45	0.32	0
1	11.41	7.92	5.51	3.85	2.69	1.89	1.33	0.94	0.66	0.47	0.34	1
2	11.41	7.96	5.57	3.91	2.75	1.94	1.37	0.97	0.69	0.49	0.35	2
3	11.42	8.00	5.63	3.97	2.81	1.99	1.41	1.01	0.72	0.52	0.37	3
4	11.42	8.05	5.69	4.03	2.86	2.04	1.46	1.04	0.75	0.54	0.39	4
5	11.42	8.09	5.74	4.09	2.92	2.09	1.50	1.08	0.78	0.56	0.41	5
6	11.43	8.13	5.80	4.15	2.98	2.14	1.55	1.12	0.81	0.59	0.43	6
7	11.43	8.17	5.86	4.22	3.04	2.20	1.59	1.16	0.84	0.62	0.45	7
8	11.43	8.22	5.92	4.28	3.10	2.25	1.64	1.20	0.88	0.64	0.47	8
9	11.43	8.26	5.98	4.34	3.16	2.31	1.69	1.24	0.91	0.67	0.50	9
10	11.43	8.30	6.04	4.41	3.23	2.37	1.74	1.28	0.95	0.70	0.52	10
11	11.44	8.34	6.10	4.48	3.29	2.43	1.79	1.33	0.99	0.73	0.55	11
12	11.44	8.39	6.17	4.55	3.36	2.49	1.85	1.38	1.03	0.77	0.57	12
13	11.44	8.43	6.23	4.61	3.43	2.55	1.90	1.42	1.07	0.80	0.60	13
14	11.44	8.48	6.29	4.68	3.50	2.62	1.96	1.47	1.11	0.84	0.63	14
15	11.45	8.52	6.36	4.76	3.57	2.68	2.02	1.53	1.15	0.88	0.67	15
16	11.45	8.57	6.42	4.83	3.64	2.75	2.08	1.58	1.20	0.92	0.70	16
17	11.46	8.61	6.49	4.90	3.71	2.82	2.15	1.64	1.25	0.96	0.73	17
18	11.47	8.66	6.56	4.98	3.79	2.89	2.21	1.69	1.30	1.00	0.77	18
19	11.48	8.71	6.63	5.06	3.87	2.97	2.28	1.76	1.35	1.05	0.81	19
20	11.49	8.76	6.70	5.14	3.95	3.04	2.35	1.82	1.41	1.10	0.85	20
21	11.50	8.82	6.78	5.22	4.03	3.12	2.42	1.88	1.47	1.15	0.90	21
22	11.51	8.87	6.85	5.31	4.12	3.20	2.50	1.95	1.53	1.20	0.94	22
23	11.52	8.92	6.93	5.39	4.20	3.29	2.57	2.02	1.59	1.25	0.99	23
24	11.53	8.97	7.00	5.48	4.29	3.37	2.65	2.09	1.66	1.31	1.04	24
25	11.54	9.03	7.08	5.56	4.38	3.46	2.74	2.17	1.72	1.37	1.09	25
26	11.55	9.08	7.15	5.65	4.47	3.55	2.82	2.25	1.79	1.43	1.15	26
27	11.56	9.13	7.23	5.74	4.57	3.64	2.91	2.33	1.87	1.50	1.21	27
28	11.57	9.18	7.31	5.83	4.66	3.73	3.00	2.41	1.94	1.57	1.27	28
29	11.58	9.24	7.39	5.92	4.76	3.83	3.09	2.50	2.02	1.64	1.33	29
30	11.59	9.29	7.47	6.02	4.86	3.93	3.19	2.59	2.11	1.72	1.40	30
31	11.60	9.35	7.55	6.11	4.96	4.03	3.28	2.68	2.19	1.79	1.47	31
32	11.61	9.40	7.63	6.21	5.06	4.14	3.39	2.78	2.28	1.88	1.55	32
33	11.62	9.46	7.72	6.31	5.17	4.24	3.49	2.88	2.37	1.96	1.63	33
34	11.63	9.52	7.80	6.41	5.28	4.35	3.60	2.98	2.47	2.05	1.71	34
35	11.64	9.57	7.89	6.52	5.39	4.47	3.71	3.09	2.57	2.15	1.80	35
36	11.66	9.63	7.98	6.62	5.50	4.59	3.83	3.20	2.68	2.25	1.89	36
37	11.67	9.69	8.07	6.73	5.62	4.71	3.95	3.32	2.79	2.35	1.99	37
38	11.69	9.76	8.16	6.84	5.74	4.83	4.07	3.44	2.91	2.46	2.09	38
39	11.70	9.82	8.25	6.95	5.87	4.96	4.20	3.56	3.03	2.58	2.20	39
40	11.72	9.88	8.35	7.07	5.99	5.09	4.33	3.69	3.15	2.70	2.31	40
41	11.74	9.95	8.45	7.19	6.12	5.23	4.47	3.83	3.28	2.82	2.43	41
42	11.77	10.02	8.55	7.31	6.26	5.37	4.61	3.97	3.42	2.96	2.56	42
43	11.79	10.09	8.65	7.43	6.40	5.51	4.76	4.12	3.57	3.09	2.69	43
44	11.82	10.16	8.76	7.56	6.54	5.66	4.91	4.27	3.72	3.24	2.83	44
45	11.84	10.24	8.87	7.69	6.68	5.82	5.07	4.43	3.88	3.39	2.98	45
46	11.88	10.32	8.98	7.83	6.84	5.98	5.24	4.60	4.04	3.56	3.14	46
47	11.91	10.40	9.10	7.97	6.99	6.15	5.41	4.77	4.22	3.73	3.30	47
48	11.95	10.49	9.22	8.12	7.16	6.32	5.59	4.96	4.40	3.91	3.48	48
49	11.99	10.58	9.34	8.27	7.33	6.50	5.78	5.15	4.59	4.10	3.67	49
50	12.04	10.67	9.48	8.43	7.51	6.70	5.98	5.35	4.80	4.30	3.87	50
51	12.10	10.78	9.62	8.59	7.69	6.89	6.19	5.57	5.01	4.52	4.08	51
52	12.16	10.89	9.76	8.77	7.89	7.10	6.41	5.79	5.24	4.74	4.30	52
53	12.23	11.01	9.92	8.95	8.09	7.32	6.64	6.03	5.48	4.99	4.55	53
54	12.31	11.13	10.08	9.14	8.31	7.56	6.88	6.28	5.74	5.25	4.80	54
55	12.40	11.27	10.26	9.35	8.53	7.80	7.14	6.55	6.01	5.52	5.08	55
56	12.50	11.42	10.44	9.56	8.77	8.06	7.41	6.83	6.30	5.82	5.38	56
57	12.61	11.58	10.64	9.79	9.03	8.33	7.70	7.13	6.61	6.13	5.70	57
58	12.74	11.75	10.85	10.04	9.30	8.63	8.02	7.45	6.94	6.47	6.04	58
59	12.88	11.94	11.09	10.31	9.59	8.94	8.35	7.80	7.30	6.84	6.41	59
60	13.05	12.15	11.34	10.59	9.91	9.28	8.71	8.18	7.69	7.24	6.82	60
61	13.23	12.39	11.61	10.90	10.25	9.65	9.10	8.58	8.11	7.67	7.26	61
62	13.44	12.65	11.92	11.24	10.62	10.05	9.52	9.02	8.57	8.14	7.75	62
63	13.68	12.94	12.25	11.61	11.03	10.48	9.98	9.51	9.07	8.66	8.28	63
64	13.95	13.26	12.62	12.02	11.47	10.96	10.48	10.04	9.62	9.23	8.87	64
65	14.27	13.63	13.03	12.48	11.97	11.49	11.04	10.62	10.23	9.86	9.52	65

Table 16 Multipliers for loss of pension commencing age 65 (females)

Age at date of trial	Multiplier calculated with allowance for population mortality and rate of return of											Age at date of trial
	0.0%	0.5%	1.0%	1.5%	2.0%	2.5%	3.0%	£3.5%	4.0%	4.5%	5.0%	
0	15.77	10.80	7.42	5.11	3.53	2.45	1.70	1.19	0.83	0.58	0.41	0
1	15.87	10.92	7.54	5.22	3.63	2.53	1.77	1.24	0.87	0.61	0.43	1
2	15.88	10.98	7.62	5.30	3.70	2.59	1.82	1.28	0.91	0.64	0.46	2
3	15.89	11.04	7.70	5.38	3.78	2.66	1.88	1.33	0.94	0.67	0.48	3
4	15.89	11.10	7.78	5.47	3.85	2.72	1.93	1.37	0.98	0.70	0.50	4
5	15.89	11.16	7.86	5.55	3.93	2.79	1.99	1.42	1.02	0.73	0.53	5
6	15.90	11.21	7.93	5.63	4.01	2.86	2.05	1.47	1.06	0.77	0.55	6
7	15.90	11.27	8.02	5.72	4.09	2.94	2.11	1.52	1.10	0.80	0.58	7
8	15.90	11.33	8.10	5.80	4.17	3.01	2.18	1.58	1.15	0.84	0.61	8
9	15.90	11.39	8.18	5.89	4.26	3.09	2.24	1.63	1.19	0.87	0.64	9
10	15.91	11.45	8.26	5.98	4.34	3.16	2.31	1.69	1.24	0.91	0.67	10
11	15.91	11.50	8.35	6.07	4.43	3.24	2.38	1.75	1.29	0.96	0.71	11
12	15.91	11.56	8.43	6.16	4.52	3.32	2.45	1.81	1.34	1.00	0.74	12
13	15.91	11.62	8.52	6.26	4.61	3.41	2.52	1.88	1.40	1.04	0.78	13
14	15.91	11.68	8.60	6.35	4.70	3.49	2.60	1.94	1.45	1.09	0.82	14
15	15.92	11.74	8.69	6.45	4.80	3.58	2.68	2.01	1.51	1.14	0.86	15
16	15.92	11.80	8.78	6.55	4.90	3.67	2.76	2.08	1.57	1.19	0.90	16
17	15.92	11.87	8.87	6.65	5.00	3.76	2.84	2.15	1.64	1.25	0.95	17
18	15.93	11.93	8.96	6.75	5.10	3.86	2.93	2.23	1.70	1.30	1.00	18
19	15.93	11.99	9.05	6.85	5.20	3.96	3.02	2.31	1.77	1.36	1.05	19
20	15.94	12.06	9.15	6.96	5.31	4.06	3.11	2.39	1.84	1.42	1.10	20
21	15.94	12.12	9.24	7.06	5.41	4.16	3.20	2.48	1.92	1.49	1.16	21
22	15.95	12.19	9.34	7.17	5.52	4.27	3.30	2.56	1.99	1.55	1.21	22
23	15.96	12.25	9.43	7.28	5.64	4.37	3.40	2.65	2.07	1.62	1.28	23
24	15.96	12.32	9.53	7.39	5.75	4.48	3.51	2.75	2.16	1.70	1.34	24
25	15.97	12.38	9.63	7.51	5.87	4.60	3.61	2.84	2.24	1.78	1.41	25
26	15.97	12.45	9.73	7.62	5.99	4.71	3.72	2.94	2.34	1.86	1.48	26
27	15.98	12.51	9.83	7.74	6.11	4.83	3.83	3.05	2.43	1.94	1.55	27
28	15.98	12.58	9.93	7.86	6.23	4.96	3.95	3.16	2.53	2.03	1.63	28
29	15.99	12.65	10.03	7.98	6.36	5.08	4.07	3.27	2.63	2.12	1.71	29
30	15.99	12.72	10.14	8.10	6.49	5.21	4.19	3.38	2.74	2.22	1.80	30
31	16.00	12.79	10.24	8.23	6.62	5.34	4.32	3.50	2.85	2.32	1.89	31
32	16.01	12.86	10.35	8.35	6.76	5.48	4.45	3.63	2.96	2.42	1.99	32
33	16.02	12.93	10.46	8.48	6.90	5.62	4.59	3.76	3.08	2.53	2.09	33
34	16.03	13.00	10.57	8.62	7.04	5.76	4.73	3.89	3.21	2.65	2.19	34
35	16.04	13.07	10.68	8.75	7.18	5.91	4.88	4.03	3.34	2.77	2.30	35
36	16.05	13.15	10.80	8.89	7.33	6.06	5.03	4.17	3.47	2.90	2.42	36
37	16.06	13.22	10.91	9.03	7.49	6.22	5.18	4.32	3.61	3.03	2.54	37
38	16.07	13.30	11.03	9.17	7.64	6.38	5.34	4.48	3.76	3.17	2.67	38
39	16.09	13.38	11.15	9.32	7.80	6.55	5.51	4.64	3.92	3.31	2.81	39
40	16.10	13.46	11.27	9.47	7.97	6.72	5.68	4.81	4.08	3.47	2.95	40
41	16.12	13.54	11.40	9.62	8.13	6.89	5.85	4.98	4.24	3.63	3.10	41
42	16.14	13.62	11.53	9.77	8.31	7.07	6.03	5.16	4.42	3.79	3.26	42
43	16.16	13.71	11.66	9.93	8.48	7.26	6.22	5.35	4.60	3.97	3.43	43
44	16.18	13.80	11.79	10.10	8.66	7.45	6.42	5.54	4.79	4.15	3.60	44
45	16.21	13.89	11.93	10.26	8.85	7.65	6.62	5.75	4.99	4.35	3.79	45
46	16.24	13.98	12.07	10.44	9.04	7.85	6.83	5.96	5.20	4.55	3.99	46
47	16.27	14.08	12.21	10.61	9.24	8.07	7.05	6.18	5.42	4.76	4.20	47
48	16.31	14.18	12.36	10.80	9.45	8.29	7.28	6.41	5.65	4.99	4.41	48
49	16.34	14.29	12.52	10.99	9.66	8.51	7.52	6.65	5.89	5.23	4.65	49
50	16.39	14.40	12.67	11.18	9.88	8.75	7.76	6.90	6.14	5.48	4.89	50
51	16.44	14.51	12.84	11.38	10.11	9.00	8.02	7.16	6.41	5.74	5.15	51
52	16.49	14.63	13.01	11.59	10.34	9.25	8.29	7.44	6.68	6.02	5.43	52
53	16.55	14.76	13.19	11.81	10.59	9.52	8.57	7.72	6.98	6.31	5.72	53
54	16.61	14.89	13.37	12.03	10.84	9.79	8.86	8.03	7.28	6.62	6.03	54
55	16.69	15.03	13.56	12.26	11.11	10.08	9.16	8.34	7.61	6.95	6.36	55
56	16.77	15.18	13.76	12.51	11.38	10.38	9.48	8.68	7.95	7.30	6.71	56
57	16.86	15.33	13.98	12.76	11.67	10.70	9.82	9.03	8.31	7.67	7.08	57
58	16.96	15.50	14.20	13.03	11.98	11.03	10.17	9.40	8.70	8.06	7.48	58
59	17.07	15.68	14.44	13.31	12.30	11.38	10.55	9.79	9.10	8.48	7.90	59
60	17.20	15.88	14.69	13.61	12.64	11.75	10.95	10.21	9.54	8.92	8.36	60
61	17.34	16.09	14.96	13.93	13.00	12.15	11.37	10.66	10.00	9.40	8.85	61
62	17.50	16.32	15.25	14.27	13.38	12.57	11.82	11.13	10.50	9.92	9.38	62
63	17.68	16.57	15.56	14.64	13.79	13.01	12.30	11.64	11.03	10.47	9.95	63
64	17.88	16.85	15.90	15.03	14.23	13.49	12.81	12.18	11.60	11.07	10.57	64
65	18.11	17.15	16.26	15.45	14.70	14.01	13.37	12.77	12.22	11.71	11.24	65

Table 17 Multipliers for loss of pension commencing age 70 (males)

Age at date of trial	Multiplier calculated with allowance for population mortality and rate of return of											Age at date of trial
	0.0%	0.5%	1.0%	1.5%	2.0%	2.5%	3.0%	£3.5%	4.0%	4.5%	5.0%	
0	7.61	5.17	3.52	2.40	1.65	1.13	0.78	0.54	0.37	0.26	0.18	0
1	7.68	5.24	3.59	2.46	1.69	1.17	0.81	0.56	0.39	0.27	0.19	1
2	7.68	5.27	3.62	2.50	1.73	1.20	0.83	0.58	0.40	0.28	0.20	2
3	7.68	5.30	3.66	2.54	1.76	1.23	0.86	0.60	0.42	0.30	0.21	3
4	7.69	5.32	3.70	2.58	1.80	1.26	0.88	0.62	0.44	0.31	0.22	4
5	7.69	5.35	3.74	2.61	1.83	1.29	0.91	0.64	0.46	0.32	0.23	5
6	7.69	5.38	3.77	2.65	1.87	1.32	0.94	0.67	0.47	0.34	0.24	6
7	7.69	5.41	3.81	2.70	1.91	1.36	0.97	0.69	0.49	0.35	0.25	7
8	7.69	5.44	3.85	2.74	1.95	1.39	0.99	0.71	0.51	0.37	0.27	8
9	7.69	5.46	3.89	2.78	1.99	1.43	1.02	0.74	0.53	0.39	0.28	9
10	7.70	5.49	3.93	2.82	2.03	1.46	1.06	0.76	0.55	0.40	0.29	10
11	7.70	5.52	3.97	2.86	2.07	1.50	1.09	0.79	0.58	0.42	0.31	11
12	7.70	5.55	4.01	2.91	2.11	1.54	1.12	0.82	0.60	0.44	0.32	12
13	7.70	5.58	4.05	2.95	2.15	1.57	1.15	0.85	0.62	0.46	0.34	13
14	7.70	5.61	4.09	3.00	2.20	1.61	1.19	0.88	0.65	0.48	0.36	14
15	7.70	5.64	4.14	3.04	2.24	1.66	1.23	0.91	0.68	0.50	0.38	15
16	7.71	5.67	4.18	3.09	2.29	1.70	1.26	0.94	0.70	0.53	0.39	16
17	7.71	5.70	4.22	3.14	2.33	1.74	1.30	0.97	0.73	0.55	0.41	17
18	7.72	5.73	4.27	3.19	2.38	1.79	1.34	1.01	0.76	0.58	0.44	18
19	7.72	5.77	4.31	3.24	2.43	1.83	1.38	1.05	0.79	0.60	0.46	19
20	7.73	5.80	4.36	3.29	2.48	1.88	1.42	1.08	0.82	0.63	0.48	20
21	7.74	5.83	4.41	3.34	2.53	1.93	1.47	1.12	0.86	0.66	0.51	21
22	7.74	5.87	4.46	3.39	2.59	1.98	1.51	1.16	0.89	0.69	0.53	22
23	7.75	5.90	4.51	3.45	2.64	2.03	1.56	1.20	0.93	0.72	0.56	23
24	7.76	5.94	4.55	3.50	2.70	2.08	1.61	1.25	0.97	0.75	0.59	24
25	7.76	5.97	4.60	3.56	2.75	2.14	1.66	1.29	1.01	0.79	0.62	25
26	7.77	6.01	4.65	3.61	2.81	2.19	1.71	1.34	1.05	0.82	0.65	26
27	7.78	6.04	4.70	3.67	2.87	2.25	1.76	1.39	1.09	0.86	0.68	27
28	7.78	6.08	4.76	3.73	2.93	2.31	1.82	1.44	1.14	0.90	0.72	28
29	7.79	6.11	4.81	3.79	2.99	2.36	1.87	1.49	1.18	0.94	0.75	29
30	7.80	6.15	4.86	3.85	3.05	2.43	1.93	1.54	1.23	0.99	0.79	30
31	7.80	6.19	4.91	3.91	3.12	2.49	1.99	1.60	1.28	1.03	0.83	31
32	7.81	6.22	4.97	3.97	3.18	2.55	2.05	1.65	1.33	1.08	0.87	32
33	7.82	6.26	5.02	4.04	3.25	2.62	2.12	1.71	1.39	1.13	0.92	33
34	7.83	6.30	5.08	4.10	3.32	2.69	2.18	1.77	1.45	1.18	0.96	34
35	7.84	6.34	5.13	4.17	3.39	2.76	2.25	1.84	1.51	1.23	1.01	35
36	7.84	6.37	5.19	4.23	3.46	2.83	2.32	1.91	1.57	1.29	1.07	36
37	7.85	6.41	5.25	4.30	3.53	2.91	2.39	1.97	1.63	1.35	1.12	37
38	7.87	6.46	5.31	4.37	3.61	2.98	2.47	2.05	1.70	1.41	1.18	38
39	7.88	6.50	5.37	4.44	3.69	3.06	2.55	2.12	1.77	1.48	1.24	39
40	7.89	6.54	5.43	4.52	3.77	3.14	2.63	2.20	1.84	1.55	1.30	40
41	7.90	6.58	5.50	4.59	3.85	3.23	2.71	2.28	1.92	1.62	1.37	41
42	7.92	6.63	5.56	4.67	3.93	3.31	2.80	2.36	2.00	1.70	1.44	42
43	7.93	6.68	5.63	4.75	4.02	3.40	2.89	2.45	2.09	1.78	1.52	43
44	7.95	6.72	5.70	4.83	4.11	3.50	2.98	2.54	2.17	1.86	1.60	44
45	7.97	6.77	5.77	4.92	4.20	3.59	3.08	2.64	2.27	1.95	1.68	45
46	7.99	6.83	5.84	5.00	4.30	3.69	3.18	2.74	2.36	2.04	1.77	46
47	8.02	6.88	5.92	5.10	4.39	3.80	3.28	2.84	2.47	2.14	1.86	47
48	8.04	6.94	6.00	5.19	4.50	3.90	3.39	2.95	2.57	2.24	1.96	48
49	8.07	7.00	6.08	5.29	4.60	4.02	3.51	3.07	2.69	2.35	2.07	49
50	8.11	7.06	6.16	5.39	4.72	4.13	3.63	3.19	2.80	2.47	2.18	50
51	8.14	7.13	6.26	5.49	4.83	4.26	3.75	3.31	2.93	2.59	2.30	51
52	8.19	7.21	6.35	5.61	4.95	4.39	3.89	3.45	3.06	2.72	2.43	52
53	8.23	7.28	6.45	5.72	5.08	4.52	4.03	3.59	3.20	2.86	2.56	53
54	8.29	7.37	6.56	5.85	5.22	4.66	4.17	3.74	3.35	3.01	2.71	54
55	8.35	7.46	6.67	5.98	5.36	4.81	4.33	3.90	3.51	3.17	2.86	55
56	8.41	7.55	6.79	6.12	5.51	4.97	4.50	4.07	3.68	3.34	3.03	56
57	8.49	7.66	6.92	6.26	5.67	5.15	4.67	4.25	3.86	3.52	3.21	57
58	8.57	7.78	7.06	6.42	5.84	5.33	4.86	4.44	4.06	3.72	3.41	58
59	8.67	7.90	7.21	6.59	6.03	5.52	5.06	4.65	4.27	3.93	3.62	59
60	8.78	8.04	7.38	6.77	6.23	5.73	5.28	4.87	4.50	4.16	3.84	60
61	8.90	8.20	7.55	6.97	6.44	5.96	5.52	5.11	4.74	4.40	4.09	61
62	9.05	8.37	7.75	7.19	6.67	6.20	5.77	5.37	5.01	4.68	4.37	62
63	9.21	8.56	7.97	7.43	6.93	6.47	6.05	5.66	5.30	4.97	4.67	63
64	9.39	8.78	8.21	7.69	7.21	6.77	6.36	5.98	5.63	5.30	5.00	64

Table 17 *continued*

65	9.60	9.02	8.48	7.98	7.52	7.09	6.69	6.33	5.98	5.66	5.37	65
66	9.84	9.29	8.78	8.30	7.86	7.45	7.07	6.71	6.38	6.07	5.78	66
67	10.12	9.60	9.11	8.66	8.24	7.85	7.48	7.14	6.82	6.52	6.23	67
68	10.43	9.94	9.49	9.06	8.67	8.29	7.94	7.62	7.31	7.02	6.75	68
69	10.78	10.33	9.91	9.51	9.14	8.79	8.46	8.15	7.86	7.59	7.33	69
70	11.19	10.77	10.38	10.02	9.67	9.35	9.04	8.75	8.48	8.22	7.98	70

Table 18 Multipliers for loss of pension commencing age 70 (females)

Age at date of trial	Multiplier calculated with allowance for population mortality and rate of return of											Age at date of trial
	0.0%	0.5%	1.0%	1.5%	2.0%	2.5%	3.0%	£3.5%	4.0%	4.5%	5.0%	
0	11.59	7.81	5.28	3.58	2.43	1.66	1.13	0.78	0.53	0.37	0.25	0
1	11.66	7.90	5.36	3.65	2.50	1.71	1.18	0.81	0.56	0.39	0.27	1
2	11.67	7.94	5.42	3.71	2.55	1.75	1.21	0.84	0.58	0.40	0.28	2
3	11.67	7.98	5.48	3.77	2.60	1.80	1.25	0.87	0.61	0.42	0.30	3
4	11.67	8.02	5.53	3.83	2.65	1.84	1.29	0.90	0.63	0.44	0.31	4
5	11.67	8.07	5.59	3.88	2.71	1.89	1.32	0.93	0.65	0.46	0.33	5
6	11.68	8.11	5.65	3.94	2.76	1.94	1.36	0.96	0.68	0.48	0.34	6
7	11.68	8.15	5.70	4.00	2.82	1.99	1.41	1.00	0.71	0.51	0.36	7
8	11.68	8.19	5.76	4.06	2.87	2.04	1.45	1.03	0.74	0.53	0.38	8
9	11.68	8.23	5.82	4.12	2.93	2.09	1.49	1.07	0.77	0.55	0.40	9
10	11.68	8.27	5.88	4.19	2.99	2.14	1.54	1.11	0.80	0.58	0.42	10
11	11.68	8.32	5.94	4.25	3.05	2.19	1.58	1.14	0.83	0.60	0.44	11
12	11.69	8.36	6.00	4.31	3.11	2.25	1.63	1.18	0.86	0.63	0.46	12
13	11.69	8.40	6.06	4.38	3.17	2.31	1.68	1.23	0.90	0.66	0.48	13
14	11.69	8.45	6.12	4.45	3.24	2.36	1.73	1.27	0.93	0.69	0.51	14
15	11.69	8.49	6.18	4.51	3.30	2.42	1.78	1.31	0.97	0.72	0.53	15
16	11.69	8.53	6.25	4.58	3.37	2.48	1.84	1.36	1.01	0.75	0.56	16
17	11.70	8.58	6.31	4.65	3.44	2.55	1.89	1.41	1.05	0.79	0.59	17
18	11.70	8.63	6.37	4.72	3.51	2.61	1.95	1.46	1.09	0.82	0.62	18
19	11.70	8.67	6.44	4.80	3.58	2.68	2.01	1.51	1.14	0.86	0.65	19
20	11.71	8.72	6.51	4.87	3.65	2.75	2.07	1.56	1.18	0.90	0.68	20
21	11.71	8.76	6.57	4.94	3.73	2.82	2.13	1.62	1.23	0.94	0.72	21
22	11.72	8.81	6.64	5.02	3.80	2.89	2.20	1.68	1.28	0.98	0.75	22
23	11.72	8.86	6.71	5.10	3.88	2.96	2.26	1.73	1.33	1.03	0.79	23
24	11.72	8.90	6.78	5.17	3.96	3.03	2.33	1.80	1.39	1.07	0.83	24
25	11.73	8.95	6.85	5.25	4.04	3.11	2.40	1.86	1.44	1.12	0.87	25
26	11.73	9.00	6.92	5.33	4.12	3.19	2.48	1.92	1.50	1.17	0.92	26
27	11.73	9.05	6.99	5.42	4.20	3.27	2.55	1.99	1.56	1.22	0.96	27
28	11.74	9.10	7.06	5.50	4.29	3.35	2.63	2.06	1.62	1.28	1.01	28
29	11.74	9.15	7.14	5.58	4.38	3.44	2.71	2.14	1.69	1.34	1.06	29
30	11.75	9.19	7.21	5.67	4.47	3.53	2.79	2.21	1.76	1.40	1.12	30
31	11.75	9.24	7.29	5.76	4.56	3.62	2.88	2.29	1.83	1.46	1.17	31
32	11.76	9.30	7.36	5.85	4.65	3.71	2.96	2.37	1.90	1.53	1.23	32
33	11.76	9.35	7.44	5.94	4.75	3.80	3.05	2.46	1.98	1.60	1.29	33
34	11.77	9.40	7.52	6.03	4.85	3.90	3.15	2.54	2.06	1.67	1.36	34
35	11.78	9.45	7.60	6.12	4.95	4.00	3.24	2.63	2.14	1.75	1.43	35
36	11.79	9.51	7.68	6.22	5.05	4.10	3.34	2.73	2.23	1.83	1.50	36
37	11.80	9.56	7.76	6.32	5.15	4.21	3.45	2.83	2.32	1.91	1.58	37
38	11.81	9.62	7.85	6.42	5.26	4.32	3.55	2.93	2.42	2.00	1.66	38
39	11.82	9.67	7.93	6.52	5.37	4.43	3.66	3.03	2.52	2.09	1.74	39
40	11.83	9.73	8.02	6.62	5.48	4.55	3.78	3.14	2.62	2.19	1.83	40
41	11.84	9.79	8.11	6.73	5.60	4.66	3.89	3.26	2.73	2.29	1.92	41
42	11.85	9.85	8.20	6.84	5.72	4.79	4.01	3.37	2.84	2.39	2.02	42
43	11.87	9.91	8.29	6.95	5.84	4.91	4.14	3.50	2.96	2.50	2.12	43
44	11.89	9.98	8.39	7.07	5.96	5.04	4.27	3.62	3.08	2.62	2.23	44
45	11.91	10.04	8.49	7.18	6.09	5.18	4.41	3.76	3.21	2.74	2.35	45
46	11.93	10.11	8.59	7.30	6.23	5.32	4.55	3.89	3.34	2.87	2.47	46
47	11.95	10.18	8.69	7.43	6.36	5.46	4.69	4.04	3.48	3.01	2.60	47
48	11.98	10.25	8.79	7.56	6.50	5.61	4.84	4.19	3.63	3.15	2.74	48
49	12.01	10.33	8.90	7.69	6.65	5.76	5.00	4.35	3.78	3.30	2.88	49
50	12.04	10.41	9.02	7.82	6.80	5.92	5.16	4.51	3.95	3.46	3.03	50
51	12.07	10.49	9.13	7.97	6.96	6.09	5.33	4.68	4.11	3.62	3.19	51
52	12.11	10.58	9.26	8.11	7.12	6.26	5.51	4.86	4.29	3.80	3.36	52
53	12.16	10.67	9.38	8.26	7.29	6.44	5.70	5.05	4.48	3.98	3.54	53
54	12.20	10.77	9.51	8.42	7.46	6.63	5.89	5.25	4.68	4.18	3.74	54
55	12.26	10.87	9.65	8.58	7.65	6.82	6.09	5.45	4.89	4.38	3.94	55
56	12.31	10.97	9.79	8.75	7.84	7.03	6.31	5.67	5.11	4.60	4.16	56
57	12.38	11.09	9.94	8.93	8.04	7.24	6.53	5.90	5.34	4.84	4.39	57
58	12.45	11.21	10.10	9.12	8.24	7.46	6.77	6.14	5.59	5.08	4.63	58
59	12.54	11.34	10.27	9.32	8.47	7.70	7.02	6.40	5.85	5.35	4.90	59
60	12.63	11.48	10.45	9.53	8.70	7.95	7.28	6.68	6.13	5.63	5.18	60
61	12.74	11.63	10.64	9.75	8.95	8.22	7.56	6.97	6.43	5.93	5.49	61
62	12.85	11.80	10.85	9.99	9.21	8.50	7.86	7.28	6.74	6.26	5.81	62
63	12.99	11.98	11.07	10.24	9.49	8.81	8.18	7.61	7.09	6.61	6.17	63
64	13.13	12.18	11.31	10.52	9.79	9.13	8.52	7.97	7.45	6.98	6.55	64

Table 18 *continued*

65	13.30	12.40	11.57	10.81	10.12	9.48	8.89	8.35	7.85	7.39	6.96	65
66	13.49	12.64	11.85	11.13	10.46	9.85	9.29	8.77	8.28	7.83	7.42	66
67	13.70	12.89	12.15	11.47	10.84	10.25	9.71	9.21	8.75	8.31	7.91	67
68	13.93	13.18	12.48	11.84	11.24	10.69	10.18	9.70	9.25	8.83	8.45	68
69	14.20	13.50	12.85	12.24	11.68	11.16	10.68	10.22	9.80	9.41	9.03	69
70	14.49	13.84	13.24	12.68	12.16	11.68	11.22	10.80	10.40	10.03	9.68	70

Table 19   Multipliers for pecuniary loss for life (males)

Age at date of trial	Multiplier calculated with allowance for projected mortality from the 1998-based population projections and rate of return of										Age at date of trial
	0.0%	0.5%	1.0%	1.5%	2.0%	2.5%	3.0%	£3.5%	4.0%	4.5%	5.0%	
0	79.84	65.45	54.50	46.07	39.50	34.30	30.14	26.77	24.01	21.72	19.80	0
1	79.24	65.10	54.31	45.99	39.48	34.32	30.18	26.83	24.07	21.79	19.87	1
2	78.26	64.44	53.87	45.69	39.27	34.18	30.08	26.76	24.02	21.75	19.84	2
3	77.27	63.77	53.41	45.37	39.05	34.02	29.98	26.68	23.97	21.71	19.82	3
4	76.28	63.09	52.95	45.05	38.83	33.87	29.87	26.60	23.91	21.67	19.79	4
5	75.28	62.41	52.48	44.72	38.60	33.70	29.75	26.52	23.85	21.63	19.75	5
6	74.28	61.72	52.00	44.39	38.36	33.54	29.63	26.43	23.79	21.58	19.72	6
7	73.27	61.02	51.51	44.04	38.12	33.36	29.51	26.34	23.72	21.53	19.68	7
8	72.27	60.32	51.02	43.70	37.87	33.19	29.38	26.25	23.65	21.48	19.64	8
9	71.27	59.62	50.52	43.34	37.62	33.00	29.24	26.15	23.58	21.42	19.60	9
10	70.26	58.91	50.02	42.99	37.36	32.82	29.11	26.05	23.50	21.37	19.56	10
11	69.26	58.20	49.51	42.62	37.10	32.62	28.97	25.94	23.43	21.31	19.51	11
12	68.25	57.48	49.00	42.25	36.83	32.43	28.82	25.84	23.34	21.24	19.46	12
13	67.25	56.77	48.49	41.88	36.56	32.23	28.67	25.72	23.26	21.18	19.41	13
14	66.24	56.05	47.97	41.50	36.28	32.02	28.52	25.61	23.17	21.11	19.36	14
15	65.25	55.33	47.45	41.12	36.00	31.81	28.36	25.49	23.08	21.04	19.31	15
16	64.25	54.61	46.92	40.74	35.71	31.60	28.20	25.37	22.99	20.97	19.25	16
17	63.26	53.88	46.39	40.35	35.43	31.39	28.04	25.25	22.90	20.90	19.19	17
18	62.28	53.17	45.87	39.96	35.14	31.17	27.88	25.13	22.80	20.83	19.14	18
19	61.31	52.46	45.35	39.57	34.85	30.96	27.72	25.00	22.71	20.76	19.08	19
20	60.34	51.75	44.82	39.18	34.56	30.74	27.55	24.88	22.61	20.68	19.03	20
21	59.37	51.03	44.29	38.79	34.26	30.52	27.39	24.75	22.52	20.61	18.97	21
22	58.40	50.32	43.75	38.39	33.96	30.29	27.21	24.62	22.41	20.53	18.91	22
23	57.43	49.59	43.21	37.98	33.65	30.05	27.03	24.48	22.31	20.45	18.84	23
24	56.45	48.86	42.66	37.56	33.33	29.81	26.84	24.33	22.19	20.36	18.77	24
25	55.48	48.12	42.10	37.13	33.01	29.56	26.65	24.18	22.08	20.26	18.71	25
26	54.50	47.38	41.54	36.71	32.68	29.30	26.45	24.03	21.95	20.17	18.62	26
27	53.53	46.64	40.97	36.27	32.34	29.04	26.25	23.87	21.83	20.07	18.54	27
28	52.55	45.89	40.40	35.83	32.00	28.77	26.04	23.70	21.70	19.96	18.46	28
29	51.57	45.14	39.82	35.38	31.65	28.50	25.82	23.53	21.56	19.86	18.37	29
30	50.59	44.39	39.23	34.92	31.29	28.22	25.60	23.35	21.42	19.74	18.28	30
31	49.61	43.62	38.63	34.45	30.92	27.92	25.37	23.17	21.27	19.62	18.18	31
32	48.62	42.86	38.03	33.98	30.55	27.63	25.13	22.98	21.12	19.50	18.08	32
33	47.64	42.08	37.42	33.49	30.16	27.32	24.88	22.78	20.95	19.36	17.97	33
34	46.65	41.30	36.81	33.00	29.77	27.00	24.63	22.57	20.78	19.23	17.86	34
35	45.66	40.52	36.18	32.50	29.37	26.68	24.36	22.36	20.61	19.08	17.74	35
36	44.66	39.72	35.55	31.99	28.95	26.34	24.09	22.13	20.42	18.93	17.61	36
37	43.67	38.93	34.90	31.47	28.53	26.00	23.81	21.90	20.23	18.77	17.48	37
38	42.67	38.13	34.26	30.95	28.11	25.65	23.52	21.66	20.03	18.60	17.34	38
39	41.68	37.33	33.61	30.42	27.67	25.29	23.22	21.42	19.83	18.43	17.19	39
40	40.70	36.52	32.95	29.88	27.23	24.93	22.92	21.17	19.62	18.25	17.04	40
41	39.71	35.72	32.30	29.34	26.79	24.56	22.62	20.91	19.40	18.07	16.89	41
42	38.73	34.92	31.64	28.80	26.33	24.18	22.30	20.64	19.18	17.88	16.73	42
43	37.75	34.11	30.97	28.25	25.87	23.80	21.98	20.37	18.95	17.69	16.56	43
44	36.77	33.30	30.30	27.69	25.41	23.41	21.65	20.09	18.71	17.49	16.39	44
45	35.80	32.49	29.62	27.12	24.93	23.00	21.31	19.80	18.47	17.27	16.21	45
46	34.82	31.68	28.94	26.54	24.44	22.59	20.96	19.50	18.21	17.05	16.02	46
47	33.84	30.85	28.25	25.96	23.95	22.17	20.59	19.19	17.94	16.82	15.82	47
48	32.86	30.02	27.54	25.36	23.44	21.74	20.22	18.87	17.66	16.58	15.61	48
49	31.87	29.19	26.83	24.76	22.92	21.29	19.84	18.54	17.38	16.33	15.39	49
50	30.89	28.35	26.12	24.14	22.39	20.83	19.44	18.19	17.07	16.07	15.15	50
51	29.91	27.51	25.40	23.52	21.85	20.37	19.03	17.84	16.76	15.79	14.91	51
52	28.93	26.67	24.67	22.90	21.31	19.89	18.62	17.48	16.45	15.51	14.66	52
53	27.96	25.84	23.95	22.27	20.76	19.41	18.20	17.11	16.12	15.22	14.41	53
54	27.00	25.01	23.23	21.64	20.21	18.93	17.78	16.73	15.79	14.93	14.14	54
55	26.06	24.18	22.51	21.01	19.66	18.44	17.34	16.35	15.45	14.62	13.87	55
56	25.12	23.36	21.79	20.37	19.10	17.95	16.91	15.96	15.10	14.31	13.59	56
57	24.20	22.55	21.08	19.75	18.54	17.46	16.47	15.57	14.75	14.00	13.31	57
58	23.30	21.76	20.38	19.13	18.00	16.97	16.03	15.18	14.40	13.68	13.03	58
59	22.42	20.99	19.69	18.52	17.45	16.48	15.60	14.79	14.05	13.37	12.74	59
60	21.56	20.23	19.01	17.91	16.91	16.00	15.16	14.40	13.69	13.05	12.45	60
61	20.72	19.47	18.34	17.31	16.37	15.51	14.72	14.00	13.34	12.72	12.16	61
62	19.88	18.72	17.67	16.71	15.83	15.02	14.28	13.60	12.97	12.39	11.85	62
63	19.05	17.98	17.00	16.10	15.28	14.53	13.83	13.19	12.60	12.05	11.54	63
64	18.22	17.23	16.33	15.49	14.73	14.02	13.37	12.77	12.21	11.70	11.22	64

Table 19 continued

65	17.40	16.49	15.65	14.88	14.17	13.51	12.91	12.34	11.82	11.34	10.89	65
66	16.58	15.74	14.97	14.26	13.60	12.99	12.43	11.91	11.42	10.97	10.54	66
67	15.76	14.99	14.28	13.63	13.02	12.46	11.94	11.45	11.00	10.58	10.18	67
68	14.94	14.24	13.60	13.00	12.44	11.93	11.44	11.00	10.58	10.18	9.82	68
69	14.14	13.51	12.92	12.37	11.86	11.39	10.95	10.53	10.15	9.78	9.44	69
70	13.36	12.78	12.25	11.75	11.29	10.86	10.45	10.07	9.71	9.38	9.07	70
71	12.60	12.09	11.60	11.15	10.73	10.34	9.96	9.62	9.29	8.98	8.69	71
72	11.89	11.42	10.98	10.57	10.19	9.83	9.49	9.17	8.87	8.59	8.33	72
73	11.20	10.78	10.39	10.02	9.67	9.34	9.04	8.75	8.47	8.21	7.97	73
74	10.56	10.18	9.83	9.49	9.18	8.88	8.60	8.33	8.08	7.85	7.62	74
75	9.95	9.61	9.29	8.99	8.70	8.43	8.18	7.94	7.71	7.49	7.28	75
76	9.37	9.07	8.78	8.50	8.25	8.00	7.77	7.55	7.34	7.14	6.95	76
77	8.81	8.54	8.28	8.04	7.80	7.58	7.37	7.17	6.98	6.80	6.63	77
78	8.28	8.04	7.80	7.58	7.37	7.17	6.98	6.80	6.63	6.47	6.31	78
79	7.78	7.56	7.35	7.15	6.96	6.78	6.61	6.45	6.29	6.14	6.00	79
80	7.29	7.10	6.91	6.73	6.56	6.40	6.25	6.10	5.96	5.83	5.70	80
81	6.83	6.66	6.49	6.33	6.18	6.04	5.90	5.77	5.64	5.52	5.40	81
82	6.39	6.24	6.09	5.95	5.81	5.68	5.56	5.44	5.33	5.22	5.11	82
83	5.98	5.85	5.71	5.59	5.47	5.35	5.24	5.14	5.03	4.93	4.84	83
84	5.60	5.48	5.37	5.25	5.15	5.04	4.94	4.85	4.76	4.67	4.58	84
85	5.25	5.14	5.04	4.94	4.84	4.75	4.66	4.57	4.49	4.41	4.34	85
86	4.92	4.82	4.73	4.64	4.56	4.48	4.40	4.32	4.25	4.17	4.10	86
87	4.62	4.53	4.45	4.37	4.30	4.22	4.15	4.08	4.02	3.95	3.89	87
88	4.34	4.27	4.19	4.12	4.05	3.99	3.92	3.86	3.80	3.75	3.69	88
89	4.08	4.01	3.94	3.88	3.82	3.76	3.71	3.65	3.60	3.54	3.49	89
90	3.81	3.75	3.70	3.64	3.59	3.53	3.48	3.44	3.39	3.34	3.30	90
91	3.54	3.49	3.44	3.39	3.35	3.30	3.26	3.21	3.17	3.13	3.09	91
92	3.29	3.24	3.20	3.16	3.11	3.07	3.03	3.00	2.96	2.92	2.89	92
93	3.05	3.01	2.98	2.94	2.90	2.87	2.83	2.80	2.77	2.74	2.71	93
94	2.83	2.79	2.76	2.73	2.70	2.66	2.63	2.61	2.58	2.55	2.52	94
95	2.62	2.59	2.56	2.53	2.50	2.48	2.45	2.42	2.40	2.37	2.35	95
96	2.42	2.40	2.37	2.35	2.32	2.30	2.28	2.26	2.23	2.21	2.19	96
97	2.25	2.23	2.20	2.18	2.16	2.14	2.12	2.10	2.08	2.07	2.05	97
98	2.09	2.07	2.05	2.03	2.02	2.00	1.98	1.96	1.95	1.93	1.91	98
99	1.94	1.93	1.91	1.90	1.88	1.86	1.85	1.83	1.82	1.81	1.79	99
100	1.81	1.80	1.78	1.77	1.75	1.74	1.73	1.71	1.70	1.69	1.68	100

Table 20 Multipliers for pecuniary loss for life (females)

Age at date of trial	Multiplier calculated with allowance for projected mortality from the 1998-based population projections and rate of return of											Age at date of trial
	0.0%	0.5%	1.0%	1.5%	2.0%	2.5%	3.0%	£3.5%	4.0%	4.5%	5.0%	
0	84.01	68.28	56.45	47.42	40.45	34.97	30.63	27.13	24.27	21.92	19.95	0
1	83.36	67.90	56.24	47.32	40.41	34.98	30.66	27.17	24.33	21.98	20.01	1
2	82.38	67.25	55.81	47.04	40.22	34.85	30.57	27.12	24.29	21.95	19.99	2
3	81.38	66.59	55.37	46.74	40.02	34.72	30.48	27.05	24.24	21.92	19.97	3
4	80.38	65.93	54.92	46.44	39.81	34.58	30.38	26.98	24.20	21.88	19.95	4
5	79.38	65.25	54.47	46.13	39.60	34.43	30.28	26.91	24.14	21.85	19.92	5
6	78.38	64.57	54.00	45.81	39.38	34.28	30.17	26.83	24.09	21.81	19.89	6
7	77.37	63.89	53.54	45.49	39.16	34.12	30.06	26.76	24.03	21.77	19.86	7
8	76.37	63.20	53.07	45.16	38.93	33.96	29.95	26.68	23.98	21.73	19.83	8
9	75.36	62.51	52.59	44.83	38.70	33.80	29.83	26.59	23.92	21.68	19.80	9
10	74.36	61.82	52.11	44.50	38.46	33.63	29.71	26.51	23.85	21.64	19.77	10
11	73.35	61.12	51.62	44.15	38.22	33.46	29.59	26.42	23.79	21.59	19.73	11
12	72.35	60.42	51.13	43.81	37.98	33.28	29.46	26.32	23.72	21.54	19.69	12
13	71.34	59.72	50.64	43.46	37.73	33.10	29.33	26.23	23.65	21.49	19.65	13
14	70.34	59.01	50.14	43.10	37.47	32.92	29.20	26.13	23.58	21.43	19.61	14
15	69.34	58.31	49.63	42.74	37.21	32.73	29.06	26.03	23.50	21.38	19.57	15
16	68.34	57.60	49.13	42.38	36.95	32.54	28.92	25.93	23.43	21.32	19.53	16
17	67.34	56.89	48.62	42.01	36.68	32.34	28.78	25.82	23.35	21.26	19.48	17
18	66.34	56.17	48.10	41.64	36.41	32.14	28.63	25.71	23.26	21.20	19.43	18
19	65.35	55.46	47.58	41.26	36.13	31.94	28.48	25.60	23.18	21.13	19.39	19
20	64.35	54.74	47.06	40.88	35.85	31.73	28.32	25.48	23.09	21.07	19.33	20
21	63.35	54.01	46.53	40.49	35.56	31.52	28.16	25.36	23.00	21.00	19.28	21
22	62.36	53.28	45.99	40.09	35.27	31.30	28.00	25.23	22.90	20.92	19.22	22
23	61.36	52.55	45.45	39.69	34.97	31.07	27.83	25.10	22.80	20.84	19.16	23
24	60.36	51.81	44.90	39.28	34.66	30.84	27.65	24.97	22.70	20.76	19.10	24
25	59.35	51.06	44.35	38.86	34.35	30.60	27.47	24.83	22.59	20.68	19.03	25
26	58.35	50.32	43.79	38.44	34.02	30.35	27.28	24.68	22.48	20.59	18.97	26
27	57.35	49.57	43.22	38.01	33.70	30.10	27.09	24.54	22.36	20.50	18.89	27
28	56.35	48.81	42.65	37.58	33.37	29.85	26.89	24.38	22.24	20.40	18.82	28
29	55.35	48.06	42.08	37.14	33.03	29.59	26.69	24.22	22.12	20.31	18.74	29
30	54.35	47.30	41.49	36.69	32.68	29.32	26.48	24.06	21.99	20.20	18.66	30
31	53.35	46.53	40.91	36.24	32.33	29.05	26.26	23.89	21.85	20.09	18.57	31
32	52.35	45.76	40.32	35.78	31.97	28.76	26.04	23.71	21.71	19.98	18.48	32
33	51.35	44.99	39.72	35.31	31.61	28.48	25.81	23.53	21.57	19.87	18.38	33
34	50.35	44.22	39.11	34.84	31.24	28.18	25.58	23.34	21.42	19.74	18.28	34
35	49.35	43.44	38.50	34.36	30.86	27.88	25.34	23.15	21.26	19.62	18.18	35
36	48.35	42.66	37.89	33.87	30.47	27.57	25.09	22.95	21.10	19.49	18.07	36
37	47.36	41.87	37.27	33.38	30.08	27.26	24.84	22.75	20.93	19.35	17.96	37
38	46.36	41.09	36.64	32.88	29.68	26.94	24.58	22.53	20.76	19.21	17.84	38
39	45.36	40.29	36.01	32.38	29.27	26.61	24.31	22.32	20.58	19.06	17.72	39
40	44.37	39.50	35.38	31.86	28.86	26.27	24.03	22.09	20.39	18.90	17.59	40
41	43.37	38.70	34.73	31.34	28.44	25.93	23.75	21.86	20.20	18.74	17.46	41
42	42.38	37.90	34.09	30.82	28.01	25.57	23.46	21.62	20.00	18.58	17.32	42
43	41.39	37.10	33.43	30.29	27.57	25.21	23.16	21.37	19.80	18.40	17.17	43
44	40.40	36.29	32.78	29.75	27.13	24.85	22.86	21.12	19.58	18.23	17.02	44
45	39.41	35.49	32.11	29.20	26.67	24.47	22.55	20.85	19.36	18.04	16.86	45
46	38.42	34.67	31.44	28.65	26.21	24.09	22.23	20.58	19.13	17.85	16.70	46
47	37.43	33.86	30.77	28.09	25.75	23.70	21.90	20.31	18.90	17.64	16.53	47
48	36.45	33.05	30.09	27.52	25.27	23.30	21.56	20.02	18.65	17.44	16.35	48
49	35.47	32.23	29.41	26.95	24.79	22.89	21.21	19.73	18.40	17.22	16.16	49
50	34.49	31.41	28.72	26.37	24.30	22.48	20.86	19.42	18.14	17.00	15.97	50
51	33.52	30.59	28.03	25.79	23.81	22.05	20.50	19.11	17.88	16.77	15.77	51
52	32.55	29.78	27.34	25.20	23.30	21.62	20.13	18.80	17.60	16.53	15.56	52
53	31.59	28.96	26.65	24.61	22.80	21.19	19.75	18.47	17.32	16.28	15.35	53
54	30.63	28.14	25.95	24.01	22.28	20.74	19.37	18.14	17.03	16.03	15.12	54
55	29.68	27.33	25.25	23.41	21.76	20.29	18.98	17.80	16.73	15.77	14.89	55
56	28.73	26.51	24.55	22.80	21.24	19.84	18.58	17.45	16.42	15.50	14.66	56
57	27.79	25.70	23.85	22.19	20.71	19.38	18.18	17.09	16.11	15.22	14.41	57
58	26.86	24.90	23.15	21.58	20.18	18.91	17.77	16.73	15.79	14.94	14.16	58
59	25.95	24.11	22.46	20.98	19.65	18.44	17.36	16.37	15.47	14.65	13.91	59
60	25.05	23.32	21.77	20.38	19.12	17.98	16.94	16.00	15.14	14.36	13.64	60
61	24.16	22.54	21.09	19.77	18.58	17.50	16.52	15.63	14.81	14.06	13.38	61
62	23.27	21.76	20.39	19.16	18.04	17.02	16.09	15.24	14.46	13.75	13.10	62
63	22.38	20.97	19.69	18.53	17.48	16.52	15.64	14.84	14.10	13.43	12.80	63
64	21.47	20.17	18.98	17.90	16.91	16.01	15.18	14.43	13.73	13.09	12.50	64

APIL Guide to Fatal Accidents

Table 20 *continued*

65	20.56	19.35	18.25	17.24	16.32	15.48	14.70	13.99	13.34	12.73	12.17	65
66	19.64	18.53	17.51	16.57	15.72	14.93	14.21	13.54	12.93	12.36	11.83	66
67	18.72	17.69	16.76	15.89	15.10	14.37	13.70	13.08	12.50	11.97	11.47	67
68	17.80	16.86	16.00	15.21	14.48	13.80	13.18	12.60	12.07	11.57	11.10	68
69	16.89	16.04	15.25	14.52	13.85	13.23	12.65	12.12	11.62	11.16	10.73	69
70	16.01	15.23	14.51	13.85	13.23	12.66	12.13	11.64	11.17	10.74	10.34	70
71	15.15	14.44	13.79	13.19	12.62	12.10	11.61	11.16	10.73	10.33	9.96	71
72	14.33	13.69	13.10	12.55	12.03	11.55	11.11	10.69	10.30	9.93	9.58	72
73	13.55	12.98	12.44	11.93	11.46	11.03	10.62	10.23	9.87	9.53	9.21	73
74	12.81	12.29	11.80	11.34	10.91	10.51	10.14	9.79	9.45	9.14	8.85	74
75	12.10	11.63	11.19	10.77	10.38	10.02	9.67	9.35	9.04	8.76	8.49	75
76	11.42	11.00	10.59	10.22	9.86	9.53	9.22	8.92	8.64	8.38	8.13	76
77	10.77	10.38	10.02	9.68	9.36	9.06	8.77	8.50	8.25	8.00	7.77	77
78	10.13	9.79	9.46	9.15	8.86	8.59	8.33	8.08	7.85	7.63	7.42	78
79	9.52	9.21	8.92	8.64	8.38	8.13	7.90	7.67	7.46	7.26	7.07	79
80	8.93	8.65	8.39	8.14	7.91	7.68	7.47	7.27	7.08	6.90	6.72	80
81	8.36	8.12	7.88	7.66	7.45	7.25	7.06	6.88	6.70	6.54	6.38	81
82	7.83	7.61	7.40	7.20	7.01	6.83	6.66	6.49	6.34	6.19	6.04	82
83	7.32	7.12	6.94	6.76	6.59	6.43	6.27	6.13	5.99	5.85	5.72	83
84	6.85	6.68	6.51	6.35	6.20	6.06	5.92	5.78	5.66	5.54	5.42	84
85	6.43	6.27	6.12	5.98	5.84	5.71	5.59	5.47	5.35	5.24	5.14	85
86	6.04	5.90	5.77	5.64	5.52	5.40	5.29	5.18	5.07	4.97	4.88	86
87	5.70	5.57	5.45	5.34	5.23	5.12	5.02	4.92	4.83	4.73	4.65	87
88	5.40	5.29	5.18	5.07	4.97	4.88	4.78	4.69	4.61	4.52	4.44	88
89	5.13	5.03	4.93	4.84	4.74	4.66	4.57	4.49	4.41	4.33	4.26	89
90	4.88	4.78	4.69	4.61	4.52	4.44	4.36	4.29	4.21	4.14	4.08	90
91	4.60	4.52	4.44	4.36	4.28	4.21	4.14	4.07	4.01	3.94	3.88	91
92	4.31	4.24	4.17	4.10	4.03	3.96	3.90	3.84	3.78	3.72	3.67	92
93	4.02	3.95	3.89	3.83	3.77	3.71	3.65	3.60	3.55	3.50	3.45	93
94	3.73	3.67	3.61	3.56	3.51	3.46	3.41	3.36	3.31	3.27	3.22	94
95	3.45	3.40	3.35	3.30	3.26	3.21	3.17	3.13	3.09	3.05	3.01	95
96	3.18	3.14	3.10	3.06	3.02	2.98	2.94	2.91	2.87	2.84	2.80	96
97	2.93	2.90	2.86	2.83	2.79	2.76	2.73	2.69	2.66	2.63	2.60	97
98	2.71	2.68	2.64	2.61	2.58	2.56	2.53	2.50	2.47	2.45	2.42	98
99	2.51	2.48	2.45	2.43	2.40	2.38	2.35	2.33	2.30	2.28	2.26	99
100	2.34	2.31	2.29	2.27	2.24	2.22	2.20	2.18	2.16	2.14	2.12	100

Table 21 Multipliers for loss of earnings to pension age 55 (males)

Age at date of trial	Multiplier calculated with allowance for projected mortality from the 1998-based population projections and rate of return of											Age at date of trial
	0.0%	0.5%	1.0%	1.5%	2.0%	2.5%	3.0%	£3.5%	4.0%	4.5%	5.0%	
16	38.25	34.79	31.75	29.08	26.73	24.65	22.81	21.17	19.70	18.40	17.22	16
17	37.26	33.97	31.07	28.52	26.26	24.26	22.48	20.90	19.48	18.21	17.07	17
18	36.28	33.15	30.39	27.96	25.79	23.87	22.15	20.62	19.25	18.01	16.90	18
19	35.30	32.34	29.71	27.39	25.32	23.47	21.82	20.34	19.01	17.82	16.74	19
20	34.33	31.52	29.03	26.81	24.83	23.06	21.47	20.05	18.77	17.61	16.56	20
21	33.35	30.70	28.34	26.23	24.34	22.64	21.12	19.75	18.51	17.39	16.38	21
22	32.38	29.88	27.64	25.63	23.83	22.22	20.76	19.44	18.25	17.17	16.19	22
23	31.40	29.04	26.93	25.03	23.32	21.77	20.38	19.12	17.97	16.93	15.98	23
24	30.43	28.21	26.21	24.41	22.79	21.32	19.99	18.78	17.69	16.68	15.77	24
25	29.45	27.37	25.49	23.79	22.25	20.86	19.59	18.44	17.39	16.43	15.55	25
26	28.47	26.52	24.76	23.16	21.71	20.39	19.18	18.08	17.08	16.16	15.31	26
27	27.49	25.68	24.02	22.52	21.15	19.90	18.76	17.71	16.76	15.88	15.07	27
28	26.52	24.82	23.28	21.87	20.58	19.40	18.32	17.33	16.42	15.58	14.81	28
29	25.54	23.96	22.52	21.21	20.00	18.89	17.87	16.94	16.07	15.27	14.54	29
30	24.56	23.10	21.76	20.54	19.41	18.37	17.41	16.53	15.71	14.95	14.25	30
31	23.58	22.23	21.00	19.85	18.80	17.83	16.93	16.10	15.33	14.62	13.95	31
32	22.60	21.36	20.22	19.16	18.18	17.28	16.44	15.66	14.94	14.26	13.64	32
33	21.62	20.48	19.43	18.46	17.55	16.71	15.93	15.21	14.53	13.90	13.31	33
34	20.64	19.60	18.64	17.74	16.91	16.13	15.41	14.73	14.10	13.51	12.96	34
35	19.66	18.71	17.84	17.02	16.25	15.54	14.87	14.25	13.66	13.11	12.59	35
36	18.67	17.82	17.02	16.28	15.58	14.93	14.32	13.74	13.20	12.69	12.21	36
37	17.69	16.92	16.21	15.53	14.90	14.30	13.74	13.22	12.72	12.25	11.81	37
38	16.71	16.02	15.38	14.77	14.20	13.66	13.15	12.67	12.22	11.79	11.39	38
39	15.72	15.12	14.54	14.00	13.49	13.01	12.55	12.11	11.70	11.31	10.94	39
40	14.74	14.21	13.70	13.22	12.77	12.34	11.93	11.54	11.17	10.82	10.48	40
41	13.77	13.30	12.86	12.43	12.03	11.65	11.29	10.94	10.61	10.30	10.00	41
42	12.79	12.39	12.00	11.63	11.28	10.95	10.63	10.33	10.03	9.75	9.49	42
43	11.81	11.47	11.14	10.82	10.52	10.23	9.95	9.69	9.43	9.19	8.96	43
44	10.83	10.54	10.27	10.00	9.74	9.49	9.26	9.03	8.81	8.60	8.40	44
45	9.86	9.62	9.38	9.16	8.95	8.74	8.54	8.35	8.16	7.98	7.81	45
46	8.88	8.68	8.49	8.31	8.14	7.97	7.80	7.64	7.49	7.34	7.19	46
47	7.90	7.74	7.59	7.45	7.31	7.17	7.04	6.91	6.79	6.66	6.55	47
48	6.92	6.80	6.68	6.57	6.46	6.36	6.25	6.15	6.05	5.96	5.86	48
49	5.94	5.85	5.76	5.68	5.60	5.52	5.44	5.37	5.29	5.22	5.15	49
50	4.95	4.89	4.83	4.77	4.72	4.66	4.60	4.55	4.50	4.45	4.40	50
51	3.97	3.93	3.89	3.85	3.81	3.78	3.74	3.71	3.67	3.64	3.60	51
52	2.98	2.96	2.94	2.91	2.89	2.87	2.85	2.83	2.81	2.79	2.77	52
53	1.99	1.98	1.97	1.96	1.95	1.94	1.93	1.92	1.91	1.90	1.90	53
54	1.00	0.99	0.99	0.99	0.99	0.99	0.98	0.98	0.98	0.98	0.97	54

Table 22   Multipliers for loss of earnings to pension age 55 (females)

Age at date of trial	Multiplier calculated with allowance for projected mortality from the 1998-based population projections and rate of return of											Age at date of trial
	0.0%	0.5%	1.0%	1.5%	2.0%	2.5%	3.0%	£3.5%	4.0%	4.5%	5.0%	
16	38.60	35.09	32.02	29.32	26.94	24.84	22.97	21.32	19.84	18.52	17.33	16
17	37.61	34.27	31.34	28.76	26.48	24.45	22.65	21.05	19.62	18.33	17.18	17
18	36.61	33.45	30.66	28.19	26.00	24.06	22.32	20.77	19.39	18.14	17.02	18
19	35.62	32.62	29.97	27.61	25.52	23.65	21.98	20.49	19.15	17.94	16.85	19
20	34.63	31.79	29.27	27.03	25.03	23.24	21.63	20.19	18.90	17.73	16.67	20
21	33.64	30.95	28.56	26.43	24.52	22.81	21.27	19.89	18.64	17.51	16.48	21
22	32.65	30.11	27.85	25.83	24.01	22.37	20.90	19.57	18.37	17.28	16.29	22
23	31.65	29.27	27.13	25.21	23.48	21.93	20.52	19.24	18.09	17.04	16.08	23
24	30.66	28.42	26.40	24.59	22.95	21.47	20.12	18.90	17.79	16.78	15.86	24
25	29.67	27.57	25.67	23.95	22.40	21.00	19.72	18.55	17.49	16.52	15.63	25
26	28.67	26.71	24.93	23.31	21.85	20.51	19.30	18.19	17.18	16.25	15.40	26
27	27.68	25.85	24.18	22.66	21.28	20.02	18.87	17.81	16.85	15.96	15.15	27
28	26.69	24.98	23.42	22.00	20.70	19.51	18.42	17.43	16.51	15.66	14.88	28
29	25.70	24.11	22.66	21.33	20.11	19.00	17.97	17.02	16.15	15.35	14.61	29
30	24.71	23.24	21.89	20.65	19.51	18.47	17.50	16.61	15.79	15.02	14.32	30
31	23.72	22.36	21.11	19.96	18.90	17.92	17.02	16.18	15.40	14.68	14.02	31
32	22.73	21.48	20.33	19.26	18.28	17.37	16.52	15.74	15.01	14.33	13.70	32
33	21.74	20.59	19.54	18.55	17.64	16.80	16.01	15.28	14.60	13.96	13.36	33
34	20.75	19.71	18.74	17.83	16.99	16.21	15.48	14.80	14.17	13.57	13.02	34
35	19.76	18.81	17.93	17.10	16.33	15.61	14.94	14.31	13.72	13.17	12.65	35
36	18.77	17.92	17.11	16.36	15.66	15.00	14.38	13.80	13.26	12.75	12.26	36
37	17.79	17.01	16.29	15.61	14.97	14.37	13.81	13.28	12.78	12.31	11.86	37
38	16.80	16.11	15.46	14.85	14.27	13.73	13.22	12.74	12.28	11.85	11.44	38
39	15.81	15.20	14.62	14.08	13.56	13.07	12.61	12.18	11.76	11.37	11.00	39
40	14.82	14.29	13.78	13.29	12.83	12.40	11.99	11.59	11.22	10.87	10.53	40
41	13.84	13.37	12.92	12.50	12.09	11.71	11.34	10.99	10.66	10.35	10.04	41
42	12.85	12.45	12.06	11.69	11.34	11.00	10.68	10.37	10.08	9.80	9.53	42
43	11.87	11.52	11.19	10.87	10.57	10.28	10.00	9.73	9.48	9.23	8.99	43
44	10.88	10.59	10.31	10.04	9.78	9.53	9.30	9.07	8.85	8.63	8.43	44
45	9.90	9.66	9.42	9.20	8.98	8.77	8.57	8.38	8.19	8.01	7.84	45
46	8.91	8.72	8.53	8.34	8.17	7.99	7.83	7.67	7.51	7.36	7.22	46
47	7.93	7.77	7.62	7.47	7.33	7.19	7.06	6.93	6.81	6.68	6.57	47
48	6.94	6.82	6.70	6.59	6.48	6.37	6.27	6.17	6.07	5.97	5.88	48
49	5.95	5.86	5.78	5.69	5.61	5.53	5.46	5.38	5.31	5.23	5.16	49
50	4.96	4.90	4.84	4.78	4.73	4.67	4.62	4.56	4.51	4.46	4.41	50
51	3.98	3.94	3.90	3.86	3.82	3.79	3.75	3.71	3.68	3.65	3.61	51
52	2.99	2.96	2.94	2.92	2.90	2.88	2.86	2.84	2.82	2.80	2.78	52
53	1.99	1.98	1.97	1.96	1.95	1.94	1.94	1.93	1.92	1.91	1.90	53
54	1.00	1.00	0.99	0.99	0.99	0.99	0.98	0.98	0.98	0.98	0.97	54

Table 23 Multipliers for loss of earnings to pension age 60 (males)

Age at date of trial	Multiplier calculated with allowance for projected mortality from the 1998-based population projections and rate of return of											Age at date of trial
	0.0%	0.5%	1.0%	1.5%	2.0%	2.5%	3.0%	£3.5%	4.0%	4.5%	5.0%	
16	42.93	38.59	34.85	31.60	28.79	26.33	24.18	22.29	20.62	19.15	17.84	16
17	41.94	37.79	34.20	31.08	28.36	25.98	23.90	22.06	20.43	19.00	17.72	17
18	40.96	36.99	33.55	30.55	27.93	25.63	23.61	21.82	20.24	18.84	17.59	18
19	39.98	36.20	32.91	30.03	27.50	25.28	23.32	21.59	20.05	18.68	17.45	19
20	39.01	35.40	32.25	29.49	27.06	24.92	23.02	21.34	19.84	18.51	17.32	20
21	38.04	34.61	31.60	28.95	26.61	24.55	22.72	21.09	19.63	18.34	17.17	21
22	37.07	33.80	30.93	28.40	26.16	24.17	22.40	20.83	19.42	18.15	17.02	22
23	36.09	32.99	30.26	27.84	25.69	23.78	22.07	20.55	19.19	17.96	16.86	23
24	35.12	32.18	29.58	27.27	25.21	23.38	21.74	20.27	18.95	17.76	16.69	24
25	34.14	31.36	28.89	26.69	24.72	22.97	21.39	19.98	18.70	17.55	16.51	25
26	33.17	30.54	28.19	26.10	24.23	22.55	21.04	19.67	18.45	17.33	16.33	26
27	32.20	29.71	27.49	25.51	23.72	22.12	20.67	19.36	18.18	17.11	16.13	27
28	31.22	28.88	26.79	24.90	23.20	21.67	20.29	19.04	17.90	16.87	15.93	28
29	30.25	28.05	26.07	24.29	22.68	21.22	19.90	18.70	17.61	16.62	15.71	29
30	29.27	27.21	25.35	23.66	22.14	20.76	19.50	18.36	17.31	16.36	15.49	30
31	28.29	26.36	24.62	23.03	21.59	20.28	19.09	18.00	17.00	16.09	15.25	31
32	27.32	25.51	23.88	22.39	21.03	19.79	18.66	17.63	16.68	15.80	15.00	32
33	26.34	24.66	23.13	21.73	20.46	19.29	18.22	17.24	16.34	15.51	14.74	33
34	25.36	23.80	22.38	21.07	19.88	18.78	17.77	16.84	15.98	15.19	14.46	34
35	24.38	22.94	21.61	20.40	19.28	18.25	17.30	16.43	15.62	14.87	14.17	35
36	23.40	22.07	20.84	19.71	18.67	17.71	16.82	16.00	15.24	14.53	13.87	36
37	22.42	21.19	20.06	19.02	18.05	17.15	16.32	15.55	14.84	14.17	13.55	37
38	21.44	20.31	19.27	18.31	17.42	16.59	15.82	15.10	14.43	13.80	13.22	38
39	20.46	19.43	18.48	17.60	16.77	16.01	15.29	14.62	14.00	13.42	12.87	39
40	19.48	18.55	17.69	16.88	16.12	15.42	14.75	14.14	13.56	13.01	12.50	40
41	18.51	17.67	16.88	16.15	15.46	14.81	14.20	13.63	13.10	12.60	12.12	41
42	17.54	16.78	16.07	15.41	14.78	14.19	13.64	13.12	12.62	12.16	11.72	42
43	16.57	15.89	15.25	14.66	14.09	13.56	13.06	12.58	12.13	11.71	11.31	43
44	15.60	15.00	14.43	13.90	13.39	12.91	12.46	12.03	11.62	11.24	10.87	44
45	14.63	14.10	13.60	13.12	12.67	12.25	11.84	11.46	11.09	10.74	10.41	45
46	13.66	13.20	12.76	12.34	11.94	11.57	11.21	10.86	10.54	10.23	9.93	46
47	12.69	12.29	11.91	11.55	11.20	10.87	10.55	10.25	9.96	9.69	9.42	47
48	11.72	11.38	11.05	10.74	10.44	10.15	9.88	9.62	9.37	9.12	8.89	48
49	10.74	10.46	10.18	9.92	9.66	9.42	9.19	8.96	8.74	8.54	8.33	49
50	9.77	9.53	9.30	9.08	8.87	8.67	8.47	8.28	8.10	7.92	7.75	50
51	8.80	8.61	8.42	8.24	8.07	7.90	7.73	7.58	7.42	7.28	7.13	51
52	7.83	7.67	7.53	7.38	7.24	7.11	6.98	6.85	6.73	6.61	6.49	52
53	6.86	6.74	6.62	6.51	6.41	6.30	6.20	6.10	6.00	5.91	5.82	53
54	5.88	5.80	5.71	5.63	5.55	5.47	5.40	5.32	5.25	5.18	5.11	54
55	4.91	4.85	4.79	4.74	4.68	4.62	4.57	4.52	4.46	4.41	4.36	55
56	3.94	3.90	3.86	3.82	3.79	3.75	3.72	3.68	3.65	3.61	3.58	56
57	2.96	2.94	2.92	2.90	2.88	2.86	2.84	2.82	2.80	2.78	2.76	57
58	1.98	1.97	1.96	1.95	1.94	1.93	1.92	1.92	1.91	1.90	1.89	58
59	1.00	0.99	0.99	0.99	0.99	0.98	0.98	0.98	0.98	0.97	0.97	59

Table 24   Multipliers for loss of earnings to pension age 60 (females)

Age at date of trial	Multiplier calculated with allowance for projected mortality from the 1998-based population projections and rate of return of											Age at date of trial
	0.0%	0.5%	1.0%	1.5%	2.0%	2.5%	3.0%	£3.5%	4.0%	4.5%	5.0%	
16	43.38	38.99	35.19	31.90	29.05	26.56	24.38	22.47	20.78	19.29	17.97	16
17	42.39	38.18	34.54	31.38	28.62	26.21	24.10	22.24	20.60	19.14	17.84	17
18	41.40	37.38	33.89	30.85	28.19	25.86	23.81	22.00	20.40	18.98	17.72	18
19	40.41	36.57	33.23	30.31	27.75	25.50	23.52	21.76	20.21	18.82	17.58	19
20	39.42	35.76	32.57	29.77	27.30	25.13	23.21	21.51	20.00	18.65	17.44	20
21	38.43	34.95	31.89	29.21	26.85	24.76	22.90	21.25	19.78	18.47	17.29	21
22	37.43	34.12	31.21	28.65	26.38	24.37	22.58	20.98	19.56	18.28	17.14	22
23	36.44	33.30	30.53	28.08	25.90	23.97	22.25	20.71	19.33	18.09	16.97	23
24	35.45	32.47	29.84	27.50	25.42	23.56	21.90	20.42	19.08	17.88	16.80	24
25	34.46	31.64	29.13	26.91	24.92	23.14	21.55	20.12	18.83	17.67	16.62	25
26	33.46	30.80	28.43	26.31	24.41	22.72	21.19	19.81	18.57	17.45	16.43	26
27	32.47	29.96	27.71	25.70	23.90	22.28	20.81	19.49	18.30	17.21	16.23	27
28	31.48	29.11	26.99	25.09	23.37	21.83	20.43	19.16	18.02	16.97	16.02	28
29	30.49	28.27	26.27	24.47	22.84	21.37	20.03	18.82	17.72	16.72	15.80	29
30	29.50	27.41	25.53	23.83	22.29	20.90	19.63	18.47	17.42	16.46	15.57	30
31	28.51	26.56	24.79	23.19	21.74	20.42	19.21	18.11	17.10	16.18	15.33	31
32	27.52	25.70	24.05	22.54	21.17	19.92	18.78	17.73	16.77	15.89	15.08	32
33	26.53	24.84	23.29	21.88	20.60	19.42	18.34	17.34	16.43	15.59	14.82	33
34	25.55	23.97	22.53	21.21	20.01	18.90	17.88	16.94	16.08	15.28	14.54	34
35	24.56	23.10	21.76	20.54	19.41	18.37	17.41	16.53	15.71	14.95	14.25	35
36	23.57	22.23	20.99	19.85	18.80	17.83	16.93	16.10	15.33	14.61	13.95	36
37	22.59	21.35	20.21	19.15	18.18	17.27	16.43	15.65	14.93	14.26	13.63	37
38	21.60	20.47	19.42	18.44	17.54	16.70	15.92	15.20	14.52	13.89	13.30	38
39	20.62	19.58	18.62	17.73	16.90	16.12	15.40	14.72	14.09	13.50	12.95	39
40	19.63	18.69	17.82	17.00	16.24	15.52	14.86	14.23	13.65	13.10	12.58	40
41	18.65	17.80	17.01	16.26	15.57	14.91	14.30	13.73	13.19	12.68	12.20	41
42	17.67	16.91	16.19	15.52	14.88	14.29	13.73	13.20	12.71	12.24	11.80	42
43	16.69	16.01	15.36	14.76	14.19	13.65	13.14	12.66	12.21	11.78	11.38	43
44	15.71	15.10	14.53	13.99	13.48	13.00	12.54	12.11	11.69	11.31	10.94	44
45	14.73	14.20	13.69	13.21	12.76	12.33	11.92	11.53	11.16	10.81	10.47	45
46	13.75	13.28	12.84	12.42	12.02	11.64	11.28	10.93	10.60	10.29	9.99	46
47	12.77	12.37	11.98	11.62	11.27	10.94	10.62	10.31	10.02	9.74	9.48	47
48	11.79	11.45	11.12	10.81	10.50	10.22	9.94	9.67	9.42	9.18	8.94	48
49	10.81	10.52	10.25	9.98	9.72	9.48	9.24	9.01	8.80	8.59	8.38	49
50	9.84	9.60	9.37	9.14	8.93	8.72	8.52	8.33	8.15	7.97	7.80	50
51	8.86	8.66	8.48	8.29	8.12	7.95	7.78	7.63	7.47	7.32	7.18	51
52	7.88	7.73	7.58	7.43	7.29	7.15	7.02	6.89	6.77	6.65	6.53	52
53	6.90	6.78	6.67	6.56	6.45	6.34	6.24	6.14	6.04	5.94	5.85	53
54	5.92	5.84	5.75	5.67	5.59	5.51	5.43	5.35	5.28	5.21	5.14	54
55	4.94	4.88	4.82	4.76	4.71	4.65	4.60	4.54	4.49	4.44	4.39	55
56	3.96	3.92	3.88	3.85	3.81	3.77	3.74	3.70	3.67	3.63	3.60	56
57	2.98	2.95	2.93	2.91	2.89	2.87	2.85	2.83	2.81	2.79	2.77	57
58	1.99	1.98	1.97	1.96	1.95	1.94	1.93	1.92	1.91	1.90	1.90	58
59	1.00	0.99	0.99	0.99	0.99	0.98	0.98	0.98	0.98	0.98	0.97	59

Table 25 Multipliers for loss of earnings to pension age 65 (males)

Age at date of trial	Multiplier calculated with allowance for projected mortality from the 1998-based population projections and rate of return of											Age at date of trial
	0.0%	0.5%	1.0%	1.5%	2.0%	2.5%	3.0%	£3.5%	4.0%	4.5%	5.0%	
16	47.44	42.17	37.69	33.87	30.59	27.76	25.32	23.20	21.35	19.74	18.31	16
17	46.45	41.39	37.07	33.38	30.20	27.45	25.07	23.00	21.20	19.61	18.21	17
18	45.48	40.62	36.46	32.89	29.81	27.14	24.83	22.80	21.03	19.48	18.10	18
19	44.51	39.84	35.84	32.39	29.41	26.83	24.57	22.60	20.87	19.35	18.00	19
20	43.53	39.07	35.22	31.89	29.01	26.50	24.31	22.39	20.70	19.21	17.89	20
21	42.57	38.29	34.59	31.39	28.60	26.17	24.05	22.17	20.53	19.07	17.77	21
22	41.60	37.50	33.96	30.88	28.19	25.84	23.77	21.95	20.34	18.92	17.65	22
23	40.62	36.71	33.32	30.35	27.76	25.49	23.49	21.72	20.15	18.76	17.52	23
24	39.65	35.92	32.67	29.82	27.33	25.13	23.19	21.48	19.95	18.60	17.38	24
25	38.68	35.12	32.01	29.28	26.88	24.76	22.89	21.23	19.75	18.42	17.24	25
26	37.71	34.32	31.35	28.74	26.43	24.39	22.58	20.97	19.53	18.25	17.09	26
27	36.73	33.51	30.68	28.18	25.97	24.01	22.26	20.70	19.31	18.06	16.94	27
28	35.76	32.70	30.01	27.62	25.50	23.61	21.93	20.43	19.08	17.86	16.77	28
29	34.79	31.89	29.32	27.05	25.02	23.21	21.59	20.14	18.84	17.66	16.60	29
30	33.81	31.07	28.64	26.47	24.53	22.80	21.24	19.85	18.59	17.45	16.42	30
31	32.84	30.25	27.94	25.88	24.03	22.37	20.88	19.54	18.32	17.23	16.23	31
32	31.86	29.42	27.23	25.28	23.52	21.94	20.51	19.22	18.05	16.99	16.03	32
33	30.89	28.59	26.52	24.67	23.00	21.49	20.13	18.89	17.77	16.75	15.82	33
34	29.91	27.75	25.80	24.05	22.47	21.03	19.73	18.55	17.48	16.50	15.60	34
35	28.93	26.90	25.07	23.42	21.92	20.56	19.32	18.20	17.17	16.23	15.37	35
36	27.95	26.05	24.34	22.78	21.37	20.08	18.90	17.83	16.85	15.95	15.12	36
37	26.97	25.20	23.60	22.13	20.80	19.58	18.47	17.45	16.52	15.66	14.87	37
38	25.99	24.35	22.85	21.48	20.22	19.08	18.03	17.06	16.17	15.36	14.60	38
39	25.01	23.49	22.09	20.81	19.64	18.56	17.57	16.66	15.82	15.04	14.32	39
40	24.04	22.63	21.33	20.14	19.04	18.03	17.10	16.24	15.45	14.71	14.03	40
41	23.07	21.77	20.57	19.46	18.44	17.50	16.62	15.82	15.07	14.37	13.73	41
42	22.10	20.91	19.80	18.77	17.83	16.95	16.13	15.38	14.67	14.02	13.41	42
43	21.14	20.04	19.02	18.08	17.20	16.39	15.63	14.92	14.27	13.65	13.08	43
44	20.17	19.17	18.24	17.37	16.56	15.81	15.11	14.45	13.84	13.27	12.73	44
45	19.21	18.30	17.45	16.66	15.92	15.22	14.58	13.97	13.40	12.87	12.37	45
46	18.25	17.42	16.65	15.93	15.26	14.62	14.03	13.47	12.95	12.45	11.99	46
47	17.28	16.54	15.85	15.20	14.58	14.01	13.46	12.95	12.47	12.02	11.59	47
48	16.32	15.66	15.03	14.45	13.90	13.37	12.88	12.42	11.98	11.56	11.17	48
49	15.35	14.77	14.21	13.69	13.19	12.73	12.28	11.86	11.46	11.09	10.73	49
50	14.39	13.87	13.38	12.92	12.48	12.06	11.67	11.29	10.93	10.59	10.27	50
51	13.42	12.97	12.54	12.14	11.75	11.38	11.03	10.70	10.38	10.07	9.78	51
52	12.46	12.07	11.70	11.35	11.01	10.69	10.38	10.09	9.80	9.54	9.28	52
53	11.50	11.17	10.85	10.55	10.26	9.98	9.71	9.46	9.21	8.98	8.75	53
54	10.55	10.27	10.00	9.74	9.50	9.26	9.03	8.81	8.60	8.40	8.20	54
55	9.60	9.37	9.14	8.93	8.72	8.52	8.33	8.14	7.96	7.79	7.62	55
56	8.65	8.46	8.28	8.10	7.93	7.77	7.61	7.45	7.31	7.16	7.02	56
57	7.70	7.55	7.40	7.26	7.13	7.00	6.87	6.74	6.62	6.51	6.39	57
58	6.75	6.64	6.53	6.42	6.31	6.21	6.11	6.01	5.92	5.82	5.73	58
59	5.80	5.72	5.64	5.56	5.48	5.40	5.32	5.25	5.18	5.11	5.04	59
60	4.85	4.79	4.74	4.68	4.62	4.57	4.52	4.46	4.41	4.36	4.31	60
61	3.90	3.86	3.82	3.79	3.75	3.72	3.68	3.65	3.61	3.58	3.55	61
62	2.94	2.92	2.90	2.88	2.85	2.83	2.81	2.79	2.77	2.76	2.74	62
63	1.97	1.96	1.95	1.94	1.93	1.92	1.91	1.91	1.90	1.89	1.88	63
64	0.99	0.99	0.99	0.98	0.98	0.98	0.98	0.98	0.97	0.97	0.97	64

Table 26 Multipliers for loss of earnings to pension age 65 (females)

Age at date of trial	Multiplier calculated with allowance for projected mortality from the 1998-based population projections and rate of return of											Age at date of trial
	0.0%	0.5%	1.0%	1.5%	2.0%	2.5%	3.0%	£3.5%	4.0%	4.5%	5.0%	
16	48.06	42.69	38.13	34.24	30.91	28.04	25.56	23.41	21.54	19.89	18.45	16
17	47.07	41.91	37.52	33.76	30.52	27.74	25.32	23.22	21.38	19.77	18.35	17
18	46.08	41.13	36.89	33.26	30.13	27.42	25.07	23.02	21.22	19.64	18.25	18
19	45.08	40.34	36.27	32.76	29.73	27.10	24.81	22.81	21.06	19.51	18.14	19
20	44.09	39.54	35.63	32.25	29.32	26.77	24.55	22.60	20.88	19.37	18.03	20
21	43.10	38.75	34.99	31.73	28.90	26.44	24.27	22.38	20.70	19.22	17.91	21
22	42.11	37.95	34.34	31.21	28.48	26.09	23.99	22.15	20.52	19.07	17.79	22
23	41.12	37.14	33.69	30.68	28.04	25.73	23.70	21.91	20.32	18.91	17.65	23
24	40.12	36.33	33.02	30.13	27.60	25.37	23.40	21.66	20.12	18.74	17.52	24
25	39.13	35.52	32.36	29.58	27.15	25.00	23.10	21.41	19.91	18.57	17.37	25
26	38.14	34.70	31.68	29.03	26.69	24.62	22.78	21.15	19.69	18.39	17.22	26
27	37.15	33.88	31.00	28.46	26.22	24.22	22.45	20.87	19.46	18.20	17.06	27
28	36.16	33.05	30.31	27.89	25.74	23.82	22.12	20.59	19.23	18.00	16.89	28
29	35.17	32.22	29.62	27.31	25.25	23.41	21.77	20.30	18.98	17.79	16.72	29
30	34.18	31.39	28.92	26.72	24.75	23.00	21.42	20.00	18.73	17.58	16.54	30
31	33.19	30.56	28.21	26.12	24.25	22.57	21.05	19.69	18.46	17.35	16.34	31
32	32.20	29.72	27.50	25.51	23.73	22.13	20.68	19.37	18.19	17.12	16.14	32
33	31.21	28.88	26.78	24.90	23.21	21.68	20.29	19.04	17.91	16.87	15.93	33
34	30.22	28.03	26.06	24.28	22.67	21.22	19.90	18.70	17.61	16.62	15.71	34
35	29.24	27.18	25.32	23.64	22.12	20.74	19.49	18.35	17.31	16.35	15.48	35
36	28.25	26.33	24.59	23.00	21.57	20.26	19.07	17.98	16.99	16.08	15.24	36
37	27.27	25.47	23.84	22.36	21.00	19.77	18.64	17.61	16.66	15.79	14.99	37
38	26.28	24.61	23.09	21.70	20.43	19.26	18.20	17.22	16.31	15.49	14.72	38
39	25.30	23.75	22.33	21.03	19.84	18.74	17.74	16.81	15.96	15.17	14.44	39
40	24.32	22.88	21.57	20.35	19.24	18.22	17.27	16.40	15.59	14.84	14.15	40
41	23.34	22.01	20.79	19.67	18.63	17.67	16.79	15.97	15.21	14.50	13.85	41
42	22.36	21.14	20.02	18.98	18.01	17.12	16.29	15.53	14.81	14.15	13.53	42
43	21.38	20.27	19.23	18.27	17.38	16.55	15.78	15.07	14.40	13.78	13.20	43
44	20.41	19.39	18.44	17.56	16.74	15.97	15.26	14.60	13.97	13.39	12.85	44
45	19.43	18.51	17.64	16.84	16.08	15.38	14.72	14.11	13.53	12.99	12.48	45
46	18.46	17.62	16.84	16.10	15.42	14.77	14.17	13.60	13.07	12.57	12.10	46
47	17.48	16.73	16.02	15.36	14.74	14.15	13.60	13.08	12.59	12.13	11.70	47
48	16.51	15.84	15.21	14.61	14.05	13.52	13.02	12.55	12.10	11.68	11.28	48
49	15.54	14.94	14.38	13.85	13.34	12.87	12.42	11.99	11.58	11.20	10.84	49
50	14.57	14.04	13.55	13.07	12.63	12.20	11.80	11.42	11.05	10.71	10.38	50
51	13.60	13.14	12.71	12.29	11.90	11.52	11.16	10.82	10.50	10.19	9.89	51
52	12.63	12.24	11.86	11.50	11.16	10.83	10.51	10.21	9.93	9.65	9.39	52
53	11.67	11.33	11.01	10.70	10.40	10.11	9.84	9.58	9.33	9.09	8.86	53
54	10.70	10.42	10.14	9.88	9.63	9.39	9.15	8.93	8.71	8.51	8.31	54
55	9.74	9.50	9.27	9.05	8.84	8.64	8.44	8.25	8.07	7.90	7.72	55
56	8.77	8.58	8.40	8.22	8.04	7.88	7.71	7.56	7.40	7.26	7.12	56
57	7.81	7.66	7.51	7.37	7.23	7.09	6.96	6.84	6.71	6.59	6.48	57
58	6.84	6.73	6.61	6.50	6.39	6.29	6.19	6.09	5.99	5.90	5.81	58
59	5.88	5.79	5.71	5.63	5.55	5.47	5.39	5.32	5.24	5.17	5.10	59
60	4.91	4.85	4.79	4.73	4.68	4.62	4.57	4.51	4.46	4.41	4.36	60
61	3.94	3.90	3.86	3.82	3.79	3.75	3.72	3.68	3.65	3.61	3.58	61
62	2.96	2.94	2.92	2.90	2.88	2.86	2.84	2.82	2.80	2.78	2.76	62
63	1.98	1.97	1.96	1.95	1.94	1.93	1.93	1.92	1.91	1.90	1.89	63
64	1.00	0.99	0.99	0.99	0.99	0.98	0.98	0.98	0.98	0.97	0.97	64

Table 27   Multipliers for loss of earnings to pension age 70 (males)

Age at date of trial	Multiplier calculated with allowance for projected mortality from the 1998-based population projections and rate of return of											Age at date of trial
	0.0%	0.5%	1.0%	1.5%	2.0%	2.5%	3.0%	£3.5%	4.0%	4.5%	5.0%	
16	51.72	45.48	40.25	35.85	32.13	28.96	26.26	23.93	21.92	20.18	18.66	16
17	50.73	44.71	39.66	35.39	31.77	28.68	26.04	23.76	21.79	20.07	18.57	17
18	49.75	43.95	39.07	34.93	31.41	28.40	25.82	23.58	21.65	19.96	18.49	18
19	48.78	43.20	38.48	34.47	31.05	28.12	25.59	23.41	21.51	19.85	18.40	19
20	47.81	42.44	37.88	34.00	30.68	27.83	25.36	23.23	21.37	19.74	18.31	20
21	46.84	41.68	37.28	33.53	30.31	27.53	25.13	23.04	21.22	19.62	18.21	21
22	45.87	40.91	36.68	33.05	29.93	27.23	24.89	22.85	21.06	19.50	18.11	22
23	44.90	40.14	36.06	32.56	29.54	26.92	24.64	22.65	20.90	19.37	18.01	23
24	43.93	39.36	35.44	32.06	29.14	26.59	24.38	22.44	20.73	19.23	17.90	24
25	42.96	38.59	34.82	31.56	28.73	26.27	24.11	22.22	20.56	19.09	17.78	25
26	41.99	37.80	34.18	31.05	28.31	25.93	23.84	22.00	20.38	18.94	17.66	26
27	41.02	37.01	33.55	30.53	27.89	25.58	23.56	21.77	20.19	18.78	17.53	27
28	40.04	36.22	32.90	30.00	27.46	25.23	23.27	21.53	19.99	18.62	17.40	28
29	39.07	35.43	32.25	29.46	27.02	24.87	22.97	21.28	19.79	18.45	17.26	29
30	38.10	34.63	31.59	28.92	26.57	24.50	22.66	21.03	19.57	18.27	17.11	30
31	37.12	33.82	30.92	28.37	26.11	24.11	22.34	20.76	19.35	18.09	16.96	31
32	36.15	33.01	30.25	27.81	25.64	23.72	22.01	20.49	19.12	17.90	16.79	32
33	35.17	32.20	29.57	27.23	25.16	23.32	21.68	20.20	18.88	17.69	16.62	33
34	34.20	31.38	28.88	26.65	24.68	22.91	21.33	19.91	18.63	17.48	16.44	34
35	33.22	30.55	28.18	26.07	24.18	22.49	20.97	19.60	18.37	17.26	16.25	35
36	32.24	29.72	27.47	25.47	23.67	22.05	20.60	19.29	18.10	17.03	16.05	36
37	31.26	28.88	26.76	24.86	23.15	21.61	20.21	18.96	17.82	16.78	15.84	37
38	30.28	28.05	26.04	24.24	22.62	21.15	19.82	18.62	17.52	16.53	15.62	38
39	29.30	27.21	25.32	23.62	22.08	20.69	19.42	18.27	17.22	16.27	15.39	39
40	28.33	26.37	24.59	22.99	21.53	20.21	19.01	17.91	16.91	16.00	15.16	40
41	27.36	25.53	23.86	22.35	20.98	19.73	18.59	17.54	16.59	15.71	14.91	41
42	26.40	24.69	23.13	21.71	20.42	19.24	18.16	17.17	16.26	15.42	14.65	42
43	25.43	23.84	22.39	21.06	19.85	18.73	17.71	16.78	15.91	15.12	14.38	43
44	24.47	22.99	21.64	20.40	19.27	18.22	17.26	16.37	15.56	14.80	14.10	44
45	23.51	22.14	20.89	19.74	18.67	17.70	16.79	15.96	15.19	14.47	13.81	45
46	22.55	21.29	20.13	19.06	18.07	17.16	16.31	15.53	14.80	14.13	13.50	46
47	21.59	20.43	19.36	18.37	17.46	16.61	15.82	15.09	14.40	13.77	13.18	47
48	20.63	19.57	18.58	17.67	16.83	16.04	15.31	14.63	13.99	13.39	12.84	48
49	19.66	18.70	17.80	16.96	16.19	15.46	14.78	14.15	13.56	13.00	12.48	49
50	18.70	17.83	17.01	16.25	15.53	14.87	14.24	13.66	13.11	12.59	12.11	50
51	17.74	16.95	16.21	15.52	14.87	14.26	13.69	13.15	12.65	12.17	11.72	51
52	16.79	16.08	15.41	14.79	14.20	13.64	13.12	12.63	12.17	11.73	11.32	52
53	15.84	15.21	14.61	14.05	13.52	13.02	12.54	12.10	11.67	11.27	10.90	53
54	14.89	14.33	13.80	13.30	12.83	12.38	11.95	11.55	11.17	10.80	10.46	54
55	13.96	13.46	12.99	12.55	12.13	11.73	11.35	10.98	10.64	10.31	10.00	55
56	13.02	12.59	12.18	11.79	11.42	11.06	10.73	10.41	10.10	9.81	9.53	56
57	12.09	11.72	11.37	11.03	10.70	10.39	10.10	9.81	9.54	9.29	9.04	57
58	11.17	10.86	10.55	10.26	9.98	9.71	9.45	9.21	8.97	8.74	8.53	58
59	10.26	9.99	9.73	9.48	9.25	9.02	8.80	8.58	8.38	8.18	8.00	59
60	9.35	9.12	8.91	8.70	8.50	8.31	8.12	7.94	7.77	7.60	7.44	60
61	8.43	8.25	8.08	7.91	7.74	7.58	7.43	7.28	7.14	7.00	6.86	61
62	7.52	7.38	7.24	7.10	6.97	6.84	6.72	6.60	6.48	6.37	6.26	62
63	6.61	6.50	6.39	6.28	6.18	6.08	5.98	5.89	5.80	5.71	5.62	63
64	5.69	5.61	5.53	5.45	5.37	5.30	5.22	5.15	5.08	5.01	4.95	64
65	4.77	4.71	4.65	4.60	4.54	4.49	4.44	4.39	4.34	4.29	4.24	65
66	3.84	3.80	3.76	3.73	3.69	3.66	3.62	3.59	3.56	3.52	3.49	66
67	2.90	2.88	2.86	2.84	2.82	2.80	2.78	2.76	2.74	2.72	2.70	67
68	1.95	1.94	1.93	1.92	1.91	1.90	1.90	1.89	1.88	1.87	1.86	68
69	0.99	0.98	0.98	0.98	0.98	0.97	0.97	0.97	0.97	0.97	0.96	69

Table 28   Multipliers for loss of earnings to pension age 70 (females)

Age at date of trial	Multiplier calculated with allowance for projected mortality from the 1998-based population projections and rate of return of											Age at date of trial
	0.0%	0.5%	1.0%	1.5%	2.0%	2.5%	3.0%	£3.5%	4.0%	4.5%	5.0%	
16	52.57	46.18	40.84	36.34	32.54	29.31	26.55	24.18	22.14	20.36	18.82	16
17	51.58	45.42	40.25	35.88	32.18	29.03	26.33	24.01	22.01	20.26	18.74	17
18	50.58	44.65	39.65	35.42	31.82	28.75	26.11	23.84	21.87	20.15	18.65	18
19	49.59	43.88	39.05	34.95	31.46	28.46	25.89	23.66	21.73	20.04	18.57	19
20	48.60	43.10	38.44	34.47	31.08	28.17	25.66	23.48	21.58	19.93	18.48	20
21	47.61	42.32	37.83	33.99	30.70	27.87	25.42	23.29	21.43	19.81	18.38	21
22	46.62	41.54	37.21	33.50	30.31	27.56	25.17	23.09	21.28	19.68	18.28	22
23	45.63	40.75	36.58	33.00	29.91	27.24	24.91	22.89	21.11	19.55	18.17	23
24	44.63	39.96	35.95	32.49	29.51	26.91	24.65	22.68	20.94	19.41	18.06	24
25	43.64	39.16	35.31	31.98	29.09	26.58	24.38	22.46	20.76	19.27	17.94	25
26	42.65	38.36	34.66	31.46	28.67	26.23	24.10	22.23	20.58	19.11	17.82	26
27	41.65	37.56	34.01	30.93	28.24	25.88	23.82	22.00	20.39	18.96	17.69	27
28	40.66	36.75	33.35	30.39	27.80	25.52	23.52	21.75	20.19	18.79	17.55	28
29	39.67	35.94	32.69	29.85	27.35	25.16	23.22	21.50	19.98	18.62	17.41	29
30	38.68	35.13	32.02	29.30	26.90	24.78	22.91	21.25	19.77	18.44	17.26	30
31	37.69	34.31	31.35	28.74	26.43	24.40	22.59	20.98	19.54	18.26	17.11	31
32	36.70	33.49	30.67	28.17	25.96	24.00	22.26	20.70	19.31	18.06	16.94	32
33	35.71	32.67	29.98	27.60	25.48	23.60	21.92	20.42	19.07	17.86	16.77	33
34	34.73	31.84	29.28	27.01	24.99	23.19	21.57	20.13	18.82	17.65	16.59	34
35	33.74	31.01	28.58	26.42	24.49	22.76	21.22	19.82	18.57	17.43	16.41	35
36	32.76	30.18	27.88	25.82	23.98	22.33	20.85	19.51	18.30	17.20	16.21	36
37	31.77	29.34	27.17	25.22	23.47	21.89	20.47	19.19	18.02	16.97	16.01	37
38	30.79	28.50	26.45	24.60	22.94	21.44	20.08	18.85	17.73	16.72	15.79	38
39	29.81	27.66	25.72	23.98	22.40	20.98	19.68	18.51	17.44	16.46	15.57	39
40	28.83	26.81	24.99	23.35	21.86	20.50	19.27	18.15	17.13	16.19	15.33	40
41	27.85	25.96	24.26	22.71	21.30	20.02	18.85	17.78	16.81	15.91	15.09	41
42	26.87	25.11	23.51	22.06	20.74	19.52	18.42	17.40	16.47	15.62	14.83	42
43	25.89	24.26	22.77	21.40	20.16	19.02	17.97	17.01	16.13	15.32	14.57	43
44	24.92	23.40	22.01	20.74	19.57	18.50	17.52	16.61	15.77	15.00	14.29	44
45	23.95	22.54	21.25	20.07	18.98	17.97	17.05	16.19	15.40	14.67	13.99	45
46	22.97	21.68	20.48	19.39	18.37	17.43	16.57	15.76	15.02	14.33	13.69	46
47	22.00	20.81	19.71	18.69	17.75	16.88	16.07	15.32	14.62	13.97	13.37	47
48	21.04	19.94	18.93	18.00	17.13	16.32	15.56	14.86	14.21	13.60	13.03	48
49	20.07	19.07	18.15	17.29	16.49	15.74	15.04	14.39	13.78	13.21	12.68	49
50	19.10	18.20	17.36	16.57	15.84	15.15	14.51	13.91	13.34	12.81	12.31	50
51	18.14	17.33	16.56	15.85	15.18	14.55	13.96	13.40	12.88	12.39	11.93	51
52	17.18	16.45	15.76	15.11	14.51	13.93	13.39	12.89	12.41	11.96	11.53	52
53	16.23	15.57	14.95	14.37	13.82	13.31	12.82	12.36	11.92	11.51	11.12	53
54	15.27	14.69	14.14	13.62	13.13	12.66	12.22	11.81	11.41	11.04	10.68	54
55	14.32	13.81	13.32	12.86	12.42	12.01	11.62	11.24	10.89	10.55	10.22	55
56	13.37	12.92	12.50	12.09	11.71	11.34	10.99	10.66	10.34	10.04	9.75	56
57	12.42	12.04	11.67	11.32	10.98	10.66	10.35	10.06	9.78	9.51	9.25	57
58	11.48	11.15	10.83	10.53	10.24	9.96	9.69	9.44	9.19	8.96	8.73	58
59	10.54	10.26	9.99	9.73	9.48	9.25	9.02	8.80	8.59	8.38	8.19	59
60	9.59	9.36	9.14	8.92	8.72	8.52	8.33	8.14	7.96	7.79	7.62	60
61	8.65	8.46	8.28	8.10	7.93	7.77	7.61	7.46	7.31	7.16	7.02	61
62	7.71	7.56	7.41	7.27	7.14	7.00	6.87	6.75	6.63	6.51	6.40	62
63	6.76	6.65	6.53	6.42	6.32	6.22	6.12	6.02	5.92	5.83	5.74	63
64	5.81	5.73	5.64	5.56	5.48	5.41	5.33	5.26	5.19	5.12	5.05	64
65	4.86	4.80	4.74	4.68	4.63	4.57	4.52	4.47	4.42	4.37	4.32	65
66	3.90	3.86	3.83	3.79	3.75	3.72	3.68	3.65	3.61	3.58	3.55	66
67	2.94	2.92	2.90	2.88	2.85	2.83	2.81	2.79	2.77	2.76	2.74	67
68	1.97	1.96	1.95	1.94	1.93	1.92	1.91	1.90	1.90	1.89	1.88	68
69	0.99	0.99	0.99	0.98	0.98	0.98	0.98	0.98	0.97	0.97	0.97	69

Table 29 Multipliers for loss of pension commencing age 55 (males)

Age at date of trial	Multiplier calculated with allowance for projected mortality from the 1998-based population projections and rate of return of											Age at date of trial
	0.0%	0.5%	1.0%	1.5%	2.0%	2.5%	3.0%	£3.5%	4.0%	4.5%	5.0%	
0	25.94	18.26	12.90	9.16	6.53	4.67	3.35	2.42	1.75	1.27	0.93	0
1	26.07	18.44	13.10	9.34	6.69	4.81	3.47	2.52	1.83	1.33	0.98	1
2	26.07	18.53	13.23	9.48	6.83	4.93	3.58	2.60	1.90	1.39	1.03	2
3	26.07	18.63	13.36	9.63	6.96	5.06	3.68	2.70	1.98	1.46	1.08	3
4	26.07	18.72	13.50	9.77	7.10	5.18	3.80	2.79	2.06	1.52	1.13	4
5	26.07	18.81	13.63	9.92	7.24	5.31	3.91	2.89	2.14	1.59	1.19	5
6	26.06	18.90	13.76	10.06	7.39	5.44	4.03	2.99	2.23	1.66	1.25	6
7	26.06	18.99	13.90	10.21	7.53	5.58	4.15	3.09	2.31	1.74	1.31	7
8	26.05	19.08	14.03	10.36	7.68	5.72	4.27	3.20	2.41	1.82	1.37	8
9	26.05	19.17	14.17	10.52	7.83	5.86	4.40	3.31	2.50	1.90	1.44	9
10	26.04	19.26	14.31	10.67	7.99	6.00	4.53	3.43	2.60	1.98	1.51	10
11	26.03	19.35	14.45	10.83	8.15	6.15	4.66	3.54	2.70	2.07	1.59	11
12	26.03	19.45	14.59	10.99	8.31	6.30	4.80	3.67	2.81	2.16	1.67	12
13	26.02	19.54	14.73	11.15	8.47	6.46	4.94	3.80	2.92	2.26	1.75	13
14	26.01	19.63	14.88	11.31	8.64	6.62	5.09	3.93	3.04	2.36	1.84	14
15	26.01	19.73	15.02	11.48	8.81	6.78	5.24	4.06	3.16	2.47	1.93	15
16	26.00	19.82	15.17	11.65	8.98	6.95	5.40	4.21	3.29	2.58	2.03	16
17	26.00	19.92	15.32	11.83	9.16	7.13	5.56	4.35	3.42	2.69	2.13	17
18	26.00	20.02	15.47	12.00	9.35	7.30	5.73	4.51	3.56	2.81	2.23	18
19	26.00	20.12	15.63	12.19	9.54	7.49	5.90	4.66	3.70	2.94	2.35	19
20	26.01	20.23	15.79	12.37	9.73	7.68	6.08	4.83	3.85	3.08	2.47	20
21	26.01	20.33	15.95	12.56	9.93	7.87	6.26	5.00	4.00	3.22	2.59	21
22	26.02	20.44	16.12	12.75	10.13	8.07	6.45	5.18	4.17	3.36	2.72	22
23	26.02	20.54	16.28	12.95	10.33	8.28	6.65	5.36	4.33	3.51	2.86	23
24	26.03	20.65	16.44	13.14	10.54	8.48	6.85	5.55	4.51	3.67	3.00	24
25	26.03	20.75	16.61	13.34	10.75	8.70	7.06	5.74	4.69	3.84	3.15	25
26	26.03	20.86	16.78	13.54	10.97	8.92	7.27	5.95	4.88	4.01	3.31	26
27	26.03	20.97	16.95	13.75	11.19	9.14	7.49	6.16	5.07	4.19	3.48	27
28	26.03	21.07	17.12	13.96	11.42	9.37	7.72	6.37	5.28	4.38	3.65	28
29	26.03	21.18	17.29	14.17	11.65	9.61	7.95	6.60	5.49	4.58	3.83	29
30	26.03	21.28	17.46	14.38	11.88	9.85	8.19	6.83	5.71	4.79	4.03	30
31	26.03	21.39	17.64	14.60	12.12	10.09	8.43	7.07	5.94	5.00	4.23	31
32	26.02	21.49	17.81	14.81	12.36	10.35	8.69	7.32	6.18	5.23	4.44	32
33	26.02	21.60	17.99	15.04	12.61	10.60	8.95	7.57	6.42	5.47	4.66	33
34	26.01	21.70	18.17	15.26	12.86	10.87	9.22	7.84	6.68	5.71	4.90	34
35	26.00	21.80	18.34	15.48	13.11	11.14	9.49	8.11	6.95	5.97	5.14	35
36	25.99	21.90	18.52	15.71	13.37	11.42	9.77	8.39	7.23	6.24	5.40	36
37	25.98	22.00	18.70	15.94	13.64	11.70	10.07	8.68	7.51	6.52	5.67	37
38	25.97	22.11	18.88	16.18	13.90	11.99	10.37	8.99	7.81	6.81	5.95	38
39	25.96	22.21	19.06	16.42	14.18	12.29	10.68	9.30	8.13	7.12	6.25	39
40	25.95	22.31	19.25	16.66	14.46	12.59	11.00	9.63	8.45	7.44	6.56	40
41	25.95	22.42	19.44	16.91	14.75	12.91	11.33	9.97	8.79	7.78	6.89	41
42	25.94	22.53	19.64	17.16	15.05	13.23	11.67	10.32	9.15	8.13	7.24	42
43	25.94	22.65	19.83	17.42	15.35	13.57	12.02	10.68	9.52	8.50	7.61	43
44	25.94	22.76	20.03	17.69	15.66	13.91	12.39	11.06	9.90	8.89	7.99	44
45	25.94	22.88	20.24	17.96	15.98	14.26	12.77	11.46	10.30	9.29	8.40	45
46	25.94	22.99	20.44	18.23	16.31	14.63	13.16	11.86	10.72	9.72	8.82	46
47	25.94	23.11	20.65	18.51	16.64	15.00	13.56	12.28	11.16	10.16	9.27	47
48	25.94	23.22	20.86	18.79	16.98	15.38	13.97	12.72	11.61	10.62	9.74	48
49	25.94	23.34	21.07	19.08	17.32	15.77	14.40	13.17	12.08	11.11	10.24	49
50	25.93	23.46	21.29	19.37	17.68	16.17	14.84	13.64	12.58	11.62	10.76	50
51	25.94	23.58	21.51	19.67	18.04	16.59	15.29	14.13	13.09	12.16	11.31	51
52	25.95	23.72	21.74	19.98	18.42	17.02	15.77	14.65	13.63	12.72	11.89	52
53	25.97	23.86	21.98	20.31	18.81	17.47	16.27	15.19	14.21	13.32	12.51	53
54	26.01	24.01	22.24	20.65	19.22	17.95	16.79	15.75	14.81	13.95	13.17	54
55	26.06	24.18	22.51	21.01	19.66	18.44	17.34	16.35	15.45	14.62	13.87	55

Table 30　Multipliers for loss of pension commencing age 55 (females)

Age at date of trial	Multiplier calculated with allowance for projected mortality from the 1998-based population projections and rate of return of											Age at date of trial
	0.0%	0.5%	1.0%	1.5%	2.0%	2.5%	3.0%	£3.5%	4.0%	4.5%	5.0%	
0	29.68	20.74	14.56	10.27	7.27	5.17	3.70	2.65	1.91	1.38	1.00	0
1	29.80	20.93	14.76	10.46	7.45	5.33	3.82	2.76	1.99	1.45	1.06	1
2	29.81	21.03	14.91	10.62	7.60	5.46	3.94	2.85	2.07	1.51	1.11	2
3	29.81	21.14	15.06	10.78	7.75	5.60	4.06	2.95	2.16	1.58	1.17	3
4	29.80	21.24	15.21	10.94	7.90	5.74	4.18	3.06	2.24	1.65	1.22	4
5	29.80	21.35	15.36	11.10	8.06	5.88	4.30	3.16	2.33	1.73	1.28	5
6	29.80	21.45	15.51	11.27	8.22	6.02	4.43	3.27	2.43	1.81	1.35	6
7	29.79	21.55	15.66	11.44	8.38	6.17	4.56	3.39	2.52	1.89	1.42	7
8	29.79	21.66	15.82	11.61	8.55	6.33	4.70	3.51	2.62	1.97	1.49	8
9	29.78	21.76	15.97	11.78	8.72	6.48	4.84	3.63	2.73	2.06	1.56	9
10	29.77	21.86	16.13	11.95	8.89	6.64	4.98	3.75	2.84	2.15	1.64	10
11	29.77	21.97	16.29	12.13	9.07	6.81	5.13	3.88	2.95	2.25	1.72	11
12	29.76	22.07	16.45	12.31	9.25	6.98	5.29	4.02	3.07	2.35	1.81	12
13	29.75	22.18	16.61	12.49	9.43	7.15	5.44	4.16	3.19	2.45	1.90	13
14	29.75	22.29	16.77	12.68	9.62	7.33	5.61	4.30	3.32	2.56	1.99	14
15	29.74	22.39	16.94	12.86	9.81	7.51	5.77	4.45	3.45	2.68	2.09	15
16	29.74	22.50	17.10	13.05	10.00	7.70	5.95	4.61	3.59	2.80	2.19	16
17	29.73	22.61	17.27	13.25	10.20	7.89	6.12	4.77	3.73	2.93	2.30	17
18	29.73	22.72	17.44	13.45	10.41	8.09	6.31	4.94	3.88	3.06	2.42	18
19	29.73	22.83	17.62	13.65	10.61	8.29	6.50	5.11	4.03	3.19	2.54	19
20	29.72	22.94	17.79	13.85	10.83	8.49	6.69	5.29	4.19	3.34	2.67	20
21	29.72	23.06	17.96	14.06	11.04	8.71	6.89	5.47	4.36	3.49	2.80	21
22	29.71	23.17	18.14	14.26	11.26	8.92	7.10	5.66	4.54	3.65	2.94	22
23	29.70	23.28	18.32	14.48	11.48	9.14	7.31	5.86	4.72	3.81	3.08	23
24	29.70	23.39	18.50	14.69	11.71	9.37	7.53	6.07	4.91	3.98	3.24	24
25	29.69	23.50	18.68	14.91	11.94	9.60	7.75	6.28	5.10	4.16	3.40	25
26	29.68	23.61	18.86	15.13	12.18	9.84	7.98	6.50	5.30	4.34	3.57	26
27	29.67	23.72	19.04	15.35	12.42	10.09	8.22	6.72	5.51	4.54	3.75	27
28	29.66	23.83	19.23	15.58	12.66	10.34	8.46	6.96	5.73	4.74	3.93	28
29	29.65	23.95	19.42	15.81	12.91	10.59	8.72	7.20	5.96	4.96	4.13	29
30	29.64	24.06	19.61	16.04	13.17	10.85	8.98	7.45	6.20	5.18	4.34	30
31	29.63	24.17	19.80	16.28	13.43	11.12	9.24	7.71	6.45	5.41	4.55	31
32	29.62	24.29	19.99	16.52	13.70	11.40	9.52	7.98	6.70	5.65	4.78	32
33	29.61	24.40	20.18	16.76	13.97	11.68	9.80	8.25	6.97	5.91	5.02	33
34	29.60	24.51	20.38	17.01	14.24	11.97	10.10	8.54	7.25	6.17	5.27	34
35	29.59	24.63	20.58	17.26	14.52	12.27	10.40	8.84	7.54	6.45	5.53	35
36	29.58	24.74	20.78	17.51	14.81	12.57	10.71	9.15	7.84	6.74	5.81	36
37	29.57	24.86	20.98	17.77	15.11	12.88	11.03	9.47	8.15	7.04	6.10	37
38	29.56	24.98	21.18	18.03	15.40	13.21	11.36	9.80	8.48	7.36	6.40	38
39	29.55	25.09	21.39	18.30	15.71	13.53	11.70	10.14	8.82	7.69	6.72	39
40	29.54	25.21	21.60	18.57	16.02	13.87	12.05	10.50	9.17	8.04	7.06	40
41	29.53	25.33	21.81	18.85	16.34	14.22	12.41	10.86	9.54	8.40	7.42	41
42	29.53	25.45	22.03	19.13	16.67	14.57	12.78	11.24	9.92	8.78	7.79	42
43	29.52	25.58	22.24	19.41	17.00	14.94	13.17	11.64	10.32	9.18	8.18	43
44	29.52	25.70	22.47	19.71	17.34	15.31	13.56	12.05	10.74	9.59	8.59	44
45	29.51	25.83	22.69	20.00	17.69	15.70	13.97	12.47	11.17	10.03	9.02	45
46	29.51	25.96	22.92	20.30	18.05	16.10	14.40	12.92	11.62	10.48	9.48	46
47	29.51	26.09	23.15	20.61	18.42	16.50	14.83	13.37	12.09	10.96	9.96	47
48	29.51	26.23	23.39	20.93	18.79	16.92	15.29	13.85	12.58	11.46	10.47	48
49	29.52	26.37	23.63	21.25	19.18	17.36	15.76	14.35	13.10	11.99	11.00	49
50	29.53	26.51	23.88	21.59	19.57	17.80	16.24	14.86	13.63	12.54	11.56	50
51	29.54	26.66	24.14	21.93	19.98	18.27	16.75	15.40	14.20	13.12	12.16	51
52	29.57	26.81	24.40	22.28	20.41	18.75	17.27	15.96	14.78	13.73	12.78	52
53	29.59	26.98	24.67	22.64	20.84	19.24	17.82	16.54	15.40	14.37	13.45	53
54	29.63	27.15	24.96	23.02	21.29	19.76	18.39	17.16	16.05	15.05	14.15	54
55	29.68	27.33	25.25	23.41	21.76	20.29	18.98	17.80	16.73	15.77	14.89	55

Table 31 Multipliers for loss of pension commencing age 60 (males)

Age at date of trial	Multiplier calculated with allowance for projected mortality from the 1998-based population projections and rate of return of											Age at date of trial
	0.0%	0.5%	1.0%	1.5%	2.0%	2.5%	3.0%	£3.5%	4.0%	4.5%	5.0%	
0	21.29	14.76	10.28	7.18	5.04	3.54	2.50	1.77	1.26	0.90	0.64	0
1	21.39	14.91	10.43	7.32	5.16	3.65	2.59	1.84	1.32	0.94	0.68	1
2	21.39	14.99	10.54	7.44	5.27	3.74	2.67	1.91	1.37	0.99	0.71	2
3	21.39	15.06	10.64	7.55	5.37	3.84	2.75	1.98	1.43	1.03	0.75	3
4	21.39	15.13	10.75	7.66	5.48	3.93	2.83	2.05	1.48	1.08	0.79	4
5	21.39	15.21	10.85	7.77	5.59	4.03	2.92	2.12	1.54	1.13	0.83	5
6	21.38	15.28	10.96	7.89	5.70	4.13	3.00	2.19	1.60	1.18	0.87	6
7	21.38	15.35	11.07	8.00	5.81	4.23	3.09	2.27	1.67	1.23	0.91	7
8	21.37	15.43	11.17	8.12	5.93	4.34	3.18	2.35	1.73	1.28	0.95	8
9	21.37	15.50	11.28	8.24	6.04	4.44	3.28	2.43	1.80	1.34	1.00	9
10	21.36	15.57	11.39	8.36	6.16	4.55	3.38	2.51	1.87	1.40	1.05	10
11	21.36	15.65	11.50	8.49	6.28	4.67	3.48	2.60	1.95	1.46	1.10	11
12	21.35	15.72	11.61	8.61	6.41	4.78	3.58	2.69	2.03	1.53	1.16	12
13	21.34	15.79	11.73	8.74	6.53	4.90	3.69	2.78	2.11	1.60	1.22	13
14	21.34	15.87	11.84	8.87	6.66	5.02	3.80	2.88	2.19	1.67	1.28	14
15	21.33	15.94	11.96	9.00	6.79	5.15	3.91	2.98	2.28	1.74	1.34	15
16	21.32	16.02	12.07	9.13	6.93	5.27	4.03	3.08	2.37	1.82	1.41	16
17	21.32	16.09	12.19	9.27	7.06	5.40	4.15	3.19	2.46	1.90	1.48	17
18	21.32	16.18	12.31	9.41	7.21	5.54	4.27	3.30	2.56	1.99	1.55	18
19	21.32	16.26	12.44	9.55	7.35	5.68	4.40	3.42	2.66	2.08	1.63	19
20	21.33	16.34	12.57	9.69	7.50	5.82	4.53	3.54	2.77	2.17	1.71	20
21	21.33	16.43	12.69	9.84	7.65	5.97	4.67	3.66	2.88	2.27	1.80	21
22	21.33	16.51	12.82	9.99	7.81	6.12	4.81	3.79	3.00	2.38	1.89	22
23	21.33	16.59	12.95	10.14	7.96	6.27	4.96	3.93	3.12	2.48	1.98	23
24	21.33	16.68	13.08	10.29	8.12	6.43	5.10	4.06	3.24	2.60	2.08	24
25	21.33	16.76	13.21	10.45	8.29	6.59	5.26	4.21	3.37	2.71	2.19	25
26	21.33	16.84	13.34	10.60	8.45	6.76	5.42	4.35	3.51	2.84	2.30	26
27	21.33	16.93	13.48	10.76	8.62	6.93	5.58	4.51	3.65	2.96	2.41	27
28	21.33	17.01	13.61	10.92	8.79	7.10	5.75	4.66	3.80	3.10	2.53	28
29	21.32	17.09	13.75	11.09	8.97	7.28	5.92	4.83	3.95	3.24	2.66	29
30	21.32	17.18	13.88	11.25	9.15	7.46	6.10	5.00	4.11	3.38	2.79	30
31	21.32	17.26	14.02	11.42	9.33	7.64	6.28	5.17	4.27	3.53	2.93	31
32	21.31	17.34	14.16	11.59	9.51	7.83	6.47	5.35	4.44	3.69	3.08	32
33	21.30	17.42	14.29	11.76	9.70	8.03	6.66	5.54	4.62	3.86	3.23	33
34	21.29	17.50	14.43	11.93	9.89	8.22	6.86	5.73	4.80	4.03	3.39	34
35	21.28	17.58	14.57	12.10	10.09	8.43	7.06	5.93	4.99	4.21	3.56	35
36	21.27	17.66	14.70	12.28	10.28	8.63	7.27	6.13	5.19	4.40	3.74	36
37	21.25	17.74	14.84	12.46	10.48	8.85	7.48	6.35	5.39	4.60	3.92	37
38	21.24	17.81	14.98	12.64	10.69	9.06	7.70	6.57	5.61	4.80	4.12	38
39	21.23	17.89	15.12	12.82	10.90	9.29	7.93	6.79	5.83	5.02	4.32	39
40	21.21	17.97	15.27	13.01	11.11	9.51	8.17	7.03	6.06	5.24	4.54	40
41	21.20	18.05	15.42	13.20	11.33	9.75	8.41	7.27	6.30	5.48	4.77	41
42	21.19	18.14	15.57	13.39	11.55	9.99	8.66	7.53	6.56	5.72	5.01	42
43	21.19	18.22	15.72	13.59	11.78	10.24	8.92	7.79	6.82	5.98	5.26	43
44	21.18	18.31	15.87	13.79	12.02	10.50	9.19	8.06	7.09	6.25	5.52	44
45	21.17	18.39	16.02	14.00	12.26	10.76	9.47	8.35	7.38	6.53	5.80	45
46	21.16	18.48	16.18	14.20	12.50	11.03	9.75	8.64	7.67	6.83	6.09	46
47	21.15	18.56	16.34	14.41	12.75	11.30	10.04	8.94	7.98	7.14	6.39	47
48	21.14	18.65	16.49	14.62	13.00	11.58	10.34	9.25	8.30	7.46	6.71	48
49	21.13	18.73	16.65	14.84	13.26	11.87	10.65	9.58	8.63	7.79	7.05	49
50	21.12	18.82	16.81	15.06	13.52	12.16	10.97	9.91	8.98	8.15	7.41	50
51	21.11	18.91	16.98	15.28	13.79	12.47	11.30	10.26	9.34	8.52	7.78	51
52	21.10	19.00	17.15	15.51	14.07	12.79	11.64	10.63	9.72	8.90	8.17	52
53	21.11	19.10	17.33	15.75	14.36	13.11	12.00	11.01	10.12	9.32	8.59	53
54	21.12	19.21	17.51	16.01	14.66	13.46	12.38	11.41	10.54	9.75	9.04	54
55	21.14	19.33	17.71	16.27	14.98	13.82	12.77	11.83	10.98	10.21	9.51	55
56	21.18	19.46	17.92	16.55	15.31	14.20	13.19	12.28	11.45	10.70	10.01	56
57	21.23	19.61	18.16	16.85	15.67	14.60	13.63	12.75	11.95	11.22	10.56	57
58	21.32	19.79	18.42	17.18	16.05	15.03	14.11	13.26	12.49	11.79	11.14	58
59	21.43	20.00	18.70	17.53	16.47	15.50	14.62	13.81	13.07	12.39	11.77	59
60	21.56	20.23	19.01	17.91	16.91	16.00	15.16	14.40	13.69	13.05	12.45	60

APIL Guide to Fatal Accidents

Table 32 Multipliers for loss of pension commencing age 60 (females)

Age at date of trial	Multiplier calculated with allowance for projected mortality from the 1998-based population projections and rate of return of											Age at date of trial
	0.0%	0.5%	1.0%	1.5%	2.0%	2.5%	3.0%	£3.5%	4.0%	4.5%	5.0%	
0	24.92	17.16	11.87	8.24	5.74	4.02	2.82	1.99	1.41	1.00	0.71	0
1	25.02	17.31	12.03	8.40	5.88	4.14	2.92	2.07	1.47	1.05	0.75	1
2	25.02	17.40	12.15	8.52	6.00	4.24	3.01	2.14	1.53	1.10	0.79	2
3	25.02	17.49	12.28	8.65	6.12	4.35	3.10	2.22	1.59	1.15	0.83	3
4	25.02	17.57	12.40	8.78	6.24	4.46	3.19	2.29	1.66	1.20	0.87	4
5	25.01	17.66	12.52	8.91	6.37	4.57	3.29	2.38	1.72	1.25	0.91	5
6	25.01	17.74	12.64	9.04	6.49	4.68	3.39	2.46	1.79	1.31	0.96	6
7	25.00	17.83	12.77	9.18	6.62	4.80	3.49	2.54	1.86	1.37	1.01	7
8	25.00	17.92	12.89	9.31	6.75	4.92	3.59	2.63	1.94	1.43	1.06	8
9	24.99	18.00	13.02	9.45	6.89	5.04	3.70	2.72	2.01	1.49	1.11	9
10	24.99	18.09	13.15	9.59	7.02	5.16	3.81	2.82	2.09	1.56	1.17	10
11	24.98	18.17	13.27	9.73	7.16	5.29	3.92	2.92	2.18	1.63	1.22	11
12	24.97	18.26	13.40	9.88	7.30	5.42	4.04	3.02	2.26	1.70	1.28	12
13	24.97	18.35	13.53	10.02	7.45	5.56	4.16	3.12	2.35	1.78	1.35	13
14	24.96	18.43	13.67	10.17	7.60	5.69	4.28	3.23	2.45	1.86	1.42	14
15	24.96	18.52	13.80	10.32	7.75	5.83	4.41	3.34	2.54	1.94	1.49	15
16	24.95	18.61	13.94	10.47	7.90	5.98	4.54	3.46	2.65	2.03	1.56	16
17	24.95	18.70	14.07	10.63	8.06	6.13	4.68	3.58	2.75	2.12	1.64	17
18	24.94	18.79	14.21	10.79	8.22	6.28	4.82	3.71	2.86	2.21	1.72	18
19	24.94	18.88	14.35	10.95	8.38	6.44	4.96	3.84	2.97	2.31	1.81	19
20	24.93	18.97	14.49	11.11	8.55	6.60	5.11	3.97	3.09	2.42	1.90	20
21	24.93	19.06	14.63	11.27	8.72	6.76	5.26	4.11	3.22	2.53	1.99	21
22	24.92	19.16	14.78	11.44	8.89	6.93	5.42	4.25	3.34	2.64	2.09	22
23	24.92	19.25	14.92	11.61	9.06	7.10	5.58	4.40	3.48	2.76	2.19	23
24	24.91	19.34	15.07	11.78	9.24	7.28	5.75	4.55	3.62	2.88	2.30	24
25	24.90	19.43	15.21	11.95	9.42	7.46	5.92	4.71	3.76	3.01	2.42	25
26	24.89	19.52	15.36	12.13	9.61	7.64	6.09	4.87	3.91	3.14	2.54	26
27	24.88	19.61	15.51	12.31	9.80	7.83	6.27	5.04	4.06	3.29	2.66	27
28	24.87	19.70	15.66	12.49	9.99	8.02	6.46	5.22	4.23	3.43	2.80	28
29	24.86	19.79	15.81	12.67	10.19	8.22	6.65	5.40	4.39	3.59	2.93	29
30	24.85	19.88	15.96	12.86	10.39	8.42	6.85	5.59	4.57	3.75	3.08	30
31	24.84	19.97	16.11	13.04	10.59	8.63	7.05	5.78	4.75	3.91	3.23	31
32	24.83	20.06	16.27	13.24	10.80	8.84	7.26	5.98	4.94	4.09	3.39	32
33	24.82	20.16	16.42	13.43	11.01	9.06	7.48	6.19	5.13	4.27	3.56	33
34	24.81	20.25	16.58	13.62	11.23	9.28	7.70	6.40	5.34	4.46	3.74	34
35	24.79	20.34	16.74	13.82	11.45	9.51	7.93	6.62	5.55	4.66	3.93	35
36	24.78	20.43	16.90	14.03	11.68	9.75	8.16	6.85	5.77	4.87	4.12	36
37	24.77	20.52	17.06	14.23	11.90	9.99	8.40	7.09	6.00	5.09	4.33	37
38	24.76	20.62	17.23	14.44	12.14	10.23	8.65	7.34	6.24	5.32	4.54	38
39	24.74	20.71	17.39	14.65	12.38	10.49	8.91	7.59	6.49	5.56	4.77	39
40	24.73	20.80	17.56	14.86	12.62	10.75	9.18	7.86	6.74	5.80	5.01	40
41	24.72	20.90	17.73	15.08	12.87	11.01	9.45	8.13	7.01	6.06	5.26	41
42	24.71	21.00	17.90	15.30	13.12	11.28	9.73	8.41	7.29	6.34	5.52	42
43	24.70	21.09	18.07	15.53	13.38	11.56	10.02	8.71	7.58	6.62	5.80	43
44	24.69	21.19	18.24	15.76	13.65	11.85	10.32	9.01	7.89	6.92	6.09	44
45	24.68	21.29	18.42	15.99	13.92	12.15	10.63	9.33	8.20	7.23	6.39	45
46	24.67	21.39	18.60	16.23	14.19	12.45	10.95	9.65	8.53	7.56	6.71	46
47	24.66	21.49	18.79	16.47	14.48	12.76	11.28	9.99	8.88	7.90	7.05	47
48	24.66	21.60	18.97	16.72	14.77	13.08	11.62	10.34	9.23	8.26	7.40	48
49	24.66	21.70	19.16	16.97	15.07	13.41	11.97	10.71	9.61	8.64	7.78	49
50	24.66	21.82	19.36	17.23	15.37	13.75	12.34	11.09	10.00	9.03	8.17	50
51	24.66	21.93	19.56	17.49	15.69	14.11	12.71	11.49	10.40	9.44	8.59	51
52	24.67	22.05	19.77	17.77	16.01	14.47	13.11	11.90	10.83	9.88	9.03	52
53	24.68	22.18	19.98	18.05	16.35	14.85	13.52	12.33	11.28	10.34	9.49	53
54	24.71	22.31	20.20	18.34	16.70	15.24	13.94	12.78	11.75	10.82	9.99	54
55	24.73	22.45	20.43	18.64	17.06	15.64	14.38	13.25	12.24	11.33	10.51	55
56	24.77	22.59	20.67	18.95	17.43	16.07	14.84	13.75	12.76	11.86	11.06	56
57	24.81	22.75	20.92	19.28	17.82	16.51	15.33	14.26	13.30	12.43	11.64	57
58	24.87	22.92	21.18	19.62	18.23	16.97	15.84	14.81	13.88	13.04	12.27	58
59	24.95	23.11	21.47	19.99	18.66	17.46	16.37	15.39	14.49	13.68	12.93	59
60	25.05	23.32	21.77	20.38	19.12	17.98	16.94	16.00	15.14	14.36	13.64	60

Table 33 Multipliers for loss of pension commencing age 65 (males)

Age at date of trial	Multiplier calculated with allowance for projected mortality from the 1998-based population projections and rate of return of											Age at date of trial
	0.0%	0.5%	1.0%	1.5%	2.0%	2.5%	3.0%	£3.5%	4.0%	4.5%	5.0%	
0	16.79	11.47	7.86	5.41	3.73	2.58	1.79	1.25	0.87	0.61	0.43	0
1	16.87	11.58	7.98	5.51	3.82	2.66	1.86	1.30	0.91	0.64	0.45	1
2	16.87	11.64	8.06	5.60	3.90	2.73	1.91	1.34	0.95	0.67	0.48	2
3	16.87	11.70	8.14	5.68	3.98	2.79	1.97	1.39	0.99	0.70	0.50	3
4	16.87	11.75	8.22	5.76	4.06	2.86	2.03	1.44	1.03	0.73	0.52	4
5	16.86	11.81	8.30	5.85	4.14	2.93	2.09	1.49	1.07	0.76	0.55	5
6	16.86	11.87	8.38	5.94	4.22	3.01	2.15	1.54	1.11	0.80	0.58	6
7	16.86	11.92	8.46	6.02	4.30	3.08	2.21	1.60	1.15	0.84	0.61	7
8	16.85	11.98	8.54	6.11	4.39	3.16	2.28	1.65	1.20	0.87	0.64	8
9	16.85	12.04	8.63	6.20	4.47	3.24	2.35	1.71	1.25	0.91	0.67	9
10	16.84	12.09	8.71	6.29	4.56	3.32	2.42	1.77	1.30	0.95	0.70	10
11	16.83	12.15	8.79	6.39	4.65	3.40	2.49	1.83	1.35	0.99	0.74	11
12	16.83	12.20	8.88	6.48	4.74	3.48	2.56	1.89	1.40	1.04	0.77	12
13	16.82	12.26	8.96	6.57	4.84	3.57	2.64	1.96	1.46	1.09	0.81	13
14	16.82	12.32	9.05	6.67	4.93	3.65	2.72	2.03	1.51	1.13	0.85	14
15	16.81	12.38	9.14	6.77	5.03	3.75	2.80	2.10	1.57	1.18	0.89	15
16	16.81	12.43	9.23	6.87	5.13	3.84	2.88	2.17	1.64	1.24	0.94	16
17	16.80	12.49	9.32	6.97	5.23	3.93	2.97	2.24	1.70	1.29	0.99	17
18	16.80	12.55	9.41	7.07	5.33	4.03	3.06	2.32	1.77	1.35	1.03	18
19	16.80	12.62	9.50	7.18	5.44	4.13	3.15	2.40	1.84	1.41	1.09	19
20	16.80	12.68	9.60	7.29	5.55	4.24	3.24	2.49	1.91	1.48	1.14	20
21	16.80	12.75	9.70	7.40	5.66	4.34	3.34	2.58	1.99	1.54	1.20	21
22	16.80	12.81	9.80	7.51	5.77	4.45	3.44	2.67	2.07	1.61	1.26	22
23	16.80	12.87	9.89	7.62	5.89	4.56	3.54	2.76	2.15	1.69	1.32	23
24	16.80	12.94	9.99	7.74	6.01	4.68	3.65	2.86	2.24	1.76	1.39	24
25	16.80	13.00	10.09	7.85	6.13	4.79	3.76	2.96	2.33	1.84	1.46	25
26	16.80	13.06	10.19	7.97	6.25	4.91	3.87	3.06	2.42	1.92	1.53	26
27	16.79	13.13	10.29	8.09	6.37	5.03	3.99	3.17	2.52	2.01	1.61	27
28	16.79	13.19	10.39	8.21	6.50	5.16	4.11	3.28	2.62	2.10	1.69	28
29	16.78	13.25	10.49	8.33	6.63	5.29	4.23	3.39	2.72	2.19	1.77	29
30	16.78	13.31	10.59	8.45	6.76	5.42	4.36	3.51	2.83	2.29	1.86	30
31	16.77	13.38	10.70	8.57	6.89	5.55	4.48	3.63	2.95	2.39	1.95	31
32	16.76	13.44	10.80	8.70	7.03	5.69	4.62	3.76	3.06	2.50	2.05	32
33	16.75	13.50	10.90	8.83	7.16	5.83	4.75	3.89	3.18	2.61	2.15	33
34	16.74	13.55	11.00	8.95	7.30	5.97	4.89	4.02	3.31	2.73	2.26	34
35	16.73	13.61	11.10	9.08	7.44	6.12	5.04	4.16	3.44	2.85	2.37	35
36	16.71	13.67	11.21	9.21	7.59	6.27	5.19	4.30	3.57	2.98	2.48	36
37	16.70	13.73	11.31	9.34	7.73	6.42	5.34	4.45	3.72	3.11	2.61	37
38	16.68	13.78	11.41	9.47	7.88	6.57	5.49	4.60	3.86	3.25	2.74	38
39	16.67	13.84	11.52	9.61	8.03	6.73	5.65	4.76	4.01	3.39	2.87	39
40	16.65	13.90	11.62	9.74	8.19	6.90	5.82	4.92	4.17	3.54	3.01	40
41	16.64	13.95	11.73	9.88	8.35	7.06	5.99	5.09	4.34	3.70	3.16	41
42	16.63	14.01	11.84	10.03	8.51	7.24	6.17	5.27	4.51	3.86	3.32	42
43	16.61	14.07	11.95	10.17	8.67	7.41	6.35	5.45	4.69	4.04	3.48	43
44	16.60	14.13	12.06	10.31	8.84	7.59	6.54	5.64	4.87	4.22	3.66	44
45	16.59	14.19	12.17	10.46	9.01	7.78	6.73	5.83	5.06	4.40	3.84	45
46	16.57	14.25	12.28	10.61	9.19	7.97	6.93	6.03	5.26	4.60	4.03	46
47	16.56	14.31	12.40	10.76	9.36	8.16	7.13	6.24	5.47	4.81	4.23	47
48	16.54	14.37	12.51	10.92	9.54	8.36	7.34	6.45	5.69	5.02	4.44	48
49	16.52	14.42	12.62	11.07	9.73	8.56	7.55	6.68	5.91	5.24	4.66	49
50	16.50	14.48	12.74	11.22	9.91	8.77	7.78	6.91	6.14	5.48	4.89	50
51	16.48	14.54	12.85	11.38	10.10	8.98	8.00	7.14	6.39	5.72	5.13	51
52	16.47	14.60	12.97	11.55	10.30	9.20	8.24	7.39	6.64	5.98	5.39	52
53	16.46	14.67	13.10	11.72	10.50	9.43	8.49	7.65	6.91	6.25	5.66	53
54	16.45	14.74	13.23	11.89	10.72	9.67	8.75	7.92	7.19	6.53	5.94	54
55	16.46	14.82	13.36	12.08	10.94	9.92	9.01	8.21	7.48	6.83	6.25	55
56	16.47	14.90	13.51	12.27	11.17	10.18	9.30	8.51	7.79	7.15	6.57	56
57	16.50	15.00	13.67	12.48	11.42	10.46	9.60	8.83	8.13	7.49	6.92	57
58	16.55	15.13	13.85	12.71	11.69	10.76	9.92	9.17	8.48	7.86	7.30	58
59	16.62	15.27	14.06	12.96	11.98	11.08	10.27	9.54	8.87	8.26	7.70	59
60	16.71	15.43	14.28	13.23	12.29	11.43	10.65	9.93	9.28	8.68	8.14	60
61	16.82	15.61	14.52	13.52	12.62	11.80	11.04	10.35	9.72	9.14	8.61	61
62	16.94	15.81	14.77	13.83	12.97	12.19	11.47	10.81	10.20	9.64	9.12	62
63	17.08	16.02	15.05	14.16	13.35	12.60	11.92	11.28	10.70	10.16	9.66	63
64	17.23	16.24	15.34	14.51	13.75	13.04	12.39	11.80	11.24	10.73	10.25	64
65	17.40	16.49	15.65	14.88	14.17	13.51	12.91	12.34	11.82	11.34	10.89	65

Table 34   Multipliers for loss of pension commencing age 65 (females)

Age at date of trial	Multiplier calculated with allowance for projected mortality from the 1998-based population projections and rate of return of											Age at date of trial
	0.0%	0.5%	1.0%	1.5%	2.0%	2.5%	3.0%	£3.5%	4.0%	4.5%	5.0%	
0	20.26	13.75	9.36	6.40	4.39	3.02	2.09	1.45	1.01	0.70	0.49	0
1	20.34	13.87	9.49	6.52	4.50	3.11	2.16	1.50	1.05	0.74	0.52	1
2	20.34	13.94	9.59	6.62	4.59	3.19	2.23	1.56	1.09	0.77	0.54	2
3	20.34	14.01	9.69	6.72	4.68	3.27	2.29	1.61	1.14	0.80	0.57	3
4	20.33	14.08	9.78	6.82	4.77	3.35	2.36	1.67	1.18	0.84	0.60	4
5	20.33	14.15	9.88	6.92	4.87	3.43	2.43	1.73	1.23	0.88	0.63	5
6	20.33	14.21	9.97	7.02	4.96	3.52	2.50	1.79	1.28	0.92	0.66	6
7	20.32	14.28	10.07	7.13	5.06	3.61	2.58	1.85	1.33	0.96	0.69	7
8	20.32	14.35	10.17	7.23	5.16	3.70	2.66	1.91	1.38	1.00	0.73	8
9	20.31	14.42	10.27	7.34	5.26	3.79	2.73	1.98	1.44	1.05	0.76	9
10	20.31	14.49	10.37	7.45	5.37	3.88	2.82	2.05	1.49	1.09	0.80	10
11	20.30	14.56	10.47	7.56	5.47	3.98	2.90	2.12	1.55	1.14	0.84	11
12	20.30	14.62	10.57	7.67	5.58	4.08	2.99	2.19	1.62	1.19	0.88	12
13	20.29	14.69	10.68	7.78	5.69	4.18	3.07	2.27	1.68	1.25	0.93	13
14	20.29	14.76	10.78	7.90	5.81	4.28	3.17	2.35	1.75	1.30	0.98	14
15	20.28	14.83	10.89	8.01	5.92	4.39	3.26	2.43	1.82	1.36	1.02	15
16	20.28	14.90	10.99	8.13	6.04	4.50	3.36	2.51	1.89	1.42	1.07	16
17	20.27	14.97	11.10	8.25	6.16	4.61	3.46	2.60	1.96	1.49	1.13	17
18	20.27	15.05	11.21	8.38	6.28	4.72	3.56	2.69	2.04	1.55	1.18	18
19	20.26	15.12	11.32	8.50	6.40	4.84	3.67	2.79	2.12	1.62	1.24	19
20	20.26	15.19	11.43	8.63	6.53	4.96	3.78	2.88	2.21	1.70	1.31	20
21	20.25	15.26	11.54	8.75	6.66	5.08	3.89	2.98	2.30	1.77	1.37	21
22	20.25	15.33	11.65	8.88	6.79	5.21	4.00	3.09	2.39	1.85	1.44	22
23	20.24	15.41	11.76	9.01	6.92	5.33	4.12	3.19	2.48	1.93	1.51	23
24	20.23	15.48	11.88	9.14	7.06	5.47	4.24	3.31	2.58	2.02	1.59	24
25	20.22	15.55	11.99	9.28	7.20	5.60	4.37	3.42	2.68	2.11	1.66	25
26	20.21	15.62	12.11	9.41	7.34	5.74	4.50	3.54	2.79	2.20	1.75	26
27	20.20	15.69	12.22	9.55	7.48	5.88	4.63	3.66	2.90	2.30	1.83	27
28	20.19	15.76	12.34	9.69	7.63	6.02	4.77	3.79	3.01	2.41	1.92	28
29	20.18	15.83	12.46	9.83	7.78	6.17	4.91	3.92	3.13	2.51	2.02	29
30	20.17	15.90	12.58	9.97	7.93	6.32	5.06	4.05	3.26	2.63	2.12	30
31	20.16	15.98	12.69	10.12	8.09	6.48	5.21	4.19	3.39	2.74	2.23	31
32	20.15	16.05	12.81	10.26	8.24	6.64	5.36	4.34	3.52	2.86	2.34	32
33	20.14	16.12	12.94	10.41	8.40	6.80	5.52	4.49	3.66	2.99	2.45	33
34	20.13	16.19	13.06	10.56	8.57	6.97	5.68	4.64	3.81	3.13	2.57	34
35	20.12	16.26	13.18	10.72	8.73	7.14	5.85	4.80	3.96	3.26	2.70	35
36	20.10	16.33	13.30	10.87	8.90	7.31	6.02	4.97	4.11	3.41	2.83	36
37	20.09	16.40	13.43	11.03	9.08	7.49	6.20	5.14	4.27	3.56	2.97	37
38	20.07	16.47	13.56	11.18	9.25	7.67	6.38	5.32	4.44	3.72	3.12	38
39	20.06	16.55	13.68	11.35	9.43	7.86	6.57	5.50	4.62	3.89	3.28	39
40	20.05	16.62	13.81	11.51	9.62	8.05	6.76	5.69	4.80	4.06	3.44	40
41	20.03	16.69	13.94	11.67	9.80	8.25	6.96	5.89	4.99	4.24	3.61	41
42	20.02	16.76	14.07	11.84	9.99	8.45	7.17	6.09	5.19	4.43	3.79	42
43	20.00	16.83	14.20	12.01	10.19	8.66	7.38	6.30	5.39	4.63	3.98	43
44	19.99	16.91	14.34	12.19	10.39	8.87	7.60	6.52	5.61	4.83	4.17	44
45	19.98	16.98	14.47	12.36	10.59	9.09	7.82	6.75	5.83	5.05	4.38	45
46	19.96	17.05	14.61	12.54	10.80	9.31	8.05	6.98	6.06	5.28	4.60	46
47	19.95	17.13	14.75	12.73	11.01	9.54	8.29	7.22	6.30	5.51	4.83	47
48	19.94	17.21	14.89	12.91	11.22	9.78	8.54	7.47	6.56	5.76	5.07	48
49	19.93	17.29	15.03	13.10	11.45	10.02	8.80	7.74	6.82	6.02	5.33	49
50	19.92	17.37	15.18	13.30	11.67	10.27	9.06	8.01	7.09	6.29	5.59	50
51	19.92	17.45	15.33	13.49	11.91	10.53	9.33	8.29	7.38	6.58	5.88	51
52	19.92	17.54	15.48	13.70	12.15	10.80	9.62	8.58	7.68	6.88	6.17	52
53	19.92	17.63	15.64	13.91	12.40	11.07	9.91	8.89	7.99	7.19	6.49	53
54	19.93	17.73	15.81	14.13	12.65	11.36	10.22	9.21	8.32	7.52	6.82	54
55	19.94	17.83	15.98	14.35	12.92	11.65	10.54	9.54	8.66	7.87	7.17	55
56	19.95	17.93	16.15	14.58	13.19	11.96	10.87	9.89	9.02	8.24	7.54	56
57	19.98	18.05	16.34	14.83	13.48	12.28	11.21	10.26	9.40	8.63	7.93	57
58	20.02	18.17	16.54	15.08	13.78	12.62	11.58	10.64	9.80	9.04	8.35	58
59	20.07	18.32	16.75	15.35	14.10	12.98	11.97	11.05	10.23	9.48	8.80	59
60	20.14	18.47	16.98	15.64	14.44	13.35	12.37	11.49	10.68	9.95	9.28	60
61	20.22	18.64	17.22	15.95	14.79	13.75	12.80	11.94	11.16	10.45	9.80	61
62	20.31	18.82	17.47	16.26	15.16	14.16	13.25	12.42	11.67	10.97	10.34	62
63	20.39	19.00	17.73	16.58	15.54	14.59	13.72	12.92	12.20	11.53	10.91	63
64	20.48	19.17	17.99	16.91	15.92	15.03	14.20	13.45	12.75	12.11	11.52	64
65	20.56	19.35	18.25	17.24	16.32	15.48	14.70	13.99	13.34	12.73	12.17	65

Table 35 Multipliers for loss of pension commencing age 70 (males)

Age at date of trial	Multiplier calculated with allowance for projected mortality from the 1998-based population projections and rate of return of											Age at date of trial
	0.0%	0.5%	1.0%	1.5%	2.0%	2.5%	3.0%	£3.5%	4.0%	4.5%	5.0%	
0	12.53	8.43	5.68	3.85	2.61	1.78	1.21	0.83	0.57	0.39	0.27	0
1	12.59	8.51	5.77	3.92	2.67	1.83	1.25	0.86	0.60	0.41	0.29	1
2	12.59	8.55	5.83	3.98	2.73	1.88	1.29	0.89	0.62	0.43	0.30	2
3	12.59	8.59	5.88	4.04	2.78	1.92	1.33	0.92	0.64	0.45	0.31	3
4	12.59	8.64	5.94	4.10	2.84	1.97	1.37	0.96	0.67	0.47	0.33	4
5	12.59	8.68	6.00	4.16	2.89	2.02	1.41	0.99	0.70	0.49	0.35	5
6	12.58	8.72	6.06	4.22	2.95	2.07	1.45	1.02	0.72	0.51	0.36	6
7	12.58	8.76	6.12	4.28	3.01	2.12	1.50	1.06	0.75	0.54	0.38	7
8	12.57	8.80	6.18	4.35	3.07	2.17	1.54	1.10	0.78	0.56	0.40	8
9	12.57	8.84	6.24	4.41	3.13	2.23	1.59	1.13	0.81	0.58	0.42	9
10	12.56	8.88	6.30	4.48	3.19	2.28	1.63	1.17	0.85	0.61	0.44	10
11	12.56	8.92	6.36	4.54	3.25	2.34	1.68	1.21	0.88	0.64	0.46	11
12	12.55	8.96	6.42	4.61	3.32	2.39	1.73	1.26	0.91	0.67	0.49	12
13	12.55	9.00	6.48	4.67	3.38	2.45	1.78	1.30	0.95	0.70	0.51	13
14	12.54	9.05	6.54	4.74	3.45	2.51	1.84	1.35	0.99	0.73	0.54	14
15	12.54	9.09	6.60	4.81	3.52	2.58	1.89	1.39	1.03	0.76	0.56	15
16	12.53	9.13	6.67	4.88	3.59	2.64	1.95	1.44	1.07	0.79	0.59	16
17	12.53	9.17	6.73	4.95	3.66	2.70	2.00	1.49	1.11	0.83	0.62	17
18	12.53	9.22	6.80	5.03	3.73	2.77	2.06	1.54	1.15	0.87	0.65	18
19	12.53	9.26	6.87	5.10	3.80	2.84	2.13	1.60	1.20	0.91	0.68	19
20	12.53	9.31	6.94	5.18	3.88	2.91	2.19	1.65	1.25	0.95	0.72	20
21	12.53	9.36	7.00	5.26	3.96	2.98	2.26	1.71	1.30	0.99	0.75	21
22	12.53	9.40	7.07	5.34	4.04	3.06	2.32	1.77	1.35	1.03	0.79	22
23	12.52	9.45	7.14	5.42	4.12	3.14	2.39	1.83	1.40	1.08	0.83	23
24	12.52	9.49	7.21	5.50	4.20	3.21	2.47	1.90	1.46	1.13	0.87	24
25	12.52	9.54	7.28	5.58	4.28	3.29	2.54	1.96	1.52	1.18	0.92	25
26	12.51	9.58	7.36	5.66	4.36	3.37	2.61	2.03	1.58	1.23	0.96	26
27	12.51	9.63	7.43	5.74	4.45	3.46	2.69	2.10	1.64	1.29	1.01	27
28	12.51	9.67	7.50	5.83	4.54	3.54	2.77	2.17	1.71	1.34	1.06	28
29	12.50	9.72	7.57	5.91	4.63	3.63	2.85	2.25	1.77	1.40	1.11	29
30	12.49	9.76	7.64	6.00	4.72	3.72	2.94	2.33	1.85	1.47	1.17	30
31	12.48	9.80	7.71	6.08	4.81	3.81	3.02	2.41	1.92	1.53	1.23	31
32	12.48	9.84	7.79	6.17	4.90	3.90	3.11	2.49	1.99	1.60	1.29	32
33	12.47	9.89	7.86	6.26	5.00	4.00	3.20	2.57	2.07	1.67	1.35	33
34	12.45	9.93	7.93	6.35	5.09	4.09	3.30	2.66	2.15	1.74	1.42	34
35	12.44	9.97	8.00	6.44	5.19	4.19	3.39	2.75	2.24	1.82	1.49	35
36	12.43	10.00	8.07	6.53	5.29	4.29	3.49	2.85	2.32	1.90	1.56	36
37	12.41	10.04	8.14	6.62	5.39	4.40	3.59	2.94	2.42	1.99	1.64	37
38	12.40	10.08	8.21	6.71	5.49	4.50	3.70	3.04	2.51	2.07	1.72	38
39	12.38	10.12	8.29	6.80	5.59	4.61	3.80	3.15	2.61	2.16	1.80	39
40	12.37	10.16	8.36	6.89	5.70	4.72	3.91	3.25	2.71	2.26	1.89	40
41	12.35	10.19	8.43	6.99	5.81	4.83	4.03	3.36	2.81	2.36	1.98	41
42	12.34	10.23	8.51	7.09	5.92	4.95	4.14	3.48	2.92	2.46	2.08	42
43	12.32	10.27	8.58	7.19	6.03	5.06	4.26	3.60	3.04	2.57	2.18	43
44	12.30	10.31	8.66	7.28	6.14	5.19	4.39	3.72	3.16	2.68	2.29	44
45	12.29	10.35	8.73	7.38	6.26	5.31	4.51	3.84	3.28	2.80	2.40	45
46	12.27	10.39	8.81	7.49	6.37	5.44	4.64	3.97	3.41	2.93	2.52	46
47	12.25	10.42	8.88	7.59	6.49	5.56	4.78	4.11	3.54	3.05	2.64	47
48	12.23	10.46	8.96	7.69	6.61	5.70	4.91	4.25	3.68	3.19	2.77	48
49	12.21	10.49	9.03	7.79	6.73	5.83	5.05	4.39	3.82	3.33	2.90	49
50	12.18	10.52	9.11	7.90	6.86	5.97	5.20	4.54	3.96	3.47	3.04	50
51	12.16	10.56	9.18	8.00	6.98	6.10	5.35	4.69	4.12	3.62	3.19	51
52	12.14	10.59	9.26	8.11	7.11	6.25	5.50	4.85	4.28	3.78	3.35	52
53	12.12	10.63	9.34	8.22	7.25	6.40	5.66	5.01	4.45	3.95	3.51	53
54	12.11	10.67	9.43	8.34	7.39	6.55	5.82	5.18	4.62	4.12	3.69	54
55	12.10	10.72	9.51	8.46	7.53	6.71	6.00	5.36	4.80	4.31	3.87	55
56	12.09	10.77	9.61	8.58	7.68	6.88	6.18	5.55	5.00	4.50	4.07	56
57	12.10	10.83	9.71	8.72	7.84	7.06	6.37	5.75	5.20	4.71	4.28	57
58	12.13	10.91	9.83	8.87	8.02	7.26	6.58	5.97	5.43	4.94	4.50	58
59	12.17	11.00	9.96	9.03	8.21	7.47	6.80	6.20	5.67	5.18	4.75	59
60	12.22	11.10	10.11	9.21	8.41	7.69	7.04	6.45	5.92	5.44	5.01	60
61	12.28	11.22	10.26	9.40	8.63	7.93	7.29	6.72	6.20	5.72	5.29	61
62	12.36	11.35	10.43	9.61	8.86	8.18	7.56	7.00	6.49	6.02	5.60	62
63	12.44	11.48	10.61	9.82	9.10	8.45	7.85	7.30	6.80	6.34	5.92	63
64	12.53	11.62	10.80	10.04	9.36	8.73	8.15	7.62	7.13	6.68	6.27	64

Table 35 *continued*

65	12.63	11.78	11.00	10.28	9.62	9.02	8.47	7.96	7.49	7.05	6.65	65
66	12.74	11.94	11.20	10.53	9.91	9.33	8.80	8.31	7.86	7.44	7.05	66
67	12.86	12.11	11.43	10.79	10.21	9.67	9.16	8.70	8.26	7.86	7.48	67
68	12.99	12.30	11.67	11.08	10.53	10.02	9.55	9.11	8.70	8.32	7.96	68
69	13.15	12.52	11.94	11.39	10.89	10.41	9.97	9.56	9.18	8.82	8.48	69
70	13.36	12.78	12.25	11.75	11.29	10.86	10.45	10.07	9.71	9.38	9.07	70

Table 36   Multipliers for loss of pension commencing age 70 (females)

Age at date of trial	Multiplier calculated with allowance for projected mortality from the 1998-based population projections and rate of return of											Age at date of trial
	0.0%	0.5%	1.0%	1.5%	2.0%	2.5%	3.0%	£3.5%	4.0%	4.5%	5.0%	
0	15.76	10.53	7.06	4.75	3.21	2.17	1.48	1.01	0.69	0.47	0.32	0
1	15.82	10.63	7.16	4.84	3.29	2.24	1.53	1.05	0.72	0.49	0.34	1
2	15.82	10.68	7.24	4.92	3.35	2.29	1.57	1.08	0.75	0.52	0.36	2
3	15.82	10.73	7.31	4.99	3.42	2.35	1.62	1.12	0.78	0.54	0.38	3
4	15.82	10.79	7.38	5.07	3.49	2.41	1.67	1.16	0.81	0.56	0.40	4
5	15.82	10.84	7.45	5.14	3.56	2.47	1.72	1.20	0.84	0.59	0.42	5
6	15.81	10.89	7.53	5.22	3.63	2.53	1.77	1.24	0.87	0.62	0.44	6
7	15.81	10.94	7.60	5.29	3.70	2.59	1.82	1.28	0.91	0.64	0.46	7
8	15.80	10.99	7.67	5.37	3.77	2.66	1.88	1.33	0.94	0.67	0.48	8
9	15.80	11.05	7.75	5.45	3.85	2.72	1.93	1.38	0.98	0.70	0.50	9
10	15.80	11.10	7.82	5.53	3.92	2.79	1.99	1.42	1.02	0.73	0.53	10
11	15.79	11.15	7.90	5.61	4.00	2.86	2.05	1.47	1.06	0.77	0.56	11
12	15.79	11.20	7.98	5.69	4.08	2.93	2.11	1.52	1.10	0.80	0.58	12
13	15.78	11.26	8.05	5.78	4.16	3.00	2.17	1.58	1.15	0.84	0.61	13
14	15.78	11.31	8.13	5.86	4.24	3.08	2.24	1.63	1.19	0.87	0.64	14
15	15.77	11.36	8.21	5.95	4.32	3.15	2.30	1.69	1.24	0.91	0.67	15
16	15.77	11.42	8.29	6.04	4.41	3.23	2.37	1.75	1.29	0.95	0.71	16
17	15.76	11.47	8.37	6.13	4.50	3.31	2.44	1.81	1.34	1.00	0.74	17
18	15.76	11.52	8.45	6.22	4.59	3.39	2.51	1.87	1.39	1.04	0.78	18
19	15.75	11.58	8.53	6.31	4.68	3.48	2.59	1.93	1.45	1.09	0.82	19
20	15.75	11.63	8.62	6.40	4.77	3.56	2.67	2.00	1.51	1.14	0.86	20
21	15.74	11.69	8.70	6.49	4.86	3.65	2.75	2.07	1.57	1.19	0.90	21
22	15.74	11.74	8.78	6.59	4.96	3.74	2.83	2.14	1.63	1.24	0.95	22
23	15.73	11.79	8.87	6.69	5.05	3.83	2.91	2.22	1.69	1.30	0.99	23
24	15.72	11.85	8.95	6.78	5.15	3.93	3.00	2.29	1.76	1.35	1.04	24
25	15.72	11.90	9.04	6.88	5.25	4.02	3.09	2.37	1.83	1.41	1.10	25
26	15.71	11.95	9.12	6.98	5.36	4.12	3.18	2.46	1.90	1.48	1.15	26
27	15.70	12.01	9.21	7.08	5.46	4.22	3.27	2.54	1.98	1.54	1.21	27
28	15.69	12.06	9.30	7.19	5.57	4.32	3.37	2.63	2.06	1.61	1.27	28
29	15.68	12.11	9.38	7.29	5.68	4.43	3.47	2.72	2.14	1.68	1.33	29
30	15.67	12.17	9.47	7.39	5.79	4.54	3.57	2.81	2.22	1.76	1.39	30
31	15.66	12.22	9.56	7.50	5.90	4.65	3.67	2.91	2.31	1.84	1.46	31
32	15.65	12.27	9.65	7.61	6.01	4.76	3.78	3.01	2.40	1.92	1.54	32
33	15.64	12.33	9.74	7.72	6.13	4.88	3.89	3.11	2.49	2.00	1.61	33
34	15.62	12.38	9.83	7.83	6.25	5.00	4.01	3.22	2.59	2.09	1.69	34
35	15.61	12.43	9.92	7.94	6.37	5.12	4.12	3.33	2.69	2.18	1.77	35
36	15.60	12.48	10.01	8.05	6.49	5.24	4.24	3.44	2.80	2.28	1.86	36
37	15.59	12.53	10.10	8.16	6.61	5.37	4.37	3.56	2.91	2.38	1.95	37
38	15.57	12.58	10.20	8.28	6.74	5.50	4.50	3.68	3.02	2.49	2.05	38
39	15.56	12.64	10.29	8.40	6.87	5.63	4.63	3.81	3.14	2.60	2.15	39
40	15.54	12.69	10.38	8.52	7.00	5.77	4.76	3.94	3.27	2.71	2.26	40
41	15.53	12.74	10.48	8.64	7.13	5.91	4.90	4.07	3.39	2.83	2.37	41
42	15.51	12.79	10.57	8.76	7.27	6.05	5.04	4.21	3.53	2.96	2.49	42
43	15.49	12.84	10.67	8.88	7.41	6.20	5.19	4.36	3.67	3.09	2.61	43
44	15.48	12.89	10.76	9.01	7.55	6.35	5.34	4.51	3.81	3.23	2.74	44
45	15.46	12.94	10.86	9.13	7.70	6.50	5.50	4.66	3.96	3.37	2.87	45
46	15.45	13.00	10.96	9.26	7.84	6.66	5.66	4.82	4.11	3.52	3.01	46
47	15.43	13.05	11.06	9.39	7.99	6.82	5.82	4.99	4.28	3.67	3.16	47
48	15.42	13.10	11.16	9.53	8.15	6.98	5.99	5.16	4.44	3.84	3.32	48
49	15.40	13.16	11.26	9.66	8.30	7.15	6.17	5.33	4.62	4.01	3.48	49
50	15.39	13.21	11.37	9.80	8.46	7.33	6.35	5.52	4.80	4.19	3.66	50
51	15.38	13.27	11.47	9.94	8.63	7.51	6.54	5.71	4.99	4.37	3.84	51
52	15.37	13.33	11.58	10.08	8.80	7.69	6.73	5.91	5.19	4.57	4.03	52
53	15.36	13.39	11.69	10.23	8.97	7.88	6.94	6.11	5.40	4.78	4.23	53
54	15.36	13.45	11.81	10.39	9.15	8.08	7.15	6.33	5.62	4.99	4.44	54
55	15.35	13.52	11.93	10.54	9.34	8.28	7.36	6.55	5.85	5.22	4.67	55
56	15.36	13.59	12.05	10.71	9.53	8.50	7.59	6.79	6.08	5.46	4.91	56
57	15.37	13.67	12.18	10.88	9.73	8.72	7.82	7.03	6.33	5.71	5.16	57
58	15.38	13.75	12.32	11.06	9.94	8.95	8.07	7.29	6.60	5.98	5.43	58
59	15.42	13.85	12.47	11.25	10.16	9.20	8.34	7.57	6.88	6.27	5.72	59
60	15.46	13.96	12.63	11.45	10.40	9.46	8.62	7.86	7.18	6.57	6.02	60
61	15.51	14.08	12.81	11.67	10.65	9.73	8.91	8.17	7.50	6.90	6.35	61
62	15.56	14.20	12.98	11.89	10.90	10.01	9.21	8.49	7.83	7.24	6.70	62
63	15.62	14.32	13.16	12.11	11.16	10.31	9.53	8.82	8.18	7.60	7.06	63
64	15.66	14.44	13.33	12.33	11.43	10.60	9.85	9.17	8.54	7.97	7.45	64

Table 36 *continued*

65	15.70	14.55	13.51	12.56	11.69	10.90	10.18	9.52	8.92	8.36	7.85	65
66	15.74	14.66	13.68	12.78	11.96	11.21	10.53	9.90	9.31	8.78	8.28	66
67	15.78	14.78	13.86	13.02	12.25	11.54	10.89	10.28	9.73	9.21	8.74	67
68	15.83	14.90	14.05	13.27	12.55	11.88	11.27	10.70	10.17	9.68	9.23	68
69	15.90	15.05	14.26	13.54	12.87	12.25	11.68	11.14	10.65	10.19	9.76	69
70	16.01	15.23	14.51	13.85	13.23	12.66	12.13	11.64	11.17	10.74	10.34	70

Table 37 Discounting factors for term certain

Term	0.5%	1.0%	1.5%	2.0%	2.5%	3.0%	3.5%	4.0%	4.5%	5.0%	Term
				Factor to discount value of multiplier for a period of deferment							
1	0.9950	0.9901	0.9852	0.9804	0.9756	0.9709	0.9662	0.9615	0.9569	0.9524	1
2	0.9901	0.9803	0.9707	0.9612	0.9518	0.9426	0.9335	0.9246	0.9157	0.9070	2
3	0.9851	0.9706	0.9563	0.9423	0.9286	0.9151	0.9019	0.8890	0.8763	0.8638	3
4	0.9802	0.9610	0.9422	0.9238	0.9060	0.8885	0.8714	0.8548	0.8386	0.8227	4
5	0.9754	0.9515	0.9283	0.9057	0.8839	0.8626	0.8420	0.8219	0.8025	0.7835	5
6	0.9705	0.9420	0.9145	0.8880	0.8623	0.8375	0.8135	0.7903	0.7679	0.7462	6
7	0.9657	0.9327	0.9010	0.8706	0.8413	0.8131	0.7860	0.7599	0.7348	0.7107	7
8	0.9609	0.9235	0.8877	0.8535	0.8207	0.7894	0.7594	0.7307	0.7032	0.6768	8
9	0.9561	0.9143	0.8746	0.8368	0.8007	0.7664	0.7337	0.7026	0.6729	0.6446	9
10	0.9513	0.9053	0.8617	0.8203	0.7812	0.7441	0.7089	0.6756	0.6439	0.6139	10
11	0.9466	0.8963	0.8489	0.8043	0.7621	0.7224	0.6849	0.6496	0.6162	0.5847	11
12	0.9419	0.8874	0.8364	0.7885	0.7436	0.7014	0.6618	0.6246	0.5897	0.5568	12
13	0.9372	0.8787	0.8240	0.7730	0.7254	0.6810	0.6394	0.6006	0.5643	0.5303	13
14	0.9326	0.8700	0.8118	0.7579	0.7077	0.6611	0.6178	0.5775	0.5400	0.5051	14
15	0.9279	0.8613	0.7999	0.7430	0.6905	0.6419	0.5969	0.5553	0.5167	0.4810	15
16	0.9233	0.8528	0.7880	0.7284	0.6736	0.6232	0.5767	0.5339	0.4945	0.4581	16
17	0.9187	0.8444	0.7764	0.7142	0.6572	0.6050	0.5572	0.5134	0.4732	0.4363	17
18	0.9141	0.8360	0.7649	0.7002	0.6412	0.5874	0.5384	0.4936	0.4528	0.4155	18
19	0.9096	0.8277	0.7536	0.6864	0.6255	0.5703	0.5202	0.4746	0.4333	0.3957	19
20	0.9051	0.8195	0.7425	0.6730	0.6103	0.5537	0.5026	0.4564	0.4146	0.3769	20
21	0.9006	0.8114	0.7315	0.6598	0.5954	0.5375	0.4856	0.4388	0.3968	0.3589	21
22	0.8961	0.8034	0.7207	0.6468	0.5809	0.5219	0.4692	0.4220	0.3797	0.3418	22
23	0.8916	0.7954	0.7100	0.6342	0.5667	0.5067	0.4533	0.4057	0.3634	0.3256	23
24	0.8872	0.7876	0.6995	0.6217	0.5529	0.4919	0.4380	0.3901	0.3477	0.3101	24
25	0.8828	0.7798	0.6892	0.6095	0.5394	0.4776	0.4231	0.3751	0.3327	0.2953	25
26	0.8784	0.7720	0.6790	0.5976	0.5262	0.4637	0.4088	0.3607	0.3184	0.2812	26
27	0.8740	0.7644	0.6690	0.5859	0.5134	0.4502	0.3950	0.3468	0.3047	0.2678	27
28	0.8697	0.7568	0.6591	0.5744	0.5009	0.4371	0.3817	0.3335	0.2916	0.2551	28
29	0.8653	0.7493	0.6494	0.5631	0.4887	0.4243	0.3687	0.3207	0.2790	0.2429	29
30	0.8610	0.7419	0.6398	0.5521	0.4767	0.4120	0.3563	0.3083	0.2670	0.2314	30
31	0.8567	0.7346	0.6303	0.5412	0.4651	0.4000	0.3442	0.2965	0.2555	0.2204	31
32	0.8525	0.7273	0.6210	0.5306	0.4538	0.3883	0.3326	0.2851	0.2445	0.2099	32
33	0.8482	0.7201	0.6118	0.5202	0.4427	0.3770	0.3213	0.2741	0.2340	0.1999	33
34	0.8440	0.7130	0.6028	0.5100	0.4319	0.3660	0.3105	0.2636	0.2239	0.1904	34
35	0.8398	0.7059	0.5939	0.5000	0.4214	0.3554	0.3000	0.2534	0.2143	0.1813	35
36	0.8356	0.6989	0.5851	0.4902	0.4111	0.3450	0.2898	0.2437	0.2050	0.1727	36
37	0.8315	0.6920	0.5764	0.4806	0.4011	0.3350	0.2800	0.2343	0.1962	0.1644	37
38	0.8274	0.6852	0.5679	0.4712	0.3913	0.3252	0.2706	0.2253	0.1878	0.1566	38
39	0.8232	0.6784	0.5595	0.4619	0.3817	0.3158	0.2614	0.2166	0.1797	0.1491	39
40	0.8191	0.6717	0.5513	0.4529	0.3724	0.3066	0.2526	0.2083	0.1719	0.1420	40
41	0.8151	0.6650	0.5431	0.4440	0.3633	0.2976	0.2440	0.2003	0.1645	0.1353	41
42	0.8110	0.6584	0.5351	0.4353	0.3545	0.2890	0.2358	0.1926	0.1574	0.1288	42
43	0.8070	0.6519	0.5272	0.4268	0.3458	0.2805	0.2278	0.1852	0.1507	0.1227	43
44	0.8030	0.6454	0.5194	0.4184	0.3374	0.2724	0.2201	0.1780	0.1442	0.1169	44
45	0.7990	0.6391	0.5117	0.4102	0.3292	0.2644	0.2127	0.1712	0.1380	0.1113	45
46	0.7950	0.6327	0.5042	0.4022	0.3211	0.2567	0.2055	0.1646	0.1320	0.1060	46
47	0.7910	0.6265	0.4967	0.3943	0.3133	0.2493	0.1985	0.1583	0.1263	0.1009	47
48	0.7871	0.6203	0.4894	0.3865	0.3057	0.2420	0.1918	0.1522	0.1209	0.0961	48
49	0.7832	0.6141	0.4821	0.3790	0.2982	0.2350	0.1853	0.1463	0.1157	0.0916	49
50	0.7793	0.6080	0.4750	0.3715	0.2909	0.2281	0.1791	0.1407	0.1107	0.0872	50
51	0.7754	0.6020	0.4680	0.3642	0.2838	0.2215	0.1730	0.1353	0.1059	0.0831	51
52	0.7716	0.5961	0.4611	0.3571	0.2769	0.2150	0.1671	0.1301	0.1014	0.0791	52
53	0.7677	0.5902	0.4543	0.3501	0.2702	0.2088	0.1615	0.1251	0.0970	0.0753	53
54	0.7639	0.5843	0.4475	0.3432	0.2636	0.2027	0.1560	0.1203	0.0928	0.0717	54
55	0.7601	0.5785	0.4409	0.3365	0.2572	0.1968	0.1508	0.1157	0.0888	0.0683	55
56	0.7563	0.5728	0.4344	0.3299	0.2509	0.1910	0.1457	0.1112	0.0850	0.0651	56
57	0.7525	0.5671	0.4280	0.3234	0.2448	0.1855	0.1407	0.1069	0.0814	0.0620	57
58	0.7488	0.5615	0.4217	0.3171	0.2388	0.1801	0.1360	0.1028	0.0778	0.0590	58
59	0.7451	0.5560	0.4154	0.3109	0.2330	0.1748	0.1314	0.0989	0.0745	0.0562	59
60	0.7414	0.5504	0.4093	0.3048	0.2273	0.1697	0.1269	0.0951	0.0713	0.0535	60
61	0.7377	0.5450	0.4032	0.2988	0.2217	0.1648	0.1226	0.0914	0.0682	0.0510	61
62	0.7340	0.5396	0.3973	0.2929	0.2163	0.1600	0.1185	0.0879	0.0653	0.0486	62
63	0.7304	0.5343	0.3914	0.2872	0.2111	0.1553	0.1145	0.0845	0.0625	0.0462	63
64	0.7267	0.5290	0.3856	0.2816	0.2059	0.1508	0.1106	0.0813	0.0598	0.0440	64
65	0.7231	0.5237	0.3799	0.2761	0.2009	0.1464	0.1069	0.0781	0.0572	0.0419	65
66	0.7195	0.5185	0.3743	0.2706	0.1960	0.1421	0.1033	0.0751	0.0547	0.0399	66
67	0.7159	0.5134	0.3688	0.2653	0.1912	0.1380	0.0998	0.0722	0.0524	0.0380	67
68	0.7124	0.5083	0.3633	0.2601	0.1865	0.1340	0.0964	0.0695	0.0501	0.0362	68
69	0.7088	0.5033	0.3580	0.2550	0.1820	0.1301	0.0931	0.0668	0.0480	0.0345	69
70	0.7053	0.4983	0.3527	0.2500	0.1776	0.1263	0.0900	0.0642	0.0459	0.0329	70
71	0.7018	0.4934	0.3475	0.2451	0.1732	0.1226	0.0869	0.0617	0.0439	0.0313	71
72	0.6983	0.4885	0.3423	0.2403	0.1690	0.1190	0.0840	0.0594	0.0420	0.0298	72
73	0.6948	0.4837	0.3373	0.2356	0.1649	0.1156	0.0812	0.0571	0.0402	0.0284	73

Table 37 *continued*

74	0.6914	0.4789	0.3323	0.2310	0.1609	0.1122	0.0784	0.0549	0.0385	0.0270	74
75	0.6879	0.4741	0.3274	0.2265	0.1569	0.1089	0.0758	0.0528	0.0368	0.0258	75
76	0.6845	0.4694	0.3225	0.2220	0.1531	0.1058	0.0732	0.0508	0.0353	0.0245	76
77	0.6811	0.4648	0.3178	0.2177	0.1494	0.1027	0.0707	0.0488	0.0337	0.0234	77
78	0.6777	0.4602	0.3131	0.2134	0.1457	0.0997	0.0683	0.0469	0.0323	0.0222	78
79	0.6743	0.4556	0.3084	0.2092	0.1422	0.0968	0.0660	0.0451	0.0309	0.0212	79
80	0.6710	0.4511	0.3039	0.2051	0.1387	0.0940	0.0638	0.0434	0.0296	0.0202	80

Table 38   Multipliers for pecuniary loss for term certain

Term	0.5%	1.0%	1.5%	2.0%	2.5%	3.0%	3.5%	4.0%	4.5%	5.0%	Term
			Multiplier for regular frequent payments for a term certain at rate of return of								
1	1.00	1.00	0.99	0.99	0.99	0.99	0.98	0.98	0.98	0.98	1
2	1.99	1.98	1.97	1.96	1.95	1.94	1.93	1.92	1.91	1.91	2
3	2.98	2.96	2.93	2.91	2.89	2.87	2.85	2.83	2.81	2.79	3
4	3.96	3.92	3.88	3.85	3.81	3.77	3.74	3.70	3.67	3.63	4
5	4.94	4.88	4.82	4.76	4.70	4.65	4.59	4.54	4.49	4.44	5
6	5.91	5.82	5.74	5.66	5.58	5.50	5.42	5.35	5.27	5.20	6
7	6.88	6.76	6.65	6.54	6.43	6.32	6.22	6.12	6.02	5.93	7
8	7.84	7.69	7.54	7.40	7.26	7.12	6.99	6.87	6.74	6.62	8
9	8.80	8.61	8.42	8.24	8.07	7.90	7.74	7.58	7.43	7.28	9
10	9.75	9.52	9.29	9.07	8.86	8.66	8.46	8.27	8.09	7.91	10
11	10.70	10.42	10.15	9.88	9.63	9.39	9.16	8.93	8.72	8.51	11
12	11.65	11.31	10.99	10.68	10.39	10.10	9.83	9.57	9.32	9.08	12
13	12.59	12.19	11.82	11.46	11.12	10.79	10.48	10.18	9.90	9.63	13
14	13.52	13.07	12.64	12.23	11.84	11.46	11.11	10.77	10.45	10.14	14
15	14.45	13.93	13.44	12.98	12.54	12.12	11.72	11.34	10.98	10.64	15
16	15.38	14.79	14.24	13.71	13.22	12.75	12.30	11.88	11.48	11.11	16
17	16.30	15.64	15.02	14.43	13.88	13.36	12.87	12.41	11.97	11.55	17
18	17.22	16.48	15.79	15.14	14.53	13.96	13.42	12.91	12.43	11.98	18
19	18.13	17.31	16.55	15.83	15.17	14.54	13.95	13.39	12.87	12.38	19
20	19.03	18.14	17.30	16.51	15.78	15.10	14.46	13.86	13.30	12.77	20
21	19.94	18.95	18.03	17.18	16.39	15.65	14.95	14.31	13.70	13.14	21
22	20.84	19.76	18.76	17.83	16.97	16.17	15.43	14.74	14.09	13.49	22
23	21.73	20.56	19.48	18.47	17.55	16.69	15.89	15.15	14.46	13.82	23
24	22.62	21.35	20.18	19.10	18.11	17.19	16.34	15.55	14.82	14.14	24
25	23.50	22.13	20.87	19.72	18.65	17.67	16.77	15.93	15.16	14.44	25
26	24.38	22.91	21.56	20.32	19.19	18.14	17.18	16.30	15.48	14.73	26
27	25.26	23.68	22.23	20.91	19.71	18.60	17.59	16.65	15.80	15.01	27
28	26.13	24.44	22.90	21.49	20.21	19.04	17.97	16.99	16.09	15.27	28
29	27.00	25.19	23.55	22.06	20.71	19.47	18.35	17.32	16.38	15.52	29
30	27.86	25.94	24.20	22.62	21.19	19.89	18.71	17.64	16.65	15.75	30
31	28.72	26.67	24.83	23.17	21.66	20.30	19.06	17.94	16.91	15.98	31
32	29.58	27.41	25.46	23.70	22.12	20.69	19.40	18.23	17.16	16.19	32
33	30.43	28.13	26.07	24.23	22.57	21.08	19.73	18.51	17.40	16.40	33
34	31.27	28.85	26.68	24.74	23.01	21.45	20.04	18.78	17.63	16.59	34
35	32.12	29.56	27.28	25.25	23.43	21.81	20.35	19.04	17.85	16.78	35
36	32.95	30.26	27.87	25.74	23.85	22.16	20.64	19.28	18.06	16.96	36
37	33.79	30.95	28.45	26.23	24.26	22.50	20.93	19.52	18.26	17.13	37
38	34.62	31.64	29.02	26.70	24.65	22.83	21.20	19.75	18.45	17.29	38
39	35.44	32.32	29.58	27.17	25.04	23.15	21.47	19.97	18.64	17.44	39
40	36.26	33.00	30.14	27.63	25.42	23.46	21.73	20.19	18.81	17.58	40
41	37.08	33.67	30.69	28.08	25.78	23.76	21.97	20.39	18.98	17.72	41
42	37.89	34.33	31.23	28.52	26.14	24.06	22.21	20.59	19.14	17.86	42
43	38.70	34.98	31.76	28.95	26.49	24.34	22.45	20.78	19.30	17.98	43
44	39.51	35.63	32.28	29.37	26.83	24.62	22.67	20.96	19.44	18.10	44
45	40.31	36.27	32.80	29.78	27.17	24.88	22.89	21.13	19.58	18.21	45
46	41.10	36.91	33.30	30.19	27.49	25.15	23.10	21.30	19.72	18.32	46
47	41.90	37.54	33.80	30.59	27.81	25.40	23.30	21.46	19.85	18.43	47
48	42.69	38.16	34.30	30.98	28.12	25.64	23.49	21.62	19.97	18.53	48
49	43.47	38.78	34.78	31.36	28.42	25.88	23.68	21.77	20.09	18.62	49
50	44.25	39.39	35.26	31.74	28.72	26.11	23.86	21.91	20.20	18.71	50
51	45.03	40.00	35.73	32.10	29.00	26.34	24.04	22.05	20.31	18.79	51
52	45.80	40.60	36.20	32.47	29.28	26.56	24.21	22.18	20.42	18.87	52
53	46.57	41.19	36.66	32.82	29.56	26.77	24.37	22.31	20.51	18.95	53
54	47.34	41.78	37.11	33.17	29.82	26.97	24.53	22.43	20.61	19.03	54
55	48.10	42.36	37.55	33.51	30.08	27.17	24.69	22.55	20.70	19.10	55
56	48.86	42.93	37.99	33.84	30.34	27.37	24.83	22.66	20.79	19.16	56
57	49.61	43.50	38.42	34.17	30.59	27.56	24.98	22.77	20.87	19.23	57
58	50.36	44.07	38.84	34.49	30.83	27.74	25.12	22.88	20.95	19.29	58
59	51.11	44.63	39.26	34.80	31.06	27.92	25.25	22.98	21.03	19.34	59
60	51.85	45.18	39.67	35.11	31.29	28.09	25.38	23.07	21.10	19.40	60
61	52.59	45.73	40.08	35.41	31.52	28.26	25.50	23.17	21.17	19.45	61
62	53.33	46.27	40.48	35.70	31.74	28.42	25.62	23.26	21.24	19.50	62
63	54.06	46.81	40.88	36.00	31.95	28.58	25.74	23.34	21.30	19.55	63
64	54.79	47.34	41.26	36.28	32.16	28.73	25.85	23.42	21.36	19.59	64
65	55.52	47.86	41.65	36.56	32.36	28.88	25.96	23.50	21.42	19.64	65
66	56.24	48.39	42.02	36.83	32.56	29.02	26.07	23.58	21.47	19.68	66
67	56.95	48.90	42.40	37.10	32.75	29.16	26.17	23.65	21.53	19.72	67

Table 38 *continued*

68	57.67	49.41	42.76	37.36	32.94	29.30	26.27	23.73	21.58	19.75	68
69	58.38	49.92	43.12	37.62	33.13	29.43	26.36	23.79	21.63	19.79	69
70	59.09	50.42	43.48	37.87	33.31	29.56	26.45	23.86	21.68	19.82	70
71	59.79	50.91	43.83	38.12	33.48	29.68	26.54	23.92	21.72	19.85	71
72	60.49	51.41	44.17	38.36	33.65	29.80	26.63	23.98	21.76	19.88	72
73	61.19	51.89	44.51	38.60	33.82	29.92	26.71	24.04	21.80	19.91	73
74	61.88	52.37	44.85	38.83	33.98	30.03	26.79	24.10	21.84	19.94	74
75	62.57	52.85	45.18	39.06	34.14	30.15	26.87	24.15	21.88	19.97	75
76	63.26	53.32	45.50	39.29	34.30	30.25	26.94	24.20	21.92	19.99	76
77	63.94	53.79	45.82	39.51	34.45	30.36	27.01	24.25	21.95	20.02	77
78	64.62	54.25	46.14	39.72	34.60	30.46	27.08	24.30	21.99	20.04	78
79	65.29	54.71	46.45	39.93	34.74	30.56	27.15	24.35	22.02	20.06	79
80	65.97	55.16	46.75	40.14	34.88	30.65	27.21	24.39	22.05	20.08	80

APPENDIX 5

FURTHER READING

General texts

1. *Kemp & Kemp on Damages* (Sweet & Maxwell, looseleaf)
    The whole of volume 2 is devoted to fatal accidents. However, as the editors note, this is a section that would benefit from rewriting.

2. *Butterworths Personal Injury Litigation Service* (Butterworths, looseleaf)
    This section on fatal accidents is in volume 1. Criminal injuries compensation is dealt with in volume 4.

3. *McGreggor on Damages* (Sweet & Maxwell, 16th edn, 1999)
    Chapter 34 deals with torts causing death. Kemp recommends this as the best account of the subject.

4. *Munkman on Personal Injuries and Death* (Butterworths, 10th edn, 1996)
    Issues relating to damages arising from death are dealt with throughout. A new edition is expected in early 2003.

5. *Charlesworth and Perry on Negligence* (Sweet & Maxwell, 10th edn, 2002)
    Chapter 15 contains a succinct discussion in relation to issues relating to death and causes of action.

6. William Norris QC and Edward Bishop, 'The Impact of the Human Rights Act 1998 on Personal Injury Law and Practice', [2000] JPIL 73.

7. A series of articles by Colin Ettinger in the APIL Newsletter. vol 10, issues 5 and 6, vol 11, issue 1 and vol 12, issue 1.

Specific texts

8. Michael Yelton *Fatal Accidents – A Practical Guide to Compensation* (Sweet & Maxwell, 1998)
    A useful guide. The primary difficulty is that the text pre-dates the Civil Procedure Rules 1998.

9. Mary Duncan and Christine Marsh *Fatal Accident Claims* (Fourmat Publishing, 1993)
    Now somewhat dated.

Guides to procedure

10. Hendy, Day, Buchan and Kennedy *Personal Injury Practice* 3rd edn (Butterworths, 2000)
    Fatal accidents are dealt with in Chapter 29.

11. Gordon Exall *Personal Injury Litigation* 3rd edn (Cavendish, 2002)
    There is a short section on fatal accidents in chapter 2.

Law Commission Reports

12.   Law Com No 263 *Claims for Wrongful Death* (1999)
      Contains a useful summary of history and current law together with a useful
      discussion of the problem areas.

INDEX

References are to paragraph numbers. References in italics refer to page numbers of the appendices